A Companion to Cultural M

A Companion to Cultural Memory Studies

Edited by
Astrid Erll · Ansgar Nünning

in collaboration with
Sara B. Young

De Gruyter

ISBN 978-3-11-022998-1

Library of Congress Cataloging-in-Publication Data

A companion to cultural memory studies / edited by Astrid Erll, Ansgar Nünning.
p. cm. – (Earlier ed. published as: Cultural memory studies : an international and interdisciplinary handbook / edited by Astrid Erll, Ansgar Nünning in collaboration with Sara B. Young. 2008.)
Includes bibliographical references and index.
ISBN 978-3-11-022998-1 (pbk. : alk. paper)
1. Culture. 2. Memory – Cross-cultural studies. 3. Collective memory. I. Erll, Astrid. II. Nünning, Ansgar. III. Cultural memory studies.
HM621.C8534 2010
306.01–dc22

2010012403

Bibliographic information published by the Deutsche Nationalbibliothek

The Deutsche Nationalbibliothek lists this publication in the Deutsche Nationalbibliografie; deatailed bibliographic data are available in the Internet at http://dnb.d-nb.de abrufbar.

Printing and binding: AZ Druck und Datentechnik GmbH, Kempten
∞ Printed on acid-free paper

Printed in Germany

www.degruyter.com

Preface and Acknowledgements

This book first appeared as a hardback volume in the de Gruyter series Media and Cultural Memory under the title *Cultural Memory Studies: An International and Interdisciplinary Handbook*. With its aim to provide a concise and accessible overview of existing approaches to the study of cultural memory it seems to have struck a nerve with scholars working in this flourishing and multifarious research field. The present *Companion to Cultural Memory Studies* therefore reissues the original articles in an affordable paperback edition, making it accessible to a larger audience.

Cultural memory studies came into being at the beginning of the twentieth century, with the works of Maurice Halbwachs on *mémoire collective*. In the course of the last two decades this area of research has witnessed a veritable boom in various countries and disciplines. As a consequence, the study of the relations between culture and memory has diversified into a broad range of approaches. Today, the complex issue of cultural memory is remarkably interdisciplinary: Concepts of cultural memory circulate in history, the social and political sciences, philosophy and theology, psychology, the neurosciences, and psychoanalysis, as well as in literary and media studies. Sometimes these concepts converge; at other times they seem to exclude one another; and all too often, researchers in one discipline seem to take no notice of the work done in neighboring disciplines. Moreover, cultural memory studies is a decidedly international field: Important concepts have been generated in France, Germany, Great Britain, Italy, Canada, the United States, and the Netherlands. At the same time, however, we have seen how nationally specific academic traditions and language barriers have tended to impede the transfer of knowledge about cultural memory.

This volume proceeds from the assumption that, more often than not, the meaning and operational value of concepts of cultural memory differ between diverse disciplines, disparate academic cultures, and different historical periods. With the move towards greater interdisciplinarity, the exchange of such concepts has considerably intensified. Through constant appropriation, translation, and reassessment across various fields, concepts of cultural memory have acquired new meanings, opening up new horizons of research in the humanities as well as in the social and in the natural sciences. To the extent that their meaning must, therefore, be constantly renegotiated, a sustained enquiry into these concepts and a survey of the latest research in cultural memory studies canfoster a self-reflexive approach to this burgeoning and increasingly diverse field, providing a theoretical, conceptual and methodological backbone for any project concerned with questions of cultural memory.

The aim of this companion is to offer the first truly integrated survey of this interdisciplinary and international field of cultural memory studies. The concise presentation of its main concepts is intended not only to offer readers a unique overview of current research in the field; it is also meant to serve as a forum for bringing together approaches from areas as varied as neurosciences and literary history, thus adding further contour and depth to this emergent field of study.

***

Our debts are many, and it is a great pleasure to acknowledge them. Our thanks go, first of all, to the many individual authors who contributed to this volume. It was a wonderful experience to collaborate on this project with researchers from numerous countries and disciplines. We are grateful for their willingness to present their research in the admittedly very concise format of this companion. Moreover, we would like to thank the editors of the de Gruyter publishing house, Heiko Hartmann and especially Manuela Gerlof, thanks to whose dedication this paperback volume can now appear.

We are also very grateful to Anna-Lena Flügel, Meike Hölscher, and Jan Rupp, who helped prepare the original manuscript for publication. Many articles had to be translated into English, and we thank Anna-Lena Flügel for her translation from French, Stephanie Wodianka for her counsel on all things Italian, and Sara B. Young for providing all the translations from German. To her go our most cordial thanks: Without her, this volume would not exist. She did an absolutely excellent job, from the critical reading and careful editing of the articles to her well-crafted translations and skilled guidance in the overall language and style of the volume.

Wassenaar and Giessen, February 2010,
Astrid Erll and Ansgar Nünning

Table of Contents

IV. Psychological Memory Studies

V. Literature and Cultural Memory

VI. Media and Cultural Memory

Cultural Memory Studies: An Introduction

ASTRID ERLL

1. Towards a Conceptual Foundation for Cultural Memory Studies

Over the past two decades, the relationship between culture and memory has emerged in many parts of the world as a key issue of interdisciplinary research, involving fields as diverse as history, sociology, art, literary and media studies, philosophy, theology, psychology, and the neurosciences, and thus bringing together the humanities, social studies, and the natural sciences in a unique way. The importance of the notion of cultural memory is not only documented by the rapid growth, since the late 1980s, of publications on specific national, social, religious, or family memories, but also by a more recent trend, namely attempts to provide overviews of the state of the art in this emerging field and to synthesize different research traditions. Anthologies of theoretical texts, such as *The Collective Memory Reader* (Olick et al.), as well as the launch of the new journal *Memory Studies* testify to the need to bring focus to this broad discussion and to consider the theoretical and methodological standards of a promising, but also as yet incoherent and dispersed field (cf. Olick; Radstone; Erll). The present handbook represents the shared effort of forty-one authors, all of whom have contributed over the past years, from a variety of disciplinary perspectives, to the development of this nascent field, and it is part of the effort to consolidate memory studies into a more coherent discipline. It is a first step on the road towards a conceptual foundation for the kind of memory studies which assumes a decidedly cultural and social perspective.

"Cultural" (or, if you will, "collective," "social") memory is certainly a multifarious notion, a term often used in an ambiguous and vague way. Media, practices, and structures as diverse as myth, monuments, historiography, ritual, conversational remembering, configurations of cultural knowledge, and neuronal networks are nowadays subsumed under this wide umbrella term. Because of its intricacy, cultural memory has been a highly controversial issue ever since its very conception in Maurice Halbwachs's studies on *mémoire collective* (esp. 1925, 1941, 1950). His contemporary Marc Bloch accused Halbwachs of simply transferring concepts from individual psychology to the level of the collective, and even today scholars continue to challenge the notion of collective or cultural memory, claiming, for example, that since we have well-established concepts like "myth," "tradition," and "individual memory," there is no need for a further, and often misleading, addition to the existing repertoire (cf. Gedi and Elam). What these criticisms overlook, of course, is that it is exactly the umbrella quality of these relatively new usages of "memory" which helps us see the (sometimes functional, sometimes analogical, sometimes metaphorical) relationships between such phenomena as ancient myths and the personal recollection of recent experience, and which enables disciplines as varied as psychology, history, sociology, and literary studies to engage in a stimulating dialogue.

This handbook is based on a broad understanding of cultural memory, suggesting as a provisional definition "the interplay of present and past in socio-cultural contexts." Such an understanding of the term allows for an inclusion of a broad spectrum of phenomena as possible objects of cultural memory studies—ranging from individual acts of remembering in a social context to group memory (of family, friends, veterans, etc.) to national memory with its "invented traditions," and finally to the host of transnational *lieux de mémoire* such as the Holocaust and 9/11. At the same time, cultural memory studies is not restricted to the study of those ways of making sense of the past which are intentional and performed through narrative, and which go hand in hand with the construction of identities—although this very nexus (intentional remembering, narrative, identity) has certainly yielded the lion's share of research in memory studies so far. The field thus remains open for the exploration of unintentional and implicit ways of cultural remembering (see Welzer, this volume) or of inherently non-narrative, for example visual or bodily, forms of memory.

But if the range of themes and objects of memory studies is virtually limitless (everything is, somehow, related to memory), then what makes our new field distinct? With Alon Confino, I would argue that it is not the infinite multitude of possible *topics* which characterizes cultural memory studies, but instead its *concepts*: the specific ways of conceiving of themes and of approaching objects. However, despite two decades of intensive research, the design of a conceptual toolbox for cultural memory studies is still at a fledgling stage, because (to quote Confino in this volume) memory studies is currently "more practiced than theorized"—and practiced, at that, within an array of different disciplines and national academic cultures, with their own vocabularies, methods, and traditions. What we need is to take a survey of the concepts used in memory studies and, in doing so, cross intellectual and linguistic boundaries.

Even a cursory look at the host of different terminologies which have emerged from memory studies since Maurice Halbwachs will shed light on the challenges faced by those who are searching for a conceptual foundation for the field: *mémoire collective*/collective memory, *cadres sociaux*/social frameworks of memory, social memory, *mnemosyne*, *ars memoriae*, *loci et imagines*, *lieux de mémoire*/sites of memory, invented traditions, myth, *memoria*, heritage, commemoration, *kulturelles Gedächtnis*, communicative memory, generationality, postmemory. The list could go on.

What this wealth of existing concepts shows, first of all, is that cultural memory is not the object of one single discipline, but a transdisciplinary phenomenon. There is no such thing as a privileged standpoint or approach for memory research (for the systematic and historic reasons for this, see sections 2 and 3 of this article). Cultural memory studies is a field to which many disciplines contribute, using their specific methodologies and perspectives. This makes for its terminological richness, but also for its disjointedness. At the same time, it has been clear since its very inception that the study of cultural memory can only be successful if it is based on cooperation among different disciplines. Cultural memory studies is therefore not merely a multidisciplinary field, but fundamentally an interdisciplinary project. Many exciting forms of collaboration have already been fostered. And indeed, the strongest and most striking studies in cultural memory are based on interdisciplinary exchange—between media studies and cultural history (J. Assmann; A. Assmann), history and sociology (Olick), neuroscience and social psychology (Welzer; Markowitsch), cognitive psychology and history (Manier and Hirst) or social psychology and linguistics (Echterhoff; all this volume). An even more intensified dialogue among disciplines will help uncover the manifold intersections of memory and culture. This, however, requires a very sensitive handling of terminology and a careful discrimination of the specific disciplinary uses of certain concepts and of their literal, metaphorical, or metonymical implications (see section 2).

2. Establishing the Framework: Dimensions, Levels, and Modes of Cultural Memory

If we want to establish a framework for cultural memory studies, working on concepts is inevitable. In the following I will propose some basic definitions and conceptual differentiations which may help to prevent misunderstanding and resolve some of the controversies which have been sparked time and again within and about cultural memory studies.

(a) *Dimensions of Culture and Memory: Material, Social, and Mental*

Arguably the most important and by far most frequently used key concept of cultural memory studies is the contentious term *mémoire collective* (collective memory), which was brought into the discussion by Maurice Halbwachs in the 1920s. Our choice of "*cultural* memory" for the title of this handbook is due, in the first place, to the highly controversial nature of Halbwachs's term and the many wrong associations it seems to trigger in those who are new to the field. Secondly, according to the definition given above, the term "*cultural* memory" accentuates the connection of memory on the one hand and socio-cultural contexts on the other. However, the term "cultural" does not designate a specific affinity to Cultural Studies as conceived and practiced by the Birmingham School (although this discipline has certainly contributed to cultural memory studies). Our notion of culture is instead more rooted in the German tradition of the study of cultures (*Kulturwissenschaft*) and in anthropology, where culture is defined as a community's specific way of life, led within its self-spun webs of meaning (cf. Geertz).

According to anthropological and semiotic theories, culture can be seen as a three-dimensional framework, comprising social (people, social relations, institutions), material (artifacts and media), and mental aspects (culturally defined ways of thinking, mentalities) (cf. Posner). Understood in this way, "*cultural* memory" can serve as an umbrella term which comprises "*social* memory" (the starting point for memory research in the social sciences), "*material* or *medial* memory" (the focus of interest in literary and media studies), and "*mental* or *cognitive* memory" (the field of expertise in psychology and the neurosciences). This neat distinction is of course merely a heuristic tool. In reality, all three dimensions are involved in the making of cultural memories. Cultural memory studies is therefore characterized by the transcending of boundaries. Some scholars look at the interplay of material and social phenomena (for example, memorials and the politics of memory; see Meyer); others scrutinize the intersections of material and mental phenomena (as in the history of mentalities; see Confino); still others study the relation of cognitive and social phenomena (as in conversational remembering; see Middleton and Brown; all this volume).

(b) *Levels of Memory: Individual and Collective*

It is important to realize that the notions of "cultural" or "collective" memory proceed from an operative metaphor. The concept of "remembering" (a cognitive process which takes place in individual brains) is metaphorically transferred to the level of culture. In this metaphorical sense, scholars speak of a "nation's memory," a "religious community's memory," or even of "literature's memory" (which, according to Renate Lachmann, is its intertextuality). This crucial distinction between two aspects of cultural memory studies is what Jeffrey K. Olick draws our attention to when he maintains that "two radically different concepts of culture are involved here, one that sees culture as a subjective category of meanings contained in people's minds versus one that sees culture as patterns of publicly available symbols objectified in society" (336). In other words, we have to differentiate between two levels on which culture and memory intersect: the individual and the collective or, more precisely, the level of the cognitive on the one hand, and the levels of the social and the medial on the other.

The first level of cultural memory is concerned with biological memory. It draws attention to the fact that no memory is ever purely individual, but always inherently shaped by collective contexts. From the people we live with and from the media we use, we acquire schemata which help us recall the past and encode new experience. Our memories are often triggered as well as shaped by external factors, ranging from conversation among friends to books and to places. In short, we remember in socio-cultural contexts. With regard to this first level, "memory" is used in a literal sense, whereas the attribute "cultural" is a metonymy, standing for the "socio-cultural contexts and their influence on memory." It is especially within oral history, social psychology, and the neurosciences that cultural memory is understood according to this first aspect of the term.

The second level of cultural memory refers to the symbolic order, the media, institutions, and practices by which social groups construct a shared past. "Memory," here, is used metaphorically. Societies do not remember literally; but much of what is done to reconstruct a shared past bears some resemblance to the processes of individual memory, such as the selectivity and perspectivity inherent in the creation of versions of the past according to present knowledge and needs. In cultural history and the social sciences, much research has been done with regard to this second aspect of collective memory, the most influential concepts to have emerged being Pierre Nora's *lieux de mémoire* and Jan and Aleida Assmann's *kulturelles Gedächtnis.*

The two forms of cultural memory can be distinguished from each other on an analytical level; but in practice the cognitive and the social/medial continuously interact. There is no such thing as pre-cultural individual memory; but neither is there a Collective or Cultural Memory (with capital letters) which is detached from individuals and embodied only in media and institutions. Just as socio-cultural contexts shape individual memories, a "memory" which is represented by media and institutions must be actualized by individuals, by members of a community of remembrance, who may be conceived of as *points de vue* (Maurice Halbwachs) on shared notions of the past. Without such actualizations, monuments, rituals, and books are nothing but dead material, failing to have any impact in societies.

As is always the case with metaphors, some features can be transferred with a gain in insight, others cannot. The notion of cultural memory has quite successfully directed our attention to the close connection that exists between, say, a nation's version of its past and its version of national identity. That memory and identity are closely linked on the individual level is a commonplace that goes back at least to John Locke, who maintained that there is no such thing as an essential identity, but that identities have to be constructed and reconstructed by acts of memory, by remembering who one was and by setting this past Self in relation to the present Self. The concept of cultural memory has opened the way to studying these processes at a collective level. More problematic is the migration of concepts between the individual and social levels when it comes to trauma studies. Wulf Kansteiner and Harald Weilnböck (this volume) show the (ethical) pitfalls of attempting to conflate processes of the individual psyche with the medial and social representation of the past.

To sum up, cultural memory studies is decidedly concerned with social, medial, *and* cognitive processes, and their ceaseless interplay. In the present volume, this fact is mirrored not only by the dedication of different sections to (clusters of) different disciplines (history, social sciences, psychology, literary and media studies) which have an expertise with regard to one specific level of cultural memory, but also by the incorporation of as many approaches as possible which go beyond those boundaries. Readers will therefore discover numerous cross-connections between the paths taken in the individual parts of this book.

(c) *Modes of Memory: The "How" of Remembering*

The last distinction to be made in this introduction—that between different modes of remembering—is one which aims to confront another source of vehement dispute within and about memory studies. One of Halbwachs's less felicitous legacies is the opposition between history and memory. Halbwachs conceives of the former as abstract, totalizing, and "dead," and of the latter as particular, meaningful, and "lived." This polarity, itself a legacy of nineteenth-century historicism and its discontents, was taken up and popularized by Pierre Nora, who also distinguishes polemically between history and memory and positions his *lieux de mémoire* in between. Studies on "history vs. memory" are usually loaded with emotionally charged binary oppositions: good vs. bad, organic vs. artificial, living vs. dead, from below vs. from above. And while the term "cultural memory" is already a multifarious notion, it is often even less clear what is meant with the collective singular of "history" (cf. Koselleck): Selective and meaningful memory vs. the unintelligible totality of *historical events*? Methodologically unregulated and identity-related memory vs. scientific, seemingly neutral and objective *historiography*? Authentic memory produced within small communities vs. ideologically charged, official *images of history*? Witnesses of the past vs. academic *historians*? The whole question of "history and/or/as memory" is simply not a very fruitful approach to cultural representations of the past. It is a dead end in memory studies, and also one of its "Achilles' heels" (see Olick, this volume).

I would suggest dissolving the useless opposition of history vs. memory in favor of a notion of different *modes of remembering* in culture. This approach proceeds from the basic insight that the past is not given, but must instead continually be re-constructed and re-presented. Thus, our memories (individual and collective) of past events can vary to a great degree. This holds true not only for *what* is remembered (facts, data), but also for *how* it is remembered, that is, for the quality and meaning the past assumes. As a result, there are different modes of remembering identical past events. A war, for example, can be remembered as a mythic event ("the war as apocalypse"), as part of political history (the First World War as "the great seminal catastrophe of the twentieth century"), as a traumatic experience ("the horror of the trenches, the shells, the barrage of gunfire," etc.), as a part of family history ("the war my great-uncle served in"), as a focus of bitter contestation ("the war which was waged by the old generation, by the fascists, by men"). Myth, religious memory, political history, trauma, family remembrance, or generational memory are different modes of referring to the past. Seen in this way, history is but yet another mode of cultural memory, and historiography its specific medium. This is not at all to lessen its importance or the merits of generations of historians. Since the early nineteenth century, the historical method has developed into the best-regulated and most reliable way of reconstructing the past (even though its specific operations have been justifiably criticized by Foucault and others, and may be complemented by other modes).

3. Genealogies and Branches of Cultural Memory Studies: The Design of This Handbook

This handbook has a historic and systematic (or diachronic and synchronic) layout. Although its main focus is on *current* research and concepts of cultural memory studies, it also provides insights into the different roots of the field. Whereas a history of thought about memory and culture would have to go back to Plato, the beginnings of a modern notion of cultural memory can be retraced to the late nineteenth and early twentieth centuries (see Olick; Straub; Marcel and Mucchielli; all this volume). The present field of research is built on the emergence of a "new wave" of cultural memory studies since the 1980s (see Confino; Harth; Fortunati and Lamberti; all this volume).

Maurice Halbwachs was the first to write explicitly and systematically about cultural memory. If one reads through the essays of this volume, there can be little doubt that his studies of *mémoire collective* have emerged as the foundational texts of today's memory studies—unequivocally accepted as such no matter what discipline or country the respective researchers call home. Halbwachs not only coined the fundamental term "collective memory"; his legacy to cultural memory studies is at least threefold. Firstly, with his concept of *cadres sociaux de la mémoire* (social frameworks of memory) he articulated the idea that individual memories are inherently shaped and will often be triggered by socio-cultural contexts, or frameworks, thus already pointing to cultural schema theories and the contextual approaches of psychology. Secondly, his study of family memory and other private practices of remembering have been an important influence for oral history. And thirdly, with his research on the memory of religious communities (in *La topographie légendaire*) he accentuated topographical aspects of cultural memory, thus anticipating the notion of *lieux de mémoire*, and he looked at communities whose memory reaches back thousands of years, thus laying the foundation for Jan and Aleida Assmann's *kulturelles Gedächtnis.*

However, although Halbwachs's work is rooted in French sociology, memory studies was an international and transdisciplinary phenomenon from the very beginning. Around 1900, scholars from different disciplines and countries became interested in the intersections between culture and memory: notably Sigmund Freud, Henri Bergson, Emile Durkheim, Maurice Halbwachs, Aby Warburg, Arnold Zweig, Karl Mannheim, Frederick Bartlett, and Walter Benjamin (see also Olick, this volume). Sometimes those scholars critically referred to one another's work (for example Halbwachs to Durkheim, or Bloch and Bartlett to Halbwachs), yet more often this early research remained unconnected. Early memory studies is thus a typical example of an emergent phenomenon, cropping up at different places at roughly the same time—a process which would be repeated in the 1980s, with the "new memory studies."

If Halbwachs is the best remembered founding father of memory studies, then Aby Warburg is arguably the most forgotten one. The German Jewish art historian was an early and energetic ambassador of the interdisciplinary study of culture (cf. Gombrich). He famously pointed out that researchers should stop policing disciplinary boundaries (*grenzpolizeiliche Befangenheit*) in order to gain insight into processes of cultural memory. Warburg—whose writings are more a quarry providing inspiration for subsequent scholars than the source of clear-cut theoretical concepts—drew attention, moreover, to the *mediality* of memory. In a great exhibition project called *Mnemosyne* (1924-28) he demonstrated how certain "pathos formulae" (*Pathosformeln*, symbols encoding emotional intensity) migrated through different art works, periods, and countries. Whereas the sociologist Halbwachs and the psychologist Frederick Bartlett (who popularized the notion of cultural schemata) laid the foundations for cultural memory studies with a view to social and cognitive levels, Warburg's legacy to present-day research is to have given an example of how cultural memory can be approached via the level of material objects.

The interest that the works by Halbwachs and others had sparked in a small community of scholars dwindled away after the Second World War. It was only in the 1980s (after the "death of history," the narrative turn, and the anthropological turn) that "collective memory," first slowly and then at breathtaking speed, developed into a buzzword not only in the academic world, but also in the political arena, the mass media, and the arts. The "new cultural memory studies" was, again, very much an emergent phenomenon, taking shape more or less concurrently in many disciplines and countries. The 1980s saw the work of the French historian Pierre Nora on national *lieux de mémoire* (see den Boer) and the publications of the German group of researchers around Jan and Aleida Assmann, who focused on media and memory in ancient societies (see Harth). In psychology, meanwhile, behavioral and purely cognitive paradigms had been superseded by ecological approaches to human memory and the study of conversational and narrative remembering (see Straub; Middleton and Brown). Historical and political changes became a catalyst for the new memory studies. Forty years after the Holocaust the generation that had witnessed the Shoah began to fade away. This effected a major change in the forms of cultural remembrance. Without organic, autobiographic memories, societies are solely dependent on media (such as monuments; see Young) to transmit experience. Issues of trauma and witnessing were not only discussed in the context of Holocaust studies, but more and more also in gender studies and postcolonial studies (see Kansteiner and Weilnböck). More recently, major transformations in global politics, such as the breakdown of the communist states and other authoritarian regimes, have brought new memory phenomena to the fore, such as the issue of "transitional justice" (see Langenohl). More generally, the shape of contemporary media societies gives rise to the assumption that—today perhaps more than ever—cultural memory is dependent on media technologies and the circulation of media products (see Esposito; Rigney; Erll; Zelizer; Zierold; all this volume).

*

In keeping with the double focus of this handbook—on genealogies and disciplinary branches—each of its six parts is concerned with historic *and* systematic aspects of cultural memory studies. Part I is dedicated to the one concept that has arguably proved most influential within the new, international and interdisciplinary memory studies: Pierre Nora's *lieux de mémoire*, which he introduced in a multivolume work of the same name, featuring French "sites of memory" (1984-92). The notion of *lieux de mémoire* quickly crossed national borders and was taken up in books about sites of memory in Italy, Germany, Canada, Central Europe, and the United States. The ubiquity of the term cannot belie the fact, however, that the *lieu de mémoire* is still one of the most inchoate and undertheorized concepts of cultural memory studies. On the one hand it lends itself particularly well to the study of a wide array of phenomena (from "places" in the literal sense to medial representations, rituals, and shared beliefs), but it is precisely because of its sheer limitless extension that the term has remained conceptually amorphous, and it would be well worth initiating another round of scholarly scrutiny (cf. Rigney). In this volume, Pim den Boer traces the roots of the *lieu* metaphor back to the ancient art of memory, its founding myth about Simonides of Ceos, and the method of *loci* and *imagines* (places and images) as we find it described in the rhetorics of Cicero and Quintilian. He uncovers the French *specificité* of Nora's concept, comments on its translatability, and considers the prospects for a comparative study of *lieux de mémoire.* Some elements of such a comparative perspective on sites of memory are provided by the following articles: Mario Isnenghi gives an insight into Italian *luoghi della memoria*; Jacques Le Rider writes about *Mitteleuropa* (Central Europe) as a site of memory; Udo J. Hebel distinguishes literary, visual, performative, material, virtual, and transnational memory sites of the United States; and Jay Winter provides a comparative view of the sites that commemorate twentieth-century wars.

Part II presents memory research rooted in cultural history. Alon Confino reveals the intellectual and methodological affiliations between memory studies and the history of mentalities, reaching back to the fathers of the Annales school, Lucien Febvre and Marc Bloch, and shows how Pierre Nora's *lieux de mémoire* emerged from this tradition. He then takes a critical look at present-day memory studies and the chances and pitfalls it offers to historians. The next three articles form a unity in many ways, not surprisingly, as they are written by members of the interdisciplinary, Heidelberg-based group of scholars who have been working on cultural memory since the 1980s. Dietrich Harth reconstructs the "invention of cultural memory" in this research context; Jan and Aleida Assmann present some of their eminently influential concepts, among them, for example, the distinction between "cultural" and "communicative" memory and between "canon" and "archive." Jürgen Reulecke delineates recent approaches to generational memory, which also have their source in the 1920s: Karl Mannheim's writings belong to the foundational texts of cultural memory studies, since memory within and between generations is a significant form of collective remembering. With the development of terms such as "generationality" and "generativity," his legacy has been updated. Vita Fortunati and Elena Lamberti complete this second part of the volume not only by giving a comprehensive overview of the wide array of concepts, but also by providing an insight into the actual practice of international and interdisciplinary cultural memory studies as carried out within the European thematic network ACUME.

Part III directs attention towards the different kinds of memory studies that have emerged in philosophy and the social sciences. Here, again, the history of memory studies and its protagonist Maurice Halbwachs get their due: Jean-Christophe Marcel and Laurent Mucchielli provide an introduction to Maurice Halbwachs's works on *mémoire collective* as a "unique type of phenomenological sociology." Jeffrey K. Olick then delineates in a grand sweep the development from Halbwachs's beginnings to the current "sociology of mnemonic practices and products." The articles by Andreas Langenohl and Erik Meyer address specific social, political, and ethical questions which have arisen out of contemporary memory politics. Langenohl provides an overview of forms of remembrance in post-authoritarian societies and elaborates on the issue of transitional justice; Meyer develops a policy studies perspective on cultural memory. The articles by Elena Esposito and Siegfried J. Schmidt represent the contributions of systems theory and radical constructivism to cultural memory studies. Esposito theorizes the powerful other side of cultural memory, namely social forgetting. This part ends with Maureen Junker-Kenny's critical recapitulation of the philosophical and hermeneutical perspective on memory, forgetting, and forgiving that was introduced by Paul Ricœur.

The inclusion of psychological concepts in part IV provides a bridge from memory studies in the humanities and the social sciences to the natural sciences. Representatives of different disciplines (including the neurosciences; psychotherapy; and narrative, social, and cognitive psychology) provide insights into their work on cultural memory. An historical perspective is assumed by Jürgen Straub, who traces the genealogy of psychological memory studies back to the late nineteenth century and charts the history of narrative psychology, up to and including its current state. Wulf Kansteiner and Harald Weilnböck take a strong stand "against the concept of cultural trauma." From a psychotherapy studies perspective they reconstruct and criticize the various uses and abuses of the concept of trauma in cultural memory studies. David Middleton and Steven D.

Brown introduce their work on conversational remembering and stress the important connection between experience and memory. David Manier and William Hirst outline what they call a "cognitive taxonomy of collective memories," thus showing how group memories are represented in individual minds. Gerald Echterhoff presents new interdisciplinary research on the relation of language and memory, which lies at the very basis of cultural memory. Hans J. Markowitsch provides an introduction to memory research in the neurosciences and discusses how the social world shapes the individual brain. Harald Welzer rounds off this part of the volume by presenting the key concepts of his inherently interdisciplinary research, which spans the field from oral history to social psychology and to the neurosciences.

Parts V and VI move on to the material and medial dimension of cultural memory. The articles in part V represent the main concepts of memory found in literary studies (cf. Erll and Nünning). Renate Lachmann shows how the ancient method of *loci imagines* is linked to literary imagination and describes her influential notion of intertextuality as the "memory of literature." With Herbert Grabes's article on the literary canon, the perspective on literature and memory moves from relations between texts to the level of the social systems which select and evaluate literary works. Max Saunders's article on "life-writing" is concerned with those literary works which are most obviously connected to cultural memory: letters, diaries, biographies, autobiographies, memoirs, etc. However, he also shows that life-writing extends beyond these genres and that individual and cultural memory can indeed be found in most literary texts. Birgit Neumann provides an overview of how memory is represented in literature, using a narratological approach to describe the forms and functions of a "mimesis of memory." Ann Rigney stresses the active and vital role that literature plays as a medium in the production of cultural memory. She understands memory as a dynamic process (rather than a static entity), in which fictional narratives can fulfill an array of different functions—as "relay stations," "stabilizers," "catalysts," "objects of recollection," or "calibrators."

With its focus on mediality and memory, Ann Rigney's article already points to the last part of the volume, which is concerned with the role of memory in media cultures. Here more than ever disciplines converge. Scholars from literary studies, history, media studies, journalism, and communication studies introduce their views on a set of questions which has emerged as one of the most basic concerns and greatest challenges of memory studies: the intersections between media and cultural memory (which, of course, also give this series its title). Cultural memory hinges on the notion of the medial, because it is only via medial externalization (from oral speech to writing, painting, or using the Internet) that individual memories, cultural knowledge, and versions of history can be shared. It is therefore no accident that many articles which have made their appearance in earlier parts of this volume could just as easily have been included in the media section. This certainly holds true for the entire section on literature, which can be viewed as one medium of cultural memory. Many other articles of this volume, such as those written by Udo J. Hebel, Jan Assmann, Aleida Assmann, Siegfried J. Schmidt, Elena Esposito, Gerald Echterhoff, and Harald Welzer, are characterized by their strong media perspective—ranging from medial sites of memory to the role of communication technologies for social forgetting and to language as a basic medium of memory.

Part VI begins with a contribution by James E. Young on what is arguably one of the most important artistic media of cultural memory—and its most intricate: the Holocaust memorial. Jens Ruchatz scrutinizes the double role of photography as medial externalization of memory and trace of the past. Barbie Zelizer writes about the connection between journalism and memory, identifying journalism, despite its strong emphasis on the present, as a memorial practice. I look at literature and film as media of cultural memory. Martin Zierold concludes this volume with a more general perspective on how memory studies might develop its focus on media cultures.

We hope that in bringing together many different voices from interdisciplinary and international memory studies and providing an overview of its history and key concepts, we will be able to give some definition to an emerging field. Most importantly, the aim of this volume is to inspire further sophisticated and exciting research by addressing scholars who are as fascinated by the possibilities of "thinking memory" as we are.

Acknowledgements

I would like to thank Ann Rigney for her critical reading and constructive comments on an earlier version of this introduction.

References

Assmann, Jan. *Das kulturelle Gedächtnis: Schrift, Erinnerung und politische Identität in frühen Hochkulturen.* Munich: Beck, 1992.

Bartlett, F. C. *Remembering: A Study in Experimental and Social Psychology.* Cambridge: Cambridge UP, 1932.

Bloch, Marc. "Memoire collective, tradition et coutume: a propos d'un livre recent." *Revue de Synthése Historique* 40 (1925): 73-83.

Confino, Alon. "Collective Memory and Cultural History: Problems of Method." *American Historical Review* 105.2 (1997): 1386-403.

Erll, Astrid. *Kollektives Gedächtnis und Erinnerungskulturen: Eine Einführung.* Stuttgart: Metzler, 2005.

Erll, Astrid and Ansgar Nünning, eds. (In collaboration with Hanne Birk, Birgit Neumann and Patrick Schmidt. *Medien des kollektiven Gedächtnisses: Konstruktivität—Historizität—Kulturspezifität.* Berlin: de Gruyter, 2004.

—., and Ansgar Nünning, eds. Gedächtniskonzepte der Literaturwissenschaft: Theoretische Grundlegung und Anwendungsperspektiven. Berlin: de Gruyter, 2005.

—. "Where Literature and Memory Meet: Towards a Systematic Approach to the Concepts of Memory in Literary Studies." *Literature, Literary History, and Cultural Memory.* REAL: Yearbook of Research in English and American Literature 21. Ed. Herbert Grabes. Tübingen: Narr, 2005. 265-98.

François, Etienne, and Hagen Schulze, eds. *Deutsche Erinnerungsorte.* 3 vols. Munich: Beck, 2001.

Gedi, Noa, and Yigal Elam. "Collective Memory: What Is It?" *History and Memory* 8.1 (1996): 30-50.

Geertz, Clifford. *The Interpretation of Cultures: Selected Essays.* London: Hutchinson, 1973.

Gombrich, Ernst H. *Aby Warburg: An Intellectual Biography.* London: Warburg Institute, 1970.

Halbwachs, Maurice. *Les cadres sociaux de la mémoire.* Paris: Alcan, 1925.

—. *On Collective Memory.* Ed. and trans. Lewis A. Coser. Chicago: U of Chicago P, 1992.

—. *La mémoire collective.* Paris: Presses Universitaires de France, 1950.

—. *La topographie légendaire des évangiles en terre sainte: Etude de mémoire collective.* Paris: Alcan, 1941.

Koselleck, Reinhart. *Futures Past: On the Semantics of Historical Time.* Trans. Keith Tribe. Cambridge: MIT Press, 1985.

Memory Studies. Andrew Hoskins, principal ed. Los Angeles: Sage, since 2008.

Nora, Pierre, ed. *Les lieux de mémoire.* 3 vols. Paris: Gallimard, 1984-92.

Olick, Jeffrey K. "Collective Memory: The Two Cultures." *Sociological Theory* 17.3 (1999): 333-48.

Olick, Jeffrey K., Vered Vinitzky-Seroussi, and Daniel Levy, eds. *The Collective Memory Reader.* Oxford: Oxford UP, 2008 (forthcoming).

Posner, Roland. "What is Culture? Toward a Semiotic Explication of Anthropological Concepts." *The Nature of Culture.* Ed. W. A. Koch. Bochum: Brockmeyer, 1989. 240-95.

Radstone, Susannah, ed. *Memory and Methodology.* Oxford: Berg, 2000.

Rigney, Ann. "Plenitude, Scarcity and the Circulation of Cultural Memory." *Journal of European Studies* 35.1-2 (2005): 209-26.

I. *Lieux de mémoire*–Sites of Memory

Loci memoriae—Lieux de mémoire

PIM DEN BOER

1. Cicero and Quintilian: *Loci memoriae*

Centuries ago a Greek poet, Simonides of Ceos, was witness to a terrible accident. The roof of the dining hall of the house of a wealthy man, Scopas in Crannon in Thessaly, collapsed and caused the death of everybody present in the hall. Simonides, who had left the hall for a moment, was the only survivor. It was not possible to identify the completely mutilated bodies. However, when asked by the mourning relatives, Simonides was able to identify the dead because he remembered who had been seated where just before the accident happened. Simonides thus realized the importance of localization for memory and discovered the importance of "places" for good memory. This Greek story about the invention of mnemotechnics circulated widely and was transmitted in Latin treatises on rhetoric.

Cicero (first century BC) mentioned Simonides's discovery (or that of "some other person," as he cautiously added), in his famous *De Oratore*:

> The best aid to clearness of memory consists in orderly arrangement [...]. [P]ersons desiring to train this faculty select localities [*loci*] and form mental images of the facts they wish to remember and store those images in the localities, with the result that the arrangement of the localities will preserve the order of the facts, and the images of the facts will designate the facts themselves [...]. (2.86.353-54)

Then Cicero makes the oft-quoted comparison that we should "employ the localities and images respectively as a wax writing tablet and the letters written on it" (2.86.354). According to Cicero "the keenest of all our senses is the sense of sight [...]" (2.87.357), and consequently what the ear hears and the intellect conceives is best preserved if the eyes help to keep it in your head. In this way the invisible takes shape in a concrete appearance. About the *loci memoriae* Cicero writes that it is well known that "one must employ a large number of localities which must be clear and defined and at moderate intervals apart, and images that are effective and sharply outlined and distinctive, with the capacity of encountering and speedily penetrating the mind" (2.87.358).

In the elaborated *Rhetorica ad Herennium* attributed to Cicero and often printed together with other works by him, but actually written by an anonymous, less brilliant author, one finds a more detailed description of *loci memoriae*. A distinction is made between two kinds of memory, one natural, the other artificial:

> The natural memory is that memory which is imbedded in our minds, born simultaneously with thought. The artificial memory is that memory which is strengthened by a kind of training and system of discipline. (16.28) The artificial memory includes backgrounds [*loci*] and images. We can grasp […,] for example, a house, an intercolumnar space, a recess, an arch or the like. (16.29) And that we may by no chance err in the number of backgrounds, each fifth background should be marked. For example, [if] in the fifth we should set a golden hand [...], it will then be easy to station like marks in each successive fifth background. (18.31)

All this seems to be mnemotechnical common knowledge in an age before the printing press. The most influential textbook on rhetoric was composed by Quintilian (first century AD). His *Institutio Oratoria* is very didactic:

> [I]t is an assistance to the memory if localities are sharply impressed upon the mind, a view the truth of which everyone may realise by practical experiment. For when we return to a place after considerable absence, we not merely recognise the place itself but remember things that we did there, and recall the persons whom we met and even the unuttered thoughts which passed through our minds when we were there before. […] Some place is chosen of the largest possible extent and characterised by the utmost possible variety, such as a spacious house divided into a number of rooms. (vol. 4, bk. 11, 2.17-18) The first thought is placed, as it were, in the forecourt; the second, let us say, in the living-room; the remainder are placed in due order all around the impluvium and entrusted not merely to bedrooms and parlours, but even to the care of statues and the like. This done, as soon as the memory of the facts requires to be revived, all these places are visited in turn […]. (vol. 4, bk. 11, 2.20)

As a good teacher Quintilian warns his audience not to overestimate the usefulness of the *loci memoriae*: "Such a practice may perhaps have been of use to those who, after an auction, have succeeded in stating what object they have sold to each buyer, their statements being checked by the books of the money-takers […]" (vol. 4, bk. 11, 2.24). However, *loci memoriae* are "of less service in learning […], [f]or thoughts do not call up the same images as material things" (vol 4, bk. 11, 2.24). Quintilian warns several times that it is impossible to represent certain things by symbols (vol. 4, bk. 11, 2.25).

2. Pierre Nora: *Lieux de mémoire* and National Identity

After the *loci memoriae* according to Cicero and Quintilian come the *lieux de mémoire* according to Nora. Collective memory, although a vague and ambivalent concept, is perhaps as fruitful and strategic for the innovation of historical research as the concept of mentality was thirty years earlier, as Nora remarked in his contribution to the French encyclopedia of *La Nouvelle Histoire* ("La mémoire collective" 401). In the *lieux de mémoire* project which started in 1977 with his inaugural seminar at the *École des Hautes Études en Sciences Sociales*, Nora has given the concept of *lieux de mémoire* not only a new meaning but also a highly successful programmatic significance.

For the ancients, the *loci memoriae* were a necessary mnemotechnics in a society without modern media (see also J. Assmann, this volume). For Cicero and Quintilian the *loci memoriae* were practical mental tools, free of ideology. *Loci memoriae* were not determined by social values, by historical views, or future expectations. Nora's *lieux de mémoire* are also mnemotechnical devices, but extremely ideological, full of nationalism, and far from being neutral or free of value judgments. Most *lieux de mémoire* were created, invented, or reworked to serve the nation-state. *Lieux de mémoire* were primarily part of the identity politics of the French nation and functioned to imprint the key notions of national history on the *outillage mental* ("set of mental tools") of the French citizens.

In his 1984 introduction to the first volume, Pierre Nora was very clear. Convinced by the perspective of a future European integration, Nora put forward without any ambiguity the necessity of inventorying the French *lieux de mémoire*: "The rapid disappearance of our national memory seemed to me to call for an inventory of the sites where it [the national memory] was selectively incarnated. Through human willpower and the work of centuries, these sites have become striking symbols: celebrations, emblems, monuments, and commemorations, but also speeches, archives, dictionaries, and museums" ("Présentation" vii).

3. French "*specificité*": Republican Universalism

In his conclusion Nora is also very clear about the special position of France. Nora seems to be convinced that there is a French *specificité*, a kind of French *Sonderweg* compared to the English monarchy and the German Empire. "The Republic distinguishes itself [from them] through an profound investment in and the systematic construction of memory which is simultaneously authoritarian, unified, exclusive, universal, and intensely historical" ("De la République" 652).

However, if one looks more closely, it seems that the French Republic is only different in one—very important—respect: universalism. The British and German *lieux de mémoire*—symbols, handbooks, dictionaries, monuments, commemorations, and expositions—were also authoritarian, unifying, exclusive, and intensely historical. The crucial element that is lacking in the British and German political regimes is this universalism, crystallized in the French Revolution and codified in the Declaration of the Rights of Man and Citizen. This universalism is typical for French republicanism and also marks the difference between the two French monarchies and the two French empires in that turbulent nineteenth century. These non-republican French regimes were as authoritarian, unified, exclusive, and historically orientated as the British and German Empires were.

4. Translating *lieux de mémoire*

Nora's project has been very successful and comparable projects and studies on national *lieux de mémoire* were recently published in Germany, Italy, Spain, and the Netherlands, and other countries will soon follow (see also Isnenghi; Hebel; and Le Rider; all this volume). Impressed by the success of this kind of historical approach easily accessible for a large audience, publishers in different countries are commissioning multi-volume series of essays on the *lieux de mémoire* of their respective nations.

The translation of the concept of *lieux de mémoire* does not pose fundamental problems in several European languages, such as Spanish and Italian, but in less Romanized European languages a fitting translation is less evident. In the English translation of the ancient rhetorical treatises in Latin, *loci memoriae* was translated as "the backgrounds of memory." The modern French concept is often translated by the more concrete expression "sites of memory." If the concept *lieux de mémoire* is used on a more abstract level a different translation in English is necessary.

In German not only the spatial designation in this context but also the term "memory" is not so easily translatable (see also Harth, this volume). The successful German series is entitled *Erinnerungsorte.* In his essay in the German series, Nora himself wrestles with the proper translation of *lieux* and uses *Herde* (centers), *Knoten* (knots), *Kreuzungen* (crossings), and even *Erinnerungsbojen* (buoys) (François and Schulze 3: 685). If a marine metaphor is chosen, perhaps "anchor" would have been more appropriate than "buoy." But even more problematic is the translation of "memory" with *Erinnerung.* This forceful modern German word—*erinneren*, "to internalize," from an older word *inneren*—has a didactical connotation and can even mean "to learn" or "to teach." Martin Luther, for example, used *erinneren* frequently in his Bible translation.

In each language a proper translation will pose different problems of translation which can be related to conceptual history. For example, in sixteenth- and seventeenth-century Flemish and Dutch, the German neologism *erinneren* was not yet accepted. Although translated in Latin as *revocare in memoriam*, it was considered to be dialect from the eastern provinces (Kiliaan 112). In the seventeenth-century authoritative Dutch Bible translation *(h)erinneren* was never used. Even in the beginning of the eighteenth century it was considered a Germanism (see Sewel 129). In Dutch, *memorie* was a common word, as was the old Dutch word *geheugen*. Due to the growing influence of the German language on Dutch in the nineteenth century, the word *herinnering* became a common Dutch word and lost its original Germanic flavor. In contemporary Dutch speech, *memorie* is not frequently used anymore and has a solemn, old-fashioned connotation. Thus, the Dutch project of four substantial volumes was appropriately entitled *Plaatsen van herinnering* (Wesseling et al.).

Lieux de mémoire is not a transnational term such as, for example, democracy. The translation problems are not just a matter of definition. In a comparative historical European perspective the positivistic reification of the concept of *lieux de mémoire* has to be avoided and an awareness of linguistic conceptual differences taken into prominent consideration.

5. Comparing *lieux de mémoire*

The next challenge will be to compare *lieux de mémoire* in different countries (den Boer and Frijhoff). Given the general European context of nation-building one may expect that the international structural similarities will be more evident than the national dissimilarities (see also Fortunati and Lamberti, this volume).

The comparative approach has two advantages. Firstly, national history will be enriched by understanding how the history of one's own nation is embedded in European and global history. A nation is never quarantined, but in a large degree determined by transnational context. Secondly, comparative research will open up transnational perspectives on the European *lieux de mémoire*. Christianity, humanism, enlightenment, and scientific development are crucial elements in European cultural history and offer a rich number of significant transnational *lieux de mémoire* such as the *ora et labora* of the Regula Benedicti, the *Imitatio Christi* of Thomas à Kempis, the *dignitas humanum* of Pico della Mirandola, the trial of Galileo Galilei, Spinoza's *Ethics*, Newton's apple, Linnaeus's taxonomy, Ranke's historical seminar, Pasteur's vaccine, Einstein's theory of relativity, or Niels Bohr's quantum mechanics, to name a few (cf. Nora, "La notion").

As *lieux de mémoire* of political European history one cannot pass over the Congress of Vienna, the peace of Versailles and Saint Germain, or the defeat of Hitler's Third Reich and the creation of an Iron Curtain. At the heyday of European nationalism, during the first half of the twentieth century, Verdun and Auschwitz present the most terrible *lieux de mémoire.*

It is remarkable to observe that even long before the disastrous outcome of nationalist rivalry and the terrible experiences of two European wars, Ernest Renan had already traced a transnational perspective. In a famous lecture about the question of what a nation is, delivered a decade after the Franco-Prussian War (1870-1871), which intensified the process of nation-building considerably, Renan prophesied: "The nations are not something eternal. They had their beginnings and they will end. A European confederation will very probably replace them. But such is not the law of the century in which we are living. At the present time, the existence of nations is a good thing, a necessity even" (53).

European nation-building has developed during successive periods of violent military confrontations and peaceful episodes of flourishing commerce. No European nation ever witnessed splendid isolation or any sort of quarantine. Nonetheless, to this day history teaching is still, generally speaking, dominated by the perspective of the nation-state. National history is often misunderstood and even occasionally disfigured by nineteenth-century national prejudice. For the Middle Ages and the early modern period, the national perspective is an anachronism that makes no sense. The comparative study of *lieux de mémoire* can help to analyze the topography of nineteenth-century national identity politics, an even more important task in the face of attempts to create "national canons" (see also the articles by A. Assmann and Grabes, this volume).

Contemporary Europe urgently needs a kind of transnational identity politics. In order to instruct their young citizens, European countries need teachers with at least a degree of knowledge, affection, and sympathy for Europe. After the *lieux de mémoire* of the nations, the future of Europe requires a new kind of *loci memoriae*: not as mnemotechnical tools to identify the mutilated corpses, not as devices of national identity politics, but to learn how to understand, to forgive, and to forget (see also Junker-Kenny, this volume).

References

Cicero. *On the Orator, Books I-II.* Trans. E. W. Sutton and H. Rackham. Cambridge: Harvard UP, 1967.

[Cicero.] *Ad. C. Herennium Libri IV de Ratione Dicendi (Rhetorica ad Herennium).* Trans. Harry Caplan. London: Heinemann, 1954.

den Boer, Pim, and Willem Frijhoff, eds. *Lieux de mémoire et identités nationales.* Amsterdam: Amsterdam UP, 1993.

François, Etienne, and Hagen Schulze, eds. *Deutsche Erinnerungsorte.* 3 vols. Munich: Beck, 2001.

Kiliaan, Cornelius. *Etymologicum teutonicae linguae: sive dictionarium Teutonico-Latinum.* Antwerp: Plantijn-Moret, 1599.

Nora, Pierre. "Entre mémoire et histoire: La problématique des lieux." *Les lieux de mémoire I: La République.* Ed. Pierre Nora. Paris: Gallimard, 1984. xv-xlii.

—. "La mémoire collective." *La Nouvelle Histoire.* Ed. Jacques Le Goff. Paris: Retz, 1978. 398-401.

—. "La notion de lieu de mémoire est-elle exportable?" *Lieux de mémoire et identités nationales.* Eds. Pim den Boer and Willem Frijhoff. Amsterdam: Amsterdam UP, 1993. 3-10.

—. "Présentation." *Les lieux de mémoire I: La République.* Ed. Pierre Nora. Paris: Gallimard, 1984. vii-xiii.

—. "De la République à la Nation." *Les lieux de mémoire I: La République.* Ed. Pierre Nora. Paris: Gallimard, 1984. 651-59.

Quintilian. *The Institutio Oratoria of Quintilian.* Vol. 4. Trans. H. E. Butler. London: Heinemann, 1961.

Renan, Ernest. "What Is a Nation?" *Becoming National: A Reader.* Eds. Geoff Eley and Ronald Grigor Suny. Oxford: Oxford UP, 1996. 41-55. Trans. of "Qu'est-ce qu'une nation?" 1882. *Oeuvres complètes d'Ernest Renan.* Ed. Henriëtte Psichari. Vol. 1. Paris: Calmann-Lévy, 1947. 887-906.

Sewel, Willem. *Nederduytsche spraakkonst.* Amsterdam: Erven J. Lescailje, 1733.

Wesseling, H. L., et al., eds. *Plaatsen van herinnering.* 4 vols. Amsterdam: Bakker, 2005-07.

Italian *luoghi della memoria*

MARIO ISNENGHI

Writing on "sites of memory" in a united Italy is set against a background of *disunited* factors and developments. Disunity is a constituent element of events, memory, and narrative.

1. From Country to State

The peninsula's great past was the original symbolic heritage through which the dawning Nation Italy took its initial form, developed as both consciousness and a project of common space, between the end of the eighteenth and the beginning of the nineteenth century. For centuries already, what other nations had seen and encountered was the past, but the past of a "land of ruins" peopled by a resigned "population of the dead." Establishing the new Nation was a matter of referring to this past from a different viewpoint. Two thousand years before, the secondary peoples of the peninsula had been unified by Rome; a few centuries before unification, between the fourteenth and sixteenth centuries, there had been a flowering of arts and culture, yet that Italy of city-states and dominions was divided politically and militarily while Europe experienced the growth of great absolute monarchies. This spelled both pre-eminence and impediment. The *Risorgimento* was born from this premise: Italy is—or rather will be, will return to being—because it was; it was founded on the memory of having been, and having been great—compared to its present lowliness. The Nation and the national State were thus conceived, establishing and legitimating themselves as a great regenerative process founded on, and made of, memory. The intellectuals and politicians who solicited this reawakening took on a maieutic role, seeking an eclipsed collective "us."

The time invested in laying the foundations spans the first seventy years of the nineteenth century, ideally framed by two great literary works expressing the predominant character of the literature and the men of letters who "invented" Italy: *I Sepolcri* ("The Sepulchres") (1807) by Ugo Foscolo, the first in a series of poet-prophets and heralds of the nation, and *Storia della letteratura italiana* ("History of Italian Literature") (1871) by Francesco De Sanctis, critic and minister, a major summing up of identity, completed as Italy's church towers—for the occasion risen to the status of civic towers, no longer controlled by mourning priests, but rather by celebrating laymen (Sanga)—rang out the conquest of Rome, thereby completing unification (De Sanctis himself recorded this). Putting the seal on this cycle we should add that in the very same year, 1871, Foscolo's remains were moved to Santa Croce, the temple of great Italians that the poet had postulated in his work in 1807.

"Oh Italians, I urge you to history," Foscolo proclaimed, opening his courses at the University of Pavia (1809), courses that undermined the regulations and mental landscapes, the traditional identity of subjects rallied to citizenship; the foreign governors soon saw the need to censure him. Foscolo was born of a Venetian father and a Greek mother, on Zakynthos, an island in the Ionian Sea, a modern Ithaca for a new Odyssean quest for a denied fatherland. Thus he had three homelands: Zakynthos, Venice, and Italy. His birth granted his poetic fantasy both classical and romantic analogies and empathies with Greece and Italy: the great civilizations of the past now fallen low, appealing to history from the nineteenth century, recruiting idealists and volunteers in sentiment and action. The move to Venice exposed the poet-citizen to further losses and deprivations, at the hands both of France, head of the "new order," and Austria, head of the ancien regime. Foscolo took on the role of exile, exiled from both his small and large homelands; this separation allowed him to associate them in memory and nostalgia, as rarely occurs unless fate consigns one to some painful, though fertile, "elsewhere." But living outside of Italy, and making it real through thought and dream, was normal for the eighteenth-century Italian patriot. This was the fate of Giuseppe Mazzini (Ridolfi): protagonist and father of the nation; author of the triple motto "Unity, Independence, Republic"; a leading force in the first Italian political party, *Giovane Italia* ("Young Italy"), in 1831; and an exile in life and death, even though he died in Italy (1872), spurned by the victorious monarchy, defeated, but not broken, living under an alias, almost like an ordinary English Mr. Brown. The Kingdom of Sardinia-Piedmont of the centuries-old Savoy dynasty became the guiding state. It achieved dominance over the national movement, either confining the democrats of the *Partito d'Azione* ("Action Party") to opposition or subordinating them to moderate monarchical initiatives, and became—when it intercepted the political diaspora from Italy to England, France, and Switzerland—itself the land of exile for several thousand refugees during the 1850s. In Turin they re-elaborated their deluded post-1848 revolutionary aspirations and the memory of their respective homelands (Tobia).

Foscolo's personal experience—from "Greek" to Venetian and from Venetian to Italian—is replicated by Ippolito Nievo in *Confessioni d'un Italiano* ("Confessions of an Italian"; Eng. trans. *The Castle of Fratta*), thus becoming the narrative path of a historical and formative novel and forming the nation, national consciousness, and citizenship in a broader than municipal context. Nievo was a great young writer who died prematurely at the age of thirty (he was one of the Garibaldi Thousand), just after having completed narrating and elaborating the entire historical cycle he had experienced. Here, too, the narrative process, in this case that of an eighty-year-old man who had experienced and describes the period of the *Risorgimento*, represents and politically welcomes a territorial and mental passage from small to large—in this case from Venetian to Italian. Reality showed this process of deconstructing and reconstructing old separate identities within a new unity to be more difficult and time consuming than in its literary depiction.

Looking towards the past to lay the foundations of Italy as a country (cf. Romano) involved not only dealing with municipalism as a permanent factor of disunity, the negative side of *civitas* and municipal energy, but also the geographic and mental centrality of the Roman Catholic church, already identified by Machiavelli in *The Prince* (1513) as the most powerful and structured anti-unity barrier. A third great divide was itself the fruit of the very process of unification, namely the discovery, identification, and accentuation of two distinct macro areas, both material and symbolic: North and South.

2. The Rivers of Memory

Recognizing "sites of memory" in a united Italy involves operating on three planes: Until 1861 the building of the Nation and the State actually proceeded by means of the selection and renewed streamlining of artifacts from the past (from an extended period of over two thousand years of history); after 1861, meaning and distance change under a second interpretative pressure, this time aimed at establishing and broadcasting the coordinates of collective memory and a public account of yesterday's events, in other words the events that led to the birth of the Kingdom of Italy (in an accelerated period of less than half a century). The third operation carried out on memory has involved historiography; this has been our task, we who over one hundred and fifty years later have come to draw the conclusions, in a period when the great tale of our origins has lost much of its aura.

Our volumes on the Italian sites of memory, written, conceived, and elaborated during the mid-1990s, did not share the emerging revisionist and anti-unitary spirit of certain environments (the municipalism, regionalism and even secessionism expressed by the new movements of the *Lega* in Veneto and Lombardy, and the clerical revanchism of a certain powerful right-wing Catholic group, *Comunione e Liberazione*, torchbearers of a counter-memory and counter-history of ancien-regime imprint). However, we were encouraged not to remain prisoners of the lofty schemes forged in post-unity public discourse, which were more a form of hegemonic pressure exerted on memory, a political operation and public usage of history, and certainly not a balanced and reliable presentation of events. As often happens, silence, omission, and oblivion are of no less importance in their own way than the emphasis placed on other facts. The concern of historians dealing with the Italian nineteenth century is, and has been, to reintegrate the political targets of oblivion, restoring importance to republicans such as Mazzini, Cattaneo and Garibaldi who "invented" the Nation and sustained the idea; but also to the clericalists who, in the name of legitimist principles and the Pope-King, had thwarted it, and blighted feelings of citizenship among the faithful *ab origine*, in other words a considerable portion of the population (then around twenty million); and to more than a few southerners who, without necessarily feeling nostalgia for the "Neapolitan homeland" and accomplices to bandits, may have struggled, and continued to struggle for some time, to subscribe to the mental adjustment necessary to experience and identify with Piedmontese occupation as national liberation. Above all, it is obviously not the task of the historian of memory to assign posthumous compensation or ideological corrections of real processes. When certain memories have the strength to impose themselves and marginalize, or even cancel others—like the post-1861 moderate, monarchical memory—they themselves become "facts" under which successive generations live, even though subordinate to forms of false consciousness. The reconstruction we sought was, therefore, that of a conflict of directions, whether open or unspoken, with victors and vanquished but without dogmatization: The waterways of history are, after all, not straight, artificial canals but instead exhibit bends, meanders, and resurgences. The waters of republican memory—but also those of anti-unitary, clerical, pro-Bourbon or pro-Austrian memory—may recede but they continue to flow underground and sometimes re-emerge.

The liberal monarchy is well represented by monuments in public squares by the "disciplined revolutionary." (In 1866, during the third war of independence, the government ordered Garibaldi to curtail his volunteers, who were setting out for Trent, as they were winning "too much" against the Austrians. The military leader of the left responded with a laconic telegram: "I obey.") In Italian imagery a different, rebel Garibaldi (Isnenghi, "Garibaldi") persisted as a counter-memory and political resource that has never been completely deactivated, lasting through several generations, made real and reactivated by the left (and during the twentieth century by the right). The Catholics prevailed in the long run: Liberalism and democracy—repudiated in the motto "be neither elector nor elected" (1861), excommunicated by the Syllabus (1864), adverted by the scandalous refusal of the early-twentieth-century "Christian Democrats" and the liquidation of the newly established *Partito Popolare Italiano* ("Popular Party of Italy") by a Vatican attracted to the "Man of Providence" Benito Mussolini—also prevailed after the Second World War under the form of a moderate popular party built on denominational foundations (cf. Tassani; Riccardi; Bravo). And this occurred precisely when the majority of Italians denied having ever been fascists, during the several decades when fascism seemed to disappear both as a real fact and as memory, becoming almost a mere "digression."

3. History and Memory

The Italian sites of memory project, though it was conceived during a period when memory appeared to be depreciated and at risk and was thus approached as a "battle for memory" (Isnenghi, "Conclusione") has therefore endeavored not to put history in a subordinate position in relation to memory. Were I to edit it today I would redress the balance even more in favor of history. In a work on memory this means insisting on the mechanisms, the players, the means of construction, the non-innocent character of memory—subjective and belonging to specific spontaneous and organized groups—and their conflicts. (We have known this since the time of Maurice Halbwachs, but today we live in an age of "invalidated memories" and the "dictatorship of witnesses.") The Savoy monarchy effectively prevailed; Turin, a northern city, marginal in relation to the rest of the peninsula—with a history, moreover, in many ways less significant than Venice, Florence, Rome, Naples or Milan—managed to take the central role in the mid-nineteenth century, during the formative phase of a country in the making, a country which had, historically, a plurality of centers and capitals. Turin—if Rome was recognized as destined to become capital—had in any case to accept and suffer the fact that, in the eyes of the world and most Italians, Rome was firstly the city of the Pope and then the city of the King.

Plurality, therefore, is a key concept; Italy was multi-centered, a public arena charged with tensions and retorts, not sufficiently well-represented by the elevated post-unitary oleography of its four great figures—Vittorio Emanuele, Cavour, Mazzini, Garibaldi—to which the most zealous even added Pius IX, the would-be "liberal pope," who should have been the mediator between "good and evil" and instead never tired of dogmatizing his own primacy and repudiating the *Risorgimento.* It was an arduous task to foster citizenship in this country, especially among an illiterate people used to believing their priests, who were induced by the ecclesiastical hierarchy during the first forty years of the Kingdom not to acknowledge the "legal Italy" that had been brought into being by a secular, often Masonic and not infrequently Jewish revolution; against this the Church offered a "real Italy," the only conceivable nation, which was that of the Guelphs. Dualism was therefore perpetuated, exhuming—and yet again exploiting the sedimentation and language of memory—the most ancient names (Guelphs and Ghibellines).

It was a decision to capitalize on an effective expression of antimony—"real Italy/legal Italy"—, flaunted for almost half a century by a considerable part of the Catholic hierarchy under three pontiffs: Pius IX, Leo XIII, and Pius X. This "real Italy" was the response of a self-referential Catholic world, resistant to the state (and incidentally not only to the "illegitimate" State) and the "legal Italy" of a liberal monarchy which had broadened, though not to any great extent, its social base in the passage (in 1976) from the governmental legacy of Cavour to the governments of the historical left, strengthened by ex-republicans and ex-followers of Garibaldi who had entered the parliamentary arena. This bi-polar image of late-nineteenth-century, post-unitary Italy, however, suffers from the absence of some interesting positions of the period such as the revanchist attitude of the Church and the intransigent clerical movement. It is also fitting to include a third Italy within this framework of competing identities that developed within public debate: the broad range of left-wing movements, the "non-repentant" remains of the Action Party, republicans and irredentists, and the newly born socialist party, especially in the 1890s when, under Andrea Costa and Filippo Turati, the socialists disassociated themselves from anarcho-socialism and entered the electoral competition. Though denying the Nation, the same Internationalists, under Bakunin, Cafiero and Merlino, ended up contributing to the definition of the arena: After several failed attempts one of them managed to assassinate Umberto I (1900). The Nation was also the Anti-Nation: The Kingdom also included its own denial of both "black" and "red." The "Italies" in conflict are substantially three. Shifting back in time, the title of a work by the national-fascist historian Gioacchino Volpe—*L'Italia in cammino* ("Italy on the Move") (1927)—suggests a conceptual framework into which we can fit the formation and conflict of subjects, identities and memories of what we can call "three Italies on the move." This framework ensured several results: the multiplicity and dialectics of the subjects in question; a division and conflict which unfolds, moreover, within the same public arena, becoming both charged and registered; and the processes of historical dynamics.

This was what we needed to underscore the specific elements of the unity-disunity of "Italy as a country," not yet finalized but *in itinere. Symbols and Myths*, *Structures and Events*, *Personalities and Dates*, variants and titles of the volumes of the Italian *Sites of Memory* project, take on and give structure and meaning to the lives of generations of "Italians." They, too, were on the move, and "on the move" does not necessarily mean going forward, united in one single direction.

The twentieth century engaged the Italians in two great historical events which can also be seen as opportunities and incentives to dissolve the disuniting factors within superior forms of unity. These were the First World War and fascism, two chapters in the transition from elitist society to mass society. The Great War—debated for ten months in the press and by the public at large, much less in Parliament—was chosen, desired but also imposed by many and on many and represents new antitheses, new dualisms, and the elaboration of new divided memories (Isnenghi, "Grande Guerra"). Victory over the "Historical Enemy"—the Habsburg Empire, Austria—created a unity never seen before and at the same time new aspects of division in experience, in representation, and in the mass of private and public accounts. Eighty years after the First World War the conflict over the pros and cons of the war, and its supporters, have not yet been appeased or become the mere object of historiographical study. Neither did the most large-scale project and endeavor towards social, political, and cultural reunification since the *Risorgimento*—fascism—manage to create unity out of differences. Not only did the dictatorship and single party allow different lines of thought to persist in a variety of fields—economy, art, concepts of city and rural life; it also retained significant powers such as the monarchy, the armed forces, and the Church, who were to promote and orchestrate the transition of the regime in 1943; in fact they primarily nourished the need and desire for *another* Italy among the antifascist minorities. Again, therefore, in researching these processes and mental redistributions the historian must maintain a balanced view of all the different levels, which at this point also include, diversely: the memory of republican and imperial Rome; a refocusing on the *Risorgimento*—excessively liberal and parliamentary in the regime's policy of memory and the object of a nostalgic countermelody for both internal and external exiles; and the memory of the "Italy of Vittorio Veneto," in other words the victorious army and D'Annunzio's "greater Italy" which Mussolini (Passerini) claimed to have "brought" to Vittorio Emanuele III when the March on Rome (Isnenghi, "Marcia") ended in Palazzo Chigi instead of in prison. The compact vision of a society reunified within a "totalitarian" State was, moreover, paradoxically crushed by the regime itself when it decided, in 1938, to annul the rights of around 40,000 citizens, those Jews who suddenly became "internal foreigners" (di Cori) though many of them—and their forefathers—had played an active role in creating the Nation.

In this necessity to contemporaneously grasp unity and disunity as permanent coordinates of Italian history the summit was reached in the Second World War. It would be impossible to disentangle the complex layers of events and memory here. There were several wars within the war, successive and intertwined, with major points of division defined by two significant moments in 1943: July 25, the end of the Mussolini government; and September 8, the armistice, in other words unconditional surrender. The *Comitato di Liberazione Nationale* ("Committee of National Liberation"), the motor of antifascist resistance and the transition from Monarchy to Republic, attempted to give a structure to the re-emerging plurality of positions and parties, yet the pressures and figures involved, in that devastated Italy between 1943 and 1945 which had ceased to believe in itself as a Great Power, created a field of tensions which included a last-minute fascism reborn in republican guise, which competed with the antifascists on the concept of Nation and fatherland, but outdid them in the name of a "new Europe." On the issues surrounding the war, in the different phases from 1940 to 1945, there are numerous essays, by witnesses such as Nuto Revelli on the "retreat from Russia," and scholars such as Marco Di Giovanni, Giorgio Rochat, Mimmo Franzinelli, Adriano Ballone, Massimo Legnani and Nicola Galleran. The second post-war period was organized—institutionally, politically, and mentally—according to two great dividing factors: the antifascism/fascism antithesis, sanctioned by the republican constitution which formally took effect in 1948, and the anticommunist/communist antithesis, which, with the Cold War, became a material constitution of greater effectiveness than the formal constitution and was never repealed in the political arena, even after 1989.

References

Bravo, Anna. "La Madonna pelegrina [The Pilgrim Madonna]." Isnenghi, *Simboli* 525-36.

Di Cori, Paola. "La leggi razziali [The Racial Laws]." Isnenghi, *Simboli* 461-76.

Isnenghi, Mario, ed. *Simboli e miti dell'Italia unita* [Symbols and Myths]. Rome: Laterza, 1996. Vol 1 of *I luoghi della memoria* [Sites of Memory]. 3 vols. 1996-97.

—, ed. *Strutture ed eventi dell'Italia unita* [Structures and Events]. Rome: Laterza, 1997. Vol. 2 of *I luoghi della memoria* [Sites of Memory]. 3 vols. 1996-97.

—. "Conclusione." Isnenghi, *Strutture* 427-74.

—. "Garibaldi." Isnenghi, *Personaggi* 25-45.

—. "La Grande Guerra [The Great War]." Isnenghi, *Strutture* 273-310.

—, ed. *L'Italie par elle meme: Lieux de mémoire italiens de 1848 à nos jours.* Paris: Editions Rue d'Ulm, 2006. Trans. of selections from *I luoghi della memoria* [Sites of Memory]. Rome: Laterza, 1996-97.

—. "La Marcia su Roma [The March on Rome]." Isnenghi, *Strutture* 311-30.

—, ed. *Personaggi e date dell'Italia unita* [Personalities and Dates]. Rome: Laterza, 1997. Vol. 3 of *I luoghi della memoria* [Sites of Memory]. 3 vols. 1996-97.

—. "La piazza [The Place]." Isnenghi, *Strutture* 41-52.

Passerini, Luisa. "Mussolini." Isnenghi, *Personaggi* 165-86.

Riccardi, Andrea. "I Papi [The Popes]." Isnenghi, *Personaggi* 401-25.

Ridolfi, Maurizio. "Mazzini." Isnenghi, *Personaggi* 3-23.

Romano, Ruggiero. *Paese Italia: Venti secoli di itentità.* Rome: Donzelli, 1994.

Sanga, Glauco. "Campane e campanili [Bells and Belltowers]." Isnenghi, *Simboli* 29-42.

Tassani, Giovanni. "L'oratorio [The Oration]." Isnenghi, *Strutture* 135-72.

Tobia, Bruno. "Le Cinque Giornate di Milano [The Five Days of Milan]." Isnenghi, *Strutture* 311-30.

Mitteleuropa as a *lieu de mémoire*

JACQUES LE RIDER

The formation of *Mitteleuropa* can be traced back to the Holy Roman Empire of the German Nation and to the first Germanic settlements east of the empire. In a direct line with Austro-Prussian dualism, entrenched at the time of Maria Theresa and Frederick II, two empires—the German *Reich* proclaimed in 1871 and the Habsburg monarchy—succeeded the Holy Roman Empire (abolished at the time of Napoleon, partially restored in 1815 in the form of the German Confederation, irrevocably destroyed by the Austro-Prussian War in 1866). In the twentieth century, the mental map of German Central Europe is marked by the geopolitical concept of *Mitteleuropa*, which is linked to the liberal nationalist ideology of Friedrich Naumann, which defined the German war aims in 1915. Naumann's ideas attenuated the pan-Germanic program by limiting it to the area of Central Europe. As a result, German-speaking historians and political scientists today tend to avoid the word *Mitteleuropa*, preferring the terms *Zentraleuropa* (closer to the French "*Europe central*" and the English "Central Europe") or *Mittelosteuropa*.

Why are *Mitteleuropa*, *Zentraleuropa*, and *Mittelosteuropa* of contemporary interest for the history of *lieux de mémoire*? Because from the Enlightenment to the Second World War, this area has, through the individual national identities, provided the center of the European continent with its identity. The twentieth century has striven to dismantle and deform *Mitteleuropa*: the First World War, Nazism and the Shoah, the Second World War, Stalinism and Neo-Stalinism. One can say that since the peace treaties of 1919-1920 and since 1945, *Mitteleuropa* as a whole has become a *lieu de mémoire*, a space of memory (*Erinnerungsraum*).

The dissemination of German culture formed a space which, from the end of the eighteenth century on, became the site of confrontation between, on the one hand, German *Kultur* and other cultural identities and, on the other hand, the German-Slavic, German-Jewish, German-Hungarian, German-Rumanian mixture. Cultural *Mitteleuropa* is thus an ambivalently defined notion. In certain contexts, it evokes the catastrophic path of Europe's destiny during the time of nationalisms and imperialisms. In other contexts, it designates a civilization of cultural mingling at the intersection of Northern and Southern Europe, halfway between Occidental Europe and Oriental Europe.

In the "center" of the European continent, other *lieux de mémoire* older than *Mitteleuropa* retain a subliminal presence, always ready to become current again. The distinction between Byzantine Europe and Central Europe, and later between Islam and Christianity, created religious and cultural borders separating the Orthodox peoples from the small islands of Islam which still exist in the Balkans, and Catholics from Protestants. These borders are *lieux de mémoire* which have often served to justify discourses of rejection (Russophobe or anti-Serbian), or to explain conflicts in the post-Communist era, particularly in the territory of the former Yugoslavia. However, the secularization of European culture renders it impossible to reduce contemporary conflicts to religious wars. These religious borders are *lieux de mémoire* manipulated by neo-nationalistic propaganda. Yet forgetting them would also be unfortunate: For example, considering attempts to define "fundamental values" and Europe's cultural identity, *Mitteleuropa* is a reminder that both Islam and Judaism have left an indelible mark on Europe, and that Byzantine Christianity is not only to be found on the Oriental edge of Europe, but instead also in its geocultural center.

Two other borders, present earlier and still existent, belong to the *lieux de mémoire* of *Mitteleuropa*. The first is that separating Russia from Central Europe. For the Slavophile Russians, the Catholic, Protestant, and non-religious Slavs of Central Europe were an exception to the rule which identified the Slavic soul with the Orthodox church. For Russian Occidentalists, Central Europe was merely a connecting passageway one had to traverse to get to Germany, France, Italy, or England. Poland, lastly, seen from the Russian perspective, occupied a place apart, as it could, after all, to a certain degree be seen as an integral part of the Russian empire. *Mitteleuropa* certainly defined itself most often in opposition to Russia, whose political and cultural regression appeared threatening from the Central European point of view. This *lieu de memoire*, namely the border between *Mitteleuropa* and Russia, could possibly reemerge, if the question of closer ties between Russia and the European Union were to be broached.

The other long-standing border which exists as a *lieu de mémoire* in Central Europe is that dividing the "Balkans" from the population of Central Europe. The *homo balkanicus* is a caricature originally conceived of by Westerners to denote a primitive European, merely picturesque within his folklore tradition but barbaric when he takes up arms. European discourses regarding "the Balkans" highlighted an Orientalism without positive characteristics. They originate from a cultural colonialism which expects Western civilization to bring a bit of order and rationality to the fragmented and underdeveloped territories. "The Balkans" were contrasted with the Southeast Central Europe of the Habsburgs. Still today, the expansion of the European Union to include the "Balkans" remains incomplete and faces difficulties, of which the symbolic constraints are not the least important.

The Western borders of Europe are not any simpler to define than its Eastern borders. Do the German-speaking countries belong to Central or Western Europe? When the German *Reich* and the Habsburg monarchy were in contact with Russia and the Ottoman Empire, they undoubtedly were a part of Central Europe. Between 1949 and 1990, the Federal Republic of Germany belonged to Western Europe, whereas the German Democratic Republic was a part of "Eastern Europe" and under Soviet influence.

In 1990, after the dissolution of the U.S.S.R., the emancipation of the Central European republics, and German reunification, Central Europe seemed to be coming to life again. After the consolidation of the European Community, the center of Europe was no longer the Berlin-Prague-Vienna-Budapest axis, but rather the axis Rotterdam-Milan. Would the Eastern enlargement of the European Union allow Europe to recover its historical center? Or would it become clear that the Central Europe in question is no longer in the center but rather at the margin of the Europe of the Treaty of Rome, and that *Mitteleuropa* now only has the status of a *lieu de mémoire*?

This *lieu de mémoire* had been the talisman of certain intellectual, anti-Soviet dissident groups. In the 1980s, György Konrád in Budapest and the Czech Milan Kundera and the Yugoslav Danilo Kis in Paris revived the discussion about *Mitteleuropa*. Kundera's text, first published in Paris in November 1983, became famous under the title of the American version from April 1984: "The Tragedy of Central Europe." Members of the anti-Soviet resistance of November 1956 in Budapest, Kundera writes, were fighting for their fatherland and for Europe. It took the repression of the Prague Spring in 1968 to awaken once again the memory of Central Europe, the myth of a Golden Age, the end of which was the time around 1900 and the 1920s.

However, the memory of Central Europe also includes fateful episodes which line the history of the "small nations" that were exposed to mortal threats. The nations of Central Europe know the experience of downfall and disappearance. The great Central European novels, namely those by Hermann Broch, Robert Musil, Jaroslav Hasek, and Franz Kafka, are meditations on the possible end of European humanity. The tragedy of Central Europe is, in short, the tragedy of Europe. When the Iron Curtain falls, Kundera concluded in his text of 1983-84, the peoples of Central Europe will realize that the culture of Europe (scientific, philosophical, literary, artistic, musical, cinematographic, audio-visual, educational and universitarian, multilingual) has ceased to be of value in the eyes of Europeans themselves, and constitutes at best only a *lieu de mémoire.*

Almost at the same time, in June 1984, the Hungarian writer György Konrád published the German version of his essay, "Der Traum von Mitteleuropa" ("The Dream of Central Europe"), first presented at a conference in Vienna in May 1984. *Mitteleuropa* for him evoked the memory of Austria-Hungary during the Belle Époque. The Central European spirit, he wrote, is a view of the world, an aesthetic sensibility that allows for complexity and multilingualism, a strategy that rests on understanding even one's deadly enemy. The Central European spirit consists of accepting plurality as a value in and of itself; it represents "another rationality," Konrád affirmed, an anti-politics, a defense of civil society against politics.

In Central Europe, the "literary republic" was long near to the heart of the *res publica.* The first configuration of the cultural identity of Central Europe appeared when Renaissance and Baroque were spreading via Vienna, Prague, Krakow, and Buda (in Hungary). This "delayed" Renaissance fused with the art and zeitgeist of the Baroque period and significantly influenced the entire Central European region. The primary factor determining the establishment of a literary republic in Europe was the reaction to the Ottoman threat, which led to the founding of the "Sodalitas litteraria Danubiana" by Conrad Celtis around 1500, unifying German, Hungarian, Slavic, Bohemian, and Wallachian humanists.

At the time of the Reformation and the Counter-Reformation, a new cultural system emerged in Northern and Central Germany, which broke with Latin and Italian Central Europe, and the Reformation called forth the first stirrings of a consciousness of national cultures, for example among the Czechs or Slovaks. In contrast, the Counter-Reformation elevated Baroque to the official style and it would be two centuries before Josephinism at the end of the eighteenth century achieved the first synthesis of German Enlightenment and Baroque, all the while endeavoring to establish German as the lingua franca in *Mitteleuropa*, after Latin, Italian, and French, which incited as a reaction the inexorable protest of the nations against this Germanization.

The production of the national through philology, which exalts the oral and written literary traditions, and through linguistics, which codifies the spelling, grammar, and vocabulary, corresponds to a German model one could call "Herderian." The diffusion of Herder's theoretical system among the peoples of Central Europe constitutes an essential stage in the formation of the cultural *Mitteleuropa.* Hungarian, Romanian, Polish, Czech, Serb, Croatian, Slovenian, etc. intellectuals, through exposure to Herder's texts, forged the conviction that love for one's fatherland is impossible without love for one's mother tongue, and that the poet is the true father of the nation, far more than the rulers who scoff at linguistic borders and only recognize dynastically defined territories.

Mitteleuropa is one of the *lieux de mémoire* that was of decisive importance in the way the "literary republic" constituted cultural and national identities. One could say that *Mitteleuropa* is the *lieu de mémoire* par excellence of a model of the production of the national through the cultural, against the pure reason of the political and military state.

Delayed by their coercion into the collectivity of the German and Habsburg empires, since the nineteenth century the historical nations of Central Europe have been demanding their emancipation, and striving to connect to earlier epochs of independence and greatness. During the twentieth century, at the time that the central empires disappeared, representations of a federal order and a cosmopolitan culture resurfaced, generally in connection with the Austrian tradition. "Central Europe is just a term which symbolizes the needs of the present," Hugo von Hofmannsthal wrote in December 1917 in his lecture on "Die österreichische Idee" (457-58). And in his notes for an article about the idea of Europe we find this definition of the *lieu de mémoire Mitteleuropa*: "Millennial struggle for Europe, millennial mission by Europe, millennial belief in Europe. For us, the Germans and Slavs and Latins who dwell on the soil of two Roman empires, chosen to bear a common destiny and inheritance—for us Europe is truly the fundamental color of the planet" (54).

Faced with the shock of the Third Reich, the Habsburg myth and, beyond that, the memory of the Holy Roman Empire of the German Nation are transformed by Joseph Roth or Stefan Zweig into a retrospective utopia of the coexistence of nations in a cosmopolitan cultural space, into a literary republic covering a vast Central European territory from Italy to the coast of the Baltic Sea.

The history of the Habsburg monarchy from this time can be interpreted as a political and socio-cultural process of harmonization of the ethnic, linguistic, and cultural plurality. Thanks to institutions which managed conflict and structured the pluralism in the form of the "Compromise" (*Ausgleich)* within the framework of each "crownland" (*Kronland*), the liberal Empire founded in 1867 on the basis of new principles attempted to improve the relationships among the nations. This is the meaning of the "Habsburg myth," which Claudio Magris has spoken of so masterfully. This ideology of the state, brought to the fore by the Habsburgs since the time when Prince Eugene referred to the monarchy as a *totum* and particularly emphasized during the time between 1866 and 1871 when Austria, removed from the Holy Roman Empire which it had long dominated and in competition with the German Empire, newly proclaimed in 1871, had to invent a new geo-political identity for itself, based on that which was left over: the territories in the East and Southeast. The Habsburg myth of a pluralistic society and a pluralistic state which provided all peoples the *Heimat* entitled to them was merely a propagandistic disguise for the battle between two hegemonic peoples, the German Austrians and the Hungarians, both fighting to defend and expand their privileges and their advantages, a struggle presented as being of general interest and "supranational" reasoning.

The comparison (flattering for Austrian Cisleithania) with the policy of Germanization pursued by the German *Reich* in its Eastern, Polish regions is an integral part of the "Habsburg myth." One also has to distinguish between the Austrian part of the Danubian Empire and the Hungarian Transleithania. The integrative force of the Habsburg model, characterized by its cultural pluralism, is incontestable in Cisleithania (even allowing for a confusion of myth and reality), but did not function in Hungary. The Slavic regions that belonged to the Hungarian part of the monarchy undoubtedly never had the feeling that they were part of a Slavic-Hungarian cultural community. The same can be said of the Romanians in Transleithania. It is Cisleithania that has romanticized the "Habsburg myth" and made it a *lieu de mémoire* of a cosmopolitan *Mitteleuropa*, in which the cultural plurality was able to form itself into a harmonic pluralism.

Since World War II, *Mitteleuropa* has become the *lieu de mémoire* of Jewish Central Europe, destroyed by the Shoah. The Jewish culture of the shtetl, the contemporary renaissance of Yiddish, and the spreading of Hasidism have drawn new maps of Central Europe. This Jewish culture of *Mitteleuropa* was also that of the Jews assimilated into the national cultures. In Prague during Kafka's time, assimilated Jews were part of both the German and the Czech cultures; in Lemberg, intellectual capital of Galicia and birthplace of Joseph Roth, they were divided between German and Polish culture; in Czernowitz, metropolis of Bukovina, the territory made famous by Paul Celan, they hesitated between assimilation into the German culture and Rumanization.

The Austrian-Marxist tradition constructed the *lieu de mémoire* of a Central Europe of the working class. The Austrian social democracy of the Habsburg era found it difficult to overcome the contradiction between "class" and "nationality." Victor Adler led a supranational, official discourse and wanted his party to become a *Reichspartei*, in opposition to nationalist currents. But from the 1890s on, even for him the nationalist arguments prevailed over internationalist class solidarity. In the Cisleithanian parliament, the Social Democratic fraction was divided into five national clubs. The trade unions tried to unite the nationalities within a factory, one branch of industry, one organization. In sum, the Austrian social democracy was a mirror image of the Habsburg monarchy: supranational in its "political myth," but in reality divided along national lines.

Mitteleuropa is a European space of memory which combines two constitutive elements of European identity: first, cultural and linguistic plurality and second, the difficulty to structure this plurality without giving in to the "holistic" temptation of a homogeneous society, the course usually followed by nationalism.

Until the 1920s, German, the lingua franca of *Mitteleuropa*, is added in some linguistic regions as an international language alongside the "national" language, occasionally in competition with another international language such as French. Gradually, with the growing sense of national consciousness and the affirmation of literary languages, German is reduced to the status of a "second language" which allows for international communication within the Central European region.

The phenomenon of true multilingualism, combining two or three languages of the Central European region, is generally limited to certain zones of contact, the children of mixed marriages, and the elites of certain metropolises (such as Trieste, Prague, Bratislava, Czernovitz, or Lemberg). It should be mentioned that cases of Polish-Lithuanian, Slovakian-Hungarian, or Austrian-Italian-Slovenian multilingualism, to name just a few possible combinations, are far less numerous than cases of multilingualism in which a Central European national language is combined with German or French. An intellectual from *Mitteleuropa* who chooses a language other than his native tongue for his literary or scholarly works seldom chooses another language of the region; only German, English, or French come into consideration.

As a *lieu de mémoire* of cultural plurality which allows multilingualism and "hybrid identities" to flourish, *Mitteleuropa* is also a *lieu de mémoire* of the degradation of nationalism, as analyzed by Gumplowicz, who depicted Central Europe as the theater of a "struggle of races" (*Rassenkampf*), a war between the various social and ethnic groups. The "race" theories of this professor at the University of Graz are dominated by a pessimism that would be worthy of Hobbes, and form the other interpretative framework for the plurality of Central Europe.

In Cisleithania, the Habsburg system had attempted to guarantee the cultural autonomy of the nationalities through constitutional compromises which controlled the balance between the ethnic-linguistic groups in each territory. In Moravia, for example, one could not simultaneously be both Czech and German, but had to choose one or the other. A majority of the Jews chose a German linguistic identity. In Cisleithania, this cohabitation without cohesion did not lead to "supranationality," but rather to a curious alloy of Habsburg citizenship and Czech, Polish, Serb, Croatian,

Slovenian, Italian, Romanian, Ruthenian, or German "private nationality." Were the Jews of the Habsburg monarchy "supranational" as well, as Joseph Roth suggested? In reality, the Jews of Austria-Hungary were swept along with everyone else in the movement affirming the individual nations and took on the language of the dominant nationality in their province.

Regarding the notion of *Mitteleuropa* from the perspectives of the different societies of the Central European region, profound divergences are evident. For most Poles, memory of *Mitteleuropa* is inextricably bound up with the successive divisions of Poland among three empires. The Poland that existed between the two world wars refused the restoration of a Central European federation and drew inspiration for being a major regional power from its own national historical references, by challenging the German enclaves within Poland maintained by the Treaty of Versailles, yet also nourishing great territorial ambitions in the East.

In Bohemia, did the national independence achieved in Saint-Germain-en-Laye do away with the nostalgia for the old Danubian order, and did Czech intellectuals in the 1920s forget the "Austroslavism" of Frantisek Palacky, that liberal Czech who insisted after 1848 that had the Habsburg monarchy not existed, it would have had to be invented, in the interest of Europe and of all mankind? In fact, the empire of the Habsburg Bohemians, which belonged to the old Holy Roman Empire, offered the best protection against Russian imperialism. The high degree of economic and political modernization achieved in Bohemia before the Second World War confirms that the Czech nationality was able to flourish in the heart of Cisleithania. But the First World War destroyed the faith that the peoples of Central Europe had in the Habsburg *Mitteleuropa*. After the summer of 1914, the Habsburgs, having betrayed their historical mission, were merely the "shining representatives" of Germany, which reduced the small nations of Central Europe to the status of oppressed peoples, as highlighted by Jaroslav Hasek's novel *The Good Soldier Švejk*.

In Hungary, a historical nation in Central Europe recaptured from the Ottomans by the Habsburgs, *Mitteleuropa* has remained a positively connotated *lieu de mémoire*. Budapest, capital of the dual monarchy after the Compromise of 1867, experienced in the last third of the nineteenth century and up until the First World War one of its most splendid periods, politically, economically, and culturally. The Treaty of Trianon, for the Hungarians a traumatic experience, is part of the reason for the idealization of the memory of *Mitteleuropa*.

Mitteleuropa is also a *lieu de mémoire* of French-German and French-Austrian tensions and conflicted relations with Italy, which, going by the "mental map" of German imperialism, was the decisive party in the fate of *Mitteleuropa*, based on the Italian territories first belonging to the Holy

Roman Empire and then the Habsburg monarchy. Since the end of the nineteenth century, French historical thought, primarily committed to the cause of the Slavic peoples, has criticized the "prison of the peoples." One of the most systematic deconstructions of the term *Mitteleuropa* comes from Ernest Denis, an expert in Czech history, friend of Benes and Masaryk, advocate of the idea of Czechoslovakia and also a defender of the idea of Yugoslavia. These negative interpretations of *Mitteleuropa* as an imperialistic German and Habsburg project corresponds to the majority opinion in France at that time. The geographer Emmanuel de Martonne, who played an eminent role in the committee that paved the way for the peace conference of 1919-20 (he suggested the borders of Hungary, Yugoslavia, Romania, Poland, and the Polish corridor), published in 1930-31 volume 4 of *Geographie universelle*, dedicated to *L'Europe Centrale.* This French concept of Central Europe, in contrast to the idea of *Mitteleuropa*, influenced the peace treaties of 1919-20 and inspired the politics of the "small entente" in Central Europe.

From the Italian perspective, the term *Mitteleuropa* evokes a debate carried out in Northeastern Italy in the time leading up to the First World War, about attempts to bring together Italians, Germans, Austrians, and Slavs in a regional community, held together by deeper links than the dynastic connections of the Habsburgs. In the 1920s, Trieste remained a hub for Austrian-Italian-Jewish-Slavic cultural contact. Under fascism, Italy tried to play a role in the foreground of Central Europe and the Balkans, but was unable to penetrate Nazi domination (see also Isnenghi, this volume).

In the years following German unification, the dissolution of the Soviet system, and the emancipation of the nations of Central Europe, one could expect *Mitteleuropa* to reconstitute itself. The French and perhaps the English might well worry that this negative *lieu de mémoire* could gain currency again and a zone of German (and Austrian) influence be re-established. In the lands that belonged to the Habsburg monarchy until 1918, *Mitteleuropa* remained the Belle Epoque, a fashionable topic re-discovered in the 1980s.

Paradoxically, at precisely the point that the expansion of the European Union to include Central Europe has been completed, *Mitteleuropa* seems to have lost its importance. But does not precisely the forgetting of this *lieu de mémoire* of Central Europe show that Europe itself has lost its memory and the markers of its identity? In the new member states of the European Union, will the feeling of being European be engulfed by the return of national emotions, by the appetite for economic and cultural globalization after decades of being trapped in the Soviet bloc, and by strategic considerations that would seem to be better guaranteed by

NATO than by Europe? Does not neo-Nazi and xenophobic populism highlight the fact that the suppression of *Mitteleuropa—lieu de mémoire* of the great catastrophes which nationalism and racism led to—does not contribute to a democratic political culture? Indeed, it is instead witness to the atrophying of historical consciousness, without which it is likely impossible to strengthen the European Union.

Translated by Anna-Lena Flügel

References

Csáky, Moritz, and Elisabeth Grossegger. *Jenseits von Grenzen: Transnationales, translokales Gedächtnis.* Vienna: Praesens, 2007.

Droz, Jacques. *L'Europe central: Evolution historique de l'idée de «Mitteleuropa».* Paris: Payot, 1960.

Europe central—Mitteleuropa. Spec. issue of *Revue germanique internationale* 1 (1994).

Hofmannsthal, Hugo von. "Die Idee Europa." 1917. *Reden und Aufsätze II, 1914-1924.* Frankfurt am Main: Fischer, 1979. 43-54. Vol. 9 of *Gesammelte Werke in zehn Einzelbänden.* Bernd Schoeller und Rudolf Hirsch, eds. 10 vols.

—. "Die österreichische Idee." 1917. *Reden und Aufsätze II, 1914-1924.* Frankfurt am Main: Fischer, 1979. 454-58. Vol. 9 of *Gesammelte Werke in zehn Einzelbänden.* Bernd Schoeller und Rudolf Hirsch, eds. 10 vols.

Konrád, György. "Der Traum von Mitteleuropa." *Aufbruch nach Mitteleuropa: Rekonstruktion eines versunkenen Kontinents.* Eds. Erhard Busek and Gerhard Wilfinger. Vienna: Edition Atelier, 1986. 87-97.

Kundera, Milan."Un Occident kidnappé ou La tragédie de l'Europe central." *Le Débat* 27 (1983): 1-22. [English: Kundera, Milan. "The Tragedy of Central Europe." *New York Review of Books* 26 Apr. 1984: 33-38.]

Le Rider, Jacques. *La Mitteleuropa.* 1994. Paris: Presses Universitaires de France, 1996. [German: Le Rider, Jacques. *Mitteleuropa: Auf den Spuren eines Begriffes.* Trans. Robert Fleck. Vienna: Deuticke, 1994.]

Le Rider, Jacques, Moritz Csáky, and Monika Sommer, eds. *Transnationale Gedächtnisorte in Zentraleuropa.* Innsbruck: StudienVerlag, 2002.

Magris, Claudio. *Il mito Absburgico nella letteratura austriaca moderna.* Turin: Einaudi, 1963.

Naumann, Friedrich. *Mitteleuropa.* Berlin: Reimer, 1915.

Sites of Memory in U.S.-American Histories and Cultures

UDO J. HEBEL

1. Conceptual Frameworks and American Memory Studies

U.S.-American cultures of memory reverberate with the particular contexts and developments of North American histories since the colonial period. The proverbial newness of the so-called New World, the definitional projection of the U.S.-American republic as an unprecedented promise of universal redemption, and the manifold conflicts within the multiethnic societies of the North American continent and the United States have supported rather than limited the emergence, purposeful construction, and ongoing revision of a multivocal network of sites of memory. Theoretical approaches to interpret the political, social, and cultural power of imagined communities and invented traditions in processes of nation-building and community preservation offer the conceptual framework to assess the significance of cultural memories and collective commemorations for the formation and stabilization of a U.S.-American nation that was created rhetorically and in historical acts of political and cultural opposition. At the same time, archaeological remains of precontact achievements of the indigenous peoples of North America and traces of pre-Columbian European travelers in the Western Hemisphere serve as lasting reminders that American cultural memories do not begin in 1492 and should not be reduced to Anglocentric sites. The multidisciplinarity of American Studies and the discipline's multicultural agenda and prominent involvement in recent theoretical turns—visual, performative, spatial, virtual, transnational—provide American Studies scholars with a comprehensive vision to account for the heterogeneity of the discursive and non-discursive manifestations of American cultures of memory and to explore the political and economic competition for commemorative participation and authority in a democratic and pluralistic society. Well-established concepts of U.S.-American cultural history and American Studies scholarship such as Henry S. Commager's stress on the specific U.S.-American search for a usable past and Robert Bellah's notion of American civil religion, as well as the New Historicist understanding of U.S.-American culture as a rhetorical battlefield, connect well with sociocultural and constructivist approaches in memory studies.

2. The Cultural Work of Literary Sites of U.S.-American Memories

The beginnings of the literary construction of specifically American cultural memories run parallel to the European colonization of the North American continent in the sixteenth and seventeenth centuries. A wealth of multilingual texts preserves the wondrous moments of the first intercultural encounters as well as the ensuing conflicts between European colonists and the indigenous peoples in the northwestern, southern, and southwestern areas of the future United States. The commemorative impulse in colonial English-language literature reaches a climax of lasting ideological impact in the historiographical writings of seventeenth-century Puritan New England. The histories of William Bradford, John Winthrop, and Cotton Mather prescribe a formula for U.S.-American commemorations of an Anglocentric myth of origin revolving around the narrative of the Pilgrim Fathers' arrival at Plymouth Rock in 1620, which is still observed today as the national family holiday of Thanksgiving on the fourth Thursday in November. The intention of seventeenth-century historiographers to perpetuate the Puritan "city upon the hill" against the changing course of worldly history is best verbalized in the "General Introduction" to Cotton Mather's *Magnalia Christi Americana* (1702): "But whether *New England* may *Live* any where else or no [sic], it must *Live* in our *History*!" The determination to use historiographical scripts to exercise commemorative authority, especially in times of political crises and intercultural conflicts, can be recognized in the repeated commissioning of prominent seventeenth-century ministers and politicians to write officially sanctioned interpretations of New England history, among them most prominently Nathaniel Morton's *New Englands Memoriall* and William Hubbard's *General History of New England*. In the centuries to follow, and especially after the foundation of the U.S.-American republic, the impulse to construct historiographical sites of memory for the sake of ideological control and cultural containment continued to remain productive. George Bancroft's *History of the United States of America*, first published in 1837 and continually revised until the 1880s, still stands as one of the best examples of a long-dominant historiographic site of U.S.-American memory.

The nineteenth century, and especially the time period between the British-American War of 1812-15 and the Civil War of 1861-65, saw the publication of innumerous historical novels which acted as literary sites of memory (see Rigney, this volume) in the processes of establishing and maintaining a national U.S.-American culture and identity. Literary critics such as George Tucker, Walter Channing, Rufus Choate, John Neal, and William Gilmore Simms called for the intentional creation of a national

U.S.-American literature. The historical novels of James Fenimore Cooper, James Kirke Paulding, John Neal, Lydia Maria Child, William Gilmore Simms, John W. DeForest, and Nathaniel Hawthorne responded to the collective desire for fictional commemorations of earlier stages of colonial and national U.S.-American history. They also provided historical precedents for contemporary cultural and political issues and conflicts such as the Indian removal policy or slavery. Regional differences in the perception of American histories and identities move to the forefront towards the end of the nineteenth century when so-called plantation literature serves as a popular, though controversial, platform for the nostalgic, at times openly apologetic and racist, commemoration of the Old South and the so-called lost cause of the Southern Confederacy. The fictional recollection of the pre-Civil War South in the context of late-nineteenth- and early-twentieth-century reconciliation politics lives on in twentieth-century American visual and media culture in Hollywood classics such as *Birth of a Nation* (1915) and *Gone with the Wind* (1939), and in the internationally successful TV series *North and South* (1985-94), based on a 1980 trilogy of conventional historical novels by John Jakes. The resurgence of history in contemporary American literature—see novels by authors such as Thomas Pynchon, E. L. Doctorow, and Charles Frazier—testifies to the unbroken cultural power of fictional sites of memory.

Autobiographical writings, here read as purposeful acts of individual remembrance and collective identity construction in specific cultural and intercultural contexts (see Saunders, this volume), make for a third noteworthy corpus of literary sites of American memory. The self-dramatizing impulse of early promoters of European colonization such as John Smith, the particularly self-scrutinizing urge and exemplary format of Puritan conversion relations, and the collective self-perception of many eighteenth-century American writers fuel the early production of a large body of religious and secular life writing in British North America. The spiritual autobiographies of Thomas Shepard and Jonathan Edwards, the Indian captivity narrative of Mary Rowlandson, the travel narratives of Sarah Kemble Knight and Elizabeth Ashbridge, John Woolman's Quaker journal, William Byrd's account of daily life on a Chesapeake Bay plantation, Native American Samson Occom's narrative, and, above all, Benjamin Franklin's *Autobiography* represent the wide spectrum and cultural diversity of seventeenth- and eighteenth-century American autobiographical writing. The autobiographies of women and ethnic writers as well as the early autobiographies of representatives of religiously and politically dissenting groups illustrate the usefulness of acts of individual remembering for oppositional, if not subversive, expressions of group concerns. Olaudah Equiano's *Interesting Narrative* (1789) is the first of a long list of African

American slave narratives which preserve for the African American community and expose to white readers the plight of Southern chattel slavery and the evil of the transatlantic slave trade. Paradigmatic examples of this literary form are the narratives of Frederick Douglass and Harriot Jacobs, whose cultural work and political impact resound in the texts of twentieth-century African American activists and writers such as Martin Luther King, Malcolm X, Alice Walker, and Toni Morrison. In the twentieth century, the archive of American autobiographical writing encompasses life writings by a wide range of differently representative Americans, from Gilded Age business tycoon Andrew Carnegie to New England intellectual and cultural critic Henry Adams, from groundbreaking feminist Charlotte Perkins Gilman to Jewish American immigrant Mary Antin, from expatriate writer Gertrude Stein to Sioux chief Black Elk. The further pluralization of a once-Anglocentric, English-only U.S.-American literature in the wake of the ethnic empowerment movements since the 1960s and the canon revisions since the 1980s have given a more prominent voice to the autobiographical fiction and commemorative identity politics of ethnic writers such as N. Scott Momaday, Louise Erdrich, Maxine Hong Kingston, Richard Rodriguez, Sandra Cisneros, and bell hooks.

At the beginning of the twenty-first century, the ever-growing editorial project of The Library of America makes for a commemorative compilation of a uniquely comprehensive scope.

3. Visual Sites of Memory in an Increasingly Mediated U.S.-American History and Culture

Petroglyphs and other forms of visual rock art of precontact indigenous Pueblo cultures in the American Southwest antedate any other manifestation of visual memory in what would become U.S.-American territory. Dating back several centuries before the arrival of European colonists and continuing into the times of European-Indian contact and conflict after 1492, the pictorial art of the prehistoric Anasazi, Mogollon, Hohokam, and Fremont cultures and the post-Columbian rock art of the Navajos and Apaches are abstract, ceremonial, or representational in composition. They preserve sacred rites, mythic figures, and ancient symbols as well as specific secular and historic events such as a Spanish massacre of Southwestern tribes in the Canyon de Chelly area in Arizona. Today, visual sites of memory remain part of the ceremonial cultures of Native American tribes but also serve as an important attraction in the tourist business and commemorative industry of the national parks of the Southwest, a prominent, and probably the best-known, example being Mesa Verde.

Among visual representations of the European colonization of North America, renditions of so-called landing scenes hold a specific ideological position as commemorative constructions of pivotal moments of origin, foundation, and identity formation. The 1493 Basel woodcuts of the arrival of Christopher Columbus in the New World express European desires, projections, and cultural schemata rather than actual American realities. Theodore de Bry's widely circulated late-sixteenth-century engravings of Columbus's imperialist act of taking possession of the Western Hemisphere became the foil for later visualizations of landing scenes with a seminal impact on U.S. history. Henry Sargent's "The Landing of the Pilgrims" (1815), today displayed in Pilgrim Hall, Plymouth, Massachusetts, and John Vanderlyn's "The Landing of Christopher Columbus" (1847), still part of the permanent exhibition in the Rotunda of the U.S. Capitol in Washington, D.C., are particularly visible examples from a much larger archive of pictorial recollections of foundational moments in North American history. The crucial moment of U.S.-American national creation is enshrined in John Trumbull's painting "The Signing of the Declaration of Independence, 4 July 1776" (1820), which remains a remarkable example of the young nation's construction of a usable past by means of commissioned icons of memory. That all the works mentioned here served as points of reference for popular prints distributed by the thousands by Currier & Ives and Kellog & Kellog, the most successful producers of lithographs in the nineteenth century, illustrates the connection between U.S.-American cultures of memory on the one hand and commercial interests on the other, evident already in the nineteenth century. The popular impact of visualizations of prenational and national American histories in the nineteenth century was furthermore enhanced by the publication of widely circulated pictorial histories. Multivolume works such as John Frost's *The Pictorial History of the United States of America* (1844) and Benjamin J. Lossing's *Pictorial Field-Book of the American Revolution* (1850) framed the commemorative constitution of a U.S.-American national history and identity with a clearly marked didactic impetus in times of territorial expansion and increasing demographic pluralization.

The archive of iconic sites of U.S.-American memory includes three pre-twentieth-century pictures that deserve special attention. Paul Revere's engraving of the Boston Massacre of 1770, distributed immediately after the event in various print and broadside versions and still used today for history and children's book illustrations, has framed interpretations of the American Revolution as the archetypal struggle of liberty-loving, American colonist-citizens and common people against British military and political tyranny. Emanuel Leutze's "Washington Crossing the Delaware" (1851) has become the quintessential representation of George Washington's historical role as the larger-than-life epic hero leading the emerging U.S.-American nation into a bright future of glory and progress. Emanuel Leutze's "Westward the Course of Empire Takes Its Way (Westward Ho!)" (1861), commissioned as a mural for the U.S. Capitol in Washington, D.C., gathered for official recollection and public admiration the full repertoire of figural and scenic elements to depict the national ideology of Manifest Destiny on the eve of the Civil War. Among more recent pictorial sites of memory, Norman Rockwell's "Freedom from Want" (1943) stands out as a painting whose rendition of an (Anglo) American Thanksgiving family celebration for World War II propaganda purposes testifies to the unbroken cultural and political power of paintings even in the twentieth century.

The rise of photography as a new documentary medium in the second half of the nineteenth century changed the configuration of visual memory and initiated the conceptualization of sites of memory as part of modern U.S.-American media culture (see Ruchatz, this volume). The Civil War photography of Matthew Brady became the first major set of photographic representations of a major event in U.S.-American history. The pictures of Brady and his teams replaced to a large extent the previously classic formats and modes of memory of war, namely literature and painting, and continue to dominate the collective U.S.-American recollection of the Civil War even today. In a similar vein, Edward Curtis's late-nineteenth- and early-twentieth-century photographs of Native Americans in the West and Southwest have inscribed into U.S.-American and non-American memories alike the iconic figure of the "vanishing Indian." The social photography of Jacob Riis has preserved the promise and plight of late-nineteenth-century immigrant life in the U.S. Throughout the twentieth century, photographs have increasingly served as commemorative registers of changes and crises in U.S.-American history and culture, from Walker Evans's and Dorothea Lange's pictures of distressed farmers during the Great Depression and Ansel Adams's photographs of the endangered landscapes of the Southwest to the stills in the Zapruder film of the assassination of John F. Kennedy, photographs of war atrocities in Vietnam, and Magnum photographers' immediate capturing of the national trauma of 9/11. Newsreels and TV news coverage, the latter increasingly live and rivaled by the Internet, have inscribed into twentieth-century collective U.S.-American memory lasting, at times haunting, images of historical events and national traumas, including, for example, pictures of great moments in American sports, decisive developments and acts of World War II, the funeral of President Kennedy, the Vietnam War, the landing on the moon, the resignation of President Nixon, 9/11, and Hurricane Katrina. How movies have shaped U.S.-American cultural memory and the popular imagination of U.S.-American histories and identities since the beginning of the twentieth century can be measured by the continued appeal and commercial success of seminal filmic sites of memory such as *Birth of a Nation* (1915), *Gone with the Wind* (1939), *JFK* (1991), *Amistad* (1997), or *Pearl Harbor* (2001). The public television documentaries by Ken Burns have presented a particularly appealing commemorative panorama of American histories, cultures, and icons, from Thomas Jefferson to the Lewis and Clark expedition, and from the Civil War to Brooklyn Bridge and the Statue of Liberty.

4. Commemorative Performances and Material Displays of U.S.-American Memories

The establishment of the United States of America stirred a collective urge for the celebration of common historical achievements and for the affirmation of the newly created collective identity. The Early Republic especially saw a large variety of local, regional, and national festivities that took the scripts and repertoires of traditional religious and folk rituals and adapted them to focus on the events, figures, and documents determining the new nation. Commemorations of specific occurrences of the American Revolution, celebrations of the birthdays or inaugurations of revolutionary leaders turned presidents, and ceremonies in honor of the ratification of the Constitution governed the festive calendar of the young nation. The commemorative culture of the Early Republic and antebellum America laid the foundation for the development of a specifically U.S.-American civil religion whose politically and culturally cohesive function relies even today to a considerable extent on the lasting appeal of largely uncontested sites of national memory and collective veneration. In the nineteenth century, the Fourth of July developed into the national holiday proper, rivaled for some time by the observance of Forefathers' Day, the commemoration of the arrival of the so-called Pilgrim Fathers in Plymouth on December 22, 1620. In the decades before the Civil War, sectional strife and territorial expansion supported the divisive functionalization of national sites of memory and the emergence of more locally and regionally significant festivities, such as the commemoration of the foundation of major cities in recently acquired territories and the celebration of technological achievements such as the opening of the Erie Canal.

Post-Civil War America saw the further pluralization and commercialization of the U.S.-American landscape of performative memory. The nationwide popularity of anniversary commemorations and reenactments related to the Civil War and a host of Civil War monuments and memorials erected with different political and cultural agendas in the North and the South reduced the national significance of New England history and heritage. The battlefield of Gettysburg in Pennsylvania became the overtowering icon of national rededication and soon developed into a commercially marketed shrine of pilgrimage and collective worship which anticipated twentieth-century memory tourism and business. The emergence of African American emancipation celebrations and the formation of a diversified landscape of ethnic sites of memory, especially in the Midwest and West in the wake of mass immigration, furthermore pluralized U.S.-American festive cultures. In particular, local history pageants complicated once-monolithic Anglocentric narratives of national and cultural origins by staging the more heterogeneous histories and heritages of the respective immigrant groups. In another illustration of the fast-changing parameters of U.S.-American cultural memories, the Wild West shows of William "Buffalo Bill" Cody staged the conflicted memory of the American West with white and Indian actors for American and European audiences from the 1880s through the 1900s, while the history of westward expansion was still under way. In this context, the ceremonious dedication of the National Monument to the Forefathers near Plymouth, Massachusetts, in 1889—one year after the erection of a statue in honor of African American Revolutionary War hero Crispus Attucks in Boston—and the Plymouth tercentenary festivities of 1920, with George P. Baker's pageant *The Pilgrim Spirit* as a major tourist attraction, appear almost like belated attempts to reanimate the binding force of an exclusively Anglocentric U.S.-American memory. However, a seemingly monolithic U.S.-American festive culture was to remain politically and culturally powerful, if not dominant, well into the second half of the twentieth century. In the context of more recent debates over multiculturalism, ethnic empowerment, political correctness, and identity politics, time-honored celebrations of Columbus Day or the arrival of the Pilgrims on Plymouth Rock became the very epitome of repressive Eurocentric conceptualizations of the U.S. to advocates of a more pluralistic understanding of American histories, cultures, and identities. Monuments such as the Boston Irish Famine Memorial, unveiled and dedicated near Boston's famous Freedom Trail in 1998, document the continued urge of American ethnic groups to claim their spaces on the map of U.S.-American historical memories.

The gathering and display of U.S.-American memories in collections, archives, and museums as publicly accessible sites of memory also goes back to the early years of the U.S.-American republic. The establishment of the Library of Congress by an act of Congress in 1800 laid the foundation for the largest U.S.-American archive, whose special online section "American Memory" (http://memory.loc.gov/ammem) is to date the most comprehensive collection of U.S.-American cultural memories electronically available. The early foundation of local and state historical societies as well as of private archives of national significance such as the Massachusetts Historical Society (1791), the New York Historical Society (1804), and the American Antiquarian Society (1812) became the model for an intricate network of historical societies and heritage institutions in all states and major cities. Over the course of more than two centuries the archival politics and cultural work of these societies and archives have impacted strongly on the particular local, regional, and national memories which they endorsed and/or contested. In the ideological crisis of the 1930s, when the cultural politics of the New Deal supported the purposeful preservation of endangered historical sources for the sake of collective identity stabilization, local and state archives often became important platforms for the retrieval of commemorative materials such as African American slave narratives and work songs, the records of the Salem witchcraft trials of 1692, and Southern blues and Western cowboy music. The centerpiece of U.S.-American museum culture is the Smithsonian Institution (http://www.si.edu), which was established in 1846 and today consists of some 20 museums, most of them located on the National Mall in Washington, D.C. Recurring controversies over particular commemorative exhibits such as the display of World War II B-29 atomic bomber "Enola Gay" in 1994/95, and the discussions about the location, architecture, and museum concepts of recently opened museums such as the National Museum of the American Indian and of still-to-be-built museums such as the National Museum of African American History and Culture illustrate the far-reaching political implications of museums as particularly visible and influential sites of memory in contemporary multiethnic U.S.-American culture.

The National Mall in Washington, D.C. is the heart of U.S.-American civil religion and the central site of national U.S.-American museum and memory culture. Designed in its basic outline by Washington architect Pierre L'Enfant in the 1790s, the National Mall today serves as the prime destination for national(ist) pilgrimages of U.S.-American citizens and as a tourist attraction for both American and international visitors. In a larger topographical and symbolic context, the Mall connects the major buildings of the three branches of government, the White House, the Capitol, and the Supreme Court. Besides the museums of the Smithsonian Institution, important national organizations such as the National Archives, the famous monuments erected in honor of George Washington, Thomas

Jefferson, Abraham Lincoln, and Franklin Delano Roosevelt, as well as major national war memorials such as the World War II Memorial, the Korean War Memorial, and the Vietnam Veterans Memorial are all located on or close to the Mall. The Rotunda of the National Archives, with its ceremonial display of the sacred documents of the U.S.-American nation, and the Great Rotunda of the U.S. Capitol, with its commemorative arrangement of paintings of crucial scenes of North American history and sculptures of important U.S.-American presidents and statesmen, have become especially venerated sites of national U.S.-American memory culture and tourism. Since 1965, the "National Mall and Memorial Parks" have been part of the U.S. National Park Service and are thus linked institutionally and ideologically to an extended system of some 400 sites across the nation. Since the establishment of the first national park, Yellowstone National Park, in 1872, the U.S.-American national parks have been expressly dedicated to the preservation of the natural and historical heritage of the United States. They range from Independence Hall in Philadelphia and mythic battlefields of the American Revolution and the Civil War to landmarks of immigration history such as Ellis Island and the Statue of Liberty, as well as to New Orleans jazz clubs, birthplaces of historical figures, churches of the Civil Rights Movement in the South, and presidential libraries (see http://www.nps.gov). In addition, privately sponsored and more openly commercial sites of memory have increasingly become part of U.S.-American memory culture and business. Plimoth Plantation and Colonial Williamsburg deserve special mention, as their living history performances of everyday life in Puritan Plymouth in the 1620s and in eighteenth-century Virginia are particularly noteworthy examples of the fusion of historical didacticism and tourism governing many sites of U.S.-American memory today. Whether the active involvement of visitors in historical performances and the increasing accessibility of sites of memory both in person and via the Internet enhance the democratization of U.S.-American national memories remains open to debate.

Visual sites of U.S.-American memory and U.S.-American commemorative displays of different kinds receive additional, material circulation on coins and stamps. Among the manifold commemorative series and programs of the United States Mint (http://www.usmint.gov), the recent "50 State Quarters Program" and the "Westward Journey Nickel Series" may serve to illustrate how coins function as agents and sites in the circulation of historical and cultural memory. The first commemorative postage stamps were issued by the United States Postal Service (http://www.usps.com) in 1893 in honor of the World Columbian Exposition in Chicago and showed well-known paintings of Columbus's arrival in the "New World." Recent examples such as the "United We Stand" and

"Heroes of 2001" stamps released in the wake of 9/11 and the Benjamin Franklin stamps issued in honor of Franklin's 300th birthday in 2006 demonstrate the continued practice of remembering statesmen, artists, sports heroes, paintings, landmark buildings, national parks, and many other historical and cultural landmarks of the U.S. on stamps.

5. Transnationalization and Virtualization of Sites of U.S.-American Memories

The multiethnic and transnational histories of North America and the hemispheric, Atlantic, and Pacific contexts of North American cultures have always given national U.S.-American sites and ceremonies of commemoration a multidirectional, pluralistic dimension—notwithstanding all historical processes and official acts of repression, exclusion, erasure, and forgetting. The renaming of Custer Battlefield National Monument as Little Bighorn Battlefield National Monument in 1991 and the addition of an Indian Memorial in 2003 to the National Park Service's previous site of commemoration of the 1876 battle between General Custer's 7th U.S. Cavalry and an alliance of Plains Indians under the leadership of chiefs Sitting Bull and Crazy Horse document in exemplary fashion how transcultural and transnational memories are now surfacing more visibly from beneath the long-monolithic landscape of U.S.-American memory. The monumental dialogue in the hills of South Dakota between the four presidents enshrined in stone at Mount Rushmore National Memorial and the even more colossal figure of Crazy Horse on horseback slowly emerging since 1948 from the wooded mountain at the construction site of the Crazy Horse Memorial makes for an equally striking example of the increasingly multivocal and controversial landscape of American memories. Pivotal sites of national(ist) U.S.-American history—such as the Alamo in San Antonio, Texas, or the two major immigration stations on Ellis Island, New York, and Angel Island, California—have been giving more multivocal narratives of their transnational histories and implications. Monuments, memorials, historical markers, and national parks related to the intercultural histories and identities of specific ethnic groups such as the National Japanese American Memorial in Washington, D.C., the "Go For Broke" Japanese American War Memorial in Los Angeles, and the Manzanar War Relocation Center National Historic Site in California now display conflicted memories of U.S.-American history and immigration. The United States Holocaust Memorial Museum in Washington, D.C. shows what scholars have termed the Americanization of the Holocaust and thus a very specific manifestation of a national appropriation of an international memory. The ongoing controversies over adequate memorials at and beyond Ground Zero in New York City dramatize more than anything else the political and cultural implications of the contest for commemorative authority over 9/11 and its sites of memory. Elaborate websites offer almost unlimited virtual access to these and most of the other sites of U.S.-American memories mentioned here. Participatory structures and interactive communicative channels turn these websites into platforms of exchange and dialogue, albeit only on a virtual level. To what extent transnational accessibility and virtual interactivity will further enhance the pluralization, democratization, and commercialization of U.S.-American cultures of memory remains to be seen.

References[1]

Blight, David W. *Race and Reunion: The Civil War in American Memory*. Cambridge: Harvard UP, 2001.

Bodnar, John. *Remaking America: Public Memory, Commemoration, and Patriotism in the Twentieth Century*. Princeton: Princeton UP, 1992.

Burnham, Patricia M., and Lucretia H. Giese, eds. *Redefining American History Painting*. Cambridge: Cambridge UP, 1995.

Dubin, Steven C. *Displays of Power: Memory and Amnesia in the American Museum*. New York: New York UP, 1999.

Ethnic Autobiography. Spec. issue of *Melus* 22.4 (1997).

Gessner, Ingrid. *From Sites of Memory to Cybersights: (Re)Framing Japanese American Experiences*. Heidelberg: Winter, 2007.

Grabbe, Hans-Jürgen, and Sabine Schindler, eds. *The Merits of Memory: Concepts, Contexts, Debates*. Heidelberg: Winter, 2007.

Grainge, Paul. *Memory and Popular Film*. New York: Palgrave, 2003.

Hass, Kristin Ann. *Carried to the Wall: American Memory and the Vietnam Veterans Memorial*. Berkeley: U of California P, 1998.

Hebel, Udo J., ed. *Sites of Memory in American Literatures and Cultures*. Heidelberg: Winter, 2003.

Heller, Dana, ed. *The Selling of 9/11: How a National Tragedy Became a Commodity*. New York: Palgrave, 2005.

Henderson, Helene. *Patriotic Holidays of the United States: An Introduction to the History, Symbols, and Traditions Behind the Major Holidays and Days of Observance*. Detroit: Omnigraphics, 2006.

Hufbauer, Benjamin. *Presidential Temples: How Memorials and Libraries Shape Public Memory*. Lawrence: UP of Kansas, 2005.

[1] For a more comprehensive bibliography, see Hebel xxii-xxxii.

Kachun, Mitch. *Festivals of Freedom: Memory and Meaning in African American Emancipation Celebrations, 1808-1915*. Amherst: U of Massachusetts P, 2003.

Kammen, Michael. "Commemoration and Contestation in American Culture: Historical Perspectives." *Amerikastudien/American Studies* 48 (2003): 185-205.

—. *Mystic Chords of Memory: The Transformation of Tradition in American Culture.* New York: Knopf, 1991.

Le Beau, Brian F. *Currier & Ives: America Imagined.* Washington, D.C.: Smithsonian Institution, 2001.

Levy, Daniel, and Natan Sznaider. *The Holocaust and Memory in the Global Age.* Philadelphia: Temple UP, 2006.

Linenthal, Edward T. *Preserving Memory: The Struggle to Create America's Holocaust Museum.* New York: Columbia UP, 2001.

Linenthal, Edward T., and Tom Engelhardt, eds. *History Wars: The Enola Gay and Other Battles for the American Past.* New York: Metropolitan, 1996.

Lipsitz, George. *Time Passages: Collective Memory and American Popular Culture.* Minneapolis: U of Minnesota P, 1990.

The National Museum of the American Indian. Spec. double issue of *American Indian Quarterly* 29.3/4 (2005).

Pfitzer, Gregory M. *Picturing the Past: Illustrating Histories and the American Imagination, 1840-1900.* Washington, D.C.: Smithsonian Institution, 2002.

Rosenzweig, Roy. *The Presence of the Past: Popular Uses of History in American Life.* New York: Columbia UP, 1998.

Savage, Kirk. *Standing Soldiers, Kneeling Slaves: Race, War, and Monument in Nineteenth-Century America.* Princeton: Princeton UP, 1997.

Sayre, Robert F., ed. *American Lives: An Anthology of Autobiographical Writing.* Madison: U of Wisconsin P, 1994.

Schindler, Sabine. *Authentizität und Inszenierung: Die Vermittlung von Geschichte in amerikanischen* historic sites. Heidelberg: Winter, 2003.

Schultz, April. *Ethnicity on Parade: Inventing the Norwegian American Through Celebration.* Amherst: U of Massachusetts P, 1994.

Schwartz, Barry. *Abraham Lincoln and the Forge of National Memory.* Chicago: U of Chicago P, 2000.

Snow, Stephen E., ed. *Performing the Pilgrims: A Study of Ethnohistorical Role-Playing at Plimoth Plantation.* Jackson: U of Mississippi P, 1993.

Sturken, Marita. *Tangled Memories: The Vietnam War, the AIDS Epidemic, and the Politics of Remembering.* Berkeley: U of California P, 1997.

Toplin, Robert B. *History by Hollywood: The Use and Abuse of the American Past.* Urbana: U of Illinois P, 1996.

Travers, Len. *Celebrating the Fourth: Independence Day and the Rites of Nationalism in the Early Republic.* Amherst: U of Massachusetts P, 1997.

Waldstreicher, David. *In the Midst of Perpetual Fetes: The Making of American Nationalism, 1776-1820.* Chapel Hill: U of North Carolina P, 1997.

Weeks, Jim. *Gettysburg: Memory, Market, and an American Shrine.* Princeton: Princeton UP, 2003.

Sites of Memory and the Shadow of War

JAY WINTER

Sites of memory are places where groups of people engage in public activity through which they express "a collective shared knowledge [...] of the past, on which a group's sense of unity and individuality is based" (Assmann 15). The group that goes to such sites inherits earlier meanings attached to the event, as well as adding new meanings. Their activity is crucial to the presentation and preservation of commemorative sites. When such groups disperse or disappear, sites of memory lose their initial force, and may fade away entirely.

The term, adumbrated in a seven-volume study edited by Pierre Nora, has been extended to many different texts, from legends, to stories, to concepts. In this brief essay, I define the term more narrowly to mean physical sites where commemorative acts take place. In the twentieth century, most such sites marked the loss of life in war.

Such sites of memory are topoi with a life history. They have an initial, creative phase, when they are constructed or adapted to particular commemorative purposes. Then follows a period of institutionalization and routinization of their use. Such markings of the calendar, indicating moments of remembrance at particular places, can last for decades, or they can be abruptly halted. In most instances, the significance of sites of memory fades away with the passing of the social groups which initiated the practice.

Sites of memory operate on many levels of aggregation and touches many facets of associative life. While such sites were familiar in the ancient and medieval period, they have proliferated in more recent times. Consequently, the subject has attracted much academic and popular discussion. We therefore concentrate here on sites of memory in the epoch of the nation state, primarily in the nineteenth and twentieth centuries.

In the modern period, most sites of memory were imbedded in events marked distinctively and separately from the religious calendar. There has been, though, some overlap. Visiting a commemorative site on Armistice Day, November 11, in countries remembering the end of the 1914-18 war, is close enough to the Catholic feast of All Saints on November 2; in some countries with a large Catholic population, the two days occupy a semi-sacred space of public commemoration. First comes the visit to the cemetery; then the visit to the war memorial or other site. The day marking the end of the Second World War in Europe, May 8, is also the Saint's day of Joan of Arc. Those engaging in commemorative acts on that day may be addressing the secular celebration or the Catholic one; some celebrate the two together. Usually the site chosen to mark the day differs.

Commemoration at sites of memory is an act arising out of a conviction, shared by a broad community, that the moment recalled is both significant and informed by a moral message. Sites of memory materialize that message. Moments of national humiliation are rarely commemorated or marked in material form, though here too there are exceptions of a hortatory kind. "Never again" is the hallmark of public commemoration on the Israeli Day of Remembrance for victims of the Nazi persecution of the Jews. The shell of public buildings in Hiroshima remind everyone of the moment the city was incinerated in the first atomic attack. Where moral doubts persist about a war or public policy, commemorative sites are either hard to fix or places of contestation. That is why there is no date or place for those who want to commemorate the end of the Algerian War in France, or the end of the Vietnam War in the United States. There was no moral consensus about the nature of the conflict; hence there was no moral consensus about what was being remembered in public, and when and where were the appropriate time and place to remember it (Prost).

When the Japanese Prime Minister visits a shrine to war dead, he is honoring war criminals as well as ordinary soldiers. The same was true when President Ronald Reagan visited the German cemetery at Bitburg, where lie the remains of SS men alongside the graves of those not implicated in war crimes. And yet both places were sites of memory; contested memory; embittered memory, but memory nonetheless.

The critical point about sites of memory is that they are there as points of reference not only for those who survived traumatic events, but also for those born long after them. The word "memory" becomes a metaphor for the fashioning of narratives about the past when those with direct experience of events die off. Sites of memory inevitably become sites of second-order memory, that is, they are places where people remember the memories of others, those who survived the events marked there.

1. Commemoration and Political Power

Much of the scholarly debate about sites of memory concerns the extent to which they are instruments of the dominant political elements in a society (see Meyer, this volume). One school of opinion emphasizes the usefulness to political elites of public events at such sites establishing the legitimacy of their rule (Nora). Some such events are observed whoever is in power—witness Bastille Day in Paris or Independence Day in Philadelphia or elsewhere in the United States. But other events are closely tied to the establishment of a new regime and the overthrow of an older one: November 7 was the date in the calendar marking the Bolshevik revolution and establishing the Communist regime in power in Russia. That date symbolized the new order and its challenge to its world-wide enemies. The march past of soldiers and weapons deployed by the Soviet army in Moscow was a moment of commemoration as well as of muscular pride, demonstrating outside the Kremlin their place in Russian and world history.

This top-down approach proclaims the significance of sites of memory as a materialization of national, imperial, or political identity. Anzac Day, April 25, is celebrated as the moment when the Australian nation was born. It commemorates the landing of Australian and New Zealand troops as part of the British-led expeditionary force sent to Turkey in 1915. The fact that the landing was a failure does not diminish the iconic character of the date to Australians. It is the day, they hold, when their nation came of age (Inglis). There are many sites of memory where this day is marked. First people come to war memorials throughout Australia. Secondly, there is a state event at the Australian War Memorial in Canberra, an edifice built in the shape of Hajia Sofia in Istanbul. On the walls of this building are inscribed the names of all Australian soldiers who died in the war. Thirdly, there is an annual pilgrimage, still robustly attended in the twenty-first century, to the shores of Gallipoli itself. There, Australians mark the Gallipoli landings on the beaches where they took place.

By no means are all commemorative activities or sites of memory associated with warfare. The birthdates of monarchs or deceased presidents are marked in similar ways. Queen Victoria's birthday, May 24, was Empire Day in Britain; now (since 1999) it is celebrated as Commonwealth Day. The creation of such commemorative dates was part of a wider movement of what some scholars have termed "the invention of tradition." That is, at the end of the nineteenth century, new nation states and pre-eminent imperial powers deepened the repertoire of their ceremonial activity. Such flourishes of the majesty of power were then immediately sanctified by a spurious pedigree. To display ceremonies with a supposed link to ancient habits or forms located in a foggy and distant past created an effective cover for political innovation, instability or insecurity (MacKenzie; Hobsbawm and Ranger). Interestingly for our purposes, such traditions have only a tenuous attachment to a site, thereby increasing the flexibility of choices available to those who want to invent traditions.

This functionalist interpretation of commemoration has been challenged. A second school of scholarship emphasizes the ways that sites of memory and the public commemorations surrounding them have the potential for dominated groups to contest their subordinate status in public. However much political leaders or their agents try to choreograph commemorative activity, there is much space for subversion or creative interpretation of the official commemorative script. Armistice Day on November 11 was a moment when different groups came to war memorials, some for the celebration and others for the denigration of military values. Pacifists announced their message of "Never again" through their presence at such sites of memory; military men and their supporters used these moments and the aura of these sites to glorify the profession of arms, and to demonstrate the duty of citizens, if necessary, to give their lives for their country in a future war. The contradictions in these forms of expression on the same day and in the same places have never been resolved (Gregory; Winter).

This alternative interpretation of the political meaning of sites of memory emphasizes the multi-vocal character of remembrance and the potential for new groups with new causes to appropriate older sites of memory. From this point of view, there is always a chorus of voices in commemorations; some are louder than others, but they never sound alone. De-centering the history of commemoration ensures that we recognize the regional, local, and idiosyncratic character of such activities and the way a top-down approach must be supplemented by a bottom-up approach to the performance of scripts about the past at commemorative sites in villages, small towns, and provincial cities, as well as in the centers of political power.

Very occasionally, these dissonant voices come together, and a national moment of remembrance emerges. However on such occasions, there is no one single site of memory at which this braiding together of leaders and led takes place. One example of this diffusion of remembrance is the two-minute silence observed in Britain between 1919 and 1938 at 11:00 am on November 11. Telephonists pulled the plugs on all conversations. Traffic stopped. The normal flow of life was arrested. Then the Second World War intervened, and such disruption to war production was not in the national interest. Thereafter the two-minute silence was moved to the Sunday nearest November 11. But in the two decades between the wars, it was a moment of national reflection, located everywhere. Mass Observation, a pioneering social survey organization, asked hundreds of ordinary people in Britain what they thought about during the silence. The answer was that they thought not of the nation or of victory or of armies, but of the men who weren't there. This silence was a meditation about absence. As such it moved away from political orchestration into the realm of family history. To be sure, families commemorated their own within a wider social and political framework. But the richest texture of remembrance was always within family life. This intersection of the public and the private, the macro-historical and the micro-historical, is what has given commemoration in the twentieth century its power and its rich repertoire of forms. But the very complexity of these processes means that sites of memory are not always the foci of acts of remembrance.

In addition, some buildings can be converted into sites of memory unofficially. A cinema where workers organized a strike, a home where women created a midwifery or child care center, a school where people made homeless by a natural disaster found shelter can all be turned into sites of memory by those who lived important moments there (Hayden). Official certification is not necessary when groups of people act on their own.

2. The Business of Remembering

Unofficial sites of memory must be preserved through the time and cash of groups of people. That is a crucial defining feature of sites of memory: They cost money and time to construct or preserve. They require specialists' services—landscapers, cleaners, masons, carpenters, plumbers, and so on; they needs funding and over time, re-funding. There are two kinds of expenditure we can trace in the history of sites of memory. The first is capital expenditure; the second is recurrent expenditure.

The land for such sites must be purchased; and an appropriate symbolic form must be designed and then constructed to focus remembrance activities. The first step may require substantial sums of public money. Private land, especially in urban areas, comes at a premium. Then there are the costs of architects' fees, especially when a public competitive tender is offered, inviting proposals from professionals. Finally, once the symbolic form is chosen, it must be constructed out of selected materials and finished according to the architect's or artist's designs.

When these projects are national in character, the process of production is in the public eye. National art schools and bodies of "experts" have to have their say. Standards of "taste" and "decorum" are proclaimed. Professional interests and conflicts come into play. Much of this professional infighting is confined to national commemorative projects, but the same complex, step-wise procedure occurs on the local level, too, this time without the same level of attendant publicity. Local authorities usually take charge of these projects, and local notables can deflect plans towards their own particular visions, whatever public opinion may think about the subject.

Most of the time, public funding covers only part of the costs of commemorative objects. Public subscriptions are critical, especially in Protestant countries where the concept of utilitarian memorials is dominant. In Catholic countries, the notion of a "useful" memorial is a contradiction in terms; symbolic language and utilitarian language are deemed mutually exclusive. But the Protestant voluntary tradition has it otherwise. In Protestant countries, commemorative projects took many forms, from the sacred to the mundane: In Britain there are memorial wards in hospitals, memorial scholarships in schools and universities, alongside memorial cricket pitches and memorial water troughs for horses. In the United States and in Australia there are memorial highways. The rule of thumb is that private citizens pick up most of the tab for these memorial forms. The state provides subsidies and occasional matching grants, but the money comes out of the pockets of ordinary people. The same is true in Britain with respect to a very widely shared form of public commemoration: the purchase of paper poppies, the symbol of the Lost Generation of the First World War. These poppies are worn on the lapel, and the proceeds of the sale go to aid disabled veterans and their families.

Recurrent expenditure for sites of memory is almost always paid for by taxpayers. War cemeteries require masons and gardeners. The Imperial (now Commonwealth) War Graves Commission looks after hundreds of such cemeteries all over the world. The cost of their maintenance is a public charge. Private charities, in particular Christian groups, maintain German war cemeteries. Once constructed, memorial statues, cemeteries, or highways also become public property, and require public support to prevent them from decomposing. They are preserved as sites of commemorative activity.

Much of this activity is directed towards inviting the public to remember in public. This means directing the public towards particular sites of remembrance. Some of them are nearby their homes. In Britain and France there are war memorials in every city, in every town, and in every village; it is there that Armistice Day ceremonies are held annually. Churches throughout Europe of all denominations have memorial plaques to those who died in war. Special prayers were added to the Jewish prayer book to commemorate the victims of the Nazis in the Second World War, and later, those who died on active service in the Israeli army.

Remembrance in local houses of worship or at war memorials required that the public travel a short distance from their homes to sites of remembrance. But given the scale of losses in the two world wars, and the widely dispersed cemeteries around the world in which lie the remains of millions of such men and women, the business of remembrance also entails international travel. Such voyages start as pilgrimage; many are mixed with tourism (Lloyd). But in either case, there are train and boat journeys to take; hotel rooms to reserve; guides to hire; flowers to lay at graves; trinkets and mementos to purchase. In some places, museums have arisen to tell more of the story the pilgrims have come to hear and to share. There too money is exchanged along with the narratives and the symbols of remembrance.

This mixture of the sacred and the profane is hardly an innovation. It is merely a secular form of the kind of pilgrimage, for example, that made San Juan de Compostela in Spain the destination of millions of men and women in the Middle Ages who came to honor the conventionally designated resting place of the remains of one of the original Apostles. Pilgrimage to war cemeteries is public commemoration over long, sometimes very long, distances. Where does pilgrimage stop and tourism take over? It is impossible to say, but in all cases, the business of remembrance remains just that—a business.

3. Aesthetic Redemption

The life history of sites of memory is described by more than political gestures and material tasks. Frequently a site is also an art form, the art of creating, arranging, and interpreting signifying practices. This field of action can be analyzed on two different levels: The first is aesthetic; the second is semiotic. The two are intimately related.

Some national commemorative forms are distinctive. Others are shared by populations in many countries. The figure of Marianne as the national symbol affixed to thousands of town halls throughout France could not be used in Germany or Britain. The German Iron Cross, on commemorative plaques, denotes the location and the tradition in which commemoration is expressed. Germany's heroes' forests or fortresses are also imbricated in Teutonic history.

At times the repertoire of one country's symbols overlap with that of others, even when they were adversaries. After the First World War, the first industrialized war fought among fully industrialized nations, many commemorative forms adopted medieval notation. Throughout Europe, the revolutionary character of warfare was marked by a notation of a backward-looking kind. Medieval images of heroic and saintly warriors recaptured a time when combat was between individuals, rather than the impersonal and unbalanced duel between artillery and human flesh. The war in the air took on the form and romance of chivalry. On the losing and the winning sides, medievalism flourished. We can see these traces clearly in stained glass windows in many churches, where the site of memory for the two world wars takes on a meaning by virtue of its proximity to older religious images and objects. Twentieth-century warfare thus takes on a sacred coloration when its sites of memory are located within a sacred grammar and a sacred building.

Until very late in the twentieth century, on war memorials the human form survived. In some instances, classical images of male beauty were chosen to mark the "lost generation"; others adopted more stoical and emphatically un-triumphalist poses of men in uniform. In most cases, victory was either partially or totally eclipsed by a sense of overwhelming loss. Within this aesthetic landscape, traditional Christian motifs were commonplace. The form of the grieving mother—Stabat Mater—brought women into the local and national constellation of grief.

In Protestant countries, the aesthetic debate took on a quasi-religious character. War memorials with crosses on them offended some Protestants, who believed that the Reformation of the sixteenth century precluded such "Catholic" notation. Obelisks were preferable, and relatively inexpensive, too. In France, war memorials were by law restricted to public and not church grounds, though many local groups found a way around this proscription. In schools and universities, the location of such memorials touched on such issues. Some were placed in sacred space, in chapels; semi-sacred space, around chapels; or in secular space. Public thoroughfares and train stations also housed such lists of men who had died in war. Placement signified meaning.

Twentieth-century warfare democratized bereavement. Previously armies were composed of mercenaries, volunteers and professionals. After 1914, Everyman went to war. The social incidence of war losses was thereby transformed. In Britain, France and Germany, virtually every household had lost someone—a father, a son, a brother, a cousin, a friend. Given the nature of static warfare on the Western front, many—perhaps half—of those killed had no known grave. Consequently commemorative forms highlighted names above all. The names of the dead were all that remained of them, and chiseled in stone or etched on plaques, these names were the foci of public commemoration both on the local and the national scale.

Sites of memory preserved the names of those who were gone. In some rare cases—Australia is one of them—war memorials listed the names of all those who served. This notation was a constant rebuke to those who passed the site knowing full well that their names were not inscribed on the memorial. Most of the time, though, the dead were the names that mattered, so much so that alphabetical order replaced social order. The overwhelming majority of war memorials list those who died in this way. A small minority listed men by rank, and some listed men by the date or year of death. But sites of memory were built for the survivors, for the families of those who were not there, and these people needed easy access to the sole signifier left to them—the name of the dead person.

This essential practice of naming set the pattern for commemorative forms after the Second World War and beyond. After 1945, names were simply added to Great War memorials. This was partly in recognition of the links between the two twentieth-century conflicts; partly it was a matter of economy. After the Vietnam War, naming still mattered, and First World War forms inspired memorials, most notably Maya Lin's Vietnam Veterans' Memorial in Washington. Her work clearly drew on Sir Edwin Lutyens's memorial to the missing on the River Somme at Thiepval, inaugurated in 1932.

By the latter decades of the twentieth century, artistic opinion and aesthetic tastes had changed sufficiently to make abstraction the key language of commemorative expression. Statues and installations thereby escaped from specific national notation and moved away from the earlier emphasis upon the human figure. The exception to the rule is Soviet commemorative art, which resolutely stuck to the path of heroic romanticism in marking out the meaning of what they called the Great Patriotic War. In many instances in Western Europe, but by no means all, forms which suggested absence or nothingness replaced classical, religious, or romantic notions in commemorative art.

This shift was noticeable in Holocaust remembrance. Holocaust sites of memory—concentration and extermination camps, in particular, but also places where Jews had lived before the Shoah—could not be treated in the same way as sites commemorating the dead of the two world wars (see Young, this volume). The first difficulty was the need to avoid Christian notation to represent a Jewish catastrophe. The second was the allergy of observant Jews to representational art, either forbidden or resisted within Orthodox Jewish tradition. The third was the absence of any sense of uplift, of meaning, of purpose in the deaths of the victims. Those who died in the Holocaust may have affirmed their faith thereby, but what is the meaning in the murder of one million children? To a degree, their deaths meant nothing, and therefore the Holocaust meant nothing.

Representing nothing became a challenge met in particular ways. Some artists provided installation art which literally vanished through the presence of visitors. Others projected photographs of the vanished world onto the facades of still erect buildings, occupied by non-Jews. Others adopted post-modern forms to suggest disorientation, void, emptiness. Daniel Libeskind's Jewish annex to the Berlin Historical Museum is one such site. It has been likened to a Jewish star taken apart, or a lightning bolt in stone and glass. Whatever metaphor one chooses, it is a disturbing, tilted, non-linear representation of the unrepresentable.

Since the 1970s, commemoration of the Second World War has become braided together with commemoration of the Holocaust. This presented aesthetic as well as social and political challenges. Great War commemorative forms had sought out some meaning, some significance in the enormous loss of life attending that conflict. There was an implicit warning in many of these monuments. "Never again" was their ultimate meaning. But "never" had lasted a bare twenty years. Thus after the Second World War, the search for meaning became infinitely more complex. And the fact that more civilians than soldiers died in the Second World War made matters even more difficult to configure in art.

Finally, the extreme character of the Second World War challenged the capacity of art—any art—to express a sense of loss when it is linked to genocidal murder or thermonuclear destruction. We have mentioned how Auschwitz defied conventional notations of "meaning," though some individuals continue to try to rescue redemptive elements from it. The same is true for the atomic destruction of Hiroshima and Nagasaki. Sites of memory are places where people affirm their faith that history has a meaning. What kind of site is appropriate where the majority of people see no meaning at all in the events being marked in time and in space? Ignoring Auschwitz or Hiroshima is impossible, but locating them within earlier commemorative structures or gestures is either problematic or absurd or both.

4. Ritual

Public commemoration is an activity defined by the gestures and words of those who come together at sites of memory to recall particular aspects of the past, their past. Such moments are rarely the simple reflection of a fixed text, a script rigidly prepared by political leaders determined to fortify their position of power. Inevitably, commemoration overlaps with political conflicts, but it can never be reduced to a direct function of power relationships.

There are at least three stages in the history of rituals surrounding public commemoration. The first we have already dealt with: the construction of a commemorative form. But there are two other levels in the life history of monuments which need attention. The second is the grounding of ritual action in the calendar, and the routinization of such activities; the third is their transformation or their disappearance as active sites of memory.

One case in point may illustrate this trajectory. The date of July 1, 1916 is not a national holiday in Britain, but it marks the date of the opening of the British offensive on the river Somme, an offensive which symbolized the terrible character of industrial warfare. On that day the British army suffered the highest casualty totals in its history; on that day a volunteer army, and the society that had created it, were introduced to the full terrors of twentieth-century warfare. To this day, groups of people come to the Somme battlefields to mark this day, without national legislation to enable them to do so. Theirs are locally defined rituals. A party of Northumberland men and women bring their bagpipes and mark the moment when the Battle of the Somme began at a gigantic crater they purchased to ensure it would not be ploughed over and forgotten. Others from Newfoundland go to the still extant trench system at Beaumont Hamel where their ancestors were slaughtered on July 1, 1916. There is a bronze caribou at the site to link this place to the landscape from which the men of Newfoundland—then a British colony—came as volunteers to fight for King and country. In France November 11 is a national holiday, but not in Britain. Legislation codifies activities the origins and force of which lie on the local level. After 1939, remembrance of the Great War dead was located on the closest Sunday to November 11. What mattered most about this is that churches became the sites where remembrance occurred. The ritual of Protestant churches domesticated war remembrance, and blunted its appeal. There is still today (2006) a movement to return war remembrance to where it belongs, in the midst of life, on whatever day the eleventh of November happens to fall.

Public commemoration flourishes within the orbit of civil society. This is not true in countries where dictatorships rule; Stalinist Russia smashed civil society to a point that it could not sustain commemorative activity independent of the party and the state (Merridale). But elsewhere, local associations matter. And so do families. Commemorative ritual survives when it is inscribed within the rhythms of community and, in particular, family life. Public commemoration lasts when it draws about overlaps between national history and family history. Most of those who take the time to engage in the rituals of remembrance bring with them memories of family members touched by these vast events. This is what enables people born long after wars and revolutions to commemorate them as essential parts of their own lives. For example, children born in the aftermath of the First World War told the story of their family upbringing to grandchildren born sixty or seventy years later. This transmission of childhood memories over two or sometimes three generations gives family stories a power which is translated at times into activity—the activity of remembrance (Winter and Sivan).

There are occasions when the household itself becomes a site of memory. The great German sculptor and artist Käthe Kollwitz kept the room of her dead son as a kind of shrine, just as it was when he volunteered for war in 1914. In Paris, there is a public housing project in a working-class neighborhood, where above every apartment door is listed the name of a soldier who died in the Great War. This is their home too, the metaphoric residence of those who were denied the chance the rest of us have of living and dying one at a time.

This framework of family transmission of narratives about the past is an essential part of public commemoration. It also helps us understand why some commemorative forms are changed or simply fade away. When the link between family life and public commemoration is broken, a powerful prop of remembrance is removed. Then, in a short time, remembrance atrophies and fades away. Public reinforcements may help keep alive the ritual and practice of commemoration. But the event becomes hollow when removed from the myriad small-scale social units that breathed life into it in the first place.

At that moment, commemorative sites and practices can be revived and re-appropriated. The same sites used for one purpose can be used for another. But most of the time, sites of memory live through their life cycle, and like the rest of us, inevitably fade away.

This natural process of dissolution closes the circle on sites of memory and the public commemoration which occurs around them. And rightly so, since they arise out of the needs of groups of people to link their lives with salient events in the past. When that need vanishes, so does the glue that holds together the social practice of commemoration. Then collective memories fade away, and sites of memory decompose, or simply fade into the landscape. Let me offer two instances of this phenomenon. For decades the national war memorial in Dublin, designed by Sir Edwin Lutyens, was completely overgrown with grass. No one could tell what it was, and this was no accident. That 100,000 Irishmen died for Britain's King and country was not an easy matter to interpolate in Irish history after 1918. But with the waning of sectarian violence in the latter decades of the twentieth century, the grass was cut and the monument reappeared, as if out of thin air. Sites of memory vanish, to be sure, but they can be conjured up again when people decide once again to mark the moment they commemorate. At other times, resurrection is more difficult. For years I asked my students at Cambridge what did they see at the first intersection into town from the railway station. Most answered nothing at all. What they did not see was the town war memorial, a victorious soldier striding back home, right at the first traffic light into town. They did not see it because it had no meaning to them. It was simply white noise in stone. For them to see it, someone had to point it out, and others had to organize acts of remembrance around it. Without such an effort, sites of memory vanish into thin air and stay there.

We have reached, therefore, a quixotic conclusion. Public commemoration is both irresistible and unsustainable. Constructing sites of memory is a universal social act, and yet these very sites are as transitory as are the groups of people who create and sustain them. Time and again people have come together at particular places, in front of particular sites of memory, to seek meaning in vast events in the past and try to relate them to their own smaller networks of social life. These associations are bound to dissolve, to be replaced by other forms, with other needs, and other histories. At that point, the characteristic trajectory of sites of memory, bounded by their creation, institutionalization, and decomposition, comes to an end.

References

Assmann, Jan. "Kollektives Gedächtnis und kulturelle Identität." *Kultur und Gedächtnis.* Eds. Jan Assmann and Tonio Hölscher. Frankfurt am Main: Suhrkamp, 1988. 9-19. [English: Assmann, Jan. "Collective Memory and Cultural Identity." Trans. John Czaplicka. *New German Critique* 65 (1995): 125-33.]

Gregory, Adrian. *The Silence of Memory.* Leamington Spa: Berg, 1994.

Hayden, Dolores. *The Power of Place.* Cambridge: MIT Press, 1992.

Hobsbawm, Eric, and Terence Ranger, eds. *The Invention of Tradition.* Cambridge: Cambridge UP, 1986.

Inglis, Ken. "World War One Memorials in Australia." *Guerres mondiales et conflits contemporains* 167 (1992): 51-58.

Lloyd, David W. *Battlefield Tourism: Pilgrimage and the Commemoration of the Great War in Britain, Australia, and Canada, 1919-1939.* Oxford: Berg, 1998.

MacKenzie, John, ed. *Imperialism and Popular Culture.* Manchester: Manchester UP, 1986.

Merridale, Catherine. "War, Death and Remembrance in Soviet Russia." *War and Remembrance in the Twentieth Century.* Eds. Jay Winter and Emmanuel Sivan. Cambridge: Cambridge UP, 1999. 61-83.

Nora, Pierre, ed. *Les lieux de mémoire.* 3 vols. Paris: Gallimard, 1984-92.

Prost, Antoine. "The Algerian War in French Collective Memory." *War and Remembrance in the Twentieth Century.* Eds. Jay Winter and Emmanuel Sivan. Cambridge: Cambridge UP, 1999. 161-76.

Winter, Jay. *Sites of Memory, Sites of Mourning: The Great War in European Cultural History.* Cambridge: Cambridge UP, 1999.

Winter, Jay, and Emmanuel Sivan. "Setting the Framework." *War and Remembrance in the Twentieth Century.* Eds. Jay Winter and Emmanuel Sivan. Cambridge: Cambridge UP, 1999. 1-40.

II. Memory and Cultural History

Memory and the History of Mentalities

ALON CONFINO

Between memory and the history of mentalities there are intellectual and methodological affiliations, though not straight connections. These affiliations began within a milieu of French scholars, notably Maurice Halbwachs and Marc Bloch, that originated at the first half of the twentieth century the modern study of memory and of mentalities. Affiliations continued to be present in the second half of the century in the work of Pierre Nora, who was a member of a succeeding French historical generation. While his magisterial project *Les lieux de mémoire* signaled the beginning of present-day memory studies, the links between memory and mentalities have been since mostly overlooked, as memory studies has been influenced by other trends in the humanities.

Today the link between memory and mentalities may serve as a call for the scholar to expand the interpretative, explanatory, and narrative potential of the notion of memory, while at the same time to exercise methodological rigor. Thinking of memory in association with mentalities may be useful in order to raise new questions, to make new connections, and to be aware of the interpretative problems and potentials in exploring the notion of memory.

The link between memory and the history of mentalities was evident from the beginning of modern memory studies. The French sociologist Maurice Halbwachs was the first to have used the concept of collective memory systematically in a seminal work, *Les cadres sociaux de la mémoire*, published in 1925. Halbwachs's fundamental contribution was to establish the connection between a social group and collective memory, and he argued that every memory is carried by a specific social group limited in space and time (see also Marcel and Mucchielli, this volume). After the First World War he received a Chair of Pedagogy and Sociology at the University of Strasbourg, where he met the celebrated historians Lucien Febvre and especially Marc Bloch, the fathers of the Annales school. They expressed vivid interest in Halbwachs's ideas, and a close professional friendship developed. When they founded in 1929 the journal *Annales d'histoire économique et sociales* Halbwachs became a member of the editorial board.

Febvre and Bloch called for a new kind of history that explored, beyond the usual political history of states and kings, the social and economic structures of a society as well as its "mental tools" (*outillage mental*), namely, the system of beliefs and collective emotions with which people in the past understood and gave meaning to their world. This history of mentalities (*histoire des mentalités*) provided a whole new approach to the study of the past, as it took seriously the history of collective representations, myths, and images. The history of collective memory—of how societies remember their past, how they represent it and lie about it—was viewed as one important part of this endeavor. Bloch published in 1924 his classic *Les Rois thaumaturges* about the "beliefs and fables" around Medieval royal healing rites, in which he used terms such as "collective ideas" and "collective representations." In the mid-1920s he started to use the term "collective memory." In 1925 he wrote a favorable review of Halbwachs's *Les cadres sociaux de la mémoire*.

The history of mentalities never possessed a clear and comprehensive body of theoretical work, and was more practiced than theorized, also by Bloch and Febvre. It was often justifiably criticized, which is beyond the scope of this entry. The same is true for the term *histoire des sensibilité*, or history of sensibilities, an offshoot of history of mentalities, coined later by Lucien Febvre to describe the study of collective psychology and reconstitution of emotions and habits of mind. What links memory and the history of mentalities therefore was not a set of clear-cut theoretical rules. Rather, it was the combination of path-breaking work, simultaneously conceived by scholars who made up an intellectual milieu, to study human society by exploring collective representations and beliefs of people in the past by using historical and sociological tools.

Pierre Nora was a member of a later generation of Annalistes, conscious of the school's traditions and also of its new directions. In 1974 he edited together with Jacques Le Goff *Faire de l'histoire*, a manifesto about a new kind of history that nonetheless took as its starting point the Annales. In a volume of similar intent published in 1978, this time explicitly called *La nouvelle histoire*, he wrote the entry on memory. He was explicit about the association between memory and mentality, and began his entry in the following words: "To talk today of collective memory raises the same genre of difficulties and mobilizes basically the same stakes that the word 'mentalités' raised thirty years ago" ("Mémoire collective" 398). By that time, the Annales as a school of historical study lost its cohesiveness and domination. But Nora's interest in memory continued in a sense a certain affiliation between memory and mentality that had always been present within the Annales and French historical thought: Thus the study of collective representations was transformed by Nora to the study of collective representations of the past, of memory.

From Halbwachs to Bloch and Febvre and up to Nora, the history of memory was linked with the history of mentalities within a shared French scholarly and intellectual milieu. But the new history of memory in the last generation, while keeping a seminal place for Nora's project, has had a distinctly different character that is not centered in France. Memory studies have been transnational and international in their scope, interests, origins, and historiographical foundation. They have been influenced by the growing interest in the Holocaust; by new approaches to nationhood and to the ways nations construct their pasts; and by a diffused body of work called cultural studies, which often centered on issues of identity (including, among others, postcolonialism and gender studies).

In this context, the link between memory and history of mentalities became less important and visible, and was indeed forgotten. The common way scholars now describe the evolution of memory studies is to begin with Halbwachs, jump some fifty years straight to Nora, and then, depending on the interpretative taste and topic, to place their study within a relevant historiography on, say, national memory or the Holocaust. This recent historiographical evolution overlooks then an important part in the history of memory. In the meantime, memory studies itself was at one and the same time a central topic of scholarly exploration as well as in the midst of what seemed like a theoretical crisis. In this interpretative context it was suggested to think of memory anew by associating it with the history of mentalities (Confino, "Collective Memory").

By the mid-1990s the notion of "memory" had taken its place as a leading term, perhaps *the* leading term, in cultural history. Used with various degrees of sophistication, the notion of memory, more practiced than theorized, has been used to denote very different things which nonetheless share a topical common denominator: the ways in which people construct a sense of the past. As such, it has contributed tremendously to our historical knowledge. Memory studies uncovered new knowledge about the past, and brought to the fore topics that were simply not known a generation ago. One example will suffice here. Memory studies demolished the venerated view that Germans after 1945 were silent over the war and the extermination of the Jews. We know today that this view was a historians' invention. Instead, there existed in West Germany (where, in contrast to East Germany, there was an open public sphere) a lively debate on National Socialism in the local and private spheres, as well as in public and political life. It is difficult to underestimate the significance of this finding to the way we now understand postwar West German society.

But the benefit of richness cannot hide a sense that the term "memory" is depreciated by surplus use, while memory studies lacks a clear focus and, perhaps, has become predictable. It has a number of critical articles on method and theory, but not a systematic evaluation of the field's problems, approaches, and objects of study. It often follows a familiar and routine formula, as yet another event, its memory, and appropriation is investigated. Memories are described, following the interpretative zeitgeist of the humanities, as "contested," "multiple," and "negotiated." It is correct, of course, but it also sounds trite by now. The details of the plot are different in each case, but the formula is the same. We know that a study of memory undertakes to explore how people imagine the past, not how the past actually happened, though this in itself is not a new undertaking. Thus the often-made contention that the past is constructed not as fact but as a cultural artifact to serve the interest of a particular community may still be considered by some a *dernier cri*, but one cannot possibly present it anymore *pour épater les historiens.*

In this context, thinking about the lost connection between memory and the history of mentalities provides an imaginative way to think of memory as a notion of historical method and explanation. The study of memory and the history of mentalities appear to share a common purpose and agenda, as well as a sense of fashionableness and crisis. Jacques Le Goff described the history of mentalities as "a novelty and already devalued by excessive use [...]. It represents a new area of research, a trail to be blazed, and yet, at the same time, doubts are raised as to its scientific, conceptual, and epistemological validity. Fashion has seized upon it, and yet it seems already to have gone out of fashion. Should we revive or bury the history of mentalities?" (166). It sounds like a description of the current state of the history of memory. Similar to the study of memory, the history of mentalities was denounced as an empty rhetoric. Like the history of mentalities, a great appeal of the history of memory appears to be its vagueness. And both histories have by themselves no additional explanatory value; their value depends on the problems posed and methods used.

But the history of mentality is useful not only in order to outline the dangers faced by the new history of memory. There is a great advantage in thinking of the history of memory as the history of collective mentality. This way of reasoning resists the topical definition of the field and, conversely, uses memory to explore broader questions about the role of the past in society. The history of memory is useful and interesting to show not only how the past is represented in, say, a single museum but about the historical mentality of people in the past, about the commingled beliefs, practices, and symbolic representations that make people's perceptions of the past. This kind of history of memory is part of the history of mentalities as described by Robert Mandrou: It aims at "reconstructing the patterns of behavior, expressive forms and modes of silence into which worldviews and collective sensibilities are translated. The basic elements of this research are representations and images, myths and values recognized or tolerated by groups or the entire society, and which constitute the content of collective psychologies."

Memory as a study of collective mentality provides a comprehensive view of culture and society that is so often missing in the history of memory whose fragmentary tendency is to focus on distinct memories. The history of mentality attempted, in theory if not in practice, to outline the mental horizons of society as a whole, to link elite and popular culture, state indoctrination and habits of mind, within a single cultural world. This is a useful corrective for the history of memory, a field that is inclined to isolate memories instead of placing them in relations to one another and to society as a whole.

This approach emphasizes that collective memory is an exploration of a shared identity that unites a social group, be it a family or a nation, whose members nonetheless have different interests and motivations. And it emphasizes that the crucial issue in the history of memory is not how a past is represented, but why it was received or rejected. For every society sets up images of the past. Yet to make a difference in a society it is not enough for a certain past to be selected. It must steer emotions, motivate people to act, be received; in short, it must become a socio-cultural mode of action. Why is it that some pasts triumph while others fail? Why do people prefer one image of the past over another? The answers to these questions lead us to formulate hypotheses and perhaps draw conclusions about historical mentality.

Thinking of memory in association with the history of mentalities invites the scholar to give memory a certain anarchic quality that will take it beyond the sphere of ideas, ideology, and state and public representations, and into the ways people acted, shaped, internalized, and changed images of the past. An anarchic quality that locates memory not only in monuments and museums, but also in the ways people make it part of how and why they act in the world. This kind of history sees its task not simply to explore how people remember the past after the fact, but how memory structures behavior and thoughts.

Differently put, it means to place memory within a broader history that takes cognizance of the coexisting diversity of social times. This argument, in a sense, takes us back to Halbwachs's classic *Les cadres sociaux de la mémoire*, whose fundamental idea was of the "multiplicity of social times." The various ways by which memories become linked is a consequence of the various ways in which people are associated to given groups, be they religious, family, professional, local, or national. Different registers of memory determine the relative importance of a memory for the individual and for the group. This approach to memory views it as one cultural practice put in relations with other practices that together make up a mental horizon of society.

For close to a century now, the notions of mentality and then memory have fascinated scholars. What has been the source of this powerful attraction for two concepts that were after all so ambiguous, even tricky? The answer lies in their two shared basic characteristics. The first is to have dramatically expanded the territory of historical investigation and imagination in a way that called into question some cherished assumptions about historical reconstruction of the past. This, more than anything else, links the two notions. Mentalities had this effect on political history in the previous century and memory had this effect on social history in the last generation.

This comes into sharp focus when we consider the recent history of the notion of memory. When Nora conceived his memory project in the late 1970s and early 1980s, it reflected a wider disciplinary transformation. Broadly speaking, we can talk of an interpretative shift from "society" to "culture" and "memory." It began in the early 1980s as a gradual yet not brisk shift. By the 1990s, however, the notion of "society"—as it had been practiced by social historians along the twentieth century and particularly after 1945—was swept away by the interpretative onslaught of memory and cultural studies. The notion of society, broadly speaking, was based on a linear concept of history developing forward along one temporal timeline and privileging social and economical topics interpreted in terms of their function and structure. The notion of "culture," in contrast, is based on a multi-temporal concept of history where past and present commingle and coalesce, capturing simultaneously different and opposing narratives and privileging topics of representation and memory interpreted in terms of experience, negotiation, agency, and shifting relationship. This shift put at the center the historicity of history writing. It became central to the project of historical understanding to emphasize the historian's act of construction and interpretation of the past. And under these circumstances, it became inevitable to explore how people (including historians) construct their collective representations of the past.

The second and closely related characteristic is that mentality and memory call for interpretation. Of course, every historical topic is interpretable. But economic trends in the nineteenth-century British coal industry do not call for interpretation in the same way that Holocaust memory does. Sources and analysis of memory and mentality lay bare the process of construction of the past and therefore the practice of the historian. That is one important reason that the notions of memory and mentality expanded the investigation of the past, and were paradigmatic to major interpretative shifts in historical studies. While expanding the territory of historical investigation, they at the same time made this territory less defined and the methods of historical analysis less precise. But this is not necessarily negative: Well-defined disciplinary borders are important but can also be limiting. Expanding the historian's territory resulted in broadening the tools, subject matters, and questions of historical analysis. And it also shaped, in the last generation or so, a period when historians write with less certitude than previous generations, and with more self reflection and experimentation, about reconstructing the past.

And here—in the unbearable lightness of interpretation—lies the risk of memory and mentality as methods of inquiry, and also the promise of their relations. They call for interpretation, which can be facile and superficial. To find a meaningful trend in the serial data of coal production in nineteenth-century Britain is much more time consuming, and involves an extended period of research, collection, and analysis of evidence. But a representation of memory is different. It is as if it does not require an interpretative effort from the historian, and the sources seem to speak for themselves. Of course, no such thing exists. The challenge of the historian is to resist this unbearable lightness of interpretation. It is rather to sift meaning from memory via methods and theories, via interrogations of the use of evidence, of narrative, and of sources. Here lies today the potential of memory and the history of mentalities to set our historical imagination free, as they have done for a century.

References

Bloch, Marc. "Memoire collective, tradition et coutume: a propos d'un livre recent." *Revue de Synthése Historique* 40 (1925): 73-83.

Confino, Alon. "Collective Memory and Cultural History: Problems of Method." *American Historical Review* 105.2 (1997): 1386-403.

—. *Germany As a Culture of Remembrance: Promises and Limits of Writing History.* Chapel Hill: U of North Carolina P, 2006.

Febvre, Lucien. "Comment reconstituer la vie affective d'autrefois? La sensibilité et l'histoire." *Annales d'histoire sociale* 3 (1941): 5-20. Rpt. in *A New Kind of History: From the Writings of Febvre.* Ed. Peter Burke. Trans. K. Folca. London: Routledge, 1973. 12-26.

Halbwachs, Maurice. *Les cadres sociaux de la mémoire.* Paris: Alcan, 1925.

—. *On Collective Memory.* 1925. Ed. and trans. Lewis A. Coser. Chicago: U of Chicago P, 1992.

Le Goff, Jacques. "Mentalities: A History of Ambiguities." *Constructing the Past: Essays in Historical Methodology.* Eds. Jacques Le Goff and Pierre Nora. Cambridge: Cambridge UP, 1984. 166-80. Trans. of "Les Mentalité: Une Histoire ambiguë." *Faire de l'histoire.* Eds. Jacques Le Goff and Pierre Nora. Vol. 3. Paris: Gallimard, 1974.

Mandrou, Robert. "Histoire/L'histoire des mentalities." *Encyclopaedia Universalis* 1971. Paris: Encyclopaedia Universalis France, 1985. 9: 366.

Nora, Pierre. "Mémoire collective." *La nouvelle histoire.* Eds. Jacques Le Goff, Roger Chartier and Jacques Revel. Paris: Retz, 1978. 398-401.

—, ed. *La République.* Paris: Gallimard, 1984. Vol. 1 of *Les lieux de mémoire.* 7 vols. 1984-92.

—, ed. *La Nation.* Paris: Gallimard, 1986. Vols. 2-4 of *Les lieux de mémoire.* 7 vols. 1984-92.

—, ed. *Les France.* Paris: Gallimard, 1992. Vols. 5-7 of *Les lieux de mémoire.* 7 vols. 1984-92.

The Invention of Cultural Memory

DIETRICH HARTH

1. Guiding Metaphors and Concepts

One can often observe that certain words and terms common in daily usage contain, like trace elements, metaphorically coded clues to a semantic deep structure, the investigative explication of which can shed light on hidden connections. For example, the lexical field "*Erinnerung-Gedächtnis-Gedenken*" (remembering-memory-remembrance) refers not only to a conditioning process of internalization (*Innerlich-Machen*) but also to the cognitive processing of that which is "internalized." This suggests a dynamic relationship between passive as well as active attainments of learning, knowledge processing, and meaning-making which allows us to use "*Gedächtnis*" and "*Erinnerung*" as interlinked key terms in a wide variety of multi-dimensional contexts. This possibility of a transdisciplinary terminological freedom is encouraged by the descriptive strategies of neuroscientific and recent psychological memory research. In these fields the "net" metaphor is used in order to illustrate the coordinative and cooperative activities of memory in the—*sit venia verbo*—antiphon of inner (neuronal) and external (social) voices (Markowitsch; Welzer; see also their articles, this volume). In the terminology of sociological memory studies based on systems theory, the metaphor of the net, in marked contrast to the expression "archive," takes on the function of a cybernetic explanatory model which promises insights regarding the procedural dynamics of mnemonic practices in various social systems (Esposito 337ff.).

The metaphor of the net evokes the work of knotting together loose ends to interlacements and thereby offers an image for the coordinative and cooperative continuity in the action plan of interdisciplinary research programs. What this metaphor leaves aside are the hierarchies and other vertically organized structures of subordination. However, what it encourages is something I would like to call an "epistemology of relations." By this I mean a path to knowledge that draws attention to the relations (*Beziehungen*) between the elements by means of their connections (*Verknüpfungen*) and interactions, in order to use these interrelations to be able to probe the forces of gravity that operate within a particular socio-cultural field (Bourdieu).

It is by no means surprising that the epistemology of relations, albeit only partly discernible, is also tangent to the examples of wordplay which thematize "*kulturelles Gedächtnis*" (see the articles by A. and J. Assmann, this volume). The "connective structure" which Jan Assmann discusses in the introduction to his principal work on cultural theory (*Das kulturelle Gedächtnis* 16f.) uses the metaphor of connection, which, in a sort of homologous reflection, connects the descriptive language to the inner form of that being described. To put it more simply, Assmann argues that every culture connects every one of its individual subjects on the basis of shared norms (rules) and stories (memories; *Erinnerungen*) to the experience of a commonly inhabited meaningful world. It is only because of this experience that individuals are able to frame their personal identity through the orientating symbols of identity of their social world, symbols which are embodied in the objectified forms of a commonly shared cultural tradition. In the term "connectivity" the two types of memory which are decisive for this theory meet: "*kommunikatives Gedächtnis*," active on the level of simultaneity, which connects the present and the most recent past (*Verknüpfung*); and "*kulturelles Gedächtnis*," which, like a large storehouse filled with traditional "memory figures" (*Erinnerungsfiguren*), offers various possibilities to link the present to an ancient past (*Anknüpfung*).

The imagery of the *co-nexio* at this point should bring us back to the imagery of knotting nets, to consider again some fundamental aspects. The denser the net, the more it resembles a fabric. True, the production techniques are different, but in the end, as in the knotting of rugs, the results are quite comparable. Precisely this similarity between net and fabric—the latter in the meaning of "texture" and "text"—benefits both the construction of scholarly conceptualizations and also the construction of appropriate research objects. And yet: The difference between "net" and "fabric/texture" becomes relevant when one considers the openness, flexibility, and extent of the phenomena constituted by these craft metaphors. Nets are not only more permeable and thus also more transparent than fabric; in addition they offer, as seen in the example of the World Wide Web, possibilities for linking and unlinking within seconds, without the fear of disturbing or destroying key organizing patterns. If the Heidelberg cultural theory prefers as its guiding conceptualization the textuality and fabric metaphor to the net metaphor (A. Assmann, "Was sind kulturelle Texte?"), then primarily because of an appreciation of those durable "textures" that are protected by ancient gods such as the Egyptian deity Thoth, who by his own account invented writing as an "elixir of memory and wisdom" (Plato 7).

2. Invention, Elaboration, Adjustment

Invention here does not mean creation *ex nihilo*, but is instead to be understood in the meaning of the rhetorical *inventio*, best compared to a "création par bricolage" (Bastide 103). Referring to this discipline of ancient rhetoric (also known as heuristics) connected to the process of producing written texts intended for oral presentation, Roland Barthes paraphrased ancient texts when he said it was like an argumentative "net" that one had to skillfully throw over the material if one wants to catch a successful text (*discours*) (197). This refers to the production of written texts, but is also valid in the larger framework of developing concepts for research programs, although this does of course call for a careful reconstruction of the elements that flow into the *inventio*.

A Brief Remark Regarding Linguistic Differences

The German expression "*kulturelles Gedächtnis*" is not translated here, but rather used in the original, out of a consideration of the two languages involved. Already the words "*kulturell*/cultural" have different semantic connotations in German and in English, as a glance at any common dictionary of standardized language use will show. Anglo-American usage locates "culture" as a collective term for ideas, customs, and art in the contexts of society and civilization, while the lexeme "*Kultur*" stands for the intellectual, artistic, and creative achievements of a community and is used to express the advanced development of humanity. In addition, "*Gedächtnis*" and "memory" are not only very different morphologically and etymologically, but also their standard semantics signal subtle differences which can only be hinted at here: "Memory," as force, process, or repository, primarily refers to the reproducing and recalling of learned knowledge. "*Gedächtnis*," however, stands for the capacity to store not just what is learned but also sensory impressions and "mental processes," which can then at an opportune moment be allowed to "enter one's consciousness" again. In both cases, the standard languages cleave to the scientifically and empirically questionable storage metaphor in order to give the abstractions an eidetic meaning. Simultaneously, we recognize already on this level that language as a register of "*mémoire collective*" exerts a creative force which also molds the objects of the *Kulturelles Gedächtnis* (Linke 75). The conventional storage metaphor to a certain extent forms the pre-scientific hinge between the idea of an inner *Gedächtnis* and a *Gedächtnis* which has in the course of its phylogeny become an "exteriorized memory" (Leroi-Gourhan 273-332; J. Assmann, *Das kulturelle Gedächtnis* 22, note 5), located in tools, material symbols, (writing) techniques, and institutions.

As a cultural-theoretical blueprint, the Heidelberg concept, which came to be known as "*Kulturelles Gedächtnis*," has in an astonishingly short time successfully entered into the circulation process of interdisciplinary structures (Erll 263-76). This has been the result of various factors, and certainly not solely the dexterity in knotting argumentative nets mentioned by Roland Barthes. Flexible forms of self-organization, which promote the development of informal communicative structures free of strict efficiency imperatives and cumbersome administrative regulations, are necessary conditions for the success of scholarly work in temporary academic groups with changing personnel. The author of this article, at the beginning of the teamwork in Heidelberg, had in mind the French model of the *École des Annales*, founded in the late 1920s, a community of scholars whose name stands for a widely influential reform of historiographical thinking, and whose interest in the social sciences and methodological syncretism is also reflected in the work of the Heidelberg initiative.

For a long time, Jan Assmann's Egyptological Institute in Heidelberg served as an interdisciplinary "center of gravity" for a similar policy of open association, discussion, and the initiation of projects. Here workshops, guest lectures, conferences, and lecture series were planned which all revolved around the topic of culture and memory. In response to growing interest, the cultural-studies groups meeting there were soon replaced by a transdisciplinary discussion group which for many years met on a regular basis in the *Internationales Wissenschaftsforum* of the university (a center for scholarly exchange in all areas of academic research) and which dated its unwritten charter to the time before 1933, when a distinguished generation of scholars well-known outside the university established the international reputation of the "Ruperto Carola" (University of Heidelberg). A crucial step in furthering the versatile application and interdisciplinary implementation of the concept of *Kulturelles Gedächtnis* was the volume of collected essays published by Suhrkamp in 1988 and edited by the archaeologists Jan Assmann (Egyptology) and Tonio Hölscher (Classical Archaeology): *Kultur und Gedächtnis.* This publication grew out of a lecture series organized by the discussion group on the occasion of a mnemonically prominent event, namely the 600th anniversary of the founding (in 1386) of the University of Heidelberg, with the intention of proving to the public that cultural studies and the humanities are in fact ideally suited to reflect and support the endowment of the complexities of modern life with meaning.

The group strategies and organizational frameworks indicated here cannot replace personal dedication, which of course also profits from the type of informal infrastructures mentioned above. Personal dedication in the humanities is most clearly reflected in written and printed words, and the Heidelberg initiative brought forth quite an impressive number of publications. Worth mentioning are particularly the books that appeared in the relatively short period from 1990 to 1992 and which had a profound effect on promulgating the key concept and its versatility: *Ma'at* (1990), *Kultur und Konflikt* (1990), *Kultur als Lebenswelt und Monument* (1991), *Weisheit* (1991), *Mnemosyne* (1991), *Die Erfindung des Gedächtnisses* (1991), *Das Fest und das Heilige* (1991), *Revolution und Mythos* (1992) and, last but not least, Jan Assmann's programmatic study *Das kulturelle Gedächtnis: Schrift, Erinnerung und politische Identität in frühen Hochkulturen* (1992).

The meaning of "invention" in this context has in the meantime, along the lines of Barthes's argumentative networking, gradually been worked out and intersubjectively tested on both the level of philological-historical and of comparative cultural studies. Even before the term *Kulturelles Gedächtnis* was found for the new theory, the initiators, Aleida and Jan Assmann, had launched a continuing series of interdisciplinary colloquia, under the title *Archäologie der literarischen Kommunikation.* The emblematic character of the name for this series, later established as a book series title, aptly indicates the complexity of the undertaking. The label "archaeology," particularly in this context, not only denotes the excavation work carried out by Jan Assmann and others, it is also directed towards the connectivity between death and writing characteristic of ancient Egyptian culture (J. Assmann, "Schrift, Tod und Identität"; cf. also Dupont 281f.). What is more, "archaeology" alludes to Sigmund Freud's use of the same expression as an image for the deep-hermeneutic seeking, bringing together, and restoring of dispersed fragments of individual memory.

A relation is indicated here which is explicitly discussed in the closing essay of the first volume of the *Archäologie* series in 1983 (A. Assmann and J. Assmann, "Nachwort") and five years later in "Schrift, Tradition und Kultur" (A. Assmann and J. Assmann). As in an overture, some of the main motifs of the concept of *Kulturelles Gedächtnis* are raised, and then elaborated, rendered more precise, and adjusted in later writings:

- Differentiation of oral and literal processes of transmission corresponding to the experienced time of everyday life on the one hand, and to the anamnestic time of events transcending entrenched habits ("time of solemn reflection") on the other hand;
- *Kultur* as an authoritative, symbolically coded "world of meaning";

- (Collective) memory as a repertoire and generator of values which transcend the span of a lifetime and create identity;
- Standardization of collectively accepted "self-images" (we-identities) through the "sacralization" (canonization) of religious, historic, legal, and literary traditions;
- Organization of a "script-based culture" (for example in Greek antiquity) as the origin for the active appropriation and continuation of canonized traditions, supported by annotation, explanation, and interpretation.

With these points, the new theory contested earlier literacy research that purported an equation of the alphabetic writing system with an allegedly advanced "rational" mentality (in comparison to other writing systems). In fact it is not the formal features of the written characters that are important; mental conditioning is instead much more a result of the social organization of oral and written communication processes, which include not only the institutionalization of experts and schools, but also the differentiation of such varied activities as reproduction, annotation, critique, canon creation, censorship, and the writing of literary history (J. Assmann, *Das kulturelle Gedächtnis* 87ff.). In short, it is the way the script-based culture is organized that determines which pragmatic, mnemonic, and formative functions the medium of writing can be accorded in the construction of a cultural system.

Since Jan Assmann's reading of Maurice Halbwachs in the summer of 1986 (J. Assmann, "Das kollektive Gedächtnis" 65), the main motifs sketched out above have remained central elements in the subsequent elaboration of the concept. One of the results of the Halbwachs reading was the replacement of the unwieldy composite "*Gedächtniskultur*" with the metaphorical construct "*Kulturelles Gedächtnis*" (A. Assmann and J. Assmann, "Schrift, Tradition und Kultur" 27). This was by no means merely a superficial shift, as the introduction of the new expression accompanies a conscious demarcation from Halbwachs's term "*mémoire collective*," a term the French sociologist was familiar with thanks to his teacher Émile Durkheim and the writings of Arnold van Gennep (Gierl 161ff.). In his posthumously published book *La mémoire collective*, Halbwachs assigned this term the status of a key concept which mediates between the individual and the society. He also tried to define it more exactly by distinguishing it from the historical work of the rational reconstruction of the past, which his colleague Marc Bloch, one of the founding fathers of the *École des Annales*, had taken as a starting point for his critique of the psychologistic transference of the term "*mémoire*" from the individual to the collective.

Assmann's use of the term "*Kulturelles Gedächtnis*" reflected this distinction and could thus profit from Halbwachs's theory. It was not sufficient to balance memory (*Gedächtnis*) against the scholarly reconstructions of historiography. It is true that the semantics of the term "memory" does indeed include cognitive intellectual operations, but that does not mean that the success or failure of remembering (*Erinnerungsleistung*) can be measured by the alternative "true or false?" (A. Assmann, "Wie wahr sind Erinnerungen?"). In contrast, the inherent logic of mnemonic shaping corresponds to a quasi-poietic force, as already reflected in the ancient myth of Mnemosyne, and as Halbwachs affirmed anew in the framework of his social-psychological reflections. This force, not directly visible and thus best regarded as a virtual entity, evinces a legend- and myth-creating productivity. The effectively normative, symbolically coded "truth" of a great memory figure—such as Assmann's example, the prophet Moses—is thus not to be found in the past of this religious founder, a past that can be reconstructed by comparatively rational means, but rather in the perspectives from whose vantage point later generations have interpreted and incorporated into their own self-image his history, passed down in writing, and the story of the exodus associated with his name (J. Assmann, *Herrschaft* 247-80). The example clarifies once again the twofold function of the memory metaphor (*Gedächtnismetapher*): On the one hand it designates the cognitively simplified visualization of the past, and on the other hand it provides a symbol for the formation of ideological convictions conceived in analogy to the internalization of concepts of religious belief.

A comparison of *mémoire collective* and *Kulturelles Gedächtnis* also brings important differences to light. Halbwachs was above all attempting to get to the bottom of the cognitive discrepancy between the scholarly reconstruction of the past and the experienced, that is, the lived, tradition. Assmann's concept, on the other hand, looks at the medial conditions and social structures of organization which groups and societies use to connect themselves to an objectified supply of cultural representations, available in diverse forms (for example, in writing, image, architecture, liturgy), in order to construct patterns for self-interpretation legitimized by the past.

The Heidelberg cultural theory thus does not lay weight on the formations, however created, of a collective consciousness. Rather, it differentiates, along the lines of the aforementioned dual coding of the social mneme, between the "communicative" group memory (*Gruppengedächtnis*), meant to guarantee the organization of "profane" everyday acts, and the memory of tradition (*Traditionsgedächtnis*) of the interpreting elites, which is there to keep at hand the longer-lasting, the "sacralized" world view. No doubt, with this concept of the Sacred (A. Assmann and J. Assmann,

"Schrift, Tradition und Kultur" 27), the theory of *Kulturelles Gedächtnis* holds to a schema of collective thought which includes the idea of a quasi-prophetic appeal to the living to forget neither victims nor past traditions' broken promises of salvation.

The ethical component of the Heidelberg cultural theory suggested here has a thanatological background which points to the ancient Egyptian cult of the dead and the associated forms of a monumental burial architecture enclosed in and covered with writing. Assmann sees in this culture-specific feature of the ancient Egyptian commemoration of the dead the "origin" of *Kulturelles Gedächtnis* in the symbolically embodied presence of the absent person (J. Assmann and Rack 96). Here a methodical relationship between the Heidelberg cultural theory and the fundamentals of semiotic hermeneutics à la Clifford Geertz becomes evident. That is to say, only in light of the interpretation of the signs, which can certainly be allegorizing, do the dead specters step out of the darkness of forgetting and transform themselves into ambiguous memory figures, on whose side the interpreter in the role of the *Remembrancer* (Burke 110) can hold up to his present time the debts of the past.

Thanks to Jan Assmann's sovereign mastery of this variety of hermeneutical necromancy, cultural history has gained a deep understanding not only of the ancient Egyptian religion and state, but—mediated through its Otherness—also new insights into the "history of influence" (*Wirkungsgeschichte*) of "Occidental" thought. The concept denoted by the formula "*Kulturelles Gedächtnis*" is to be understood—as is made clear by Assmann's extensive comparative cultural studies—as a *hermeneutical category*, which leads the efforts to reconstruct the historically shaped consciousness beyond that teleologically constructed realm of memory (*Gedächtnisraum*), the historical border of which is demarcated by, to use Karl Jaspers's term, the "Axial Age" (J. Assmann, *Ma'at* 11).

3. Limits of the Concept

The idea of interconnecting "culture" and "memory" is not particularly new. In 1910, Arnold van Gennep pointed to the tenacious longevity of the "*mémoire des faits d'ordre culturel*" (164), which can allow technical know-how and religious traditions, but also rules and regulations of social and political organizations, to outlast historical "expiration dates." Nor may one forget Maurice Halbwachs, important for the early history of the concept even beyond the aforementioned aspects. For sound reasons, the editor of the critical edition of *La mémoire collective* emphasizes the French sociologist's tendency to cross the conventional borders of "*mémoire psy-*

chologique" in the direction of "*mémoire culturelle*" (Namer 270f.). One must also mention Aby Warburg, who in the early twentieth century pondered the socio-cultural implications of remembering. In his posthumously published work he called attention to the dark, even "demonic," as he called it, side of the emergence of cultures, and advocated the thesis that the iconographic memory (*Bildgedächtnis*) provides the means to endure, and even to sublimate, the horrors of existence.

It was not until the 1970s that the Moscow-Tartu semiotic school (Lotman) once again established a loose affiliation between "culture" and "memory"; the Heidelberg concept drew on this at the beginning (J. Assmann, *Das kulturelle Gedächtnis* 21). A short time later the first volumes of Pierre Nora's "*lieux de mémoire*" appeared, which not only provided an encyclopedic repertoire of constructions of a nationally significant collective memory, but also reflected on the changing functions of the French memorial sites in the framework of post-traditional lifestyles (see den Boer, this volume). More recently, a group of American philosophers appealed to the historically saturated, reflective "cultural memory," in order to stand up to the vagueness and loss of history and memory disseminated in certain academic communities (Cook).

It would be futile to compare the positions mentioned here with the Heidelberg cultural theory and ask which one of these should enjoy the rights of the firstborn. The Heidelberg theory can justifiably claim to be an argumentatively well-founded theory without fulfilling the rigid demands of an orthodox system. The theory of *Kulturelles Gedächtnis* instead offers an open concept that is thus adaptable in other disciplines and which it is no rebuke to call conservative. After all, with its reconstructive path through the "great tradition" (Redfield 43ff.), its application convincingly spreads a wealth of guiding ideas before our eyes which, to name just one, albeit very important, aspect, brings together political and religious thought. The authors of the Heidelberg cultural theory have expressly linked their concept with the problems of German historical memory and have participated in controversial debates regarding appropriate forms of commemoration of the Holocaust (J. Assmann, "Das kollektive Gedächtnis" 67). This relationship of the theory of *Kulturelles Gedächtnis* to controversial questions of identity-creating politics of memory does, though, draw attention to a difficult aspect of the concept which I would like to, in closing, comment on with a critical remark.

Key elements of the Heidelberg cultural theory include the way the medium of writing is charged with the task of passing on tradition and its standardizing function. *Kultur*, in this view, unfolds as a dense fabric of writings before the eyes of those who read and are able to interpret what they read. These are both abilities acquired through learning, and in earlier times were mastered by only a few, very powerful elites, and which even today are associated with privileged access to the general culture and corresponding group loyalties. Illiteracy, inadequate mastery of the written word, and hermeneutic incompetence would, according to this understanding, exclude large majorities and entire social classes from participation in the *Kulturelles Gedächtnis* and its rewards of identity creation.

This raises the question as to the effects of a social distinction that is based on the unequal distribution of symbolic capital and thus offers only a few groups the possibility to satisfy their need for orientation through an institutionally anchored *Kulturelles Gedächtnis* kept alive by the constant care and regeneration carried out by scholars. The crucial point is that society's acceptance of norms and values does not depend on a "sacralized," written, or in any other form symbolically coded canon. The genesis and validity of values and their translation into effective practical norms is instead based on the processes of negotiation and agreement that are part of common experience. This refers to communicative practices that would be overstrained with charges to safeguard memory and create identity, and yet which nonetheless hold to cultural standards, while not immunizing themselves against alternative interests through the "sacralization" of a cultural canon. This sort of defense of cultural standards is transverse to the distinction between everyday memory (*Alltagsgedächtnis*) and sacred memory (*Festtagsgedächtnis*), and does not require an appeal to identity. In general, it is sufficient if the members of a group or society can explain why they keep to their effectively operating self-images and are not interested in any other, without necessarily needing to denigrate or despise alternative kinds of cultural experience (Waldron).

Revised article based on a translation by Sara B. Young

References

Assmann, Aleida. "Was sind kulturelle Texte?" *Literaturkanon—Medienereignis—Kultureller Text: Formen interkultureller Kommunikation und Übersetzung.* Ed. Andreas Poltermann. Berlin: Schmidt, 1995. 232-44.

—. "Wie wahr sind Erinnerungen?" *Das soziale Gedächtnis: Geschichte, Erinnerung, Tradierung.* Ed. Harald Welzer. Hamburg: Hamburger Edition, 2001. 103-22.

Assmann, Aleida, and Jan Assmann. Nachwort. *Schrift und Gedächtnis.* Archäologie der literarischen Kommunikation I. Eds. Aleida Assmann, Jan Assmann and Christof Hardmeier. Munich: Fink, 1983. 265-84.

—. "Schrift, Tradition und Kultur." *Zwischen Festtag und Alltag: Zehn Beiträge zum Thema 'Mündlichkeit und Schriftlichkeit'*. Ed. Wolfgang Raible. Tübingen: Narr 1988. 25-49.

Assmann, Jan. *Herrschaft und Heil: Politische Theologie in Altägypten, Israel und Europa.* Munich: Hanser, 2000.

—. "Das kollektive Gedächtnis zwischen Körper und Schrift: Zur Gedächtnistheorie von Maurice Halbwachs." *Erinnerung und Gesellschaft/Mémoire et Société: Hommage à Maurice Halbwachs (1877-1945).* Eds. Hermann Krapoth and Denis Laborde. Wiesbaden: VS Verlag, 2005. 65-83.

—. *Das kulturelle Gedächtnis: Schrift, Erinnerung und politische Identität in frühen Hochkulturen.* Munich: Beck, 1992.

—. *Ma'at: Gerechtigkeit und Unsterblichkeit im Alten Ägypten.* Munich: Beck, 1990.

—. "Schrift, Tod und Identität: Das Grab als Vorschule der Literatur im alten Ägypten." *Schrift und Gedächtnis.* Archäologie der literarischen Kommunikation I. Eds. Aleida Assmann, Jan Assmann and Christof Hardmeier. Munich: Fink, 1983. 64-93.

Assmann, Jan, and Tonio Hölscher, eds. *Kultur und Gedächtnis.* Frankfurt am Main: Suhrkamp, 1988.

Assmann, Jan, and Jochen Rack. "Totenrituale: Einübungen in das Hinausdenken über die eigene Lebenszeit." *Lettre International* 72 (2006): 95-99.

Barthes, Roland. "L'ancienne rhétorique: Aide-mémoire." *Communications* 16 (1970): 172-223.

Bastide, Roger. "Mémoire collective et sociologie du bricolage." *L'Année Sociologique* 21 (1970): 65-108.

Bourdieu, Pierre. *Raisons pratiques: Sur la théorie de l'action.* Paris: Seuil, 1994.

Burke, Peter. "History as Social Memory." *Memory, History, Culture and the Mind.* Ed. Thomas Butler. Oxford: Blackwell, 1989. 96-113.

Cook, Patricia, ed. *Philosophical Imagination and Cultural Memory: Appropriating Historical Traditions.* Durham: Duke UP, 1993.

Dupont, Florence. *L'invention de la literature: De l'ivresse grecque au livre latin.* Paris: La Découverte, 1994.

Erll, Astrid. "Literatur und kulturelles Gedächtnis: Zur Begriffs- und Forschungsgeschichte, zum Leistungsvermögen und zur literaturwissenschaftlichen Relevanz eines neuen Paradigmas der Kulturwissenschaft." *Literaturwissenschaftliches Jahrbuch* 43 (2002): 249-76.

Esposito, Elena. *Soziales Vergessen: Formen und Medien des Gedächtnisses der Gesellschaft.* Frankfurt am Main: Suhrkamp, 2002.

Gierl, Walter. "Zwischen Traum und Legende: Wie Maurice Halbwachs unsere Erinnerungsformen einkreist." *Erinnerung und Gesell-*

schaft/Mémoire et Société: Hommage à Maurice Halbwachs (1877-1945). Jahrbuch für Sozialgeschichte. Eds. Hermann Krapoth and Denis Laborde. Wiesbaden: VS Verlag, 2005. 153-218.

Halbwachs, Maurice. *La mémoire collective.* Paris: Michel, 1997.

Leroi-Gourhan, André. *Hand und Wort: Die Evolution von Technik, Sprache und Kunst.* Trans. Michael Bischoff. Frankfurt am Main: Suhrkamp, 1988.

Linke, Angelika. "Kulturelles Gedächtnis: Linguistische Perspektiven auf ein kulturwissenschaftliches Forschungsfeld." *Brisante Semantik: Neuere Konzepte und Forschungsergebnisse einer kulturwissenschaftlichen Linguistik.* Eds. Dietrich Busse et al. Tübingen: Niemeyer, 2005. 65-85.

Lotman, Jurij M., and B. A. Uspensky. "On the Semiotic Mechanism of Culture." *New Literary History* IX (1978): 211-32.

Markowitsch, Hans J. *Neuropsychologie des Gedächtnisses.* Göttingen: Hogrefe, 1992.

Namer, Gérard. Postface. *La mémoire collective.* By Maurice Halbwachs. Paris: Michel, 1997. 237-95.

Plato. "Phaidros 274c-278b." *Schrift und Gedächtnis.* Archäologie der literarischen Kommunikation I. Eds. Aleida Assmann, Jan Assmann and Christof Hardmeier. Munich: Fink, 1983. 7-9.

Redfield, Robert. *The Little Community and Peasant Society and Culture.* Chicago: U of Chicago P, 1960.

van Gennep, Arnold. *La formation des Légendes.* Paris: Flammarion, 1910.

Waldron, Jeremy. "Cultural Identity and Civic Responsibility." *Citizenship in Diverse Societies.* Eds. Will Kymlicka and Wayne Norman. Oxford: Oxford UP, 2000. 155-74.

Welzer, Harald. *Das kommunikative Gedächtnis: Eine Theorie der Erinnerung.* Munich: Beck, 2002.

Canon and Archive

Aleida Assmann

1. The Dynamics of Cultural Memory between Remembering and Forgetting

Over the last decade, the conviction has grown that culture is intrinsically related to memory. Jurij Lotman and Boris Uspenskij have defined culture as "the memory of a society that is not genetically transmitted" (3) but, we may add, by external symbols. Through culture, humans create a temporal framework that transcends the individual life span relating past, present, and future. Cultures create a contract between the living, the dead, and the not yet living. In recalling, iterating, reading, commenting, criticizing, discussing what was deposited in the remote or recent past, humans participate in extended horizons of meaning-production. They do not have to start anew in every generation because they are standing on the shoulders of giants whose knowledge they can reuse and reinterpret. As the Internet creates a framework for communication across wide distances in space, cultural memory creates a framework for communication across the abyss of time.

When thinking about memory, we must start with forgetting. The dynamics of individual memory consists in a perpetual interaction between remembering and forgetting (see also Esposito, this volume). In order to remember some things, other things must be forgotten. Our memory is highly selective. Memory capacity is limited by neural and cultural constraints such as focus and bias. It is also limited by psychological pressures, with the effect that painful or incongruent memories are hidden, displaced, overwritten, and possibly effaced. On the level of cultural memory, there is a similar dynamic at work. The continuous process of forgetting is part of social normality. As in the head of the individual, also in the communication of society much must be continuously forgotten to make place for new information, new challenges, and new ideas to face the present and future. Not only individual memories are irretrievably lost with the death of their owners, also a large part of material possessions and remains are lost after the death of a person when households are dissolved and personal belongings dispersed in flea markets, trashed, or recycled.

When looking more closely at these cultural practices, we can distinguish between two forms of forgetting, a more active and a more passive one. *Active* forgetting is implied in intentional acts such as trashing and destroying. Acts of forgetting are a necessary and constructive part of internal social transformations; they are, however, violently destructive when directed at an alien culture or a persecuted minority. Censorship has been a forceful if not always successful instrument for destroying material and mental cultural products. The *passive* form of cultural forgetting is related to non-intentional acts such as losing, hiding, dispersing, neglecting, abandoning, or leaving something behind. In these cases the objects are not materially destroyed; they fall out of the frames of attention, valuation, and use. What is lost but not materially destroyed may be discovered by accident at a later time in attics and other obscure depots, or eventually be dug up again by more systematic archaeological search. Sir Thomas Browne, a physician of the seventeenth century with a philosophical mind, was convinced that the unremarkable traces of the past have a better chance of being preserved than the ostentatious monuments of emperors. With respect to some antique urns which were unearthed in his Norfolk neighborhood, he commented: "Time which antiquates Antiquities, and hath an art to make dust of all things, hath yet spared these *minor* Monuments" (279). The German writer F. G. Jünger has defined this type of reversible or "halfway" forgetting as "preservative forgetting" (*Verwahrensvergessen*). Archaeology is an institution of cultural memory that retrieves lost objects and defunct information from a distant past, forging an important return path from cultural forgetting to cultural memory.

If we concede that forgetting is the normality of personal and cultural life, then remembering is the exception, which—especially in the cultural sphere—requires special and costly precautions. These precautions take the shape of cultural institutions. As forgetting, remembering also has an active and a passive side. The institutions of active memory preserve the *past as present* while the institutions of passive memory preserve the *past as past.* The tension between the pastness of the past and its presence is an important key to understanding the dynamics of cultural memory. These two modes of cultural memory may be illustrated by different rooms of the museum. The museum presents its prestigious objects to the viewers in representative shows which are arranged to catch attention and make a lasting impression. The same museum also houses storerooms stuffed with other paintings and objects in peripheral spaces such as cellars or attics which are not publicly presented. In the following, I will refer to the actively circulated memory that keeps the past present as the *canon* and the passively stored memory that preserves the past past as the *archive.*

This important distinction can be further explained by a reference to the cultural historian Jakob Burckhardt. He divided the remains of former historical periods into two categories: "messages" and "traces." By "messages" he meant texts and monuments that were addressed to posterity, whereas "traces" carry no similar address. Burckhardt mistrusted the messages, which are usually written and effectively staged by the carriers of power and state institutions; he considered them tendentious and therefore misleading. The unintentional traces, on the other hand, he cherished as unmediated testimonies of a former era that can tell a counter-history to the one propagated by the rulers. If we modify Burckhardt's distinction somewhat, we can perhaps generalize it. Cultural memory contains a number of cultural messages that are addressed to posterity and intended for continuous repetition and re-use. To this active memory belong, among other things, works of art, which are destined to be repeatedly re-read, appreciated, staged, performed, and commented. This aspiration, of course, cannot be realized for all artistic artifacts; only a small percentage acquire this status through a complex procedure which we call canonization. At the other end of the spectrum, there is the storehouse for cultural relicts. These are not unmediated; they have only lost their immediate addressees; they are de-contextualized and disconnected from their former frames which had authorized them or determined their meaning. As part of the archive, they are open to new contexts and lend themselves to new interpretations.

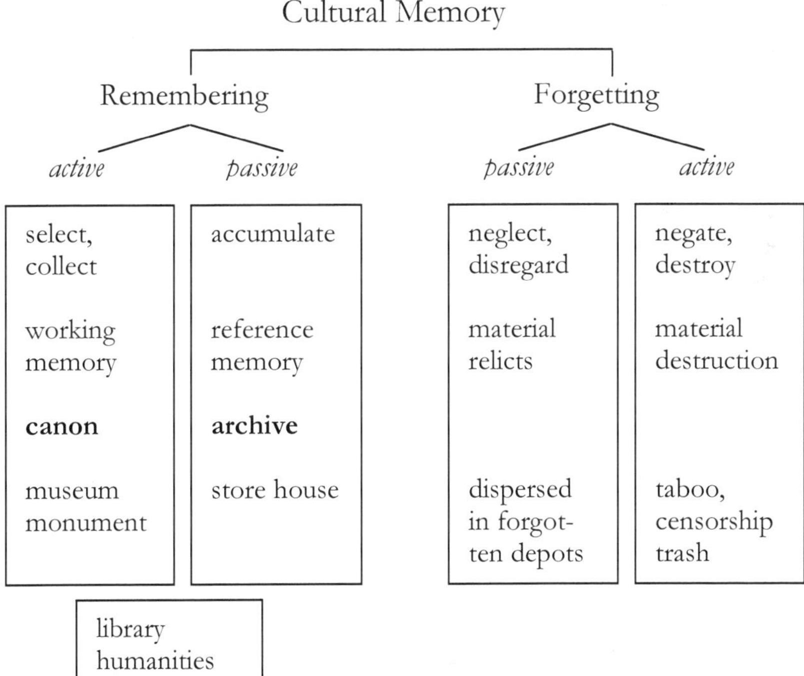

2. Cultural Working Memory: The Canon

The active dimension of cultural memory supports a collective identity and is defined by a notorious shortage of space. It is built on a small number of normative and formative texts, places, persons, artifacts, and myths which are meant to be actively circulated and communicated in ever-new presentations and performances. The working memory stores and reproduces the cultural capital of a society that is continuously recycled and re-affirmed. Whatever has made it into the active cultural memory has passed rigorous processes of selection, which secure for certain artifacts a lasting place in the cultural working memory of a society. This process is called canonization. The word means "sanctification"; to endow texts, persons, artifacts, and monuments with a sanctified status is to set them off from the rest as charged with the highest meaning and value. Elements of the canon are marked by three qualities: selection, value, and duration. Selection presupposes decisions and power struggles; ascription of value endows these objects with an aura and a sacrosanct status; duration in cultural memory is the central aim of the procedure. A canon is not a hit-list; it is instead independent of historical change and immune to the ups and downs of social taste. The canon is not built up anew by every generation; on the contrary, it outlives the generations who have to encounter and reinterpret it anew according to their time. This constant interaction with the small selection of artifacts keeps them in active circulation and maintains for this small segment of the past a continuous presence.

There are three core areas of active cultural memory: religion, art, and history. The term "canon" belongs to the history of religion; it is used there to refer to a text or a body of texts that is decreed to be sacred and must not be changed nor exchanged for any other text. The canonized text is a stable reference that is used over centuries and millennia in continuous acts of reverence, interpretation, and liturgical practice. Canonization is also a term for the transformation of martyrs of the Christian church into saints. These saints are remembered not only by stories and images but also by their names, which are inscribed into the calendar and reused for the naming of those who are born on these respective days. A Christian church is an institution of the active cultural memory. With its stone tablets and commemorative sculptures on the walls, especially old churches are unique memorial spaces that span several centuries. This cultural memory is kept alive also by architectural styles, traditions of images, and continuously and periodically repeated liturgical rites and practices.

When the religious canon was translated into the arts in secular modernity, it became a canon of classics. This canon is not as fixed and closed as the religious canon but open to changes and exchanges. Sacrosanct writers such as Milton and Nobel laureates such as T. S. Eliot have lost much of their former prestige during the last thirty years. In the postcolonial era, the Western literary canon is hotly contested and undergoing considerable transformations (see also Grabes, this volume). Although canons change, they remain indispensable tools for education; without them academic fields cannot be established, university curricula cannot be taught. The canon of classical texts is not only taught from generation to generation but also performed on the stages of theaters and in the concert halls. A canon of paintings and artifacts is repeatedly presented in museums and traveling exhibitions, and literary classics are stable elements in the book market. It is only a tiny segment of the vast history of the arts that has the privilege of repeated presentation and reception which ensures its aura and supports its canonical status.

A third realm of active cultural memory is history. Nation-states produce narrative versions of their past which are taught, embraced, and referred to as their collective autobiography. National history is taught via history textbooks, which have been appropriately termed "weapons of mass instruction" (Charles Ingrao). National history is also presented in the public arena in the form of monuments and commemoration dates. To participate in a national memory is to know the key events of the nation's history, to embrace its symbols, and connect to its festive dates.

Cultural memory, then, is based on two separate functions: the presentation of a narrow selection of sacred texts, artistic masterpieces, or historic key events in a timeless framework; and the storing of documents and artifacts of the past that do not at all meet these standards but are nevertheless deemed interesting or important enough to not let them vanish on the highway to total oblivion. While emphatic appreciation, repeated performance, and continued individual and public attention are the hallmark of objects in the cultural working memory, professional preservation and withdrawal from general attention mark the contents of the reference memory. Emphatic reverence and specialized historical curiosity are the two poles between which the dynamics of cultural memory is played out.

The tension that exists between these two poles can be further illustrated by two different approaches to literary criticism. In 2003 and 2004, two books appeared on Shakespeare, one by Harold Bloom with the title *Hamlet: Poem Unlimited*, and one by his former Yale student Stephen Greenblatt with the title *Will in the World*. Both books became bestsellers, although they could not have been more contrary in their approaches, methods, aims, and premises. Bloom writes in the spirit of the canon, developing a praising style, venerating the text and its author with a semi-religious fervor. Greenblatt, on the other hand, establishes a relation of distance and estrangement to his object of research. While Bloom de-contextualizes the text to make it the object of devotion, Greenblatt places the text back in its historical context, reading it side by side with other texts of the epoch. One adopts the strategy of the canon, investing the text with existential meaning and framing it with an aura; the other adopts the strategy of the archive, aiming at destroying the aura (Greenblatt and Gallagher 12). The tension acted out between Bloom and Greenblatt is the tension between the canon and the archive, or, in other words, between the contraction of cultural memory and its expansion.

3. Cultural Reference Memory: The Archive

The institutions of passive cultural memory are situated halfway between the canon and forgetting. The archive is its central and paradigmatic institution; to understand this dimension of cultural memory, it is necessary to explore the history and function of the archive. In literary studies, the archive is a concept that, just like trauma, has moved into the center of poststructuralist and postcolonial discourse: in this career, however, it is often disconnected from the empirical institution and used in metaphorical ways as a highly suggestive trope. According to a famous statement by Foucault, the archive is "the law that determines what can be said" (186f.). To bring this statement closer to the level of empirical institutions, it can be rephrased in the following way: The archive is the basis of what can be said in the future about the present when it will have become the past.

As the paradigmatic institution of passive cultural memory, the archive is the opposite of the memorial space of the church: It is the unhallowed bureaucratic space of a clean and neatly organized repository. Archives were developed in ancient cultures together with writing systems and bureaucratic structures of organization. In their primary function, they served the ruling class with the necessary information to build up provisions for the future through stockpiling. They also served as tools for the symbolic legitimation of power and to discipline the population. Examples of such political archives are, for example, the Inquisition files or the files compiled by the East German State Security (Stasi). Archives always belonged to institutions of power: the church, the state, the police, the law, etc. Without extended archives of data, there is no state bureaucracy, no strategy to organize the future and no control over the past. Archives of data provide important tools for political power (*Herrschaftswissen*).

Time, however, quickly outdates these archives. Once they are outdated, they lose their political function and relevance, transforming them into a heap of (possibly compromising) rubbish. If they do not disappear altogether, they may enter into the new context of the historical archives. These relicts of the past are not trashed, because they are considered to be of historical or scholarly interest. The historical archive is a receptacle for documents that have fallen out of their framing institutions and can be reframed and interpreted in a new context. We must therefore distinguish between *political archives* and *historical archives*. While political archives function as an important tool for power, historical archives store information which is no longer of immediate use. They are a very recent institution, dating back to the French revolution. The revolution brought about and sealed a violent break with the past out of which not only a new future but also a new historical sense was born. Ernst Schulin speaks of "a birth of historical consciousness out of the violent break with tradition" (24). The modern idea of progress and a new form of antiquarianism, namely historical scholarship, evolved side by side. Both presuppose a break between past and present. After having withdrawn from the past its normative values and claims, it could be subjected to historical scrutiny. If power is based on the political archive, historical scholarship is based on the historical archive.

The objects in the historical archive have lost their original "place in life" (*Sitz im Leben*) and entered a new context which gives them the chance of a second life that considerably prolongs their existence. What is stored in historical archives is materially preserved and cataloged; it becomes part of an organizational structure, which allows it to be easily sourced. As part of the passive dimension of cultural memory, however, the knowledge that is stored in the archive is inert. It is stored and potentially available, but it is not interpreted. This would exceed the competence of the archivist. It is the task of others such as the academic researcher or the artist to examine the contents of the archive and to reclaim the information by framing it within a new context. The archive, therefore, can be described as a space that is located on the border between forgetting and remembering; its materials are preserved in a state of latency, in a space of intermediary storage (*Zwischenspeicher*). Thus, the institution of the archive is part of cultural memory in the passive dimension of preservation. It stores materials in the intermediary state of "no longer" and "not yet," deprived of their old existence and waiting for a new one.

Although there are many different kinds of material relicts, the past, as Margaret Atwood has put it, is largely made of paper, and paper must be taken care of. She calls archivists and librarians "the guardian angels of paper" to whom we owe thanks, because "without them there would be a lot less of the past than there is" (31-32). These guardian angels are so inconspicuous that they remain almost as invisible as the angels themselves. Other important guardian angels of transmission were the scribes who copied texts from fragile papyrus scrolls onto the much more durable carrier of parchment in late antiquity, but also the Irish monks who copied ancient classical books and stored them in their libraries although they were not part of their own tradition and they did not make use of them.

4. Embodied and Disembodied Cultural Memory

The selection criteria for what is to be remembered and circulated in the active cultural memory and what is to be merely stored are neither clear nor are they uncontested. In the modern print age of libraries, science, and the growth of encyclopedic knowledge, the storage capacity of the archive has by far exceeded that which can be translated back into active human memory. In the age of digital media, the growing rift between the amount of externalized information and internalizable knowledge becomes ever more dramatic. As the capacity of computers is doubled every two years, the external storage capacity of the digital age has expanded even further, while the human capacity for memory remains the same due to its neural constraints. Already at the beginning of the twentieth century, Georg Simmel had referred to this uncontrollable process as "the tragedy of culture."

According to Plato, the "tragedy of culture" started with the introduction of (alphabetic) writing, because this technique of notation separated the knower from the known and made knowledge available to the non-initiated. Plato argued that writing does not transmit memory but produces a memory ersatz. Though already inherent in the introduction of writing itself as a form of externalizing knowledge, the distinction between a cultural working memory and a cultural reference memory has been considerably exacerbated with the new institution of the historical archive. In Western democracies, these two functions of cultural memory have come to be more and more separated. But they are, contrary to Simmel's (or Nietzsche's) apprehensions, in no way unrelated. The two realms of cultural memory are not sealed against each other. On the contrary, they interact in different ways. The reference memory, for instance, provides a rich background for the working memory, which means that elements of the canon may be "estranged" and reinterpreted by framing them with elements of the archive (which is the method of New Historicism). Elements of the canon can also recede into the archive, while elements of the archive may be recovered and reclaimed for the canon. It is exactly this interdependence of the different realms and functions that creates the dynamics of cultural memory and keeps its energy flowing.

Although we cannot imagine a culture without an active cultural memory, we can well imagine a culture without a passive storing memory. In oral cultures in which the cultural memory is embodied and transmitted through performances and practices, material relics do not persist and accumulate. In such cultures, the range of the cultural memory is coextensive with the embodied repertoires that are performed in festive rites and repeated practices. Cultures that do not make use of writing do not produce the type of relicts that are assembled in archives. Nor do they produce a canon that can be enshrined in museums and monuments. In order to do justice to cultures based on embodied forms of transmission, UNESCO has recently created a new category, referring to their cultural capital as "intangible cultural heritage." The new law of 2003 revalorized nonverbal forms of knowledge and protects a heritage that consists of practices, dances, rituals, and performances. Diana Taylor has written eloquently on the power of the Western archive over indigenous performance in the Americas. She has drawn attention to "non-archival systems of transfer" and "indigenous embodied practice as a form of knowing as well as a system for storing and transmitting knowledge" (18). Embodied repertoires and performances cannot be fixated and stored externally; they are multiplied and continued "in a constant state of againness" (Taylor 21). In an oral culture, cultural memory that is stored in embodied practices and live performances is kept within human limits and cannot expand indefinitely.

In totalitarian states, there is also no storing memory, but for very different reasons. In such a state, as Orwell has shown in his novel *1984*, every scrap that is left over from the past has to be changed or eliminated because an authentic piece of evidence has the power to crush the official version of the past on which the rulers base their power. Orwell's protagonist Winston Smith is a paradoxical archivist who is engaged in the ongoing project of effacing traces and rewriting the sources to make them mirror the present concerns. This paranoid effort is deemed necessary for the protection of the state because an independent reference to the past can trigger a counter-history that challenges the totalitarian version of the past and undermines the state.

5. Conclusion

Total recall is only possible in the science fiction movie of Arnold Schwarzenegger. Memory, including cultural memory, is always permeated and shot through with forgetting. In order to remember anything one has to forget; but what is forgotten need not necessarily be lost forever. The canon stands for the active working memory of a society that defines and supports the cultural identity of a group. It is highly selective and, as Harold Bloom has put it, built on the principle of exclusion. The function of the archive, the reference memory of a society, provides a kind of counterbalance against the necessarily reductive and restrictive drive of the working memory. It creates a meta-memory, a second-order memory that preserves what has been forgotten. The archive is a kind of "lost-and-found office" for what is no longer needed or immediately understood. The historical archive helps us to position ourselves in time; it affords us the possibility of comparison and reflection for a retrospective historical consciousness. We must acknowledge, however, that archives are selective as well. They are in no way all-inclusive but have their own structural mechanisms of exclusion in terms of class, race, and gender. These mechanisms, however, have in recent decades become the focus of critical attention, debate, and investigation, which are themselves powerful agents of change. Luckily, there is not only intentional but also accidental preservation when hidden deposits are discovered. They are what involuntary memory is to voluntary memory. But even counting in accidental discoveries, the past remains, as Thomas Carlyle once put it, a "miserable, defective shred." While historians have to adjust their research and questions to the extension and range of the archives, literary writers may take the liberty to fill in the gaps. Atwood writes: "[T]he parts left unexplained—the gaps unfilled—I was free to invent. Since there were a lot of gaps, there is a lot of invention" (35). Toni Morrison is a writer who deals with the gaps in historical records and archives in yet another way; the gaps that she discovers are the wounds in memory itself, the scar of a trauma that resisted representation and can only belatedly, long after the deeply destructive events, become articulated in the framework of a literary text. In a novel like *Beloved*, Morrison's imaginary literary supplement to historical memory is not a filling of the gap but a marking of it.

I wanted to show that both the active and the passive realms of cultural memory are anchored in institutions that are not closed against each other but allow for mutual influx and reshuffling. This accounts for the dynamics within cultural memory and keeps it open to changes and negotiations. I also wanted to show that the archive is an institution with a history and specific functions. Like the recognition of human rights, the archive is an important achievement of civil society and perhaps not the least by which we may judge its strength.

References

Atwood, Margaret. *In Search of Alias Grace: On Writing Canadian Historical Fiction*. Ottawa: U of Ottawa P, 1997.

Bloom, Harold. *The Western Canon: The Books and School of the Ages*. New York: Harcourt Brace, 1994.

Browne, Thomas. "Hydriotaphia, Urne-Burial, or A Brief Discourse of the Sepulcrall Urnes Lately Found in Norfolk." *The Prose of Sir Thomas Browne*. Ed. Norman Endicott. New York: New York UP, 1986. 241-86.

Derrida, Jacques. *Archive Fever: A Freudian Impression*. Chicago: U of Chicago P, 1997.

Foucault, Michel. *Archäologie des Wissens*. 4th ed. Frankfurt am Main: Suhrkamp, 1990.

Gallagher, Catherine, and Stephen Greenblatt. *Practicing New Historicism*. Chicago: U of Chicago P, 2000.

Jünger, Friedrich G. *Gedächtnis und Erinnerung*. Frankfurt am Main: Klostermann, 1957.

Lotman, Jurij M., and Boris A. Uspenskij. *The Semiotics of Russian Culture*. Ed. Ann Shukman. Michigan Slavic Contributions 11. Ann Arbor: U of Michigan P, 1984.

Schulin, Ernst. "Absage an und Wiederherstellung von Vergangenheit." *Speicher des Gedächtnisses: Bibliotheken, Museen, Archive*. Eds. Moritz Csáky and Peter Stachel. Vol. 1. Vienna: Passagen, 2000. 23-39.

Simmel, Georg. "Der Begriff und die Tragödie der Kultur." *Das individuelle Gesetz: Philosophische Exkurse*. Ed. Michael Landmann. Frankfurt am Main: Suhrkamp, 1987: 116-47.

Taylor, Diana. *The Archive and the Repertoire: Performing Cultural Memory in the Americas*. Durham: Duke UP, 2005.

Veit, Ulrich, Tobias L. Kienlin, Christoph Kümmel, and Sascha Schmidt, eds. *Spuren und Botschaften: Interpretationen materieller Kultur*. New York: Waxmann, 2003.

Communicative and Cultural Memory

JAN ASSMANN

1. Memory: Individual, Social, and Cultural

Memory is the faculty that enables us to form an awareness of selfhood (identity), both on the personal and on the collective level. Identity, in its turn, is related to time. A human self is a "diachronic identity," built "of the stuff of time" (Luckmann). This synthesis of time and identity is effectuated by memory. For time, identity, and memory we may distinguish among three levels:

Level	Time	Identity	Memory
inner (neuro-mental)	inner, subjective time	inner self	individual memory
social	social time	social self, person as carrier of social roles	communicative memory
cultural	historical, mythical, cultural time	cultural identity	cultural memory

Figure 1

On the *inner level*, memory is a matter of our neuro-mental system. This is our personal memory, the only form of memory that had been recognized as such until the 1920s. On the *social level*, memory is a matter of communication and social interaction. It was the great achievement of the French sociologist Maurice Halbwachs to show that our memory depends, like consciousness in general, on socialization and communication, and that memory can be analyzed as a function of our social life (*Les cadres sociaux*; *La mémoire collective*). Memory enables us to live in groups and communities, and living in groups and communities enables us to build a memory. During these same years, psychoanalysts such as Sigmund Freud and Carl Gustav Jung were developing theories of collective memory but still adhered to the first, the inner and personal level, looking for collective memory not in the dynamics of social life but in the unconscious depths of the human psyche (see also Straub, this volume).

Aby Warburg, however, the art historian, coined the term "social memory" with regard to the third, the *cultural level*; he seems to have been the first one who treated images, that is, cultural objectivations, as carriers of memory. His main project was to study the "afterlife" (*Nachleben*) of classical antiquity in Western culture and he termed this project "Mnemosyne," the ancient Greek term for memory and the mother of the nine Muses. As an art historian, Warburg specialized in what he called *Bildgedächtnis* (iconic memory), but the general approach to reception history as a form of (cultural) memory could be applied to every other domain of symbolic forms as well (Gombrich). This is what Thomas Mann endeavored to do in his four Joseph novels, which appeared between 1933 and 1943 and which may rank as the most advanced attempt to reconstruct a specific cultural memory—in this case of people living in Palestine and Egypt in the Late Bronze Age—and, at the same time, to conjure up our European cultural memory and its Jewish foundations in times of anti-Semitism (J. Assmann, *Thomas Mann*). Neither Warburg nor Thomas Mann, however, used the term "cultural memory"; this concept has been explicitly developed only during the last twenty years. It is, therefore, only since then that the connection between time, identity, and memory in their three dimensions of the personal, the social, and the cultural has become more and more evident.

The term "communicative memory" was introduced in order to delineate the difference between Halbwachs's concept of "collective memory" and our understanding of "cultural memory" (A. Assmann). Cultural memory is a form of collective memory, in the sense that it is shared by a number of people and that it conveys to these people a collective, that is, cultural, identity. Halbwachs, however, the inventor of the term "collective memory," was careful to keep his concept of collective memory apart from the realm of traditions, transmissions, and transferences which we propose to subsume under the term "cultural memory." We preserve Halbwachs's distinction by breaking up his concept of collective memory into "communicative" and "cultural memory," but we insist on including the cultural sphere, which he excluded, in the study of memory. We are, therefore, not arguing for replacing his idea of "collective memory" with "cultural memory"; rather, we distinguish between both forms as two different modi memorandi, ways of remembering.

2. Culture as Memory

Cultural memory is a kind of institution. It is exteriorized, objectified, and stored away in symbolic forms that, unlike the sounds of words or the sight of gestures, are stable and situation-transcendent: They may be transferred from one situation to another and transmitted from one generation to another. External objects as carriers of memory play a role already on the level of personal memory. Our memory, which we possess as beings equipped with a human mind, exists only in constant interaction not only with other human memories but also with "things," outward symbols. With respect to things such as Marcel Proust's famous madeleine, or artifacts, objects, anniversaries, feasts, icons, symbols, or landscapes, the term "memory" is *not a metaphor but a metonym* based on material contact between a remembering mind and a reminding object. Things do not "have" a memory of their own, but they may remind us, may trigger our memory, because they carry memories which we have invested into them, things such as dishes, feasts, rites, images, stories and other texts, landscapes, and other "lieux de mémoire." On the social level, with respect to groups and societies, the role of external symbols becomes even more important, because groups which, of course, do not "have" a memory tend to "make" themselves one by means of things meant as reminders such as monuments, museums, libraries, archives, and other mnemonic institutions. This is what we call cultural memory (A. Assmann). In order to be able to be reembodied in the sequence of generations, cultural memory, unlike communicative memory, exists also in disembodied form and requires institutions of preservation and reembodiment.

This institutional character does not apply to what Halbwachs called collective memory and what we propose to rename communicative memory. Communicative memory is non-institutional; it is not supported by any institutions of learning, transmission, and interpretation; it is not cultivated by specialists and is not summoned or celebrated on special occasions; it is not formalized and stabilized by any forms of material symbolization; it lives in everyday interaction and communication and, for this very reason, has only a limited time depth which normally reaches no farther back than eighty years, the time span of three interacting generations. Still, there are frames, "communicative genres," traditions of communication and thematization and, above all, the affective ties that bind together families, groups, and generations.

A change of frames brings about forgetting; the durability of memories depends on the durability of social bonds and frames. In his earlier work, Halbwachs does not seem to be concerned with the social interests and power structures that are active in shaping and framing individual memories. In his last work on collective memory, however, he shows a keen awareness of institution and power. *La topographie légendaire des évangiles en terre sainte*, published in 1941 during the German occupation, deals with the transformation of Palestine into a site of Christian memory by the installment of all kinds of memorials, a process which took place after the adoption of Christianity as the state religion by the Roman empire. In this work, he crosses the border which he himself had erected between *mémoire* and *tradition* and shows to what degree this kind of official memory is dependent on theological dogma and formed by the power structure of the church.

3. Time Frames

Jan Vansina, an anthropologist who worked with oral societies in Africa, devoted an important study to the form in which they represent the past and observed a tripartite structure. The recent past, which looms large in interactive communication, recedes, as time goes by, more and more into the background. Information becomes scarcer and vaguer the further back one moves into the past. According to Vansina, this knowledge of affairs that are told and discussed in everyday communication has a limited depth in time, reaching not beyond three generations. Concerning a more remote past, there is either a total lack of information or one or two names are produced with great hesitation. For the most remote past, however, there is again a profusion of information dealing with traditions about the origin of the world and the early history of the tribe. This information, however, is not committed to everyday communication but intensely formalized and institutionalized. It exists in the forms of narratives, songs, dances, rituals, masks, and symbols; specialists such as narrators, bards, mask-carvers, and others are organized in guilds and have to undergo long periods of initiation, instruction, and examination. Moreover, it requires for its actualization certain occasions when the community comes together for a celebration. This is what we propose calling "cultural memory." In oral societies, as Vansina has shown, there is a gap between the informal generational memory referring to the recent past and the formal cultural memory which refers to the remote past, the origin of the world, and the history of the tribe, and since this gap shifts with the succession of generations, Vansina calls it the "floating gap." Historical consciousness, Vansina resumes, operates in oral societies on only two levels: the time of origins and the recent past.

Vansina's "floating gap" illustrates the difference between social and cultural frames of memory or communicative and cultural memory. The communicative memory contains memories referring to Vansina's "recent past." These are the memories that an individual shares with his contemporaries. This is what Halbwachs understood by "collective memory" and what forms the object of oral history, that branch of historical research that bases itself not on the usual written sources of historiography, but exclusively on memories gained in oral interviews. All studies in oral history confirm that even in literate societies living memory goes no further back than eighty years after which, separated by the floating gap, come, instead of myths of origin, the dates from schoolbooks and monuments.

The cultural memory is based on fixed points in the past. Even in the cultural memory, the past is not preserved as such but is cast in symbols as they are represented in oral myths or in writings, performed in feasts, and as they are continually illuminating a changing present. In the context of cultural memory, the distinction between myth and history vanishes. Not the past as such, as it is investigated and reconstructed by archaeologists and historians, counts for the cultural memory, but only the past as it is remembered. Here, in the context of cultural memory, it is the temporal horizon of cultural memory which is important. Cultural memory reaches back into the past only so far as the past can be reclaimed as "ours." This is why we refer to this form of historical consciousness as "memory" and not just as knowledge about the past. Knowledge about the past acquires the properties and functions of memory if it is related to a concept of identity. While knowledge has no form and is endlessly progressive, memory involves forgetting. It is only by forgetting what lies outside the horizon of the relevant that it performs an identity function. Nietzsche (*The Use and Abuse of History*) circumscribed this function by notions such as "plastic power" and "horizon," obviously intending the same thing for which now the term "identity" has become generally accepted.

Whereas knowledge has a universalist perspective, a tendency towards generalization and standardization, memory, even cultural memory, is local, egocentric, and specific to a group and its values.

4. Identity

The distinction of different forms of memory looks like a structure but it works more as a dynamic, creating tension and transition between the various poles. There is also much overlapping. This holds true especially with respect to the relation between memory and identity. We must certainly avoid falling victim to what Amartya Sen has described as the "identity illusion." Individuals possess various identities according to the various groups, communities, belief systems, political systems, etc. to which they belong, and equally multifarious are their communicative and cultural, in short: collective memories. On all levels, memory is an open system. Still, it is not totally open and diffuse; there are always frames that relate memory to specific horizons of time and identity on the individual, generational, political, and cultural levels. Where this relation is absent, we are not dealing with memory but with knowledge. Memory is knowledge with an identity-index, it is knowledge about oneself, that is, one's own diachronic identity, be it as an individual or as a member of a family, a generation, a community, a nation, or a cultural and religious tradition.

Groups are formed and cohere by the dynamics of association and dissociation which is always loaded (to varying degrees) with affection. Halbwachs, therefore, spoke of "*communautés affectives.*" These "affective ties" lend memories their special intensity. Remembering is a realization of belonging, even a social obligation. One has to remember in order to belong: This is also one of the most important insights in Nietzsche's *Genealogy of Morality*. Assimilation, the transition of one group into another one, is usually accompanied by an imperative to forget the memories connected with the original identity. Inversely, this kind of assimilatory forgetting is precisely what is most feared and prohibited in the book of Deuteronomy, which deals with such a change of frame between Egypt and Canaan and the first and second generations of emigrants from Egypt.

5. Institutions and Carriers

The difference between communicative and cultural memory expresses itself also in the social dimension, in the structure of participation. The participation of a group in communicative memory is diffuse. Some, it is true, know more, some less, and the memories of the old reach farther back than those of the young. However, there are no specialists of informal, communicative memory. The knowledge which is communicated in everyday interaction has been acquired by the participants along with language and social competence. The participation of a group in cultural memory, by contrast, is always highly differentiated. This applies even and especially to oral and egalitarian societies. The preservation of the cultural memory of the group was originally the task of the poets. Even today, the African griots fulfill this function of guardians of cultural memory.

The cultural memory always has its specialists, both in oral and in literate societies. These include shamans, bards, and griots, as well as priests, teachers, artists, clerks, scholars, mandarins, rabbis, mullahs, and other names for specialized carriers of memory. In oral societies, the degree of specialization of these carriers depends on the magnitude of the demands that are made of their memory. Those demands that insist on verbatim transmission are ranked highest. Here, human memory is used as a "database" in a sense approaching the use of writing: A fixed text is verbally "written" into the highly specialized and trained memory of these specialists. This is typically the case when ritual knowledge is at stake and where a ritual must strictly follow a "script," even if this script is not laid down in writing. The Rgveda constitutes the most prominent example of a codification of ritual memory based solely on oral tradition. The magnitude of this task corresponds to the social rank of the ritual specialists, the Brahmin, who form the highest caste, higher even than the aristocratic class of warriors (Kshatriya) to which the rulers belong. In traditional Rwanda, the scripts for the eighteen royal rituals had to be memorized by specialists who ranked as the highest notables of the kingdom. Error could be punished by death. Those three notables who knew by heart the full text of all eighteen rituals even partook of the divinity of the ruler (Borgeaud).

In the context of rituals, therefore, we observe the rise of the oldest systems of memorization or mnemotechniques, with or without the help of systems of notation like knotted chords, tchuringas, and other forms of pre-writing. With the invention of full-fledged systems of writing, it is interesting to see how differently various religions have behaved vis à vis this new cultural technique. In the Indo-European traditions, from the Indian Brahmins to the Celtic Druids, we observe a general distrust and shunning of writing. Memory is held to be by far the more trustworthy medium to hand down the religious (that is, ritual) knowledge to later generations. The reason normally given is that too many mistakes may creep into a text by copying. The true reason, however, seems to be that writing always implies the danger of dissemination, of giving away a secret tradition to the profane and uninitiated. This distrust in writing is still very prominent in Plato. In the ancient Near Eastern societies such as Mesopotamia, Israel, and Egypt, on the other hand, writing is eagerly grasped as an ideal medium for codifying and transmitting the sacred traditions, especially ritual scripts and recitations.

But even where the sacred tradition is committed to writing, memorization plays the central role. In ancient Egypt, a typical temple library contained no more books than may be known by heart by the specialists. Clement of Alexandria gives a vivid description of such a library. He speaks of forty-two "indispensable" or "absolutely necessary" (*pany anankaiai*) books that formed the stock of an Egyptian temple library and were all written by Thot-Hermes himself. The priests were not supposed to read and learn all of the books, but to specialize in certain genres corresponding to their rank and office. In describing a procession of these priests, Clement shows both the hierarchy of the priesthood and the structure of their library (*Stromateis* 6.4.35-37). The highest ranks are held by the *stolistes* and the *prophetes*, corresponding in Egyptian terminology to the "lector priest" and the "high priest." It is the books of the stolist that serve as a codification of ritual memory proper, complemented by what Clement calls "education." The books of the high priest, on the other hand, are said to contain normative or legal literature concerning the laws, the gods, and priestly education. The library, thus, is divided into normative knowledge, which ranks highest; ritual knowledge, which comes a close second; and general knowledge concerning astronomy, geography, poetry, biography, and medicine, which occupies the lowest rank among this canon of highly indispensable literature.

There is, however, still another sense in which the participation in cultural memory may be structured in a society. This concerns the question of restricted knowledge, of secrecy and esotericism. Every traditional society knows areas of restricted knowledge whose boundaries are not simply defined by the different capacities of human memory and understanding, but also by questions of access and initiation. In Judaism, for example, general participation is required in the Torah which every (male) member of the group is supposed to know by heart. Specialized participation concerns the world of Talmudic and Medieval commentaries, codices, and midrash, a vast body of literature that only specialists can master. Secrecy, however, shrouds the esoteric world of kabbala, to which only select adepts (and only after they have reached the age of forty) are admitted.

The participation structure of cultural memory has an inherent tendency to elitism; it is never strictly egalitarian. Some are almost forced into participation and have to prove their degree of admittance by formal exams (as in traditional China); or by the mastery of linguistic registers (as in England); or of the "*Citatenschatz des deutschen Volkes*" (treasury of German quotations) as in nineteenth-century Germany. Others remain systematically excluded from this "distinguished" knowledge, such as women in ancient Greece, traditional China, and orthodox Judaism, or the lower classes in the heyday of the German *Bildungsbürgertum* (educated bourgeoisie).

As to the media of cultural memory, a more or less pronounced tendency can be discerned towards a form of intra-cultural diglossia, corresponding to the distinction between one "great tradition" and several "little traditions" as proposed by Robert Redfield. Until the creation of modern Iwrith, the Jews had always lived in a situation of diglossia, since their "Great Tradition" was written in Hebrew and for their everyday communication they used vernacular languages such as Yiddish, Ladino, or the various languages of their host countries. To a similar or lesser degree, this situation is typical of virtually all traditional societies, be it in the form of two different languages, such as Hindu and Sanskrit or Italian and Latin, or two different linguistic varieties, such as Qur'anic and vernacular Arabic or classical and modern Chinese. Modern societies tend to diversify this binary structure by introducing more linguistic varieties according to the multiplication of cultural media such as film, broadcasting, and television. The following list with its clear-cut binary structure, therefore, does not do full justice to the modern situation:

	Communicative Memory	Cultural Memory
Content	history in the frame of autobiographical memory, recent past	mythical history, events in absolute past ("in illo tempore")
Forms	informal traditions and genres of everyday communication	high degree of formation, ceremonial communication;
Media	living, embodied memory, communication in vernacular language	mediated in texts, icons, dances, rituals, and performances of various kinds; "classical" or otherwise formalized language(s)
Time Structure	80-100 years, a moving horizon of 3-4 interacting generations	absolute past, mythical primordial time, "3000 years"
Participation Structure	diffuse	specialized carriers of memory, hierarchically structured

Figure 2

Transitions and transformations account for the dynamics of cultural memory. Two typical directions have a structural significance and should at least briefly be mentioned in this context. One concerns the transition from autobiographical and communicative memory into cultural memory, and the other concerns, within cultural memory, the move from the rear stage to the forefront, from the periphery into the center, from latency or potentiality to manifestation or actualization and vice versa. These shifts presuppose structural boundaries which are to be crossed: the boundary between embodied and mediated forms of memory, and the boundary between what we propose calling "working" and "reference memories" or "canon" and "archive" (see also A. Assmann, this volume).

References

Assmann, Aleida. "Memory, Individual and Collective." *The Oxford Handbook of Contextual Political Analysis*. Eds. Robert E. Goodin und Charles Tilly. Oxford: Oxford UP, 2006. 210-24.

Assmann, Jan. "Das kulturelle Gedächtnis." *Erwägen, Wissen, Ethik* 13 (2002): 239-47.

—. *Das kulturelle Gedächtnis: Schrift, Erinnerung und politische Identität in frühen Hochkulturen*. Beck: Munich, 1992.

—. *Thomas Mann und Ägypten: Mythos und Monotheismus in den Josephsromanen*. Munich: Beck, 2006.

Borgeaud, Philippe. "Pour une approche anthropologique de la mémoire religieuse." *La mémoire des religions*. Eds. Jean-Claude Basset and Philippe Borgeaud. Geneva: Labor et Fides, 1988. 7-20.

Clemens von Alexandria. *Stromateis*. Trans. Otto Stählin. 3 vols. Munich: Kösel & Pustet, 1936-38.

Gombrich, Ernst H. *Aby Warburg: An Intellectual Biography*. Chicago: U of Chicago P, 1986.

Halbwachs, Maurice. *Les cadres sociaux de la mémoire*. 1925. Paris: Albin Michel, 1994.

—. *On Collective Memory*. 1925. Ed. and trans. Lewis A. Coser. Chicago: U of Chicago P, 1992.

—. *La mémoire collective*. 1950. Paris: Albin Michel, 1997.

—. *La topographie légendaire des évangiles en terre sainte*. 1941. Paris: Presses universitaires de France, 1971.

Luckmann, Thomas. "Remarks on Personal Identity: Inner, Social and Historical Time." *Identity: Personal and Socio-Cultural*. Ed. Anita Jacobson-Widding. Atlantic Highlands, NJ: Humanities, 1983. 67-91.

Nietzsche, Friedrich. *On the Genealogy of Morality*. Trans. Maudemarie Clark and Alan J. Swensen. Indianapolis: Hackett, 1998.

—. *The Use and Abuse of History*. Trans. Adrian Collins. New York: Macmillan, 1957.

Redfield, Robert. *Peasant Society and Culture: An Anthropological Approach to Civilization*. Chicago: U of Chicago P, 1956.

Sen, Amartya. *Identity and Violence: The Illusion of Destiny*. New York: Norton, 2006.

Vansina, Jan. *Oral Tradition as History*. Madison: U of Wisconsin P, 1985.

Welzer, Harald. *Das kommunikative Gedächtnis*. Munich: Beck, 2002.

Generation/Generationality, Generativity, and Memory

JÜRGEN REULECKE

The term "generation" is used in public discussions in an ambiguous manner, such that several different meanings are often blended one with another. In everyday language, the term is used to refer to a member in the natural sequence of grandparents, parents, children, and grandchildren, a progression that traditionally assumes a distance between generations of about thirty years (the "pulse-rate hypothesis"). In reference to the population structure of a society, "generation" is used (although "cohort" would be the correct term) to statistically group all those born in the same year or the same five-year period or decade. A new understanding of the term which originated in the humanities and social sciences has now become common, however, which defines "generation" as a group within a society that is characterized by its members having grown up in the same particularly formative historical era. Often, such a generational identity exists throughout its members' lives due to their having experienced times of radical upheaval and new beginnings (primarily in adolescence) and as a result sharing a specific habitus (the "imprint hypothesis").

The term "generationality" gets at the particular features of this identity and has a twofold meaning. On the one hand, it refers to characteristics resulting from shared experiences that either individuals or larger "generational units" collectively claim for themselves. On the other hand, it can also mean the bundle of characteristics resulting from shared experiences that are ascribed to such units from the outside, with which members of other age groups—and often also public opinion as expressed in the media—attempt, in the interest of establishing demarcations and reducing complexity, to identify presumed generations as well as the progression of generations. This led during the twentieth century in particular to many blanket labels that caught on in public discourse in Germany, such as the "superfluous," "disinherited," "oppressed," "skeptical," or the "conformist" generations. Thus, generation and generationality are, in the end, not tangible entities but rather mental, often very zeitgeist-dependent constructs through which people, as members of a specific age group, are located or locate themselves historically, and accordingly create a we-feeling.

Linking processes of societal change to generational relations, and characterizing individual generations as, say, engines of progress or as initiators of a particular, perhaps avant-garde, style did not start until the early nineteenth century, in the wake of the experiences of upheaval during that era. As contemporaries from Goethe to Friedrich Schlegel and Schleiermacher all the way to Auguste Comte and John Stuart Mill realized, the various age groups living then perceived the rapid political, social, and technical-economic changes of their epoch differently and, as a result, assessed and reacted to them differently. In the time since, there have been numerous trends in the public discourse on generations, including arguments which in the twentieth century frequently led to demagoguery and political actionism, with slogans such as "Make way, you old men!" ("*Macht Platz, ihr Alten*!"; Gregor Strasser 1927) and "Trust no one over 30!" One could almost argue that grave changes generally lead, first immediately afterwards and then again at a distance of one to two decades, to society-wide debates about the generational background and results of these events.

Scholarly attempts at a more thorough analysis of the generation problem began in earnest in Germany around 1870 with the philosopher and statistician Gustav von Rümelin, and in particular with Ranke's student Wilhelm Dilthey. The latter strongly favored the imprint hypothesis, in that the starting point of his theory of generations was the "dependence" of particular groups of individuals on "the same significant facts and changes which emerged in the period when they were most susceptible." Shortly before World War One, Sigmund Freud introduced to the debate an additional, psychoanalytical interpretation of the role the mental generational legacy played in determining the course of individuals' lives in subsequent generations. At the end of the 1920s, the sociologist Karl Mannheim then supplied his theory of generations, which remains the operative approach today, albeit in a modified form. He distinguished between the "generational location" (*Generationslagerung*), exposure to the same historical contexts during youth, which he saw as a disposition that under certain circumstances could lead to a "generational connection" (*Generationenzusammenhang*) and "generational consciousness" (*Generationenbewußtsein*), and the groups these could feed into, the "generational units" (*Generationseinheiten*), identifiable and influential groups within a society. Mannheim compared "generation" with "class" and believed that the specific location "primarily eliminates a great number of the possible ways of experiencing, thinking, feeling, and acting and [limits] the scope of the effect of individuality to certain circumscribed possibilities" (528).

Mannheim's belief that "generation" was a quasi-objective, existent entity to which he also ascribed a fixed purpose, a "generational entelechy," has been criticized and rejected, yet to this day his other fundamental assumptions provide manifold impulses not only to the social sciences, but also in political science, the history of education, the history of mentalities, and the history of experience. In addition, the strengths of the generational approach in the context of a recent turn to cultural-historical approaches have only gradually been discovered: Studying historical contexts with the generational approach, in combination with the concept of "generationality," connects the identification of general structures and processes, especially those of various social levels, with the subjective perceptions and experiences of contemporaries, including their interpretations, spheres of action, and options for action. This achieves an at least partial dissolution of the far too heavily emphasized pair of opposites "objective vs. subjective," in favor of an integrative perspective. This view places the concrete temporality of humans, including their generational "baggage," into the context of general historical change, which the individual may face passively as well as actively. In other words: With such an approach, the individual is left his unmistakable historicity within the framework of his realm of experience as well as his life story, with a view not least towards his actions in light of the future open to him. The oft-voiced criticism of the generational approach is that it creates—through hindsight and quite arbitrarily—artificial clusters of people, and that it is oriented solely on birth years and thus reduces the continuous passage of time to segments of time constructed retrospectively. Yet this is not the case if one takes seriously as historically influential phenomena the subjective generational positioning—both the self- and the historically specific external positioning—of people during their lives, including the associated creations of meaning, interpretations, and memory, which are ever changing according to the particular stage of life.

Generational research, in the 1980s and 1990s rather narrowly limited primarily to the political and social sciences and social and everyday history, which were increasingly taking up questions of the history of mentalities, has expanded significantly due to increasing interdisciplinarity. New ideas include questions that, on the one hand, are derived from the current interdisciplinary study of culture, which is paying more attention to historical phenomena of perception, experience, and memory. On the other hand, there has also been increased collaboration between generational researchers in the humanities and the social sciences and those interested in generationality in the psychological sciences, including psychoanalysis, psychotherapy, psychosomatic medicine, and psychogerontology. In addition to this there are also the challenges that arose from the new findings of neuroscientific research, especially with respect to the research area of memory and remembering (see also Markowitsch, this volume): These motivated further efforts to investigate the complex concurrence of generationality, memory, and generativity (see below). And there was one more, rather extra-scientific, impulse: For several years, in the context of a "memory boom," new, catchy generational attributions have constantly been invented in the media, in politicians' speeches, in advertising, and in essays—from the "Generation [VW] Golf," the "Generation Berlin," and the "Generation '89" in Germany to the "Generations X," "Y," and "@" in the United States and elsewhere. Moreover, there is an age group that has recently begun, in their self-biographization or retrospective reconstruction of the course of their own lives, to position themselves generationally and speak as a generational unit, one that until this point had drawn little attention to itself: the war babies. Born in the late 1930s and early 1940s and now reaching retirement age, they are calling to memory their early childhood experiences—or these are "catching up" with them—of the bombing war, expulsion, the loss of their fathers, etc. Some of these memories are extremely traumatic, and can have grave results for their self-image, creation of aims and meaning for their lives, and mental stability. Here we see that not only—as assumed up to now throughout generational research—are the experiences from adolescence able to create a long-term generationality, but also that grave experiences in other phases of life, even in very young years, can lead to a we-feeling of special generational units.

Only slowly, however, are studies beginning to get under way which pursue the question of whether national characteristics can be determined in comparison to other societies (such as in Germany, where this is a current topic). For example, can the problem of the generational mental "baggage" of the children of war, which these then pass on in a specific manner to their children and grandchildren, be studied in international comparison and not solely in relation to the Second World War? This question lends significance to a new concept, namely that of "generativity," used to some extent as a synonym for "natality." It refers primarily to the—conscious or unconcious—examination, especially within particularly distinctive generationalities, of their ties to the diachronic sequence of "generations" in the genealogical sense of the word. Sigmund Freud alluded to this already in 1912 in his book *Totem and Taboo*, with his exhortation to consider how a generation transfers its specific mental problems to the next generation. According to Freud, no generation is capable, in the end, of hiding meaningful mental processes from the following generations. The extremes that can result range from passing the problems on in an individual manner to a massive generation break, leading to sometimes quite considerable consequences for entire societies. Especially after experiences of major upheaval, the aftershock can be felt "into the third and fourth generation," as it is said in the Old Testament. "Generational rejection," whether institutionally absorbed or revolutionary, thus belongs, according to the historian Reinhart Koselleck, to the elementary preconditions of a generation becoming aware of its historicity. How this happens in each individual case is a question of the "factual history," the potential of which is contained in each individual generativity.

It is clear that individual as well as collective forms of memory and the maintenance of memory typical of a specific period project into this central, downright existential-anthropological complex. A broad debate about the dissimilarity vs. the insoluble connection between a "communicative" and a "cultural" memory in distinct cultures of memory, about memory spaces, sites of memory, and the different "temporal *Heimate*" of age groups living together, about the mediality of memory, about competing memories and the (often generationally definable) "interpreting elites," about the changing, reshaping, or even erasure of memory has since been led in a lively interdisciplinary exchange. Age groups with distinct generationality are understood in this context as communities of experience and carriers of memory, who then can also potentially exhibit a "memorial resistance" towards the more or less official interpretations of history, since a memory that is subjectively coded as "true" or "correct" can prove to be resistant to the given images and interpretations of history of a society in which one lives.

To sum up: With the triad "generationality-generativity-memory" discussed here key anthropological facts are thus addressed, as with such memorable phrases as "*ohne Herkunft keine Zukunft*" ("without a past no future") (Odo Marquard) or "*Erfahrungsraum und Erwartungshorizont*" ("'space of experience' and 'horizon of expectation'") (Reinhart Koselleck), which—both individually and collectively—refer not only to the fundamental problem of human historicity, but are also of central importance for every concrete analysis of contemporary history. Their strongly formative experiences and the specific ways in which they process their experiences make each generation unique and unmistakable. These can, it is true, not be passed on directly, but they do indeed flow, in the form of memory contents created through later selection, attribution, interpretation, etc., into the generative succession as well as into the subjective positioning in one's own "temporal *Heimat*." They can also be a legacy intentionally offered to posterity in the form of narratives, bequeathed works, institutions, designed places, and more, and also, according to Freud (see above) engraved in subsequent generations even without an expressed intention to pass them on, although these later generations might also (consciously or unconsciously) reject, re-interpret, or erase them. The latter can happen rather casually, without particular activity or controversy, in times of upheaval and new beginnings, or with pathos, with demagogic arrogance, with great pressure and, in the extreme case, with massive force. All historical processes in concurrence with generationality, generativity, and memory can, following Koselleck, be accordingly assessed by asking whether the generational break, which is fundamentally always present as a possibility, can be bridged or not. Scholars in disciplines which work from the premise of humans' temporality understand that each generation makes its decisions based on the rich experience it is carrying forward and that which it has accumulated itself, and against the backdrop of a wide-open horizon of experience. They are thus called upon to see themselves in their own societies as communication partners who provoke stimulating as well as critical self-questioning regarding the neverending adventure that is history.

Translated by Sara B. Young

References

Assmann, Jan, and Tonio Hölscher, eds. *Kultur und Gedächtnis*. Frankfurt am Main: Suhrkamp, 1988.

Assmann, Aleida. *Erinnerungsräume: Formen und Wandlungen des kulturellen Gedächtnisses*. Munich: Beck, 1999.

Daniel, Ute. "Generationengeschichte." *Kompendium Kulturgeschichte: Theorien, Praxis, Schlüsselwörter*. Ed. Ute Daniel. 5th ed. Frankfurt am Main: Suhrkamp, 2007. 330-45.

Erll, Astrid. *Kollektives Gedächtnis und Erinnerungskulturen*. Stuttgart: Metzler, 2005.

Fogt, Helmut. *Politische Generationen: Empirische Bedeutung und theoretisches Modell*. Opladen: Westdeutscher Verlag, 1982.

Jaeger, Hans. "Generationen in der Geschichte." *Geschichte und Gesellschaft* 3 (1977): 429-52.

Jarausch, Konrad H., and Martin Sabrow, eds. *Verletztes Gedächtnis: Erinnerungskultur und Zeitgeschichte im Konflikt*. Frankfurt: Campus, 2002.

Jureit, Ulrike. *Generationenforschung*. Göttingen: Vandenhoeck & Ruprecht, 2006.

Jureit, Ulrike, and Michael Wildt. *Generationen: Zur Relevanz eines wissenschaftlichen Grundbegriffs*. Hamburg: Hamburger Edition, 2005.

Koselleck, Reinhart. *Zeitschichten: Studien zur Historik*. Frankfurt am Main: Suhrkamp, 2000.

Loewy, Hanno, and Bernhard Moltmann, eds. *Erlebnis—Gedächtnis—Sinn: Authentische und konstruierte Erinnerung*. Frankfurt am Main: Campus, 1996.

Lüscher, Kurt, and Ludwig Liegle. *Generationenbeziehungen in Familie und Gesellschaft*. Konstanz: Universitätsverlag Konstanz, 2003.

Mannheim, Karl. "Das Problem der Generationen." 1928. Rpt. in *Wissenssoziologie*. Ed. Kurt H. Wolff. Neuwied: Luchterhand, 1970. 509-65.

Platt, Kristin, and Mihran Dabag. *Generation und Gedächtnis: Erinnerungen und kollektive Identitäten*. Opladen: Leske & Budrich, 1995.

Reulecke, Jürgen, ed. *Generationalität und Lebensgeschichte im 20. Jahrhundert*. Munich: Oldenbourg, 2003.

Weigel, Sigrid. "Generation, Genealogie, Geschlecht. Zur Geschichte des Generationskonzepts und seiner wissenschaftlichen Konzeptualisierung seit Ende des 18. Jahrhunderts." *Kulturwissenschaften: Forschung—Praxis—Positionen*. Eds. Lutz Musner and Gotthard Wunberg. Vienna: WUV, 2002. 161-90.

Cultural Memory: A European Perspective

VITA FORTUNATI AND ELENA LAMBERTI

1. Cultural Memories: The Making of Europe

In recent years, memory studies has been playing a pivotal role in reshaping traditional approaches to sociological, historical, political, and cultural issues. For instance, Jeffrey Olick has shown how the idea of a memory related to the formation of the nation-state has been reshaped; as a consequence, today the old relationship between memory and nation must be rediscussed and renegotiated. On the other hand, it is the actual crisis of this value which has led to a complex re-discussion about the very meaning of memory itself. It is no coincidence that this flourishing of studies about memory has gone side by side with certain crucial historic events of the twentieth century: the decline of ideologies and the collapse of the U.S.S.R., the re-emergence of heavy historical responsibilities, and the explosion of issues related to post-colonialism, to mention just some of the key moments of our most recent history.

Hence, memory studies can offer an interesting ground for observing the making of Europe (or of the new Europe), especially if we assume that the memory-power nexus is extremely important for understanding how memory has been, over the centuries, subject to manipulation and exploitation by hegemonic states. As a matter of fact, as Francesco Remotti points out, in order to understand the processes of identity formations of a collectivity or of a nation, it is necessary to investigate the relationship between "what disappears," "what remains," and "what re-emerges." Indeed, it is only through a careful analysis of the processes which select and filter the past that we can highlight the dialectics among these three categories and avoid the dangers of an ideological manipulation of memory. Also, the aforementioned studies have suggested that to be able to live, it is true that one must also forget (see Esposito, this volume); and yet, the relationship and the dialectics between memory and forgetting are never "given" and never linear. To understand who we are, we need to establish a certain distance from those who came before us; however, we also need to establish a certain continuity. The dialectics between continuity and discontinuity in relation to our past must always be renegotiated. Halbwachs's studies on collective memory have been seminal on this point.

Hence, today what the *making of Europe* inevitably implies (in order to try and grasp the meaning of a still foggy idea of "European identity") is that such a dialectic is to be played not only within single countries, but also at the macro level of the European Union; a fact that, needless to say, clearly complicates the process. Today, however, the most interesting aspect to be stressed is the social interaction which takes place during the act of remembering: This interactive act prevents fixing and hypostatizing memory. As a consequence, it is no longer possible to passively accept a monolithic idea of collective memory, as it must be perceived as a more fluid concept. Collective memory is not just a substantial entity; we need to grasp the dynamic aspects of remembering, not the static aspects of memory, that is, its mnemonic practices.

For an individual, as well as for a nation, cultural memory is a complex and stratified entity strictly connected not only to the history and the experience of either the individual or the nation, but also to the way in which that very history and experience are read in time, individually and collectively. Each time, the past acquires new meanings and the same fact, even though it stays the same, is nevertheless shaped through remembrance; inevitably, it is juxtaposed against new backgrounds, new biographies, and new recollections. Hence, following the theoretical debate which has characterized the last decades of the twentieth century and which has undermined ontological categories and disciplinary statutes, it is possible to argue that it is no longer possible to offer a final and absolute vision of the past. The breaking of all canons, the juxtaposition of macro and micro history, the questioning of the ideas of objectivity and subjectivity in the historiographic rendering, as well as in literature, have taught us all to be prudent observers and to use the plural instead of the singular: no longer a unique "memory," but many "memories," many traces left by the same event which in time sediment in the individual consciousness, as well as in the collective consciousness, and that are often—consciously or unconsciously—hidden or removed; traces that nevertheless stay and that suddenly or predictably re-emerge each time the historical, political, or cultural context changes. It has become evident through memory studies that no unitary definition of memory exists and that memory is dynamic (see also Rigney, this volume). It is memory as a process (over the course of time) which is reshaped according to the present—hence its pivotal role in interdisciplinary studies of both the notion of historical context and that of the context of the dialectics of temporality.

Therefore, research on memory in the humanities and in literary studies has marked the breakdown of disciplinary barriers, thus giving rise to a comparison between disciplines such as history, philosophy, anthropology, social sciences, and the hard sciences. Memory is a complex subject of research, which, for its investigation, requires an orchestration drawing on various branches of knowledge.

For instance, memory studies has brought to light the crisis of history as a discipline, the difficulty of giving an ultimate meaning to the concepts of "document," "source," "truth." For these reasons, the relationship between memory and history has received more and more attention in recent years, since faith in the existence of objective historical truth has lost its hold and the idea that historical statement is a construction which draws on fictional paradigms has been put forward (White). On the other hand, memory studies has underscored how experience in no way guarantees truth because in evidence—as several studies on oral history have amply demonstrated (Hodgkin and Radstone)—subjectivity and emotion determine different viewpoints of the same historic event. It is decisive to investigate the extent to which the changed historical context conditions individual memory and how pronounced and intricate the relationship between public memory and private memory is in order to gain an understanding of the various patterns of recollection. Rather than going into the lively debate on history and memory, it will be suggested along with Raphael Samuel that in comparing the two disciplines it is more helpful from a methodological viewpoint to underline common characteristics than the differences and make use of the synergism evident in the following parallel: "Like history memory is inherently revisionist and never more chameleon than when it appears to stay the same" (x). What emerges here is an idea of non-monolithic memory, that is, of a more fluid memory: The process of memory and recollection is always the result of an interaction which, at times, is marked by strife juxtaposing the individual and the group. A metaphor often used in cultural studies to underline its vitality is that of the "battlefield," where nothing is neutral and everything is under constant discussion (Lamberti and Fortunati).

Thus this is a memory which is restored through a critical gaze towards a "contested past," which becomes the setting in which to investigate truth and above all to achieve an awareness of the present. So it is not memory as commemoration, and still less a sanctifying one but rather a memory which wants to bring to light traumatic, repressed, and censored memories and again questions dangerous stereotypes which have been lurking over some historical events. Thus in "gender studies" and in postcolonial studies what becomes pivotal is the concept of "counter-memory"—where the term "counter" emphasizes the fact that these are *other* memories belonging to minority groups and thus marginalized by the dominant cultures. Memory becomes an "act of survival," of consciousness and creativity, fundamental to the formation and rewriting of identity as both an individual and a political act. In such a perspective, memory and recollection have a critical impact, as Benjamin states, because they bring out unresolved difficulties of history and represent the most efficient protest against suffering and injustice. In this sense some of Walter Benjamin's essays are still fundamental. He underlined the dangers of a memory reaching into the past and thereby fossilizing and falsifying it: "[...] only a redeemed mankind (which) receives the fullness of its past—which is to say, only for a redeemed mankind has its past become citable in all its moments" (254).

This is truer when controversial memories of a traumatic historical event are at stake, as in the case of memories of the two world wars (see also Winter, this volume): One has to question the provenance of such recollections, from whom these recollections come, where they are remembered, and in what context. Hence, also the *discourse* on trauma always implies a dialogue between memory and oblivion, memories and counter-memories, the ethics of bearing witness and the difficulty of telling and representing (see also Kansteiner and Weilnböck, this volume). Media representations, cinema, television, photography, the visual arts (and more recently, the Internet) have been, for at least sixty years, the fundamental vehicle by means of which traumas are transmitted, judged, and remembered. Literature, in its diverse expressions, and theoretical studies have played an important role in the representation, the transmission, and the critical (or mystifying) elaboration of traumatic events. Through the analysis of these sources, a re-conceptualization of memory as a *discursive* construction, as a *culture* of memory can be inferred. Memory becomes not a mere instrument for the construction of an identity, both individual and collective, but also a method of deconstruction of those very processes leading to the definition and elaboration of individual and collective identities. In this perspective, the representation and the transmission of traumas is carried out through the deconstruction and the difficult operation of re-composing controversial, neither homogeneous nor universal memories in a dialectic relation between the responsibility of remembrance and the necessity of oblivion.

The accent placed on the possibility of "re-constructing" and representing trauma has foregrounded sources such as diaries, autobiographies, testimonies, and narrations (fictions) not only as individual expressions, but also as cultural structures exposing narratives of imagination and opposition. Dominick LaCapra insists on the difference between writing trauma and writing *about* trauma. Writing trauma means acting it out in a performative discourse or in artistic practice. Given these premises, there is a dynamic and perhaps positive aspect which links memory studies to a series of political issues which today underpin the molding of a European scenario, as they can help to sort out new strategies for assessing controversial memories of the same past.

2. Memory Studies in Europe: The Case of the European Thematic Network Project ACUME

Today, it is the European Commission that encourages transnational forms of research, such as the European Thematic Network Projects, in order to encourage communal speculations capable of bringing Europe together through the sciences and the humanities. The underpinning educational project is very ambitious and also somehow dangerous: On the one hand, promoting new forms of research capable of overcoming national boundaries is certainly a fundamental and a necessary input to work out new European educational standards at once original and updated. And yet, on the other hand, pursuing a shared European identity through new educational patterns risks inducing some sort of homologation and melting of all differences that are, instead, a precious heritage to be preserved while unifying, and not assimilated. For this reason the European Thematic Network Project ACUME, dedicated to the study of cultural memory in relation to the making of a European identity, was based on the idea that the very term "European identity" is to be considered an "open" and "dynamic" term, capable of re-negotiating itself starting from a shared set of values that the scientific and the humanistic research can certainly help to work out. In such a context, the European identity is to be perceived as a sum of various identities, both those rooted in the various national realities, and those nowadays in progress, following the new understanding of historical processes as well as the new waves of immigrations within Europe and from outside Europe. It is this idea of cultural memory that we have tried to encourage through our ACUME Network.

"Cultural Memory in European Countries: An Interdisciplinary Approach (ACUME)" was a European Thematic Network which was started in 2002 and which ended its last year of activities at the end of September 2006 (detailed information is available online at http://www.lingue.unibo.it/acume). ACUME was designed with an interdisciplinary approach to introduce the study of cultural memory to the European university curricula: The trans-European study of cultural memory was seen, in fact, as a strategic goal in order to preserve and respect local and national identities while co-operating in the making of a communal European educational system. Inevitably, such a goal implied also developing a new series of trans-national research projects fostering memory studies across disciplines.

Therefore, the intention was to bring together scholars and experts from various European countries, as well as from the associated countries, in order to encourage a deeper understanding of the very idea of cultural memory and to co-operate in a broader curricular innovation, in the spirit of the guidelines established in Bologna, Prague, Berlin, and in other and more recent education forums. The importance of focusing on this major issue is proven by the fact that the ACUME Network included partners from almost all European countries, who jointly contributed to design, develop and implement this project: We counted about 80 partner universities and associated partners (including also non-European partner institutions in North and South America, that is, in areas in which European immigrants constitute a conspicuous part of the population).

The working hypothesis of ACUME was that cultural memory has become a very important issue pervading and affecting the cultural education of old and young generations of Europeans; also, it could be conceived as a priority step towards the making of a new European identity, built upon common and shared values, but fully respecting local identities and traditions. The need to question European cultural history seems to be cogent since, in recent times, it has also been the object of ideological manipulations brought to bear on various nationalist claims in Europe (such as the Balkans, Spain, Ireland, or Italy). We were therefore aware of the fact that cultural memory is something closely linked to national identity; this is why the objective of our broader research was not so much to embalm memory, but rather to pursue a critical approach to memory. This means that all the partners involved aimed to investigate how, within the history of the various countries, there has always been a very close link between memory and power. Hence, for us, remembering meant also having a critical perspective on the past. For all these reasons, our thematic network questioned the idea of cultural memory and fully investigated all the inevitably related cultural (and historical) oblivions. For each nation there are, in fact, historical events which have played a fundamental role in the shaping of national identity and that are collectively remembered and celebrated. On the other hand, for each nation there are historical events which, due to political and ideological reasons, continue to constitute a sort of national emotional burden, a real trauma which, consciously or unconsciously, is too often "removed" and "forgotten."

What constituted a fundamental aspect of this thematic network was the fact that the partners, while carrying out their various activities and research, also carried out a survey of local situations and realities (a sort of field research); this implied a strong co-operation among European generations who were encouraged to meet and confront, by means of interviews, gathering of materials (photographs, films, documents, etc.) and similar processes of "cultural exchange." In the long term, the hope was to contribute to the creation of a possible archive of European Cultural Memories, and to the establishment of a permanent Centre for Research on Cultural Memory. This latter idea is currently being pursued by a group of ACUME partners, to encourage the study of cultural memory in lifelong learning.

The project was characterized by an interdisciplinary methodology and by a comparative approach. The areas of research and teaching were: history, history of ideas, philosophy, literature and translation studies, anthropology (folklore and ethnographic studies) and social sciences, cultural studies (cinema, media, pop culture) and gender studies, and visual arts. While developing both research and teaching activities, partners started to collaborate also with scholars in the hard sciences, especially in biology, bioinformatics, and cognitive neuroscience, further proving that memory studies works well as a catalyzer of joint research. Partners co-operating in this project encouraged students' active involvement in the discussion of new university curricula; assessed curricular innovation and developed new educational strategies at a European level; designed and tested new teaching modules, both traditional and in e-learning mode; produced Web pages on the theme of cultural memory; and produced new teaching and research materials on cultural memory, both in the form of books and e-outputs.

The project included five fields (sub-projects) of teaching and research:

1) *Cultural Amnesia*: This sub-project explored the theme of cultural amnesia. Through the analysis of an eclectic variety of documents (from canonical texts to visual records and interviews with survivors), partners investigated the double process of remembrance and oblivion that cultures experience when dealing with traumatic aspects of their history (such as Nazism and the Holocaust in Germany, the Empire politics of colonization in Great Britain, Fascism in Italy, or the Balkan quest for identity).

In particular, within this sub-project, a group of partners investigated the textual interweaving of the discourse of European memory carried out by postcolonial writers. This concern was motivated by the acknowledgement of the increasing critical attention devoted to postcolonial works in Europe. The result is that the traditional silence imposed on these voices, as well as the traditional erasure of their memories, are now abolished so that, today, the assessment of postcolonial fiction triggers a series of interesting (and even uncanny) speculations on the very issue of European identity itself. This retrieved-narrative scenario raised complex issues such as the discursive nature of memory, European memory as a performative cultural practice, and the irreducible identity of postcolonial writers.

2) *Bearing Witness*: This sub-project investigated written sources, visual documents, and oral testimonies concerning events, situations, and people who played an important role in the cultural making of each nation (including letters, diaries, autobiographies, novels, photographs, films,

documentaries, and museums and archives). The idea was to question the very act of bearing witness by combining macro and micro history, as well as the forms and times of testimonies. In particular, partners investigated traumatic memories of World War One and World War Two as useful benchmarks to bring to light uneasy questions, such as the idea of contested memories. The research was carried out by a network of scholars belonging to various areas of study, including literature, history, and visual arts; it offered an emblematic ground to further investigate the controversial and often painful idea of "reconciliation" within nation-states and Europe. Moving from the study of cultural memories of the two world wars in the various European national realities, we have become more and more convinced that acknowledging the existence of these contested memories is the first step to take to encourage the negotiation of a truly shared ethic of memory.

3) *Memory and Places*: This sub-project investigated the importance of landscape, urban sites, and various individual places (real but also always to some extent imaginary, and in some cases wholly so) in the characterization of communities of various sizes and kinds—and the ways in which places are tied to memory in its many forms. The interplay of places and memory (with its inherent components of historical and spatial "production") is a central issue at various communal levels—regional, national, and global—and can also be a strong indicator for those wanting to explore the (imagined or real) existence of a communal European identity.

Every so-called "real" space is a mere product of the storage of various significances, be they parallel, telescoped, conflicting, overlapping, exclusive, or complementary. These kinds of mixed symbolic meanings are specific to every human community. They are mostly representations of the Self and of the Other. Recollection endows these representations with various values: ethical, ideological, political, religious, social, economic. Within a particular community, these values are shared, having previously been selected, secured, and sorted through specific ritual procedures.

4) *Oral and Written History*: Cultural memories are transmitted, and in the process shaped, by "languages"; in our context, the word "language" should be very broadly defined, denoting all manner of practices, visual signs, linguistic discourses, and other modes of communication. However, as the title announces, this sub-project focused mainly upon language as texts; several other relevant communicative modes were, however, considered within the sub-projects focusing upon the memory of specific events.

The various ways in which the past and cultural practices are transmitted, and the different roles of orality and writing within the same community, have proved particularly topical areas of study within the overall project of ACUME as Western culture is going through multiple changes that arguably amount to an overall shift in world paradigm. In this context, Europe may be construed both as representatively Western, sharing features with, for instance, the U.S.A. and the so-called "global village," and as in some ways unique, presenting distinctively European manifestations of the changes involved (which are further differentiated in their respective national-historical contexts).

Crucial factors in the overall change are the technological and digital revolutions: These have challenged the codes of written discourse solidly entrenched for at least three to four hundred years (the Enlightenment) and are introducing, even within the written media, quasi-"oral" habits of thought and utterance (features which may be accommodated within the hybrid term of "oralcy"). These changes—a new balance between oral and written, and an increasingly "oral" quality within some written genres—may usefully be studied not only for their own sake, but also in the light of the earlier revolution in communication by which orality gave way to literacy as communicative dominant (first in manuscripts, latter, and massively, though print). Thus, oral and written technologies of memory, both as phenomena *per se* and as historically determined, should be studied in their diachronic as well as synchronic aspects. Therefore, this sub-project moved along both these axes in an effort to: 1. salvage specific cultural memories; 2. study the differences as well as problematic and fruitful interrelations between orality and literacy as these appear in the aforementioned two transitional periods (from the Middle Ages to Modernity, and our own time); and 3. contemplate the cognitive implications of today's digital revolution for our culture.

5) *Foundation Texts and Mythologies*: The research in this project focused on three major themes: 1. anachronisms and discontinuities of cultural memory; 2. the role of myths and foundation texts in establishing "imagined communities," including rewritings and other manipulations of European traditions; and 3. the role of specific "universal" canons (mainly Shakespeare's work) in the formation of national and European identities (see also Grabes, this volume). The coordinators and partners developed their activities along two main lines: researching the anachronisms of cultural memory and the discontinuities of European traditions; and studying cultural invention, rewriting of myths and histories, and the formation of imagined communities.

The study of cultural invention, the rewriting of myths and histories, and the formation of imaginative communities was expanded in the dissemination year by the study of the relation between spectrality and cultural memory. Spectrality has been proved to exist as an important temporal and value paradigm used both in works of literature and art but also in the process of understanding historical monuments, local historical narratives, problems of marginality and liminality in cultural studies and anthropology, and in spectacular forms of culture.

In addition to the various seminars and conferences, in its three years of activities, the European Thematic Network Project ACUME has designed, realized and promoted several outputs, which have been promoted and disseminated at a European level. These outputs offer new tools for new research and teaching on the theme of cultural memory and can be grouped in three main typologies: volumes, teaching modules, and e-materials. Also, ETNP ACUME encouraged the development of new strategies of investigation and research also in the humanities, such as networking, a practice which implies interaction and exchange of mutual synergies among scholars expert in different fields. The format offered by the European Network (grouping partners in various geographical realities) and the object of research (memory) have fruitfully combined, in turn implementing each other: Memory, which is per se a trans-disciplinary field of research, has encouraged networking, at the same time fostering new understandings and knowledge across disciplines. In such a context, it was possible also to further investigate the ontological status of memory studies itself, therefore suggesting new potentialities pertaining to this area of research. For instance, networking on memory studies offered the opportunity to open up a new dialogue with the hard sciences and to start to pursue a renewed idea of "interfacing" between the sciences and the humanities which has led to the establishment of a group of researchers belonging to six different areas of studies: social sciences, biomedical sciences, visual culture, media, humanities and literary studies, and religious studies. Scholars investigated the very idea of "memory," moving from their own expertise and using some key words which have characterized memory studies in the last twenty years: *the self*; *emotions*; *time and evolution*; *the tension between memory and oblivion*; *the context*; *information*; *memory as construction*. These words represented a sort of *fil rouge*, a powerful heuristic tool and an epistemological matrix, and enabled a discussion on the interrelations between memory and power, memory and the body, memory and trauma, memory and religion, memory and images, and memory and places, as well as the themes of oblivion and of cultural mediators (cinema, TV, advertisement, journalism, etc.). The results of this investigation are now gathered in a volume (Agazzi and Fortunati), proving the fertile role which memory studies can play in forging a new idea of Europe. Europe is an economic and institutional reality; nonetheless, defining Europe from the cultural point of view is still a major challenge, especially today when society has to cope with new flows of immigration, both inside and towards Europe. By addressing historical and political issues (such as the controversial past, cultural differences, etc.), memory studies can contribute to finding common roots while enhancing and acknowledging diversity; it can turn Europe into a dynamic workshop where new ideas can be discussed and developed and thus trigger hope for new and much-needed scenarios.

References

Agazzi, Elena, and Vita Fortunati. *Memoria e saperi: Percorsi transdisciplinari.* Rome: Meltemi, 2007.

Assmann, Aleida. *Erinnerungsräume: Formen und Wandlungen des kulturellen Gedächtnisses.* Munich: Beck, 1999.

Benjamin, Walter. "Thesis on the Philosophy of History." *Illuminations.* Trans. Harry Zohn. Ed. Hannah Arendt. New York: Schocken, 1985. 253-64.

Connerton, Paul. *How Societies Remember.* Cambridge: Harvard UP, 1989.

Felman, Shoshana, and Dori Laub. *Testimony: Crises of Witnessing in Literature, Psychoanalysis, and History.* London: Routledge, 1992.

Halbwachs, Maurice. *Les cadres sociaux de la mémoire.* 1925. Paris: Presses Universitaires de France, 1952.

—. *La mémoire collective.* 1939. Paris: Presses Universitaires de France, 1950.

Hodgkin, Katharine, and Susannah Radstone. *Contested Past: The Politics of Memory.* London: Routledge, 2003.

LaCapra, Dominick. *Writing History, Writing Trauma.* Baltimore: Johns Hopkins UP, 2001.

Lamberti, Elena, and Vita Fortunati. *Memories and Representation of War in Europe: The Case of WW1 and WW2.* New York: Rodopi, 2007.

Le Goff, Jacques. *Histoire et mémoire.* Paris: Gallimard, 1988.

Nora, Pierre, ed. *Les lieux de mémoire.* 3 vols. Paris: Gallimard, 1984-92.

Olick, Jeffrey. *States of Memory: Continuities, Conflicts and Transformations in National Retrospection.* Durham: Duke UP, 2003.

Remotti, Francesco. *Luoghi e corpi: Antropologia dello spazio, del tempo e del potere.* Turin: Bollati Boringhieri, 1993.

Samuel, Raphael. *Theatre of Memory.* Vol. 1. London: Verso, 1994.

Suleiman, Susan Rubin. *Crises of Memory and the Second World War.* Cambridge: Harvard UP, 2006.

White, Hayden. *Tropics of Discourse: Essays in Cultural Criticism.* Baltimore: Johns Hopkins UP, 1978.

III. Social, Political, and Philosophical Memory Studies

Maurice Halbwachs's *mémoire collective*

JEAN-CHRISTOPHE MARCEL AND LAURENT MUCCHIELLI

Halbwachs, born in 1877, graduate of the Paris *Ecole Normale Supérieure* (where many of France's outstanding thinkers have studied and/or taught), holder of the *agrégation* in Philosophy (1901), and of doctorates in Law and the Arts, was influenced by both Henri Bergson and Emile Durkheim (see also Olick, this volume). The former was his philosophy teacher at the Lycée Henri IV (secondary school). He later distanced himself from Bergson, his first major book on collective psychology (*Les cadres sociaux de la mémoire*, 1925) being, in a sense, the formulation of his criticism. Halbwachs discovered the thinking of Emile Durkheim and joined the group around the *Année sociologique* periodical in 1904, through François Simiand. From then on he was one of the most faithful and at the same time one of the least conformist members of the "French school of sociology." Named professor of sociology in Strasburg in 1919, he went on to the Sorbonne in 1937 and was ultimately elected to the *Collège de France* in 1944, for a new chair in "Collective Psychology." The present text is devoted to a presentation of his collective psychology, focusing on the theme of memory.

In 1918, in "La doctrine d'Emile Durkheim," Halbwachs gives his interpretation of Durkheim's scientific project and suggests ways of making the most of this legacy. His answer is collective psychology. It is a new theory, indicated by the idea of the collective consciousness:

> Collective consciousness is a spiritual reality. [...] Its action and extensions may indeed be followed into every region of each man's conscience; its influence on the soul is measured by the influence exerted on sensitive life by the higher faculties, which are the means of social thought. (410)

There are of course temperamental differences between individuals, which are the object of individual psychology. But temperaments are of little help in studying people's actions, for "their nature is entirely reworked and transformed by social life" (Halbwachs, *Esquisse* 209). Only collective psychology is able to show how motives, aspirations, emotional states, and reflective sensations are connected to collective representations stored in the memory, which is the focal point of the higher faculties of the mind (Halbwachs, "La psychologie collective").

Having reasserted the cogency of Durkheim's psychosociological theory, Halbwachs determines the cerebral mechanisms by which the collective consciousness acts on individual consciences. In 1898, in his famous article on "Individual and Collective Representations," Durkheim had attempted to respond with the theory of collective representations, postulating an unconscious social memory affecting individuals automatically without their being aware of it, and developing a specific mental life in them (Mucchielli, *La découverte*, chap. 5). Halbwachs differs from Durkheim here, and turns toward a unique type of phenomenological sociology, with three main lines of thought:

1. the social construction of individual memory;
2. the development of collective memory in intermediary groups (family and social classes);
3. collective memory at the level of entire societies and civilizations.

1. The Social Construction of Individual Memory

There does not seem to have been any essential evolution in the psychology of memory since the two seminal books, one by Théodule Ribot (*Les maladies de la mémoire*, 1881) for psychophysiology and psychopathology, the other by Henri Bergson (*Matière et mémoire*, 1896) for introspective psychology. Halbwachs is an heir of the latter, for whom there are "dominant memories, on which other memories lean, as on supportive points" (*Matière et mémoire* 186). Ribot too thought that locations used "landmarks," that is, states of consciousness serving to "measure other distances" according to their intensity. Halbwachs uses that argument to claim that those landmarks actually construct us as members of groups (*Les cadres sociaux* 125), since we try to locate memories using social frames built from our present identity. To demonstrate this, Halbwachs used several detailed examples, including dreams and language.

In *Les cadres sociaux de la mémoire* (1925), Halbwachs experiments on himself. For over four years, he analyzes his dreams "to determine whether they contain complete scenes from our past" (3) and whether there is such a thing as strictly personal memories. He confronts Freud, for whom dreams reproduce fragments of the past, and wonders whether those fragments are authentic bits of recollections. The answer is negative, since memories are precise and dated, as opposed to the reminiscences discussed by Freud. Halbwachs contrasts those impressions, mixing past and present, with precise memories implying reasoning and comparison, which is to say dialogue with an other, for his point is that the past is not really preserved in the individual memory. "Fragments" persist there, but not complete recollections. What makes them true memories are collective representations. The collective memory is made of those "instruments" used by the conscious individual to recompose a coherent image of the past.

Halbwachs also deals with the problem of aphasia, a speech disorder characterized by a loss of verbal recollections. Earlier research tended to identify neurological centers of ideation and to explain aphasia as a malfunctioning of that center. Now Halbwachs pointed out that physicians all consistently differentiate various types of aphasia, but are unable to formulate an exact classification. He first shows that aphasia, viewed by an outside observer, is characteristically the impossibility of communicating with other members of the social group. Secondly, disorders apparently similar to those produced by aphasia may be encountered in practically anyone in specific situations, as in the case of a person taking an examination who is nervous to the point of momentarily forgetting his words. At this point, one may postulate that aphasia definitely does not require the presence of brain damage, but that it is above all "a deep alteration in the relations between the individual and the group" (*Les cadres sociaux* 69).

Halbwachs finds proof of this in the writings of Henry Head. Head, observing young soldiers with head wounds who had developed disorders of an aphasic type, showed that their inability to reproduce some words pronounced in their presence was not due to the absence of mental images or of the memories corresponding to those words, but to the forgetting of the words themselves. What aphasics suffer from, then, is definitely a loss of the conventional social markers:

> All of these observations seem to indicate that what the aphasic patient lacks is not so much memories as the ability to situate them in a framework, the very frame which is provided by the social environment [...]. The loss of words [...] is only one specific manifestation of a more general incapacity: all conventional symbolism, the necessary basis of social intelligence, has become foreign to him. (Halbwachs, *Les cadres sociaux* 76-77)

Dreams, aphasia—but also mental illness—are phenomena traditionally accounted for in purely individual and biological terms. Halbwachs's work shows that people act according to the *meaning* they ascribe to their own and other people's behavior. Now the content of those meanings is provided, originally, by the conventions of the community to which the individual belongs. Memory, intelligence, and identity are constructed by a learning process within a group. Subsequently, it is in an absent or disordered relationship to that group that the causes of any individual mental disorders should be sought, instead of launching into unverifiable conjectures as to the state of an individual's brain. As Durkheim had announced, sociology is "a new view of human nature," destined to renew psychology by transcending the traditional neurobiological and psychiatric conceptions.

2. Collective Memory and Intermediate Groups

Having solved the problem of the fundamental human mechanisms of the collective memory, Halbwachs devoted his work to the main producers of that collective memory: the family, social classes, and religious communities.

A family is not merely a concatenation of individuals with shared feelings and kinship relations. Those individuals inherit a "broad conception of the family" (*Les cadres sociaux* 148), a number of social representations of *what a family should be*, and of their roles toward one another and toward their children. Those conceptions do not depend exclusively on their personal tastes and on their affectionate feelings:

> No doubt, within a given family, feelings are not always in step with kinship relations. Sometimes one loves one's grandparents as much or more than one's father or mother [...]. But one barely admits this to oneself, and *the feelings expressed are nonetheless regulated by the structure of the family*: that is what matters [...] for the conservation of the group's authority and cohesion. (Halbwachs, *Les cadres sociaux* 149, emphasis added)

To convince oneself of this, generally speaking, it suffices that we compare the different types of family structure. In ancient Roman society, it was thought normal for each individual to conclude an average of three or four marriages in a lifetime. The family was much more extended. In our modern societies, these representations are far less active. Nonetheless, the family still structures children's memory through the roles they play in shared events, and which roles they continue to play in their parents' eyes, even when they have become adults. Now this collective life, however minimal, has a memory, as is illustrated by the choice of first names, for instance, which are symbols: "[I]f they help differentiate members of a family, it is because they correspond to the group's felt need to differentiate them for itself and to agree on that differentiation" (Halbwachs, *Les cadres sociaux* 165-66).

The psychology of social classes looks at the whole of the representations produced by a human group. As soon as a group is integrated in a social space, it develops a notion of its place in society, of the society itself and of what is required for its maintenance. For the constituent element of a group is an interest, an order of ideas and concerns, no doubt reflected in personalities, but still sufficiently general and impersonal to retain their meaning and portent for all (Halbwachs, *La mémoire collective*, chap. 3). This is what each person has in mind when deciphering his own and other people's behavior.

For example, the collective working class memory is made of recollections that conform to an interpretation of the worker's condition, which may be assumed to revolve around the feeling of not participating in a dignified manner in collective life, of not participating in the establishment of its shared ideals (Halbwachs, *Esquisse* 132). Workers are not free to set the pace of their work, and are constantly subservient to the lifeless, often foul and even dangerous substances they fashion. Everything in their social life reminds them of this, including their crude lodgings, which are reminiscent of the workshop.

Nevertheless, those lodgings "harbor the family" viewed as a little society providing warm relations and in which the individual is judged according to his or her personal qualities, as opposed to the arbitrary depersonalization reigning in the world of the factory. Here originates a second idea, according to which the collective memory is also composed of what the group aspires to being or doing (in this case, retrieving some of the dignity denied it by society). This in turn explains the aspirations and modes of consumption of workers, translating the search for "increasing participation in the forms of modern civilization" (Halbwachs, *Esquisse* 182).

In *Morphologie sociale* (1938), Halbwachs states that for a group to have an idea of what it needs in order to persist, it must begin by developing as clear as possible a representation of itself. On this is based its special relation with the material forms embodying it: Their relative steadiness provides the group with tangible proof of its existence and with a basic tenet of stability. Once constructed, these spatial forms have a dynamic of their own. They change very gradually, so that while individuals live and die, society does not disappear with them. Generations go by, but villages and city neighborhoods persist.

The city neighborhood regulates the way its inhabitants get together, their movements across space, which influence tastes, needs, and customs. Similarly, economic activity, the directions in which exchanges flow, the intensity of business transactions, fluctuations in the prices of goods may all be viewed as the outcome of many collective aspirations. And, lastly, those aspirations depend on the location of markets and of places of production.

By a sort of to-and-fro movement, the social group comes into being through stable spatial images representing it. Thus, we may consider that material forms both reflect and shape the concerns of each individual inasmuch as he acts and thinks as a member of the group. In this sense, the material form of the group is the source of the "primordial" psychological life of its members. It is the spatial images which produce collectively constituted psychological states, and especially the collective representations connected with memories and stored in the collective memory.

> It should be clearly understood that the material forms of society operate [...] through our awareness of them, which we acquire as members of a group who perceive its volume, physical structure and movements within space. This represents a sort of collective thought process or perception, that might be called an *immediate given of social consciousness*, and which contrasts with every other process. (*Morphologie sociale* 182-83; emphasis added)

The importance of social morphology is justified, for behind the material forms and distribution of the population there is a whole series of psychosocial factors in operation, tied to collective thoughts and trends. However, the psychology of intermediate groups comes up against one difficulty: the intertwined motives behind the action of members of a group. For instance, it is difficult to claim that workers' desire to consume new goods is exclusively due to their need to participate more completely in the forms of modern civilization. That desire also has to do with the harried pace that urban life imposes on people. Collective psychology should therefore also view the population taken at the broadest level.

3. The Collective Memory of Societies and Civilizations

Halbwachs transposes the reasoning he applies to intermediate groups to society as a whole. It too develops "an intuitive, profound sense" of its identity (*Morphologie sociale* 176), through its hold on its body: the population. The broadest spatial structures (such as the entire national territory) express the spirit of the society and cannot be modified by specific activities, for the laws shaping the population do not change. This means that each and every social group is caught up in another current, determining the forms of the population.

Halbwachs, like Durkheim, views the density of human groups as one of the most important laws of population. Urban life is thus viewed as the most remarkable civilizational fact. In cities, collective life is more hectic; it is channeled into paths forming a circulation network of unparalleled intensity. This results in a mixture of material and mental representations causing social groups to tend more to be dissolved there. There are more occasions for people to experience extreme isolation, but also, at the same time, a more powerful collective feeling may develop, with the presence of apparently limitless masses of people. As situations are more complex, there are greater chances for individuals to be maladjusted (Halbwachs developed this idea in his work on suicide: *Les causes* 13-14).

To make the transition from material forms to an overall collective psychology, Halbwachs borrows the concept of "way of life" (*genre de vie*) from geographer Vidal de la Blache and from Simiand, defining it as "a set of customs, beliefs and ways of being resulting from men's usual occupations and from the way these are established" (*Les causes* 502). The urban way of life is opposed to the rural way of life, just as modern life is opposed to the old way of life in which collective life was both very strong and highly simplified, since there was little separation. In urban society, the spatial fragmentation causes fragmentation of social life. But movements among people are faster paced, and a greater diversity of situations is concentrated in a given time frame.

The main resulting psychological states tend to limit births. This behavior is a sort of instinctive reaction to the shortage of space characteristic of the new urban population structure. For the city demands great efforts of its residents, whose integration requires that they change many of their habits and expend their energy to "defend their life" and "prolong it" (Halbwachs, *Morphologie sociale* 127).

The lower death rate should be seen as the outcome of the will to persist and to concern oneself with the value of the individual existence, ideas which are spurred by society in its members. As for the collective memory of urban society, it is composed of recollections tied to spatial representations reflecting the way it conceives and preserves itself. For example, a nation has borders it attempts to maintain and memories attached to that spatial structure, whence the commemoration of great military victories.

In the hypothesis that social change is an ongoing attempt on society's part to adjust to its environment, and that the collective memory tells us something about the nature of that society, we can attempt to discover the laws governing its evolution. This is what Halbwachs proposes to do by studying the collective memory of Christians.

The Gospel provides the Church with a broad framework enabling Christians to fortify their faith. Scenes found on stained-glass church windows, such as the path of suffering followed by the Christ on his way from Pontius Pilate to Calvary, fill this commemorative role (Halbwachs, *La topographie légendaire*). These memories are symbols of unity, supported by spatial and temporal frames. But the collective memory is not composed of just any old memories: It contains those which, in the views of living Christians, best express the substance of the group they form. In Jerusalem itself, with its long history of upheavals and transformations, it is of course impossible to certify that the locations revealed by the Gospel are the true ones. Yet, the memory of them is retained. Generally speaking, religious groups attempt to materialize the separation between the sacred and the profane.

Similarly, the collective memory of believers is based on a reconstructed time in which Christians locate the founding events: Easter, Ascension, Christmas, and so on. This discontinuous time is not clock time or calendar time. It has evacuated some memories because the events it retains are those that best express the essence of the community of believers. This means that as members change, die, or disappear, as the spatial frames change and the concerns of the time replace past concerns, the collective memory is continually reinterpreted to fit those new conditions. It adjusts the image of old facts to the beliefs and spiritual needs of the moment. It is as if the collective memory empties itself a bit when it feels too full of differences: Some memories are evacuated as the community enters a new period of its life (Halbwachs, *La mémoire collective*, chap. 3). Conversely, new memories develop and acquire another reality because they henceforth provide individuals with the markers needed to situate themselves in the social environment of the time. For instance, Christians did not always pay attention to the path of suffering followed by Jesus on his way to crucifixion.

Halbwachs ends up defining two laws governing the evolution of the collective memory:

- *A law of fragmentation.* Occasionally several facts are located at the same place. A location may be split in two, or into fragments, or proliferate. In this case, it is as if the strength of religious devotion required several recipients into which to be poured without exhausting itself.
- *A (converse) law of concentration.* Facts that are not necessarily interrelated are located in the same or a very nearby place. Here, the concentration of locations provides believers with grand memories in some places.

References

Bergson, Henri. *Matière et mémoire.* Paris: Alcan, 1896. [English: *Matter and Memory.* 1908. Trans. Nancy Margaret Paul and W. Scott Palmer. New York: Zone, 1991.]

Halbwachs, Maurice. *Les cadres sociaux de la mémoire.* 1925. Paris: Albin Michel, 1994.

—. *Les causes du suicide.* Paris: Alcan, 1930.

—. *La classe sociale et les niveaux de vie: Recherches sur la hiérarchie des besoins dans les sociétés industrielles contemporaines.* Paris: Alcan, 1913.

—. "La doctrine d'Émile Durkheim." *Revue philosophique* 85 (1918): 353-411.

—. *Esquisse d'une psychologie des classes sociales.* 1938. Paris: Rivière, 1955.

—. *L'évolution des besoins de la classe ouvrière.* Paris: Alcan, 1933.

—. *La mémoire collective.* Paris: Presses Universitaires de France, 1950.
—. *Morphologie sociale.* 1938. Paris: Colin, 1970.
—. *La psychologie collective.* Paris: Centre de Documentation Universitaire, 1938.
—. *La topographie légendaire des évangiles en terre sainte: Etude de mémoire collective.* Paris: Alcan, 1941.
Head, Henry. "Aphasia and Kindred Disorders of Speech." *Brain* 43 (1920): 87-165.
Marcel, Jean-Christophe. "Les derniers soubresauts du rationalisme durkheimien: une théorie de «l'instinct social de survie» chez Maurice Halbwachs." *Maurice Halbwachs: Espaces, mémoires et psychologie collective.* Eds. Yves Déloye and Claudine Haroche. Paris: Publications de la Sorbonne, 2004.
—. "Mauss et Halbwachs: vers la fondation d'une psychologie collective (1920-1945)." *Sociologie et sociétés* 36.2 (2004): 73-90.
Marcel, Jean-Christophe, and Laurent Mucchielli. "Un fondement du lien social: la mémoire collective selon Maurice Halbwachs." *Technologies, idéologies, pratiques: Revue d'anthropologie des connaissances* 13.2 (1999): 63-88.
Mucchielli, Laurent. *La découverte du social: Naissance de la sociologie en France (1870-1914).* Paris: La Découverte, 1998.
—, ed. *Maurice Halbwachs et les sciences humaines de son temps.* Spec. issue of *Revue d'histoire des sciences humaines* 1.1 (1999).
—. *Mythes et histoire des sciences humaines.* Paris: La Découverte, 2004.

From Collective Memory to the Sociology of Mnemonic Practices and Products

JEFFREY K. OLICK

1. Introduction

Like sociology in general, a sociology of retrospection is concerned with how what we say and do—as individuals and together—is shaped by a not often obvious—and always changing—combination of traditions, fantasies, interests, and opportunities. One problem, however, has been finding useful concepts that do not deny important distinctions among kinds of retrospection, whether these distinctions are epistemological, institutional, or substantive. Intellectual frameworks and their attendant concepts have proliferated in recent years. In France, for instance, the "history of mentalities" has pursued a "collective psychology" approach to cultural history. Its aim—which it formulates in distinction to the high-mindedness of intellectual history and the economic and demographic foci of social history—is to grasp "the imaginary and collective perceptions of human activities as they vary from one historical period to another" (Chartier 27-30). Commemoration and historical imagery, in this approach, are parts of "the whole complex of ideas, aspirations, and feelings which links together the members of a social group" (Goldmann, qtd. in Chartier 32) and are thus important topics for investigation.

In Germany, many historians and social scientists have revived an older, philosophical concept of "historical consciousness" (*Geschichtsbewusstsein*) to guide analysis (the most important contemporary figure being Jörn Rüsen). In some versions—particularly those steeped in Hegelian abstractions about historical spirits and cultural essences unfolding in history—"historical consciousness" is nearly synonymous with collective identity per se. In other versions, "historical consciousness" refers more narrowly to the production of, and debate over, images of the past in political processes (cf. Lukacs). Here "historical consciousness" is often linked to the label "the politics of history" (*Geschichtspolitik*), which indicates both the role of history in politics and the role of politics in history (see, for example, Wolfrum; see also Meyer, this volume).

Yet another camp employs the awkward yet useful term "mnemohistory," which "[u]nlike history proper [...] is concerned not with the past as such, but only with the past as it is remembered" (Assmann 8-9). Mnemohistory calls for a theory of cultural transmission, one that helps us understand history not as "one damned thing after another," as Arthur

Lovejoy put it, nor as a series of objective stages, but as an active process of meaning-making through time, "the ongoing work of reconstructive imagination" (Assmann 14). Indeed, according to the term's inventor, "it is only through mnemohistorical reflection that history [...] becomes aware of its own function as a form of remembering" (Assmann 21). Other terms include "political myth" (Tudor), "tradition" (Shils), "public history" (Porter Benson, Brier, and Rosenzweig), "oral history" (Passerini; Thompson), and "heritage" (Lowenthal), among others. Each of these terms has its own inflection of the issue, and several label distinct scholarly literatures. While many authors using these terms have adopted "collective memory" as a more general term or label for an area of concern, others have objected that collective memory's conceptual contribution is not positive. Gedi and Elam (30), for instance, call its use "an act of intrusion [...] forcing itself like a molten rock into an earlier formation [...,] unavoidably obliterating fine distinctions." As we will see, I agree with the charge that collective memory over-totalizes a variety of retrospective products, practices, and processes. Nevertheless, as a sensitizing rather than operational concept, I believe it raises useful questions when taken as a starting point for inquiry rather than as an end point.

Despite this array of different concepts and traditions—all useful in their ways—the overwhelming majority of discussions in recent years has proceeded under the rubric of "collective memory." Like "mentality," "historical consciousness," "mnemohistory" and other terms, "collective memory"—or, alternatively, collective or social remembering—directs our attention to issues at the heart of contemporary political and social life, including the foundations of group allegiance and the ways we make sense of collective experience in time. But it does so, I think, in particularly salutary ways, perhaps paradoxically because of its very breadth and imprecision. Because of its general sensitizing powers, I use "collective memory" as the guiding concept for my own work (e.g., "Collective Memory"; *In the House of the Hangman*). However, it is important to spend some time exploring what kinds of sensitivities "collective memory" creates, and why.

2. From Individual to Collective Memory

Memory, our common sense tells us, is a fundamentally individual phenomenon. What could be more individual than remembering, which we seem to do in the solitary world of our own heads as much as in conversation with others? Even when we "reminisce," we often experience this as a process of offering up to the external world the images of the past locked away in the recesses of our own minds. We can remember by ourselves in the dark at night, as we drive alone along the highway, or as we half-listen to a conversation about something else. By the same token, lesions of the brain—caused perhaps by Alzheimer's disease or physical injury—are surely internal rather than social defects preventing us as individuals from remembering. Memory—and by extension forgetting—thus seems not just fundamentally individual, but quintessentially so, as primal and lonely as pain. What can we possibly mean, then, when we refer to social or collective memory?

Contemporary use of the term collective memory is traceable largely to the sociologist Maurice Halbwachs, who published his landmark *Social Frameworks of Memory* (*Les cadres sociaux de la mémoire*) in 1925. Halbwachs's interest in memory combined insights from two important figures in late-nineteenth-century France, philosopher Henri Bergson and sociologist Emile Durkheim, both of whom were concerned—though in very different ways—with "advances" of European "civilization." Halbwachs's Strasbourg colleague, historian Marc Bloch, also used the term collective memory in 1925 as well as in a later book on feudal society. Memory, of course, has been a major preoccupation for social thinkers since the Greeks (see especially Coleman). Yet it was not until the late nineteenth and early twentieth centuries that a distinctively social perspective on memory became prominent. The first explicit use of the term I have ever seen was by Hugo von Hofmannsthal in 1902, who referred to "the damned up force of our mysterious ancestors within us" and "piled up layers of accumulated collective memory" (qtd. in Schieder 2), though this was a poetic allusion rather than the seed of a sociological theory of memory.

In the late nineteenth century, powerful forces were pushing to overcome subjectivity, judgment, and variability in the name of science, organization, and control. Political and commercial elites, for instance, viewed the diversity of local times as a growing problem: Like different gauge railroad tracks, the diversity of times was an impediment to increasingly complex and widespread commerce and political power (see especially Kern). As a result, elites worked hard to standardize time in terms of homogeneous criteria. One good example was the establishment of time zones and Greenwich Mean Time. Scientific advances—which discovered regularities behind apparent variations—lent support to these unifying and standardizing projects. The philosophical tradition, moreover, had long favored objectivist accounts, in which empirical variety is a mere illusion behind which lie perfect conceptual unities.

Influenced in part by Romantic perceptions that this new conceptual universe was somehow sterile, the philosopher Henri Bergson rejected objectivist accounts, arguing that subjectivity is the only source of true philosophical knowledge. Like many other thinkers of the time, Bergson was concerned with increasing rationalization and the unifying force of science. Writers like Proust and Freud, for instance, became preoccupied with memory because it seemed to them that precisely in an age in which history, biography, and other forms of record keeping were ordering history in an increasingly objective and complete manner, meaningful connections to our pasts, personal or shared, seemed to be waning (see Bergson; Terdiman; Kern). As a result, Bergson undertook a radical philosophical analysis of the *experience* of time, highlighting memory as its central feature. Against accounts of memory as passive storage, he characterized remembering as active engagement. Against accounts of memory as the objective reproduction of the past, he characterized remembering as fluid and changing. Bergson thus posed the problem of memory in particularly potent ways for Halbwachs and other later theorists. His work on memory drew Halbwachs's attention to the difference between objective and subjective apprehensions of the past: Whereas new forms of record keeping measured time and recorded history in increasingly uniform and standardized ways, individual memory was still highly variable, sometimes recording short periods in intense detail and long periods in only the vaguest outline. More recently, however, Eviatar Zerubavel has demonstrated that this variable attention span characterizes social memory as well. Following Bergson, the variable *experience* of memory was for Halbwachs the real point of interest.

Like Bergson, Durkheim too considered objectivist accounts of time and space unjustified. Unlike Bergson, however, Durkheim located the variability of perceptual categories not in the vagaries of subjective experience, but in differences among forms of social organization. Where Bergson rejected objectivist and materialist accounts of time in favor of the variability of *individual* experience, Durkheim rejected such accounts by attending to the ways different *societies* produce different concepts of time: Forms of time, like other basic categories, derive neither from transcendental truths nor from material realities, but are social facts, varying not according to subjective experience but according to the changing forms of social structure. Standardization and objectivism, according to Durkheim, were central ways modernizing societies were responding to increasing levels of differentiation and individuation. By connecting cognitive order (time perception) with social order (division of labor), Durkheim thus provided for Halbwachs a *sociological* framework for studying the variability of memory raised by Bergson.

3. Halbwachs's Legacies

In his seminal work on collective memory, Halbwachs drew from Bergson's problematization of time and memory, but addressed the issue through Durkheim's sociological lens (see also Marcel and Mucchielli, this volume). Of course, there are other paths to the contemporary interest in collective or social remembering. Important examples include Russian behaviorist psychology from the early twentieth century, including the work of Vygotsky and Pavlov, among others (see Bakhurst), and the work of the British social psychologist Fredrick Bartlett (see Douglas), to name just a few.

Memory, for Halbwachs, is first of all framed in the present as much as in the past, variable rather than constant. Studying memory, as a result, is not a matter of reflecting philosophically on inherent properties of the subjective mind but of identifying its shifting social frames. Moreover, for Halbwachs memory is a matter of how minds work together in society, how their operations are not simply mediated but are structured by social arrangements: "[I]t is in society that people normally acquire their memories. It is also in society that they recall, recognize, and localize their memories" (*On Collective Memory* 38). The forms memory take vary according to social organization, and the groups to which any individual belongs are primary even in the most apparently individual remembering. But memory, following Bergson, is also a central part of social and psychic life, not just an interesting aspect of social structure.

There are, nevertheless, a number of distinct aspects of collective remembering in Halbwachs, and different kinds of collective memory research since then have emphasized various of these (see Olick, "Collective Memory"; Olick and Robbins). First, Halbwachs argued that it is impossible for individuals to remember in any coherent and persistent fashion outside of their *group contexts*; these are the necessary *social frameworks* of memory (see also Irwin-Zarecka). His favorite examples include the impossibility of being certain of any particular childhood memory: As adults, it is impossible to say whether the memory of a childhood experience is more the result of stored features of the original moment or some kind of compilation out of stored fragments, other people's retellings, and intervening experiences. The social frameworks in which we are called on to recall are inevitably tied up with what and how we recall. Groups provide us the stimulus or opportunity to recall, they shape the ways in which we do so, and often provide the materials. Following this argument, the very distinction between the individual and social components of remembering ceases to make absolute sense: "There is no point," Halbwachs argued, "in seeking where [...] [memories] are preserved in my brain or in some nook of my mind to which I alone have access: for they are recalled to me externally, and the groups of which I am a part at any time give me the means to reconstruct them [...]" (*On Collective Memory* 38). All individual remembering, that is, takes place with social materials, within social contexts, and in response to social cues. Even when we do it alone, we do so as social beings with reference to our social identities.

If all individual memory is socially framed by groups, however, groups themselves also share *publicly articulated images of collective pasts.* For this reason, Halbwachs distinguished between "autobiographical memory" and "historical memory." The former concerns the events of one's own life that one remembers because they were experienced directly. The latter refers to residues of events by virtue of which groups claim a continuous identity through time. "Historical memory" of the Civil War, for instance, is part of what it means to be an American, and is part of the collective narrative of the United States. But nobody still has "autobiographical memory" of the event. This is the more authentically Durkheimian moment in Halbwachs's theory: Durkheim developed a sociological approach to what he called "collective representations," symbols or meanings that are properties of the group whether or not any particular individual or even particular number of individuals shares them. In this sense, very few people may be able to identify key figures or events of the Civil War, but those figures or events may nonetheless be important elements of American collective memory. Whereas survey researchers may conclude that a particular image or event not remembered by very many people is no longer a part of the collective memory, for a true Durkheimian culture is not reducible to what is in people's heads.

Representations themselves, from this analytical perspective, are not to be evaluated in terms of their origins, resonance, or distribution in any particular population. Collective memory, in this sense, has a life of its own, though this need not be as metaphysical as it sounds: Work emphasizing the genuinely collective nature of social memory has demonstrated that there are long-term structures to what societies remember or commemorate that are stubbornly impervious to the efforts of individuals to escape them; powerful institutions, moreover, clearly support some histories more than others, provide narrative patterns and exemplars of how individuals can and should remember, and stimulate public memory in ways and for reasons that have little to do with the individual or aggregate neurological records. Without such a collectivist perspective, after all, it is difficult to provide good explanations of mythology, tradition, and heritage, among other long-term symbolic patterns.

Durkheimian approaches are often accused—and often rightly so—of being radically anti-individualist, conceptualizing society in disembodied terms, as an entity existing in and of itself, over and above the individuals who comprise it. Another important feature of Durkheimian sociology can be an unjustified assumption that these societies—constituted by collective representations which individuals may or may not share—are unitary. A Durkheimian approach to collective memory, thus, can lead us to attribute one collective memory or set of memories to entire, well-bounded societies. (Like all such critiques, these are based on something of a straw man version of Durkheim's positions.) While not usually—though sometimes—articulated in terms of Durkheimian theory, many contemporary political discussions about cultural heritage share such assumptions: Commemoration of certain historical events is essential, so the argument goes, to our sense of national unity; without substantial consensus on the past, social solidarity is in danger. There is either a "deep structure" or stored up legacy of shared culture which binds us together; without its pervasive influence, there is no "us" to bind.

Halbwachs was in many ways more careful than his great mentor, placing most of his emphasis on the multiple social frameworks of individual memories (see Coser). He characterized collective memory as plural, showing that shared memories can be effective markers of social differentiation. Nevertheless, Halbwachs did lay the groundwork for a genuinely collective, in addition to socially framed individualist, approach to memory. In some contrast to his discussion in which what individuals remember is determined by their group memberships but still takes place in their own minds, Halbwachs also focused on publicly available commemorative symbols, rituals, and technologies. As I just noted, some later theorists treat these symbols and representations as a vast cultural storehouse; this is a wise move, since the items in a cultural storehouse are real. Others, however, take an additional step and hypothesize a deep cultural structure, a set of rules, patterns, and resources, that generates any particular representation. In even more extreme versions, the structure of collective meanings is treated as not as *conscience collective*, but as a "collective unconscious," which does indeed have mystical overtones (cites to Jung). One need not become a metaphysician, however, to believe there is a dimension of collective remembering that is organized without direct reference to individuals.

4. From Collective Memory to the Sociology of Mnemonic Practices and Products

Perhaps the solution is to recognize that all of these factors are in play at all times: collective representations (publicly available symbols, meanings, narratives, and rituals), deep cultural structures (generative systems of rules or patterns for producing representations), social frameworks (groups and patterns of interaction), and culturally and socially framed individual memories. The kinds of questions one asks when looking at collective representations as collective representations, after all, are distinct from those one asks when looking at the individual reception of such representations or at their production. Cognitive storage processes, moreover, are pretty obviously different from official story-telling. And different theories have shown how cultural patterns (e.g., time consciousness) produce social structures (e.g., strong national identities), though other theories show just as well exactly the opposite, that social structures produce cultural patterns (e.g., memory is structured generationally).

But are individual memory, social and cultural frameworks, and collective representations really separate things? The term collective memory—with its sometimes more, sometimes less clear contrast to individual memory—seems to imply just that! But only if we forget that collective memory is merely a broad, sensitizing umbrella, and not a precise operational definition. For upon closer examination, collective memory really refers to a wide variety of *mnemonic products and practices*, often quite different from one another. The former (products) include stories, rituals, books, statues, presentations, speeches, images, pictures, records, historical studies, surveys, etc.; the latter (practices) include reminiscence, recall, representation, commemoration, celebration, regret, renunciation, disavowal, denial, rationalization, excuse, acknowledgment, and many others. Mnemonic practices—though occurring in an infinity of contexts and through a shifting multiplicity of media—are always simultaneously individual and social. And no matter how concrete mnemonic products may be, they gain their reality only by being used, interpreted, and reproduced or changed. To focus on collective memory as *a variety of products and practices* is thus to reframe the antagonism between individualist and collectivist approaches to memory more productively as a matter of moments in a dynamic process. This, to me, is the real message of Halbwachs's diverse insights.

5. Three Principles for the Analysis of Collective Memory

The foregoing excursus on Halbwachs and the origins of the collective memory concept may appear rather abstract, but it leaves us with quite concrete principles about what to look for in the diverse landscapes of memory, and about how to treat the materials we find there. First, despite the penchant of many politicians, commentators, and scholars for invoking *the* collective memory of an entire society, collective memory is far from monolithic. Collective remembering is a highly complex process, involving numerous different people, practices, materials, and themes. One need be careful, therefore, not to presume at the outset that every society has one collective memory or that it is obvious and unproblematic how (and which) public memories will be produced. It is important to remember the different demands on participants in different discursive fields, such as politics or journalism, religion or the arts, and to appreciate subtleties of context and inflection. Doing so, of course, makes it difficult to judge a whole epoch or a whole society. For me, this is no loss.

Second, the concept of collective memory often encourages us to see memory either as the authentic residue of the past or as an entirely malleable construction in the present (see especially Schwartz; Schudson). "Traditionalist" models, for instance, assimilate collective memory to heritage, patrimony, national character, and the like, and view collective memory as a bedrock for the continuity of identities. They often ask how collective memory shapes or constrains contemporary action. On the other hand, "Presentist" models assimilate collective memory to manipulation and deception, a mere tool in the arsenal of power. They ask how contemporary interests shape what images of the past are deployed in contemporary contexts and see memory as highly variable. Neither of these views, however, is a particularly insightful way to understand the complexities of remembering, which is always a fluid negotiation between the desires of the present and the legacies of the past. What parts past and present, history and memory, respectively play in this negotiation—and how they are related—is as much an empirical question as it is a theoretical one. As Barry Schwartz puts it: "Sharp opposition between history and collective memory has been our Achilles Heel, causing us to assert unwillingly, and often despite ourselves, that what is not historical must be "invented" or "constructed"—which transforms collective memory study into a kind of cynical muckraking" (personal communication).

And third—though this may just be another way of stating the first two principles—we must remember that memory is a process and not a thing, a faculty rather than a place. Collective memory is something—or rather many things—we *do*, not something—or many things—we *have*. We therefore need analytical tools sensitive to its varieties, contradictions, and dynamism. How are representations of and activities concerning the past organized socially and culturally? When and why do they change? How can we begin to untangle the diverse processes, products, and practices through which societies confront and represent aspects of their pasts?

References

Assmann, Jan. *Moses the Egyptian: The Memory of Egypt in Western Monotheism.* Cambridge: Harvard UP, 1998.

Bakhurst, David. "Social Memory in Soviet Thought." *Collective Remembering.* Eds. David Middleton and Derek Edwards. London: Sage, 1990. 203-26.

Bartlett, F. C. *Remembering: A Study in Experimental and Social Psychology.* Cambridge: Cambridge UP, 1932.

Bersgon, Henri. *Matter and Memory.* Trans. Nancy Margaret Paul and W. Scott Palmer. New York: Zone, 1990. Trans. of *Matière et mémoire.* Paris: Alcan, 1896.

Chartier, Roger. *Cultural History: Between Practices and Representatives.* Trans. Lydia G. Cochrane. Ithaca: Cornell UP, 1988.

Coleman, Janet. *Ancient and Medieval Memories: Studies in the Reconstruction of the Past.* Cambridge: Cambridge UP, 2005.

Coser, Lewis A. Introduction. *On Collective Memory.* By Maurice Halbwachs. Ed. and trans. Lewis A. Coser. Chicago: U of Chicago P, 1992. 1-34.

Douglas, Mary. *How Institutions Think.* Syracuse: Syracuse UP, 1986.

Gedi, Noa, and Yigal Elam. "Collective Memory: What Is It?" *History and Memory* 8.1 (1996): 30-50.

Goldmann, Lucien. *The Hidden God: A Study of Tragic Vision in the Pensées of Pascal and the Tragedies of Racine.* Trans. Philip Thody. London: Routledge & K. Paul; New York: Humanities, 1964.

Halbwachs, Maurice. *On Collective Memory.* 1925. Ed. and trans. Lewis A. Coser. Chicago: U of Chicago P, 1992.

Irwin-Zarecka, Iwona. *Frames of Remembrance: The Dynamics of Collective Memory.* New Brunswick, NJ: Transaction, 1994.

Kern, Stephen. *The Culture of Time and Space 1880-1918.* Cambridge: Harvard UP, 1983.

Lowenthal, David. *The Heritage Crusade and the Spoils of History.* Cambridge: Cambridge UP, 1998.

Lukacs, John. *Historical Consciousness, or, The Remembered Past.* New Brunswick, NJ: Transaction, 1994.

Olick, Jeffrey K. "Collective Memory: The Two Cultures." *Sociological Theory* 17.3 (1999): 333-48.

—. *In the House of the Hangman: The Agonies of German Defeat, 1943-1949.* Chicago: U of Chicago P, 2005.

Olick, Jeffrey K., and Joyce Robbins. "Social Memory Studies: From 'Collective Memory' to the Historical Sociology of Mnemonic Practices." *Annual Review of Sociology* 24 (1998): 105-40.

Passerini, Luisa, ed. *Memory and Totalitarianism.* New Brunswick, NJ: Transaction, 2005.

Porter Benson, Susan, Stephen Brier, and Roy Rosenzweig, eds. *Presenting the Past: Essays on History and the Public.* Philadelphia: Temple UP, 1986.

Schieder, Theodor. "The Role of Historical Consciousness in Political Action." *History and Theory* 17.4 (1978): 1-18.

Schudson, Michael. *Watergate in American Memory: How We Remember, Forget and Reconstruct the Past.* New York: Basic, 1992.

Schwartz, Barry. *Abraham Lincoln and the Forge of National Memory.* Chicago: U of Chicago P, 2000.

Shils, Edward. *Tradition.* Chicago: U of Chicago P, 1981.

Terdiman, Richard. *Present Past: Modernity and the Memory Crisis.* Ithaca: Cornell UP, 1993.

Thompson, Paul Richard. *The Voice of the Past: Oral History.* Oxford: Oxford UP, 1988.

Tudor, Henry. *Political Myth.* London: Pall Mall, 1971.

Wolfrum, Edgar. *Geschichtspolitik in der Bundesrepublik Deutschland: Der Weg zur bundesrepublikanischen Erinnerung 1948-1990.* Darmstadt: Wissenschaftliche Buchgesellschaft, 1999.

Memory in Post-Authoritarian Societies

ANDREAS LANGENOHL

1. Transitions from Authoritarianism: Democratization and the Role of Memory

The problem of how societies cope with the macro-criminal legacies of formerly authoritarian regimes and political orders has been in the focus of researchers since the middle of the twentieth century. It is intimately interwoven with questions about the necessary conditions for a successful construction of a post-authoritarian democratic order: first, how the institutional "transition from authoritarianism" can be secured, and second, how the new institutions can be culturally rooted ("democratic consolidation"). In this context, questions of memory refer to judicial, political science, and sociological questions, as well as issues of democratic theory.

Political scientists distinguish between at least three historical waves of democratization in the twentieth century. During the first wave, from the nineteenth century until after the end of World War One, European monarchies were overthrown or democratically transformed, yet this phase did not draw much attention to the question of how to remember the former regimes, although, as has become apparent in hindsight, biased memories of the war eventually contributed to the failure of the Weimar republic. The second wave of democratization set in after the end of World War Two. First, Germany, Italy, and Japan were defeated and then democratized from outside. Later on, many colonies of the European empires in Africa and Asia achieved independence and aspired to a democratic order. In contrast to the first wave, the second was shot through with questions of how to assess and remember the macro-crimes associated with fascism and national socialism, but also with imperial colonialism from the very beginning. While in Germany this question was first mainly addressed as the problem of elite continuity in public administration and of individual guilt of leading Nazis in the Nuremberg (1946) and the Auschwitz trials (1963-66), in postcolonial societies it rapidly assumed also a cultural dimension, for example by taking issue with the cultural remnants of colonialism such as the official language, arts canons, etc. The third wave of democratization encompassed Latin American, Asian, and Southern European countries (Portugal, Spain, and Greece) whose authoritarian regimes were overthrown in the course of the 1970s. It introduced the problem of a possible contradiction between politically pragmatic and juridical-morally just ways of addressing the past, as all three transitions (and especially the Spanish one) were accompanied by impunity for the perpetrators on the part of the democratic regime (Arenhövel 96-102). While this strategy was legitimate insofar as it aimed at the successful completion of the democratic transition, it also triggered reproaches by the victims of authoritarianism and therefore kept the authoritarian legacy on the agenda (cf. Roht-Arriaza). This problematic dimension has become the defining feature of the latest wave (which some subsume under the third wave), that of state-socialist societies in the 1980s and of the Republic of South Africa in 1994. These transitions are characterized by the dilemma of combining justice in a legal and a moral sense with the necessity of political and social integration of former victims and perpetrators alike (cf. Tucker).

There are several ways in which non-democratic orders can cease to exist, all of which impact upon the challenges to a successful completion of the transition, which is known as "democratic consolidation" and loosely defined as the achievement of acceptance of the new democratic institutions in the political socio-culture, that is, in attitudes and opinions toward political objects. It goes without saying that these ways, which will be discussed below, are ideal types and that most empirical cases represent mixed types.

Defeat from Outside: The case of post-war Germany stands for the classical example of the overthrowing of authoritarianism through international intervention. On the level of institution building, this greatly contributed to a rapid development of democratic institutions through denazification, import of institutions, and international control. On the cultural level, because of the lack of resistance among the population, it has been notoriously problematic for many Germans to identify with the overcoming of the authoritarian regime. This is exemplarily epitomized by the repeated debates in Germany about whether May 1945 symbolizes a liberation or a defeat. *Revolution and Resistance from Within*: Many cases of the third and the fourth waves of democratization represent the second type of transition from authoritarianism, whereby it is political groups and/or broad strata of the population that rise against the authoritarian order. Here there is a chance that the end of authoritarianism becomes part of the new democracy's foundational narrative. The challenges for a democratic consolidation arise from the dilemma that perpetrators and victims have different interests. If perpetrators or their supporters still hold influential positions in society (as happened after the end of the dictatorships in Chile and Argentina, cf. Arenhövel 81-95; Nino), the post-authoritarian government sees itself exposed to pressure to advocate impunity; if it does so, though, victims or their representatives will reproach the government for continuing the authoritarian legacy. Consequently the new democratic order is in danger of lacking either the support of powerful interest groups or public legitimacy. *Negotiated Change*: Many cases of former state-socialist countries, but also the Republic of South Africa, function as examples for a transition negotiated between representatives of the old regime and the protesters. For instance, in Poland and Hungary "round tables" were implemented in 1988 and 1989 comprising participants from the Communist system and civil society. The most extreme case of a negotiated change, close to a change from above, is the political transition from the Soviet Union to the Russian Federation, where protest movements and civil society activities did not play as much a role as ideological conflicts and power struggles among members of the political elite. Negotiated transitions have the advantage that many issues between old and new orders may be solved or at least postponed into the future, thus enabling a smooth transition and a comparably high general support for the new order in the initial stage. At the same time, though, compromises can be reached only at the expense of those groups most victimized by the authoritarian regime, the consequence being that their expectable protests against the negotiations' outcomes will be rendered in public as dysfunctional for democratic consolidation. After the U.S.S.R. had vanished, in Russia many protagonists of the radical anti-system movement of the late 1980s (the society "Memorial," for example) were reproached for holding maximalist positions, which led to a decrease in public attention and the organization's aims to advocate the cause of the victims of mass repressions and to keep their memory alive.

The international contexts of transitions to democracy play a role as regulatory framework, whose presence or absence can be decisive in regard to the success of the transition, and as cultural frame of reference. International impact has led to the demise of many authoritarian regimes in the twentieth century, such as the fascist regimes in Europe and that of Japan. Later, international pressure—by individual state actors, by international organizations such as the United Nations, or by supranational units like the European Community and later the European Union—was decisive in initiating transitions, most notably in South Africa, in some of the new states in the territory of former Yugoslavia, and in the thus far failed transitions to democracy in Afghanistan and Iraq. Furthermore it can be hypothesized that certain institutional strategies to come to terms with a criminal past—in particular, Truth and Reconciliation Commissions (cf. 2)—are being internationally diffused as best-practice models and thus becoming part of a global institutional environment for coping with mass atrocities.

The international and transnational context is also important in its quality as a frame of reference for memory practices. Since the 1990s some notable developments pointing to an internationalization of memory have taken place. First, as Levy and Sznaider have argued, the Holocaust has by now acquired a global meaning as a point of reference symbolizing that which people all over the world should avoid permitting under any circumstances. The international and especially the European dimension of Holocaust memory crystallized, for instance, in the 2002 "Stockholm International Forum on the Holocaust," which convened state representatives and government officials from more than forty countries, who passed a joint declaration condemning the massive atrocities and apologizing for the part that their nations played in bringing them about. Second, in Europe (including Russia) there are attempts to frame the memory of World War Two not only as part of national history but also of a common European history. This became evident on the occasion of the sixtieth anniversary commemorations of D-Day and May 9 in 2004 and 2005, which were conducted with the participation of many European state leaders and the Russian president. However, the European context of commemoration also creates new political schisms or deepens existing ones which have their roots also in history. This is clearly demonstrated by the boycott of the Victory Day celebrations in Moscow on May 9, 2005 by the presidents of the Baltic republics, who rejected the interpretation of Russia/the U.S.S.R. as the liberator of Europe.

2. Transitional Justice: Reckoning with a Macro-Criminal Past

As transition to democracy involves also the return to the legal state, in post-authoritarian contexts the question inevitably arises of how to deal with the macro-crimes in a legal perspective. The Nuremberg trials were a milestone in this regard, because they created the option of establishing an international legal court grounded on moral and/or ethical notions like "human rights violations," "crimes against humanity," or "war crimes." These legal bodies avoid the difficulty of applying national law retroactively and thus violating the legal maxim *nulla poena sine lege*, but are themselves faced with the problem of being recognized as legitimate which, as the International Criminal Court shows, is not the case among all nations.

What can be *gained* from transitional justice is the clear identification of victims and perpetrators, the validity of which is emphasized by legal sanctions (punishments, compensations, etc.). Furthermore, if the criteria of formality and political independence are met and broadly acknowledged, transitional justice stands in for an unbiased coping with the past. Legal courts thus can contribute to making the reckoning with the past more transparent and to equipping it with legitimacy gained from processual rationality. The main *limit* to juridical approaches to coming to terms with a macro-criminal past is that those crimes, taking into consideration the conditions of their emergence, do not resemble individual crimes on a mass scale but collective crimes. That is, they would not have taken place without the implicit support, and thus co-responsibility, of a large part of the population ("bystanders"). In addition, considerable parts of the population may have been systematically profiting from the crimes against other groups, an example being the white English-speaking citizens of the Republic of South Africa who, as a rule, did not directly participate in the subjugation of the Black majority but profited from it.

Nazi Germany is the paradigmatic example for the structure of macro-crimes, as the mass murder of the European Jews would not have occurred without the passivity, silent and not-so-silent affirmation, and profiteering of broad strata of the German population. Vice versa, individual responsibility may be hard to fix in the case of collective macro-crimes, as the example of the former Soviet Union shows: Although the Communist Party of the Soviet Union undoubtedly was a part of the system of mass repressions, the degree to which a given individual can be held responsible for the consequences of his/her actions cannot easily be established. Both these features of macro-crimes in authoritarian contexts put obstacles in the path of the juridical coping with the past, because they cast doubt on individual guilt and responsibility as exclusive or even major principles of approaching macro-crimes.

As the legal system operates within the limits set by legislation, it is always possible for the latter to circumscribe the activities of the former. For instance, the general amnesty passed in Spain in 1977 put an end to the persecution of the former regime's representatives as well as of those of the opposition (Arenhövel 96-101). In many Latin American countries amnesties and impunity were part of the negotiated changes. Also, providing compensation for the victims usually requires that a compensation law be passed. Therefore the legitimacy of juridical solutions for a macro-criminal heritage depends to a high degree on the inclination of political representatives to engage in such solutions.

The degree to which individual countries differ with respect to employing juridical means for approaching authoritarian macro-crimes can be illustrated with the following examples (cf. Elster). The focus on a persecution of perpetrators has led, for instance, to a thorough "lustration" of former members of the Communist Party in the Czech Republic, while in Poland the negotiated character of the transition shifted the focus to a so-called policy of the "thick line" (Arenhövel 102-04). The rehabilitation and compensation of victims can also be quite variegated. While rehabilitation can in principle be passed by law without examining each individual case (as happened in Russia in regard to lawsuits which had violated already Soviet law), compensation usually requires a time-consuming process in which the individual has to prove that he/she has been impaired, with the danger of becoming victimized a second time. Thus, while juridical responses to authoritarian heritages are an indispensable part of any transition to democracy, they cause their own problems and are in no way sufficient for the establishment of a stable democratic order.

These problems have triggered responses: Since the 1970s there have been numerous attempts to set up Truth and Reconciliation Commissions (TRCs). The term came from the Republic of South Africa's TRC, but has been extended to comparable ones in, for instance, Argentina, Chile, Paraguay, Peru, and Sierra Leone (cf. Kritz). These commissions have been conceptualized as an answer to challenges in post-authoritarian societies which cannot be coped with by means of justice alone. This concerns in particular the contradiction between the political imperative to integrate a society in transition—victims, perpetrators, bystanders, and profiteers—and the ethical, social, and juridical imperatives to do justice to victims and to indict perpetrators.

The example of the South African Truth and Reconciliation Commission, headed by Bishop Desmond Tutu, highlights features and consequences of those institutions (cf. Boraine and Levy). The Commission's declared aim was not to persecute perpetrators or compensate victims but to publicly acknowledge the victims' suffering and to establish this as a cornerstone of post-authoritarian national identity. Proceeding from the diagnosis that the South African nation needed a symbolic bond integrating the formerly antagonistic social groups, the potentially disturbing effects of a merely juridical coping with the past was to be absorbed by a public vindication of the suffering of victims and a public apology by the perpetrators. Under the condition that perpetrators publicly listened to the narratives of their victims and accepted their own guilt, they could be exempted from being legally charged. This procedure was supposed to contribute to recasting apartheid's representation in a series of publicly vindicated individual stories of suffering and institutionalized practices of repenting, thus promoting national reconciliation. However, the Commission was also criticized for pardoning perpetrators and not contributing to changing the social and political inequalities that had constituted apartheid. Thus, although TRCs are set up as a response to the juridical system's incapacity to resolve the social and moral tensions inherited from the authoritarian political order, they may threaten to annul the merits of a juridical ascription of individual responsibilities for macro-crimes.

3. Collective Memory and Post-Authoritarian Democratic Consolidation

The representation of macro-crimes impacts not just upon the transition from authoritarianism but also upon the consolidation of a democratic political culture. In 1946 the German philosopher Karl Jaspers published a small booklet on "The Question of Guilt" (*Die Schuldfrage*) with a view to the German macro-crimes committed during national socialism. He differentiated between four categories of guilt, which still serve as a guideline to link juridical attempts to come to terms with the past with collective and societal ways of dealing with it. According to Jaspers, individual guilt can be juridically coped with and is thus termed "criminal guilt." By contrast, "political guilt" refers to crimes committed in the name or on behalf of one's political collectivity (nation, for example), in which case a responsibility for the consequences of the crimes may be expected of all members of the collectivity in question. "Moral guilt" is a commitment toward "anybody with a human face" that befalls people in reaction to macro-crimes, and can best be analogized with the concept of shame. Finally, "metaphysical guilt" describes a relationship toward instances transcending the worldly orders (for instance, God).

This differentiation between different types of guilt highlights the different levels at stake in analyzing the impact of macro-crimes on post-authoritarian political culture. The concept of "political guilt," for instance, identifies as the flip side of social and political integration in modern "imagined communities" (Benedict Anderson) the responsibility for crimes done on behalf of the collectivity one is ascribed to. Claiming political membership in an imagined community, thus, is coincidental with agreeing to be held politically responsible for atrocities committed in the name of it. "Moral guilt," in turn, might be described as a possible motivation to work against mass atrocities wherever in the world they happen so that "the traumatic contemplation of absolute horror and absolute disregard of the fundamental norms of civilization can engender an ethics transcending the boundaries of a single nation" (Dubiel 218-19).

In the initial stage of transition, negotiations between representatives of the old and of the new regime may be instrumental in stabilizing the first years of the new democratic order. Thus it has been argued that the silence about the Nazi past in West Germany of the 1950s and 1960s helped root the young democratic order in the political socio-culture because it kept disintegrative tendencies from the agenda. However, once the democratic institutions have acquired a certain acceptance in society, silence about the past crimes may become dysfunctional and/or result in social conflicts over interpretations (Bergmann). This was the case in the

1960s in West Germany when young educated people accused their parents of remaining silent about Germany's Nazi past (Schwan). Similar processes are currently happening in Spain, where in the 1970s the decision was made to pardon state perpetrators and those members of the opposition who were involved in crimes. The swing from silence to public acknowledgement may strengthen a democracy's political culture instead of undermining the legitimacy of its institutions.

A peculiar obstacle to the emergence of democratic consolidation may be the memory of a glorious past, if it cannot be calibrated with that of a scornful past. This is the peculiarity, for instance, of post-Soviet public memory in Russia, where representations of the victory over Nazi Germany and fascist Europe tend to go along with rigid denials of the atrocities associated with Stalinism, while conversely those insisting on the memory of the GULag automatically expose themselves to the reproach of "betraying" the national memory (cf. Langenohl).

4. The Memory of Macro-Crimes in Late-Modern Democratic Societies

Since the 1990s, the issue of how to remember macro-criminal pasts has had an impact on democratic theory and theories of societal integration, the reason being that the problem of remembering collective crimes and atrocities probes some taken-for-granted assumptions about how democratic societies are held together on the symbolic level. During this period, instances of public apologies by statesmen and other political representatives of democratic countries have rapidly increased. Apart from Germany, this has involved representatives of European countries that had witnessed some form of collaboration with Nazi Germany, and also the president of the United States, who apologized for the atrocities associated with slavery. Along with these public apologies, there are ongoing discussions about how to represent such a past, be it in museums, in school and education, in historiography, or in public space. Apologizing, which on the level of human interactions can be regarded a basic mode of continuing a relationship that has been put under stress through reaffirming and renegotiating responsibilities and agency, seems to slowly be establishing itself as a way of symbolic governance on national and international levels.

This observation bears varying interpretations. First, in terms of history it indicates that most of today's democratic societies are built upon some sort of massive atrocity. This holds, of course, first of all for Germany, whose democratic order was imposed from outside and whose constitution (*Grundgesetz*) is a direct response to the macro-crimes committed against Jews, homosexuals, or Sinti and Roma. Still, it is also true, if to a lesser degree, for other countries whose history is bound up with that of Nazi Germany or features other macro-crimes, as in the formerly state-socialist or in some Latin American societies.

Second, in terms of memory the above observation illustrates that there are no unchallenged representations of the collective (especially the national) past anymore. Each particular representation of the past can be taken issue with on the grounds that it excludes certain groups. Thereby it is especially the accusation of remaining silent about the atrocities done to certain groups that can have a scandalizing effect and shatter hegemonic memory narratives. Therefore, public apologies can also be seen as reactions to the pluralization of memories and the increasing challenges that all-encompassing foundational narratives about history face.

Third, as the pluralization of modern societies does not leave much room for the articulation of a foundational narrative, recent developments in democratic theory hold that the memory of past macro-crimes done on behalf of one's own political collectivity might serve as a last resort for the symbolic-political integration of highly differentiated and increasingly transnational societies (Arenhövel 134). According to this approach, it is increasingly difficult to gain integrative impulses from a glorious past as such representations are very likely to be publicly challenged. By contrast, the representation of an ambiguous or even outspokenly criminal past may turn out to be functional for symbolic integration at the societal level, because it opens up the possibility of a negativistic mode of collective identification—late-modern political collectivities might find it easier to establish what they do not want to do to each other and to articulate "avoidance imperatives" (Dubiel 220; cf. also Booth) than to say what they essentially are.

Fourth, and more pessimistically, recent studies have turned toward the notion of "cultural trauma" (Alexander et al.; Giesen) in order to describe the *longue durée* effects of mass atrocities on social cohesion and democratic stability (see also Kansteiner and Weilnböck, this volume). According to these accounts, groups that have been massively victimized are subject to cultural trauma, as are those whose members who have committed macro-crimes: the former because the mechanism of intergenerational handing-down of traditions and value orientations has suffered a severe rupture, the latter because representations of their history shuttle between a massive distancing from the macro-criminal past and a notorious denial of it. Democratic theory will have to concentrate on empirical instances of remembrances of past macro-crimes in order to pinpoint the relationship between those memories' potential to increase the awareness for fundamental human rights violations on a global level and their power to keep victims and perpetrators of macro-crimes encapsulated in their national histories.

References

Alexander, Jeffrey, et al. *Cultural Trauma and Collective Identity*. Berkeley: U of California P, 2004.

Arenhövel, Mark. *Demokratie und Erinnerung: Der Blick zurück auf Diktatur und Menschenrechtsverbrechen*. Frankfurt am Main: Campus, 2000.

Bergmann, Werner. "Kommunikationslatenz und Vergangenheitsbewältigung." *Vergangenheitsbewältigung am Ende des 20. Jahrhunderts*. Eds. Helmut König, Michael Kohlstruck and Andreas Wöll. Opladen: Westdeutscher Verlag, 1998. 393-408.

Booth, W. James. "Communities of Memory: On Identity, Memory, and Debt." *American Political Science Review* 93.2 (1999): 249-63.

Boraine, Alex, and Janet Levy, eds. *The Healing of a Nation?* Cape Town: Justice in Transition, 1995.

Dubiel, Helmut. "Mirror-Writing of a Good Life?" *The Lesser Evil: Moral Approaches to Genocide Practices*. Eds. Helmut Dubiel and Gabriel Motzkin. London: Routledge, 2004. 211-21.

Elster, Jon. "Coming to Terms with the Past: A Framework for the Study of Justice in the Transition to Democracy." *Archives europeénnes sociologiques* 39.1 (1998): 7-48.

Giesen, Bernhard. *Triumph and Trauma*. Boulder: Paradigm, 2004.

Kritz, Neil J., ed. *Transitional Justice: How Emerging Democracies Reckon with Former Regimes*. 3 vols. Washington: U. S. Institute of Peace Press, 1995.

Langenohl, Andreas. "Political Culture in Contemporary Russia: Trapped between Glory and Guilt." *The Transition: Evaluating the Postcommunist Experience*. Ed. David W. Lovell. Aldershot: Ashgate, 2002. 96-112.

Levy, Daniel, and Natan Sznaider. *Holocaust and Memory in the Global Age*. Philadelphia: Temple UP, 2005.

Nino, Santiago. *Radical Evil on Trial*. New Haven: Yale UP, 1996.

Roht-Arriaza, Naomi, ed. *Impunity and Human Rights in International Law and Practice*. New York: Oxford UP, 1995.

Schwan, Gesine. *Politik und Schuld: Die zerstörerische Macht des Schweigens*. Frankfurt am Main: Fischer, 1997.

Tucker, Aviezer. "Paranoids May Be Persecuted: Post-Totalitarian Retroactive Justice." *Archives europeènnes sociologiques* 40.1 (1999): 56-100.

Memory and Politics

ERIK MEYER

Political science mainly focuses on aspects of memory culture insofar as it understands itself as a discipline contributing to the foundation of democratic conditions. According to this agenda and considering the success of parliamentarian democracy as a form of government on a global scale, this approach does not deal with the normality of political systems. It rather concentrates on the special case of regime change, which generally causes a confrontation with the previous regime: Wherever an abrupt transformation from pre-democratic, autocratic, or dictatorial regimes to democratic governance takes place, there is the necessity to come to terms with the past. The notion of *Vergangenheitsbewältigung*, currently used to name this process in the German discussion, is nevertheless controversial. In the course of the debate, the connection established between this term and the historical context has been transformed. Formerly only meant to signify Germany's ethical dealing with the Nazi past, *Vergangenheitsbewältigung* has turned into a generic term, referring to the abolition of dictatorship and its replacement with democratic institutions. It refers to those activities that societies and states which are committed to the principles of democracy and human rights unfold when they grapple with the crimes and the dictatorial past of the predecessor regime (König, Kohlstruck, and Wöll). Questions of guilt and responsibility are not only treated in their political and penal-juridical dimension, but also discussed in their moral and meta-physical facet. Whereas studies in democratic theory address these dimensions in their entirety, empirical investigations tend to examine institutional measures of the perpetrator-victim relationship taken by the executive, the legislative, and the judiciary.

1. Transitional Justice and Political Culture

At the international level, the subject is discussed under the term "transitional justice" and explored in historical comparative perspective (Barahona de Brito, Gonzaléz-Enriquez, and Aguilar; Elster; Kritz; see also Langenohl, this volume). Various measures concerning specific groups of persons—be they penal sanction, disqualification, or rehabilitation as well as material compensation—are tied to the temporal proximity to the fallen regime: They only make sense if they take place during the lifetime of victims and perpetrators. This dimension in a broader sense affects the relationship to other states or citizens insofar as they have suffered injustice. Thus, aspects of transitional justice may become matters of foreign policy and diplomacy. All in all, this point of view underlines the necessity of confronting the past as a precondition for functioning political systems and their ability to act in international relations.

Meanwhile, *Vergangenheitsbewältigung* is not limited to the implementation of the measures outlined so far: The concept contains the totality of actions and knowledge new democratic systems make use of with regard to the antecedent state. Sanctioning past behavior not only has a material impact, it also has symbolic significance: A standard is set, allowing an evaluation of the previous regime. Thus, its legitimacy and acceptance depends on public communication. The study of the past and the information about practices, mechanisms, and modes become elements of a discourse through which post-dictatorial societies account for their grasp of history. This process of coming to terms with history on a cognitive level includes activities, both of a developing civil society and of the political-administrative system, which impact the political public sphere, scholarly research, political education, cultural representation by means of artistic artifacts, as well as institutionalized commemoration through monuments, museums, and memorial days. The methods and the extent of coming to terms with the past can be seen as a sign of the condition of a country's political culture. The concept of political culture touches upon the issue of how members of society situate themselves with respect to the political system. Conventional political culture research defines this dimension as follows: "The political culture of a nation is the particular distribution of patterns of orientation toward political objects among the members of a nation" (Almond and Verba 14f.). From that perspective, the starting point is the assumption that the establishment of stable democratic institutions is congruent with specific individual orientations. Thus both political culture research and studies on transitional justice have an interest in transforming systems; however, they differ in that the former focuses on the continuity of attitudes and values, whereas the latter centers on aspects of political-institutional change. In this context, one can criticize the orientation on the Anglo-Saxon model of civic culture as well as the empirical evaluation of relevant attitudes by means of survey research. As a result of the research discussion, the understanding of political culture has been broadened to the extent that political culture is not only considered as a fixed scheme, but also as practice and process. Consequently, not only internalized attitudes can figure as appropriate indicators. This function is also fulfilled by externalized ideas, thus the expressional side of culture. One factor of this approach is the political-cultural dimension of *Vergangenheitsbewältigung*.

For instance, Thomas Herz and Michael Schwab-Trapp sketch a theory of political culture by means of conflicts about National Socialism in Germany. They understand controversies on the subject as conflicts of interpretation which have to be reconstructed through the use of discourse analysis. At the center of this concept is a model of political narratives, formulating the relation between a society and its history. Starting from concrete occasions, competing interpretations of the past are publicly negotiated and discussed in regard to their legitimate validity. These "conflicts unveil the fundamental components of societies [and] allow us to perceive structures of power as well as interests, norms, and values on which a society is based" (Herz and Schwab-Trapp 11). In contrast to conventional political culture research, this approach is based on a conflict-oriented perception of culture focusing on the process of negotiating shared meanings.

2. Policy for the Past and Politics of History

Particularly in the context of German historiography, one can confirm a systematic application of the notions of *Vergangenheitspolitik* ("policy for the past") and *Geschichtspolitik* ("politics of history"). Norbert Frei uses the term "policy for the past" to denote a concrete historical phenomenon, namely a political process spanning approximately half a decade. Its results are, on the one hand, regulations and measures of impunity for perpetrators and fellow travelers of the Nazi regime, aiming to reintegrate those suspected, indicted, and in many cases convicted. On the other hand, efforts were simultaneously made to create a distance, both politically and judicially, from ideological remainders of National Socialism. What is defined as "policy for the past" is constituted by three different elements: amnesty, integration, and demarcation. Whereas Frei conceptualizes "policy for the past" as a closed period of the political-judicial dimension of *Vergangenheitsbewältigung* with regard to the "Third Reich," the term is meanwhile also used in a more general form, abstracting from the concrete reference to German history. Despite this generalization, *Vergangenheitspolitik* is still dependent on the presence of involved individuals. Among the conditions mentioned, it is also possible to grasp "policy for the past" in a comparative perspective as a generic term for temporary policies by which post-dictatorial states primarily, through legal regulations, deal with problems resulting from regime change.

In contrast, the research subject *Geschichtspolitik* ("politics of history"), sketched by Edgar Wolfrum, who uses the history of the Federal Republic until 1990 as an example, is considerably wider: "While 'policy for the past' […] refers primarily to practical-political measures, which are subordinated to public-symbolic action, 'politics of history' is characterized by precisely the opposite relationship" (32). Furthermore, *Geschichtspolitik* is neither specified by coming to terms with the effects of dictatorship, nor does it depend on temporal proximity to the referring subject. Instead, it generally deals with the history of a community, whose interpretation and significance is, as assumed, always disputed. The fact that relevant interpretive controversies are politically charged results from the orientation function ascribed to history. Conflicts within the field of "politics of history" deal less with the facticity of historical reconstructions and the appropriateness of resulting interpretations than one might assume for discussion within the academic community. The interest lies instead in the meaningful connection between past, present, and future, which is often coupled with a reference of action. In this perspective, the question is not if the image of history communicated is scientifically truthful. Instead, the crucial factor is how and by whom, as well as through which means, with which intention, and which effect past experiences are brought up and become politically relevant.

By defining "politics of history" as a political domain—where different actors not only seek to provide history with their specific interests, but also use it for their political benefit—Wolfrum follows the pejorative use of the term: It often serves to mark a political-instrumental way of dealing with history and historiography which aims to influence contemporary debates. In this perspective, "politics of history" is a matter of public political communication, primarily taking place in the mass media (see also Zierold, this volume). This process reveals forces and counter-forces competing for hegemony of discourse and interpretive patterns. Thus, the approach assumes the existence of a pluralistic public, functioning as an arena for these controversies. Not only representatives of the political-administrative system are involved therein, but also individuals and groups who possess a privileged access to the political public sphere. In addition to politicians, this elite includes journalists, intellectuals, and scholars.

Wolfrum also distinguishes another dimension of the intentional instrumentalization of history and its short-term effects in political controversies of pluralistic democracies, namely the indirect consequences of publicly deliberated interpretation clashes: "Conflicts within the field of politics of history can be considered as expression of affirmation and renewal of specific value patterns, behaviour patterns as well as belief systems, which—observed in long-term perspective—frame and change political culture" (29). Hence, "politics of history" not only serves the purpose of legitimating contemporary political projects, but—in a conflicting theoretical perspective—also contributes to the negotiation and clarification of normative orientations which should be applied in society. In this context, it again becomes obvious that Wolfrum conceptualizes "politics of history" in opposition to "policy for the past" primarily as discursive practice.

Other conceptions of "policy for the past" and "politics of history" largely correspond with the understanding described above. After the so-called *Historikerstreit* ("historians' controversy") in the 1980s, the notion of "politics of history" was used to criticize the politicized perception of history by historians and politicians. With the end of the GDR dictatorship, the focus of interest has shifted towards the role of "politics of history" during the Cold War. Peter Reichel sums up with reference to the GDR: "Politics of history was [...] a convenient resource in the German conflict of systems and at the same time politically significant symbolic capital" (37). As a result, a semantic generalization can certainly be perceived, but "politics of history" as an empirical observable phenomenon still remains under ideological suspicion. This doubt does not refer to concrete political actors or systems any longer. Instead, it assumes a general instrumentalization of history by politics. In the context of cultural memory studies, this heuristic seems to be problematic: Following Maurice Halbwachs's concept of collective memory as social construction, remembrance of the past is impossible without current interests.

Nevertheless, according to concrete conflicts regarding the contemporary significance of National Socialism, the term is conceived of instead as an analytical category which can be generalized. Subsequently, Reichel understands sites of memory as a field of political activity: "Creation of monuments and ceremonial remembrance rituals as well as destruction and transformation of monuments and memorial sites thus are an important sector of symbolic politics and the pluralistic culture of memory thus constituted" (33). Insofar he recurs to the differentiation between appearance and reality, which is implicit in the concept of symbolic politics. "Politics of history," then, does not refer to the creation of collectively binding decisions, but targets a similarly significant political construction of reality. In this viewpoint, "politics of history" is close to symbolic forms such as "rituals" and "political myths," even though both are under suspicion in political science as being intentionally created (Edelman). This judgment corresponds with the assumption that symbolic politics does not constitute a communicative frame for political action, but on the contrary is a deficient mode of reality. The focus of constructing reality through "politics of history" is the dimension of legitimacy. This could be the legitimacy of collective identity, the legitimacy of a new order, or the legitimacy of political actors in a pluralistic society. As to the addressees, the belief in legitimacy can be evoked by negative differentiation from, or by positive reference to, a historic point of reference. Therefore "politics of history" and "policy for the past" can be located within the context of the theory of cultural hegemony formulated by Gramsci.

With regard to the specific case of coming to terms with the past (*Vergangenheitsbewältigung*), it is possible to identify "policy for the past" as well as "politics of history" as historical phases whose sequence Helmut König describes concisely with the phrase "from decision to communication." Quoting the example of Germany, it is therefore stated: "In the meantime, the emphasis has shifted from material policy, which is related to decision-making and resources, to discursive and symbolic dimensions of dealing with National Socialism" (König, Kohlstruck, and Wöll 11f.). And König specifies: "If collectively binding decisions with reference to politics for the past are made today and generate public interest, they try in most cases to regulate the political communication about the past" (458). To summarize, "politics of history" can be characterized as a specific type of political communication and symbolic politics and actually appears as "politics without policy." "That is to say, public debates do not refer to actions, nor do they announce actions or decisions, but in fact already constitute actions themselves" (König 463).

3. A Policy Studies Perspective on Cultures of Memory

From a cultural memory perspective, this diagnosis, however, can be thwarted: For instance, Jan Assmann distinguishes between communicative and cultural memory as—related to the event to remember—two successive "modi memorandi" (see J. Assmann, this volume). Insofar as communicative memory is shaped by the biographical horizon of the experiencing generation, Assmann presumes an epochal threshold, which is characterized by the fact that, due to the death of contemporary witnesses, vital remembrance can only be perpetuated if it is transferred into institutionalized forms. One can assume that, especially in pluralistic societies with diverging group memories, constructing tradition does not proceed without conflict. Instead, the transformation from communicative into cultural memory evokes an increased need for political decision-making.

Even though Kohlstruck, for example, conceptualizes "politics of memory" (*Erinnerungspolitik*) primarily as a communicative act, he also claims: "Without consideration of political responsibilities and decisions, institutions, and resources [...], politics of memory cannot be sufficiently investigated" (188). The contradiction between this postulate and the continuously differing concepts can be solved if one understands cultures of memory as a conventional political domain. We (Leggewie and Meyer) therefore suggest, complementary to existing conceptions of "politics of memory," a policy studies perspective. Although the scope of the subject in the pertinent literature is consistently qualified as a political field of activity, studies concentrate on the interpretation of public communication. "Politics of history," in this perspective, takes place when actors articulate interpretations of the history of a community in the political public sphere, competing for cultural hegemony. The theoretical and empirical studies in fact also broach the impact of politics on cultures of memory. But because of their concentration on the communicative dimensions of political acting, they primarily establish a vague connection: The hegemonic interpretive patterns materialize themselves in the sphere of public and official commemoration.

In slightly drastic terms, the epistemological interest of most approaches does not apply to memory culture itself: Assuming that the political character of cultures of memory in the end serves the purpose of legitimacy building, the identification of the actors' intrinsic interests is spotlighted. This central hypothesis shall not be contested. But it has to be argued that deficits result from this approach, specifically concerning the description of relevant political processes and their outcome. A change in perspective may generate insights in structuring the scope of the subject through policy-making requirements. To understand the concrete constitution of monuments, museums, or memorial sites one has to consider administrative aspects such as financial and legal preconditions as well as the interest of political systems to resolve conflicts. Therefore, we propose treating cultures of memory like other political domains and analyzing the public policy of memory.

References

Almond, Gabriel A., and Sidney Verba. *The Civic Culture: Political Attitudes and Democracy in Five Nations.* Princeton: Princeton UP, 1963.

Assmann, Jan. *Das kulturelle Gedächtnis: Schrift, Erinnerung und politische Identität in frühen Hochkulturen.* Munich: Beck, 1992.

Barahona de Brito, Alexandra, Carmen Gonzaléz-Enriquez, and Paloma Aguilar, eds. *The Politics of Memory: Transitional Justice in Democratizing Societies.* Oxford: Oxford UP, 2001.

Edelman, Murray. *The Symbolic Uses of Politics.* Urbana: U of Illinois P, 1964.

Elster, Jon. *Closing the Books: Transitional Justice in Historical Perspective.* Cambridge: Cambridge UP, 2004.

Frei, Norbert. *Adenauer's Germany and the Nazi Past: The Politics of Amnesty and Integration.* Trans. Joel Golb. New York: Columbia UP, 2002. Trans. of *Vergangenheitspolitik: Die Anfänge der Bundesrepublik und die NS-Vergangenheit.* Munich: Beck, 1996.

Herz, Thomas, and Michael Schwab-Trapp, eds. *Umkämpfte Vergangenheit: Diskurse über den Nationalsozialismus seit 1945.* Opladen: Westdeutscher Verlag, 1997.

Kohlstruck, Michael. "Erinnerungspolitik: Kollektive Identität, Neue Ordnung, Diskurshegemonie." *Politikwissenschaft als Kulturwissenschaft: Theorien, Methoden, Problemstellungen.* Ed. Birgit Schwelling. Wiesbaden: VS, 2004. 173-93.

König, Helmut. "Von der Entscheidung zur Kommunikation: Vergangenheitsbewältigung als Demokratieproblem." *Von der Bonner zur Berliner Republik: 10 Jahre Deutsche Einheit.* Eds. Roland Czada and Hellmut Wollmann. *Leviathan Sonderhefte: Zeitschrift für Sozialwissenschaft* 19 (1999): 451-66.

König, Helmut, Michael Kohlstruck, and Andreas Wöll, eds. *Vergangenheitsbewältigung am Ende des zwanzigsten Jahrhunderts. Leviathan Sonderhefte: Zeitschrift für Sozialwissenschaft* 18 (1998).

Kritz, Neil J., ed. *Transitional Justice: How Emerging Democracies Reckon with Former Regimes.* 3 vols. Washington: U. S. Institute of Peace Press, 1995.

Leggewie, Claus, and Erik Meyer. *"Ein Ort, an den man gerne geht": Das Holocaust-Mahnmal und die deutsche Geschichtspolitik nach 1989.* Munich: Hanser, 2005.

Reichel, Peter. *Politik mit der Erinnerung: Gedächtnisorte im Streit um die nationalsozialistische Vergangenheit.* Munich: Hanser, 1995.

Wolfrum, Edgar. *Geschichtspolitik in der Bundesrepublik Deutschland: Der Weg zur bundesrepublikanischen Erinnerung 1948-1990.* Darmstadt: Wissenschaftliche Buchgesellschaft, 1999.

Social Forgetting: A Systems-Theory Approach

ELENA ESPOSITO

1.

The topic of forgetting has always accompanied, like a kind of shadow, the theories and techniques of memory, and, like a shadow, it highlights the latter's dark sides and dilemmas. As far back as antiquity there was actually a widespread awareness that in order to remember it is necessary first of all to be able to forget—to forget the countless singular and irrelevant aspects of objects and events, but also the excess of accumulated memories, in order to free mnemonic capacity, and to permit the construction of new memories. Already Themistocles replied to those who offered him the wonders of mnemotechnics that he was instead interested in lethotechnics, an art that would allow him to learn and practice forgetting. And actually the various versions of the *ars memoriae* also implied some form of *ars oblivionalis*—albeit associated with a certain discontent and with inevitable practical difficulties. The topic has had a constant echo in the reflections about memory, as testified in more recent times by Nietzsche's well-known argument on the advantages and disadvantages of history (1874), which can be read as an apologia for forgetting, which is necessary especially to enable action and prevent being bound by the ties of the past.

The problem is that forgetting is a difficult and thorny matter: One can remember and remember to remember, and one can also develop techniques to help one remember, but a technique to forget becomes immediately paradoxical (Eco). It would be the same as a procedure to remember to forget, and thus a technique that denies itself. And actually the procedures proposed over the centuries to aid forgetting have always followed latently paradoxical paths—resorting usually not to the cancellation but rather to the accumulation of memories, intended to produce indirectly their neutralization. A classical tool is writing, accused since Plato, in the famous passage of the *Phaedrus* (275f.), of being a means to foster forgetting rather than remembering. Even the "memorist" studied by Luria still revealed that he put in writing what he wanted to forget, as if to free the mind from irrelevant or troublesome memories.

The difficulty of forgetting, if one considers the matter carefully, is always connected to a form of reflexivity: The one who intends to forget cannot avoid confronting himself and his own procedures of memory construction, while in the case of remembering one can persist in the illusion of only recording external data (in however inevitably defective and selective a manner). In remembering, one faces the world; in forgetting one faces oneself—a circumstance that will always create problems for all approaches that believe the two references to be independent.

2.

This is not the case with systems theory, which starts precisely from the assumption of "autology," the relativity of the world to the system observing it, which finds itself in its own field of observation. In other words, an autologic system faces a world that also includes the observing system itself, which gives up the privileged position of the external observer looking at the world from the outside (Luhmann, *Gesellschaft* 16ff.). In all of its objects, therefore, such a system finds itself and its own intervention again, and it comes as no surprise that from this reflexive point of view forgetting becomes a privileged theme, much more congenial and informative than simple non-reflexive remembering. Luhmann declares this explicitly, maintaining that the main function of memory lies in forgetting, which prevents the system from blocking itself with the accumulation of the results of former operations, and frees processing capabilities that can be open to new stimuli and new irritations. The system usually forgets, and only in exceptional cases is this forgetting inhibited in order to build up identities that remain relatively stable despite the progression of operations: These are the memories used to direct the system and to avoid always having to start everything afresh (Luhmann, *Gesellschaft* 579).

Strictly speaking, moreover, remembering and forgetting always proceed together. Without a connection of operations that allows the capture of identities and repetitions, there would not be anything to forget, but without the ability to neglect most of the details and all the particulars that deviate from the remembered identity—that is, without the ability to forget—the faculty to remember would soon be overloaded. There must be something that can be remembered, but one must forget almost everything. Remembering and forgetting get stronger or weaker at the same time: As we will see later (in section 6), memory grows when the ability to remember and the ability to forget increase contemporarily. The task of memory lies in balancing remembering and forgetting, in finding an equilibrium that allows the operations of the system to continue in a non-arbitrary way. The priority of forgetting derives from the fact that this process has to remain unnoticed: It could not work if one did not forget the continuous performance of remembering/forgetting. That is why, as we have seen, one cannot remember to forget, while there is no difficulty in remembering memories, nor in trying to remember them better.

3.

It should come as no surprise that this kind of approach does not find many points of contact in the most widespread sociological theories of memory, and in fact, systems theory explicitly distances itself from them. Their model is still the Durkheimian-oriented collective memory, famously proposed by Halbwachs to describe the memory of a group, or more specifically those memories that do not concern the most intimate and personal sphere of an individual, but are shared by all the members of the (more or less broadly defined) group. This, of course, opens up all the matters related to the supports of such shared memories (places, monuments, rituals) and to the relationship of collective and individual memory, which inevitably influence each other.

From the point of view of systems theory, however, it is the very premise of the whole formulation that cannot be accepted. Sociological theory looks for a notion of memory which refers specifically to society, and being a reflexive concept it must refer to the way society approaches itself and its own processes. It must be a social performance, which cannot be referred to external factors—we can know what happened in the past and yet not know the memories of a system that observed these events. Memory must be referred to the specific structures of the remembering system. Collective memory, then, is not social memory, because its seat and its reference are not in society, but indirectly in the consciousnesses (or in the minds) of the individuals taking part in it. We could argue, radicalizing the position of Durkheim himself, that social memory gets stronger as collective memory gets weaker. The collective consciousness of which Durkheim speaks notoriously gets weaker with the progress of social evolution: The strength and the extension of a collective consciousness decrease as society becomes more complex and autonomous, at the same time as the individuals composing it become individualized. The society then becomes more and more independent from the contents of individual consciousnesses, and the collective consciousness decreases and becomes emptier and emptier. The same happens to collective memory: The more complex the society is, the more limited collective memory is, and the increase in complexity tends to separate them more and more clearly—up to the emergence of a social memory based on social operations, aside from (more or less shared) cognitive traces and individual memories. Collective memory is a matter for social psychology; sociology has to look for something else.

4.

The first address for the study of the social organization of memory should be the *ars memoriae*, which belongs to the great apparatus of rhetoric that for many centuries constituted the foundation of social semantics. The techniques of memory, however, have always maintained the cognitive reference: All their precepts, rules, and procedures aim to increase the abilities of the individual mind to register data and notions—in an organized way, with the help of spatial references acting as the rooms and the buildings where memories were placed, and using also the passions and the emotions of the "carriers" by employing grisly, unusual, touching or sexy images. The *ars memoriae* continues to play a role in a form of memorization that uses people's minds as a "transitory depot" (*Zwischenspeicher*), an idea which is quickly discredited when, as a consequence of the printing press, the maintenance of cultural contents is progressively entrusted more and more to this other means of support. For a sociological systems theory looking for a specifically social notion of memory, the whole mnemotechnics is interesting from an historical point of view, but it cannot be the basis for the construction of the theory.

To what, then, must one turn? In this as in other cases, the most useful hints come from cybernetics and observation theory. Heinz von Foerster is still an essential reference for theories with autological foundational claims, because he formulated and described the conditions of a system that observes a world which also includes the observers, meaning that the observer realizes she or he is observed by others and by her- or himself as well (second-order observation). In this circular network of observations, memory has a central role, but obviously it cannot be a memory that passively records the events and accumulates information, because there are no events or information defined once and for all—the world of every system emerges each time from a process of elaboration (or of "computation"). Memory, in this view, does not serve to accumulate fixed memories as a sort of storehouse that would be more efficient the more materials it can include, but serves rather to eliminate the punctual aspects of the events in an ever more refined process of abstraction (Foerster 92ff., 140ff.).

The first task memory performs is actually not to preserve the events, but to select the few aspects that are considered remarkable and that allow the insertion of data and events in an already known category ("chair," "invitation to supper," etc.), forgetting everything else. Memory serves, after all, to create independence from time, that is, from the punctual realization of events, which in the form of memories become available for the system and allow the construction of always new and always different connections. Precisely by eliminating time from the events, memory can allow them to be synchronized—remembering, anticipating, making projections and reconstructions. The presupposition, however, is that it does not operate as a storage system, but rather as a computing device that does not include data but only procedures that generate the data again, and in a different way, each time. Memory does not record the past, which would be of no use and would only be an overload, but reconstructs it every time for a future projected in ever new ways.

It is interesting to note that these positions coincide to a large extent with those of recent neurophysiological research (for instance Edelman), which refuses the idea of memory as a form of replicative filing system and describes it explicitly as a procedural capability realizing a constant re-categorization. Remembrance is the actual activation of processes activated before, which never provide exactly the same answer—one remembers something different each time, and the remembering system is thereby also modified.

5.

These cues are also the starting point for systems theory, which maintains that the task of memory lies in organizing the access to information, engendering to this end an always new and always changing equilibrium of remembering and forgetting: One forgets enough to be able to fix some remembrance, and confronts the actual events with these remembrances, confirming them or modifying them in accordance with the new experiences. One could also say that the system thereby regulates the relationship of redundance and variety, of repetition and novelty, on which also depends its ability to recognize and to accept surprises. Thanks to its memory, the system has a past from which to depart in turning to what is to come—in a more or less open way (Luhmann, *Realität* 179ff.; Luhmann, *Erkenntnis*; Luhmann, *Gesellschaft* 581).

With respect to the other approaches, the difference lies mainly in the fact that one usually starts from the idea of a system facing a given world and remembering more or less faithfully part of the occurring events. The systemic approach, instead, starts from an observer whose world depends on his or her own structures of understanding and elaboration capability, that is, also on its memory: It is not memory that depends on the world, but it is the world of each system that depends on the form and on the capabilities of its memory. Memory operates by carrying out a continuous test of the coherence (*Konsistenzprüfung*) of what happens with the structures of the system, a comparison of data with memory, from which results, on the one hand, the image of reality and, on the other hand, the ability to acquire information. The world of a system, then, is more or less varied and more or less open according to the abilities and structures of its memory.

That is why, as we have seen, memory is a reflexive function, which concerns first of all the relationship of the system with itself, its self-reference: Luhmann says that it is actually a shortened expression for the recursivity of operations ("Zeit und Gedächtnis"). Memory expresses the dependence of all that happens on the elaboration capability of the system, on its structures and therefore in some extent on the past—which conditions the ability to gather and to accommodate surprises, that is, the openness of the future. And that is why forgetting becomes the primary function: It is the ability to select which produces each time the identity of the system as distinct from its environment.

6.

More concretely: Where can this memory be found when dealing with the operations of a social system? On what does the ability of one particular society to remember and to forget depend, and how does it change with socio-cultural evolution? As we have seen, the seat of this memory cannot be the minds of the people, because what we are looking for is a faculty that coincides neither with the cognitive contents of the individual nor with their sums or intersections, but rather a faculty that constitutes the presupposition for the production of cognitive contents.

We know that linguistic forms precede individual thoughts, which are constituted instead on the basis of schemes and generalizations implicit in the language one is exposed to. The words correspond to (more or less abstract) concepts that always operate on the basis of a generalization, leaving aside consideration of the specific characteristics of the object at issue: Each chair is different from every other one, but whoever knows the language identifies it as representative of the category (remembering implicitly every preceding instance). The autonomy from cognitive contents, therefore, is given in any society, including those without writing, which fixes a meaning to objects and "quasi-objects" such as rites, symbols, and myths, which allow for recall in different situations, and for the preservation of the society's identity for long periods of time, even if the participants (the "cognitive substratum") change. With the availability of a means of diffusion (the so-called technologies of communication), however, social memory becomes more and more independent, up to the turn marked by the printing press, at which point even the use of cognitive systems as a "transitory depot" was abandoned. It is to these technologies that the systemic approach refers the forms and the scope of the memory of society: It is to writing, to the printing press and later to the whole apparatus of the mass media that one must refer the social capability to remember and to forget (see Schmidt; Zierold; both this volume).

Alphabetical writing marks a first turning point, entrusting to written texts the recording of the contents of memory. Written communication has to constitute autonomously all the identities it refers to, without the possibility of relying on more or less implicit references taken for granted by the participants in the communication—as happens in oral communication, which can use without ambiguity deictic expressions or other contextual references such as "yesterday," "behind there," "your nephew," and the like. In a written text, in contrast, every reference must be specified independently of the knowledge of each single participant in the communication, yet must be understandable for all of them—that is, independently from the specific cognitive contents.

Writing alone, however, is not sufficient to impose this passage: Since the diffusion of the printing press the prevailing model of communication has remained the oral model, with writing used in a broad sense as a support for verbalization, and memory remains bound to relatively concrete references, such as the spatial order systematized by topic and practiced in rhetoric. It is only with the printing press and the subsequent enormous diffusion of written texts that communication at a distance acquires its autonomy and develops its own forms, based rather on a temporal order and being much more mobile, with references created and recreated each time: Whoever writes for the printing press does not address specific partners, and gives up the control of the situation. One does not know who will read the text, in what context or with what interests, and the text thus exposes itself to the production of meaning guided by entirely unpredictable references (the famous plurality of interpretations, where every reader can make of a text what he or she wants, producing a sense different from that of other readers and possibly also from the sense the author intended).

This means a radical change in the structure of social memory, that is, in the form of the test of coherence, which, as we have seen, is the primary task of memory: The redundance necessary to make communication work is not grounded on the presupposition that people know certain things any more, but simply on the fact that the necessary information is known and available somewhere (in a book, newspaper, or somewhere else) and thereby it is not necessary to communicate it again. Most of us today know very few things by heart, certainly less than in other, less mediatized societies, but we can access a huge range of contents, so much in fact that we often face the well-known phenomenon of information overload. One can speak, then, of many different things that enormously increase the variety of possible forms of communication—starting from the formerly impossible ability to forget a great deal without thereby losing the contents.

One can say, therefore, that the printing press strengthens and at the same time overloads social memory, allowing us to remember and simultaneously to forget much more, and therefore enabling us at the same time to retain more redundance and more variety. In this way, autonomy from the "cognitive substratum" is achieved, which initiates an autonomous evolution of semantics, on the basis of the possibility to criticize and to deviate, to interpret the communication apart from the original intent, to risk implausible forms, seeking novelty and improbability.

7.

The memory of society, regulating redundance and variety, also has the task of offering an image of reality for the corresponding system: This task, namely reality construction for society as a whole, is entrusted today to the system of mass media (Luhmann, *Gesellschaft* 591; Luhmann, *Realität* 121ff.). Memory also has to make available to the system a range of objects and references that can be presupposed in further operations, that is, the reality from which to start and which it addresses. In the case of social systems, which according to this theory are constituted of communication, these objects are the available themes, the topics one can mention and expect one's partners to be informed and able to offer contributions about. Today these themes are offered primarily by the mass media, the source nowadays of most of our data concerning the society and the world—it would be insufficient to confine oneself to the notions acquired directly, through perception or through personal knowledge. Our world is populated by people, places, and lifestyles that we will never see personally, but that are nevertheless no less real or less appropriate as topics of discussion, identification, and comparison.

The memory of our society, therefore, is constituted first of all by the mass media and ruled by their always changing forms, submitted to the iron law of the search for novelty (news). They are, however, also the only forms compatible with a memory really independent from cognitive contents, because they are able to advance and regulate communication without implying any specific identity in the minds of the participants, who remain intransparent (i.e., autonomous): The mass media offer only the themes and not opinions about them. Their construction of reality is construction of a "second reality without obligation of consent" (cf. Luhmann, *Realität*, ch.12), made out of existing or fictitious characters, of stereotypes, of notions that are known without being necessarily understood, a reality that is shared by all exactly because it is not binding. We know only what the others know, not what they think of it—in a construction that uses the identities only as points of departure for the articulation of the diversities and differences of the individual opinions. But we can communicate with almost everyone, without any need to know them or to be in the same place, sharing very little in common, but remembering more or less the same things and forgetting immediately almost everything.

References

Eco, Umberto. "An *Ars Oblivionalis*? Forget it!" *Kos* 30 (1987): 40-53.

Edelman, Gerald M. *The Remembered Past: A Biological Theory of Consciousness*. New York: Basic, 1989.

Esposito, Elena. *Soziales Vergessen: Formen und Medien des Gedächtnisses der Gesellschaft*. Trans. Alessandra Corti. Frankfurt am Main: Suhrkamp, 2002.

Foerster, Heinz von. *Observing Systems*. Seaside, CA: Intersystems, 1981.

Halbwachs, Maurice. *La mémoire collective*. Paris: Presses Universitaires de France, 1950.

Luhmann, Niklas. *Erkenntnis als Konstruktion*. Bern: Benteli, 1988.

—. *Die Gesellschaft der Gesellschaft*. Frankfurt am Main: Suhrkamp, 1997.

—. *Die Realität der Massenmedien*. Opladen: Westdeutscher Verlag, 1995.

—. "Zeit und Gedächtnis." *Soziale Systeme* 2 (1996): 307-30.

Luria, Aleksandr R. *The Mind of a Mnemonist: A Little Book about a Vast Memory*. London: Cape, 1969.

Nietzsche, Friedrich. *Unzeitgemässe Betrachtungen. Zweites Stück: Vom Nutzen und Nachteil der Historie für das Leben*. 1874. *Werke in drei Bänden*. Munich: Hanser, 1999.

Weinrich, Harald. *Gibt es eine Kunst des Vergessens?* Basel: Schwabe, 1996.

—. *Lethe: Kunst und Kritik des Vergessens*. Munich: Beck, 1997.

Memory and Remembrance: A Constructivist Approach

SIEGFRIED J. SCHMIDT

1. Introductory Remarks

For many years already, not only cultural studies scholars but also a broad public have been deeply interested in the subjects of memory and remembrance. The media, especially television, present a great number of historical movies, documentaries, and discussions concerning the last century, with its two world wars and especially with the Holocaust. Many books have examined the topic of how individuals and societies remember historical events. Yet the broad academic interest in these topics suffers from a remarkable lack of a theoretical foundation. Nearly all the crucial concepts, such as "memory," "remembrance," "culture," and "media," are rather vague, and the theoretical approaches are incompatible and in many respects normative and incomplete regarding crucial aspects, such as the role of emotions and of the media. In this article I shall thus try to outline a homogeneous theoretical basis for the scholarly discourse on memory and remembrance which is abstract enough to both provide a basis for an interdisciplinary approach to the topic and also allow for empirical studies.

2. Individual Memory

Traditional memory models have been based on ideas of storage, place, and retrieval. Recent theories in neurobiology and cognition theory prefer process-oriented models instead (see Schmidt, *Gedächtnis*). They argue that the human neuronal apparatus is determined by the connectivity of the neurons which are interconnected in complex networks. Both genome and experience specify the connectivity of the components of the neuronal system. Experiences modify the connectivity through activities which are based both on events in the system's environment as well as on system-internal processes. Complex nervous systems interconnect cortical, sensory, and motor processes, thus paving pathways that can be both stable and changeable in the distribution of excitations and the spreading of events in the system. Such pathways paved by learning processes endure as stabile properties of the brain and stabilize subsequent cortical processes. Irritations beyond such marked pathways are perceived as "new" and are emotionally connotated with uncertainty. Based on these considerations, Humberto R. Maturana has argued that memory cannot be modeled as a storage site which is located at a specific place in the brain, but must instead be seen as the establishing of relevant and enduring cognition structures which serve to constitute order in the brain and synthesize human behavior (62). The relationship of such structures with the past consists in nothing else but in the fact that they have arisen before the respective synthesis of behavior. It follows from these considerations that the function of the brain does not consist in storing past events for a shorter or longer time. Instead, it evaluates the relevance of all cognitive processes on the basis of previous experiences. Its function therefore exceeds by far the storage function, since it is in force in perception, remembrance, attention, cognition, action, and evaluation. Knowledge of presuppositions and schemata operates as the mechanism for creating order. Together with the capacity to discern between what is new and what is well known, the brain thus provides these processes with clarity and safety. (I will not comment on the numerous typologies of different memories developed in recent decades, since most of them are highly speculative.)

Memory conceived of as a function of the brain which is distributed over the whole neuronal system organizes itself on the basis of its own history; consequently it is plausible to say that it does not represent but rather constructs reality. The criteria which regulate these constructive processes can be both innate and acquired in early childhood and shaped by later experiences. Nearly all operations of our memory do not enter our consciousness. The paving of enduring pathways for the spreading of excitations and the synthesis of behavior is intrinsically connected with the normatively imprinted intensity of emotions (see Roth).

3. Remembering

Following the reasoning in these considerations, remembering can be defined as the process of activating memory functions. Gebhard Rusch has advocated the view that remembering resembles perceiving without sensory stimulation (self-stimulation) or recognizing without a perceivable object. If remembering is not modeled in terms of retrieving stored data but instead as a constructive cognitive synthesis of behavior based upon activated neuronal structures, it is easier to observe strategies which lead to an elaboration of remembrances such as completing or contextualization. The application of such strategies diminishes inconsistencies and dissonances in cognitive syntheses of behavior which are influenced by various factors such as context, relation to other people, motives and occasions for remembering and its relevance, and emotional intensity. Accordingly we have to expect a high diversity in the results of remembering processes—remembrances of "the same" are not at all the same remembrances.

Verbal elaborations which follow conscious remembrances necessarily make use of narrative schemata which are culturally determined to a high degree. Since they have been acquired by individuals during their socialization we can assume that they do not organize only the verbalization of remembrances but also already their pre-verbal elaboration. In other words: The order of the narrated event is essentially a function of the narration and not of the order of the event itself, since narrations aim at constructing coherent stories which are accepted by the audience. This construction acquires intersubjective acceptance since both sides are implicitly convinced that (in principle) everybody knows the same patterns and strategies of narration and knows which features of reliability have to be employed to render a narration authentic or true. If this happens the narrator feels a complete correspondence of past and narrated remembrance—that is to say the narrator falls prey to his own art of seduction; he is simply not able to produce a false remembrance.

As is widely known, narrating is closely connected with the construction of identity. Identity can be conceptually differentiated into a cognitive I and a social ego. Consciousness, modeled as an auto- or allo-referentially experienced referring to something as something (see Schmidt, *Geschichten*) can refer to itself, too, in a self-referential manner. Through this operation the cognitive I is constituted in terms of self-consciousness. The social ego, on the other hand, is constituted through the use of the difference between *ego* and *alter*. Therefore, identity cannot be averred as a stabile state. Instead, it results from observed references to oneself in self-observations and self-descriptions (construction of identity for oneself) and self-performances (construction of identity for others). The verbal as well as the non-verbal performance of social identity necessarily relies upon continuity and plausibility for the respective audiences. Variances in the performance must be mutually compatible and have to be accepted or at least tolerated by the audiences. That is to say: Identity is a product of successful *attribution*. Communicative self-descriptions have to orient themselves on socially accepted sense schemata and must make use of narrative schemata which the members of a society ascribe to one another as collective knowledge.

Remembering needs *occasions* and it is selective by necessity. What is remembered and what is forgotten first of all depends upon the subjective management of identity, which in turn is steered by emotions, needs, norms, and aims. Facing this playground of possibilities for the elaboration of remembrances the actor who remembers and narrates must decide on an identity policy (that is, what sort of management of remembering and narrating he will perform) with various degrees of consciousness. (On the role of media for remembrance and narration see section 6.)

Remembering as a *cognitive* process is determined by two traits: (a) Like all conscious processes remembering realizes itself as a process in the here and now (in the present) which is bound to an individual actor; in other words, the past exists only in the domain of (actor-bound) remembrances. (b) Like all other conscious processes, remembering is oriented towards and determined by an irreducible complementarity of cognition, emotion, and moral evaluation. This systemic complexity has to be taken into account as a categorical condition, not as an optional one.

Remembering needs *production* which requires occasions, demands, and gratifications, which in turn are steered by cognitions, emotions, and moral orientations and which are specified in histories and discourses (see Schmidt, *Geschichten*).

Remembering needs *performance*, that is to say, narrations of remembrances, which make use of narrative schemata as modes of socially acceptable production and performance of remembrances, of appropriate verbal instruments such as metaphors and pictures, and of optical symbolizations such as stereotypes or schematizations. We may assume that already the cognitive production of remembrances makes use of such instruments acquired during socialization (see Rusch). It seems evident that it is in the application of socially learned narrative schemata that remembrances become discursively acceptable, and that, in turn, remembrance is thus bound up with its socially expected application.

4. A Necessary Interlude: Actors and Society

In the introductory remarks I announced my intention to provide a homogeneous theoretical basis for the memory discourse. In order to fulfill this promise for the discussion of *social or collective memory*, too, I have to clarify the relationship between individuals/actors and society. For this reason I must introduce two concepts: "world model" and "culture program."

World models (in the sense of models *for* and not models *of* reality) can be characterized as long-term semantic arrangements which orient the cognitions, communications, and interactions of the members of a society. World models, which are based on categories (such as age) and their semantic differentiation (such as old/young), are a result of the successful acting and communicating of the members of a society and are in turn confirmed and approved by their successful acting and communicating. They become socially efficient through their implementation in the individual actor's mind during the socialization process. Socialization gives rise to individual actors' expectations that (in principle) all members of their society have at their disposal more or less the same knowledge as they do, and that the others expect the same; and that all others pursue specific motives and expectable aims in/with their activities. These reflexive structures, expectations in the knowledge domain, and imputations in the domain of motives and intentions serve the purpose of operative fictions which can be called "collective knowledge."

World models systematize knowledge needed for problem solutions in all dimensions which are relevant for the success and the survival of societies. Arguably the most prominent dimensions of world models are the domination of the environment, interaction with other people, acting in institutions, the domination and expression of emotions, and the handling of normative problems.

A world model can only become efficient if its emergence is concomitant with a program for socially reliable references to this model by a majority of society members. This program of socially obligatory semantic instantiations of world models, together with an emotional charge and a normative evaluation of possible references, I call "culture" or "culture program." The culture program couples the autonomous cognitive systems of actors to the communicative system. It provides continuity for problem solutions in the domain of sense and meaning, thus rendering these solutions quasi natural or self-evident—the contingency of all problem solutions is rendered invisible. This social operative fiction of commonly shared collective knowledge serves as a basis for interactions and communication and creates at the same time stability for acting and collective identity.

Societies continuously constitute themselves through an uninterrupted processing of the interaction of world models and culture programs or as the unity of the difference of world models and culture programs, which must be modeled in strict complementarity. This processing is performed by and in actors, be they individual or collective.

5. Social Memory

Whatever we do we do in terms of a positing which requires presuppositions. Positing (*Setzung*) and presuppositions are strictly complementary and constitute one another. The presuppositions of a positing can only be observed in reflexive references to the positing. This basic assumption holds true for cognitive as well as for communicative positings.

The presuppositions claimed by cognitive processes have been modeled as memory (see section 2). The presuppositions claimed for communicative positings in the context of social processes can be modeled as a culture program. That is to say, the collective knowledge which individuals mutually expect as an efficient operative fiction in communication processes orients their cognitive processes with regard to what is remembered or narrated as "the past." Similar to the modeling of memory as a structure of paved ways for the cognitive production of order in the cognitive domain, memory in the social domain can be modeled as a set of efficient knowledge structures which result from successful applications of the culture program and which are invested by the actors as presuppositions for their positings. Normally this does not happen in a conscious manner; routines and doxa are very influential in this domain. Since the culture program is not willing to learn during the act of application (otherwise it would lose its power), but is in fact changeable and dynamic over longer periods, it is reasonable to assume that references to the culture program vary from actor to actor and from time to time.

References to culture programs can only be performed by actors; accordingly, memory can only be located in actors, although no one disposes of the complete system of presuppositions provided by culture programs. That is to say that memory is not located at a specific place or completely incorporated in somebody; instead it actualizes itself through its application by actors: "A social memory can only be modeled as an operative fiction" (Zierold 128; see also Zierold, this volume).

Memory and remembering become social not by the fact that they are located at a place beyond actors, but by the fact that they become co-oriented via reflexive processes of expectations and imputations which give rise to the impression that nearly everybody in society thinks about the past in that and no other way. Therefore, in the domain of collective remembering, too, remembering can be modeled as *performance* which operates on the basis of memory as structure or competence (see Schmidt, *Lernen*).

Like individual remembering, social remembering also needs motives and occasions which are regulated by cultures of remembering; thus it can support the making of social identities over time. In order to systematize such occasions, societies have invented "remembering occasions" of different kinds, such as commemoration days, monuments, special places, or museums. Such remembering occasions which today are mostly provided by the media can only become efficient if actors actually make use of them for the purpose of remembrances—they are not remembrances themselves.

Social identity processes operate upon the basic difference of we/the others. This difference has to be accepted by the members of a society as well as by other societies; only then can it be attributed in a socially reliable way. The construction and maintenance of a social "autobiography" can only proceed in a selective way. For this reason societies as well as individual actors produce their past in terms of an active politics of remembering; that is, they transform their past in a communicative way that serves the purpose of constructing a desirable or at least tolerable self-consciousness (collective management of identity). Palliation, forgetting (in the sense of not remembering for various reasons) and repression (understood as the refusal of remembering) are appropriate instruments for the treatment of archives which—according to specific interests and motives—are used rather selectively, the more so since these archives tend to become larger and larger in media societies.

The politics of remembering, too, is steered by emotions and moral values, and it is intrinsically connected to *power*: Who is entitled to select topics and forms of remembering in the public discourse(s)? Who decides in which way narrations of remembrances rely upon relevant presuppositions in order to shape the past in the present for promising futures?

Narrations of the past are deeply influenced by negation and differences. This becomes evident when we regard the negative concepts (*Gegenbegrifflichkeit*) we use or presuppose in our own discourse, especially when it is a discourse directed against someone. Concepts such as "crime," "guilt," "expiation," "revenge," or "reparation" tell us how this strategy works.

6. Media of Remembrance—The Remembrance of the Media

The important role of media for individual and social remembering processes has already been mentioned above. At issue are "media offers" (*Medienangebote*) which elaborate remembrances as well as media offers which are (or can be) used as triggers for remembering. Media offers can only then become relevant when their subject as well as their mode of thematizing the subject are deemed socially relevant.

Before the relation between media and social remembering can be explained, however, we have to clarify the media concept. As set out on many other occasions, I conceive of the "medium" here as a compact concept which integrates four dimensions and areas of effect: 1. communication instruments (such as language and pictures); 2. technological devices (such as Internet technology on the side of receivers and producers); 3. the social dimensions of such devices (such as publishing houses or television stations); and 4. media offers which result from the coalescence of these components and can only be interpreted in relation to this context of production.

Communication instruments such as language and pictures are distinguished from media because they can be used in all media. It therefore makes sense to use the difference between communication instruments and media in order to observe and describe the differences in the uses of these instruments in the various media. One example here would be the Internet as a hybrid medium.

Both communication instruments and all media since the advent of writing have, on the one hand, expanded our forms of perception and, on the other hand, disciplined them in relation to the various medium-specific conditions of perception and use. This explains why there are literates and illiterates for every medium. For this reason, media (systems) have developed a dual effectiveness: on the one hand a semantic effectiveness by means of the manifest contents of *media offers* and on the other by means of the structural effects of instruments and orders which go considerably beyond the individual media user's capacity for control and recognition, as the Internet demonstrates so vividly.

Media offers are therefore not independent objects but instead results of rather complex production, distribution, and presentation processes following the respective economic, social, and technical conditions of media systems. In other words: Media systems are necessarily conditioned by their own system's logic. This also holds true with regard to what media actors regard as events, persons, data, or objects beyond the media systems. Through media processes, such events, persons, etc. are transformed into *media facts* which result from media-specific references to reasonable and relevant presuppositions of all activities in the respective media system. Accordingly, media systems create and distribute *media* facts. It is worthwhile to keep that in mind in all discussions about media and reality, especially with regard to alleged representations of "the past."

Media systems work as observing and describing systems which do not start from "the reality" but from former descriptions of reality which are then transformed into new description. In this sense the description of reality and the reality of description coincide. By this argument the tedious question of the relation between media and reality can be resolved. Due to their system-specific logic, media cannot represent an extra-medial reality. They can only produce and present media-specific realities—and this equally holds true for the making of a/the past.

The assumption that media provide actors and societies with information and knowledge neglects the constitutive and strictly complementary role of the recipients. Media offers do not simply and immediately transport knowledge, meanings, and values; instead they offer actors well-structured semiotic events which can be used by actors for the production of meaning, knowledge, or evaluation in their respective biographical situation—that is the reason why we know so little about the actual effectiveness of media offers.

Media systems of societies have emerged in the context of concurrent developments of technology, economics, politics, and so on. Their offers are built into recipients' lives following rather unpredictable rules and are deeply influenced by emotions and moral values. In addition, they are modified by reflexive processes: experiences may shape expectations for future media reception, effects change effects, etc. For this reason it becomes very unreasonable to forecast the effectiveness of media or media systems on remembrances and forgetting. Aleida Assmann, for example, who avers that the Internet will entail a complete loss of memory and remembrances, advocates a rather normative concept of remembering and overlooks that the media development has not only produced technical, legal, and economic problems with the storage and use of media offers for remembrance but has also opened up completely new types of archives and possibilities for constituting and using them. (For an explicit and critical commentary on this topic, see Zierold, 155-99). Backward-oriented historians do not realize that there is no (or no longer?) such a thing as "the memory" and "the remembrance" of "the society." Instead, memories and remembrances in the different social functional systems as well as in the different actors have developed, which follow different rules, react on different occasions, and apply different routines and strategies while creating their past in their presence. In addition, post-modern conditions of experiencing and narrating allow for decontextualizing and sampling narrations of remembering which therefore extricate themselves from *specific* normative and emotional claims for the authenticity of such narrations.

7. What About the Promised Coherent Theoretical Basis?

In the introduction I promised to provide the memory discourse with a coherent theoretical basis. Has this promise been realized? In my article I have shown that individual as well as social remembrances can, first, be modeled as *performance* of memory, modeled as structure, or as the ability of the brain to create order. Second, I have shown that they refer to *memo-*

ries qua presuppositions of actual positings. In the cognitive domain the presuppositions were specified as neuronally paved pathways of creating syntheses of behavior; in the social domain, the presuppositions were modeled as culture programs which constitute social identity since it is used by all society members in terms of the operative fiction of collective knowledge. Third, remembrances are shaped by specific *cultural modes and schemata* organizing experiences as well as narrations. Their common use by the members of a society basically determines the construction and the maintenance of individual as well as social identity. Fourth, individual as well as social remembrances are realized by *actors* as "places of memory"; their sociality is constituted by the expectation that everybody refers in a comparable manner to the sense orientations provided by world models and culture programs. Fifth, due to the selectivity and *contingency* of all remembrances, they need a (conscious or unconscious) identity policy of remembering which refers to the respective culture of remembering as available in the respective culture program. And lastly, individual as well as social remembrances are fundamentally influenced by media, which play a crucial role in the elaboration of remembrances in media offers and which regulate the career of topics in the public sphere.

Leaving behind the traditional dichotomy of individual vs. society and replacing it with a specific management of observing actors, processes, and their results together with the sense orientation applied in these processes helps us to recognize that society seen as the unity of the difference between world models and culture programs can realize itself only through actions and communications of actors who refer to the orientational power of these models and programs. Memories serve as instruments for remembering in terms of a present preview via a constructive glance backwards. We can either write history together or not at all, because it can only be produced, and not possessed.

References

Assmann, Aleida. "Spurloses Informationszeitalter." *Cover. Medienmagazin* 4 (2004): 74-77.

Maturana, Humberto R. *Erkennen: Die Organisation und Verkörperung von Wirklichkeit.* Braunschweig: Vieweg, 1982.

Roth, Gerhard. *Fühlen, Denken, Handeln: Wie das Gehirn unser Verhalten steuert.* Frankfurt am Main: Suhrkamp, 2001.

Rusch, Gebhard. *Erkenntnis, Wissenschaft, Geschichte: Von einem konstruktivistischen Standpunkt.* Frankfurt am Main: Suhrkamp, 1987.

Schmidt, Siegfried J., ed. *Gedächtnis: Probleme und Perspektiven der Gedächtnisforschung*. Frankfurt am Main: Suhrkamp, 1991.
—. *Geschichten & Diskurse: Abschied vom Konstruktivismus*. Reinbek: Rowohlt, 2003.
—. *Lernen, Wissen, Kompetenz, Kultur: Vorschläge zur Bestimmung von vier Unbekannten*. Heidelberg: Auer, 2005.
Zierold, Martin. *Gesellschaftliche Erinnerung: Eine medienkulturwissenschaftliche Perspektive*. Berlin: de Gruyter, 2006.

Memory and Forgetting in Paul Ricœur's Theory of the Capable Self

MAUREEN JUNKER-KENNY

The task of philosophers is, in one of Paul Ricœur's understated definitions, to be responsible for the exact formulation of specific problems ("Ethics" 279). Philosophy's contribution to human knowledge is achieved through an analysis and critique of concepts that other branches of knowledge avail of directly in their empirical enquiries; philosophy offers a reflection that leads back to the human subject presupposed, but not analyzed, by other disciplines. Its enquiries go back behind the unquestioned currency of concepts such as identity, communication, culture, integration, or memory, by distinguishing the origin, levels, and frameworks of their use. Striving to integrate them into a coherent theory, they link epistemology and ethics by reconnecting aspects such as language, agency, responsibility, and memory to the self in its receptivity and activity.

Thus, the first question I will be pursuing is what originary and irreplaceable perspective philosophy has to offer towards the problem of memory in its constitution and its personal, collective, and cultural manifestations. The investigation into Ricœur's philosophical approach yields an epistemology of history in which given events are traced back to their source of reconstruction: the individual self in its capability, finitude, and specific vulnerability (section 2). Having clarified his position regarding the condition of the possibility of historical knowledge, the second aspect to reflect on will be the subject in its capability for morality, or its "imputability." Here, the domain of the practical with its moral and political arenas is opened up. What does Ricœur's analysis of the struggle of memory with forgetting imply for the responsible subject and for an ethics of remembering? It is in the context of striving for a "policy of the just allotment of memory" (*Memory* xv) that the distinction of two kinds of forgetting becomes decisive: one that destroys traces, and one that preserves. This "*oubli de reserve*" is not only held to be constitutive of the depth dimension of the past but also harbors a productivity of its own, enabled to reopen the future in a horizon of forgiveness. Ricœur's analysis of how memory functions in that special type of active forgetting which is forgiving in its political and personal dimensions shows that an ethics of memory depends on a horizon he calls "eschatological." This is what the epilogue of *Memory, History, Forgetting* develops. The outlook it opens on the preceding phenomenological and epistemological enquiries developed in his masterly, sustained dialogue with the philosophical tradition from antiquity to the present within the first six hundred pages of *La mémoire, l'histoire, l'oubli* (*Memory, History, Forgetting*) will be the final point of my investigation (section 2).

1. Philosophy of the Self as Critical Reflection on Memory and History

How is memory constituted in the self (2.1), and what is its role within the reconstruction of history (1.2)? Ricœur develops his position in debate with the philosophical tradition since Plato, tracing back current controversies to alternative views emerging in earlier paradigms of thinking. The French hermeneut pursues as his first concern how to distinguish memory from an imagination with no corresponding reality. The mandate to distinguish between real and only apparent or false memories is part of philosophy's search for truth. The relevance of the ability to tell the difference is clear for the second theme he treats, historiography, which is committed to investigate what really happened even if the only avenue towards it are traces and testimonies, and their interpretation.

1.1 Memory as *Mneme* and as *Anamnesis* Relating to the Past

Memory, History, Forgetting starts with a comparative analysis of the basic concepts and starting points for locating the phenomenon of memory in the classical philosophical tradition. While the guiding concept for both Plato and Aristotle is the same, that of image, *eikon*, their use shows a crucial difference. For Ricœur, Plato's attempt to capture memories as present "images" (*eikon*) of a previous "imprint" (*typos*) on the wax of the soul, as in *Theaetetus*, risks being read as a misleading naturalistic account (*Memory* 9-13). By contrast, Aristotle's unequivocal attribution of the *eikon* of memory to the complex of time offers the decisive route to be followed: "All memory is of the past." Here, the "specificity of the properly *temporalising* function of memory" has been discovered, over against the Platonic emphasis on the presence of something merely absent (*Memory* 6).

The distinction found already in Plato between *mneme* and *anamnesis*, involuntary reappearance and searched-for recollection, is pursued into the modern philosophy of consciousness. Tracing the development within Husserl's phenomenological analysis of retention, modification, and reproduction, Ricœur corrects his own previously positive reception in *Time and Narrative*. While his focus then was on the constitution of time (*Memory*

109), his new problematic is that of how to achieve a faithful representation of real events in the past. Criticizing Husserl for the "dictatorship of retention" (*Memory* 117), which limits analysis to matters internal to consciousness, Ricœur is now more interested in how reproduction is achieved. The problem is how to do justice to the distance which separates us from the past in its independence from consciousness, a distance necessary in order to appropriate the past (cf. Tengelyi; Teichert).

In summary, from the beginnings of classical Greek thinking, the double shape of memory both as a receptive "cognitive" faculty in which previous elements of learning as well as events reappear unbidden, and as a "pragmatic," directed activity of recall (*Memory* 4) have been noted. This duality and the unavoidable image shape of memories make it necessary to establish criteria regarding the difference between true and false.

1.2 Reconstructing History: *Mise en intrigue* Based on Facts

The definition of memory by its reference to the past, as inaugurated by Aristotle, raises the epistemological question of how the past can be accessed. How trustworthy are involuntary and searched-for memories for the reconstruction of history? Ricœur's earliest contribution to the theory of science of historiography dates from the 1950s, when in view of the problem of evil he had already changed methodology from phenomenology to a hermeneutics of texts relating to different orders, such as literature, law, and exegesis ("Ethics" 281). The position Ricœur outlines now in his renewed dialogue especially with French theorists and practitioners of historic representation, such as Pierre Nora and Michel de Certeau, comes to the conclusion that the only way to overcome the well-rehearsed impasses and aporias in the epistemology of history is a critical trust in individual testimony (*Memory* 21). The alternatives to this solution are less convincing. I want to outline the stakes in this debate by commenting on the critique launched by Rainer Adolphi against what he sees as Ricœur's privileging of narrative over against theory, and as a naïve reclaiming of facts instead of facing up to the thoroughly interpretive nature of historical judgment (Adolphi 165-68).

Throughout the phases into which he divides the historian's work in the second part of *Memory, History, Forgetting*, such as searching for traces, selecting and combining material in order to account for causes and motivations, and venturing a coherent interpretation, the French philosopher is keen to underline the integral and irreplaceable element of *mise en intrigue* (cf. Petersdorff 136). The very question at the heart of history writing, "why" something developed, owes its answer to an individual assembly of what counts as facts for the matter in question. History is a science that answers to objectifiable criteria, but equally a subject matter to which researchers are linked by intentionality. Thus, both explanation and understanding (*compréhension*) are demanded (*Memory*, part 2: ch. 2). The object—structures, events, interactions, periods of long or short duration in the past—is marked by its connectedness with human agents and recipients. Yet the conclusion Ricœur draws from his support for the Aristotelian definition of memory by its reference to a past independent of thinking is that history writing, despite the researcher's heuristic and systematizing input, relates to the reality of a past to which it has to do justice. This task involves documentary and reconstructive accuracy as much as a sense for the unkept promises of the past, the possibilities that for contingent reasons did not come to pass. I see Ricœur as steering a careful course between three currents: (1) a positivist reduction to mere facts, without their as yet unrealized potential, (2) a naïve presupposition that we can reconstruct the past as it really happened, and (3) a deliberate suspension of judgment in a never-ending passing of the torch from one chief interpreter to the next, Hegelianism turned Historicism. Against these three alternatives, his modest-looking conclusion that "we have nothing better than memory" (*Memory* 21) is a critical restatement of the non-substitutability (*Nichthintergehbarkeit*) of subjective testimony.

The objection that this stance comes close to "naturalism," by going back to some assumed "original" fact where there are only already interpreted issues (Adolphi 164), can itself be analyzed in its presuppositions. It may be true that we cannot get back to the facts themselves, as Ranke held, since events are never naked, but always already dressed in some interpretive garb; yet, the conclusion that the only question left to ask is "Who speaks?" is not convincing, either. It overrides the possibility of individual judgment and gives up all orientation towards truth. Already in his debate in the 1980s with the position then held by Michel de Certeau, Ricœur criticized the "sociologism" of the *Annales* school and of Marxist reconstructions of history (Dosse 15). The seemingly critical question from whose perspective history is being written is at heart a resignation of the question of truth to the historicism left after the demise of the metaphysical assumptions of the Hegelian system. Ricœur's hermeneutics insists that there is a "fact" in the sense of an event as distinct from its interpretation, even if our sole access to it may be through previous understandings.

The significance of this solution to the question of criteria for the truth of memories, that all we have are testimonies and the critical assessment of their trustworthiness, becomes clear when one enquires which positions are able to refute what is known in French as "*negationnisme*," the denial of the Holocaust. Ricœur's emphasis in all interplay of interpretations on the need to measure understandings against a factual core thus reveals its critical significance for current controversies. Other examples debated include the storming of the Bastille, the question of resistance and collusion under Vichy, and May 1968. An interpretation-only theory will not esteem the possible resistance of facts, much less be able to deal with their outright denial. It is against this stance that Ricœur's insistence on memory's reference to the past and his detailed treatment of the documentary phase have to be valued, however much it is true that the significance of facts is not a natural given.

So far, the philosophical approach to memory has been able to clarify conceptual problems and to offer solutions to apparent impasses. It has shown that shifting the question of how history is reconstructed to the sociologically analyzable "who" does not help if the truth claim of such reconstructions has not been addressed. It has gone behind the seeming alternative between collective and personal memory, uncovering its roots in the early-twentieth-century polemic against a philosophy of reflection from the objectifying ideal of empirical social sciences. Exploring the appropriateness of extending the concept of memory from the individual to a plural subject by way of analogy, it has incorporated Freud's observations on blocked memory that is under the compulsion to act out instead of remember, and traced the possibility for the ideological abuse of memory to the reasons for the fragility of personal and collective identity (*Memory* 82). The advantage of being able to position current cultural debates in the history of thinking will now be turned to the field of ethics. The precision tools forged in centuries of renewed reflection on inherited problems will show their analytical edge in the contemporary setting.

2. The Ethics of Memory

The positions Ricœur has developed in the theoretical disputes about the status and accessibility of the past anticipate his ethical reflection on memory in its practical dimension. Already his attribution of types of abuse of memories to the levels of ideology (*Memory* 82) which he distinguished in the 1980s—integration of a shared world by symbol systems, legitimization of power, distortion of reality—have relevance for social ethics. The instrumentalization of memories to construct a nation's identity is a case in point. His detailed review of the shifts in Pierre Nora's argumentation across the three volumes of *Les Lieux de mémoire* (1984-1992) agrees with the historian's protest against the events of staged celebrations of remembrance that take the place of a living connection to the past. Ricœur points out the ambiguous role of the concept of national heritage (*patrimoine*) at the service of contemporary identity construal which claims local sites for a historicized present (*Memory* 410).

It is in line with his warning against the danger of a political exploitation of memory to legitimate and add surplus credibility to those in governance that Ricœur sides with Tzvetan Todorov on the question of whether the call for a just memory should take the form of a "duty to remember" (*Memory* 86). Here, the place assigned to deontology in his three-step approach to ethics will be decisive (2.1). Ricœur's initial claim that forgetting has equal standing to memory and history and forms the third mast of a three-mast ship setting out on the project of representing the past (*Memory* xvi) is fleshed out at the end of the third part. Following the epistemology of history, the final part's anthropological reflection on the "historical condition" of human existence concludes in chapter 3 with an exploration of forgetting in its two inimical forms. The ability to see memory and forgetting not in simple contradiction but as mutually enabling and constitutive factors (Askani 188) is the strength of the phenomenological method. The epilogue establishes as the horizon of the whole work an eschatology of forgiveness (2.2).

2.1 Remembering as Duty, or as Work under the Sign of Justice?

Ricœur's dissatisfaction with turning memory into an imperative has three reasons. First, already mentioned, is the danger of political instrumentalization; the second lies in the architecture of his ethics; the third in the risk of short-circuiting the relationship between memory and history. Instead of a duty to remember, he proposes terms taken from Freud: "work of memory" and "work of mourning."

In the ethics developed in *Oneself as Another*, the entry point is not the level of duty; rather, the "sieve of the norm" comes as the second step. Commenting on his attempt in his 1990 theory of the self to mediate Aristotle's ethics of striving for the good life with Kant's deontology, Ricœur would then have preferred a presentation that would proceed "from the middle […] and show that it is the normative that implies […] a basic ethics and […] an applied ethics" ("Ethics" 286). He already interprets Kant's ethics in favor of such a double orientation of deontology: towards the good will as its basis, and towards fields of application as expressed in the different formulations of the Categorical Imperative that point to the self, the other, and to political commitment. The ethics of memory would thus fall under the third, applied, level which is entitled "practical wisdom." The fact that in political life an excess both of memory and of forgetting can be observed only reinforces his conviction that it is a matter for judgment, of finding a specific answer between rule and singularity for each individual case. The need for and validity of the deontological level is presupposed, but it does not itself yield the answer in a particular setting, such as that of historical judgment ("Ethics" 289).

Calling on citizens to take on the work, not the "duty," of memory does not deny that "the moral priority belongs to the victims" (*Memory* 89). What Ricœur objects to is the immediacy of the claim to memory which in order to be able to function as a reservoir and resource needs to be kept out of any direct purposive enlistment. While agreeing with Todorov on this danger, he rejects the way in which he splits what is good for the community from what is true. I see a confirmation of Ricœur's position in his critique of the political institution of amnesty as "commanded forgetting" in the service of the stability of a state (*Memory* 452). (See also Langenohl, this volume.) The truth of memory cannot be put into a balance with any other value.

2.2 Forgiveness as the "Eschatology of Memory"

The epilogue of *Memory, History, Forgetting* provides an outlook from which the whole work needs to be reread. It uncovers the invisible thread orientating the presentation with its goal of a pacified, happy memory. If it happens, then as the result of a reconciliation that is seen as the opposite of a forgetting that effaces all the traces and is the epitome of the precarious and vulnerable position of the self. Over against such destructive forgetting figures the positive type entitled *oubli de réserve*, a forgetting that preserves.

What qualification does the term "eschatological" offer for this necessary but also receding horizon (*Memory* 413) that is not at the subject's disposal? On the one hand, Ricœur insists on the need to be aware of the limits of human reflection, not only in the sense of rejecting a totalizing view of history. More specifically, his debate with Hannah Arendt makes it quite clear that forgiveness is not a natural part of human capability, similar to promising (*Memory* 459, 486-89; Junker-Kenny and Kenny 34-41). We can take part in forgiveness because, as Ricœur states with Levinas, it is there *(il y a le pardon)* (*Memory* 466). The trust that it is there to stay is based on the analogy with a text from the New Testament, Paul's Letter to the Corinthians, in which love, stronger than death (*Memory* 506), is said to "endure" (*Memory* 468).

On the other hand, while the openness for a religious fulfillment is notable in a work that carefully justifies each methodological shift, the theological question has been raised why forgiveness is possible only in an eschatological sense. Is it an eschatological limitation of the concept of forgiveness (Böhnke; Orth) to allow for it only in hope for a new future order that cannot be realized within history? In forgiving, the ultimacy of crimes committed and the unbridgeable difference between perpetrator and victim is recognized. The immanent critique of Kant in *Oneself as Another*, while insisting on imputation as the highest form of capability, had the point of giving singularity its due. The principal criterion in his political ethics of justice and his treatment of law is the obligation to see the person as more than the sum of her acts. In the epilogue, the givenness of forgiveness enables subjects to avail of it. Could Ricœur have gone farther and imagined the chance for a new beginning also for perpetrators by distinguishing between a forgiveness that is made possible now, and an ultimate healing of the irretrievable losses left by their atrocities from beyond human powers? The word on which the work ends, *inachèvement*, "incompletion" (*Memory* 506), keeps the voyage of the three-master tied to the limits of even the best intentions. The analysis and distinction of levels and the thought-through integration of the three themes of memory, history, and a historical condition marked by both the destructive and the preserving type of forgetting are results of a reflection that only a philosophical master could provide for our most recent attempts to make sense of our condition.

References

Adolphi, Rainer. "Das Verschwinden der wissenschaftlichen Erklärung: Über eine Problematik der Theoriebildung in Paul Ricœurs Hermeneutik des historischen Bewusstseins." Breitling and Orth 141-75.

Askani, Hans-Christoph. "L'oubli fondamental comme don." *La juste mémoire: Lectures autour de Paul Ricœur.* Eds. Olivier Abel, Enrico Castelli-Gattinara, Sabina Loriga and Isabelle Ullern-Weité. Geneva: Labor et Fides, 2006. 182-206.

Barash, Jeffrey Andrew, ed. *Paul Ricœur.* Spec. issue of *Revue de Métaphysique et de Morale* 2 (2006).

Böhnke, Michael. "Die Zukunft der Vergangenheit. Zwei kritische Rückfragen an Paul Ricœurs Theorie über das Vergessen und Verzeihen." Breitling and Orth 243-48.

Breitling, Andris, and Stefan Orth, eds. *Erinnerungsarbeit: Zu Paul Ricœurs Philosophie von Gedächtnis, Geschichte und Vergessen.* Berlin: Berliner Wissenschaftsverlag, 2004.

Dosse, Francois. *Paul Ricœur, Michel de Certeau: L'Histoire: entre le dire et le faire*. Paris: L'Herne, 2006.

Greisch, Jean. "Vom Glück des Erinnerns zur Schwierigkeit des Vergebens." *Facettenreiche Anthropologie: Paul Ricœurs Reflexionen auf den Menschen*. Eds. Stefan Orth and Peter Reifenberg. Freiburg: Alber, 2004. 91-114.

Junker-Kenny, Maureen, and Peter Kenny, eds. *Memory, Narrativity, Self, and the Challenge to Think God: The Reception within Theology of the Recent Work of Paul Ricœur*. Münster: LIT, 2004.

Orth, Stefan. "Zwischen Philosophie und Theologie: Das Verzeihen." Breitling and Orth 223-36.

Petersdorff, Friedrich von. "Verstehen und historische Erklärung bei Ricœur." Breitling and Orth 127-40.

Ricœur, Paul. "Ethics and Human Capability: A Response." *Paul Ricœur and Contemporary Moral Thought*. Eds. John Wall, William Schweiker and W. David Hall. New York: Routledge, 2002. 279-90.

—. *Geschichtsschreibung und Repräsentation der Vergangenheit*. Münster: LIT, 2002.

—. *Memory, History, Forgetting*. Trans. Kathleen Blamey and David Pellauer. Chicago: U of Chicago P, 2004. Trans. of *La mémoire, l'histoire, l'oubli*. Paris: Seuil, 2000.

—. *Oneself as Another*. Trans. Kathleen Blamey. Chicago: U of Chicago P, 1992.

—. *Das Rätsel der Vergangenheit*. Göttingen: Wallstein, 1998.

—. *Time and Narrative*. Trans. Kathleen McLaughlin and David Pellauer. 3 vols. Chicago: U of Chicago P, 1984-88.

Teichert, Dieter. "Erinnerte Einbildungen und eingebildete Erinnerungen: Erinnerung und Imagination in epistemologischer Perspektive." Breitling and Orth 89-100.

Tengelyi, Laszlo. "Husserls Blindheit für das Negative? Zu Ricœurs Deutung der Abstandserfahrung in der Erinnerung." Breitling and Orth 29-40.

IV. Psychological Memory Studies

Psychology, Narrative, and Cultural Memory: Past and Present

JÜRGEN STRAUB

1. Establishing Memory Discourses in the Nineteenth Century: A Cultural-Psychological Footnote on European "Retrospective Culture" and the Development of Narrative Psychology

The emergence of memory sciences in nineteenth-century Europe was closely linked to secularization and the development of a scientific approach towards the human soul. Especially in the latter third of the nineteenth century—Hacking distinguishes the years 1874 to 1886—the prevalent idea was that the most important keys to the mental life of humans lay in human memory and recollection. It was claimed ever more often that numerous life problems could only be comprehended and worked out through an exact reconstruction of the life story of a person or history of a group (which was reified as a subject).

In the course of this profound cultural transformation, the time-honored *art* of memory (see Lachmann, this volume) became marginalized. In the center stood the *scientific* (or science-*affine*), that is, *methodical*, dealing with structures, processes, and functions of this mysterious constituent, as well as of the human physique, human psyche, and a day-to-day social and communicative, symbolically transmitted praxis. The memory sciences had the prospect of an indiscrete career which is still steadily developing to this day. Psychology—to which psychoanalysis belongs—had an important role in it from the very beginning. The advancement and the still attractive nature of the subject "memory and recollection" accompanied an equally successful psychologization of human life, and vice versa. This complex procedure was tightly connected with the narrativization of the psychic sphere. It was never very self-evident and the representative actors were in no way completely aware of it at that time, nor in the first third of the twentieth century (e.g., Bartlett). The connection, close from the very beginning, of strands of thinking of modern psychology, and especially particular branches of memory psychology, with the narrative models of the psyche and of human life in general, became fully manifest only after the so-called narrative turn in the social and cultural sciences (cf. Nash;

Polkinghorne; for a specifically psychological point of view, cf. Brockmeier; Bruner; Sarbin; Straub, *Narration*).

This innovative, highly fruitful focalization of the narrative and narration, which in the latter third of the twentieth century broke ground in numerous disciplines, as well as in trans- and interdisciplinary discourses, brought about the realization of the fundamental meaning of this language and communication form for the constitution and development of the psychic sphere (see Echterhoff, this volume). Nowadays one speaks of it in virtually all domains of psychology. Multiple psychic structures, processes, and functions cannot be sufficiently comprehended without a detailed reference to (hi)stories and the socio-cultural praxis of storytelling. Various psychic procedures and functions are narratively structured and connected in a certain way with stories, or, rather, the formal scheme of a story. As countless empirical studies have demonstrated, this connection concerns such fundamental aspects as perception and reception, thinking and judging, motivation and emotion, wishing, willing, and acting, as well as holding true for such complex social phenomena as the creation of a sense of time and history, the constitution and transformation of the Self or a personal identity, and the changes in social relations, the cohesion of groups, and whole communities. It is also valid for memory processes and recollection achievements, which in an equally important way follow the narrative structure, form, and "logic" (for an overview, see Echterhoff and Straub; also cf. Brockmeier). Recollections themselves often assume the form of a story or are at least constituents of a story, which can be narrated and has usually been repeatedly told.

In the nineteenth century, the engagement with the past and history informed a program of scientific research from which was expected not only knowledge and enlightenment but also multiple enrichments of life and betterments of performance. These scientifically founded hopes increasingly characterized public debates and the everyday awareness of the many members of modern societies. Memory research, and psychological memory research in particular, was interwoven with a kind of memory politics and ethics of recollection, which elevated the reconstruction of the past to a central activity in the context of "reason-oriented life management." Bestirring one's memory and oneself to recollect, possibly permanently and comprehensively, truthfully and exactly, became a psychological disposition which controlled and disciplined significant spheres of day-to-day activities and was embraced by a growing number of people. From this behavioral regulator one expected manifold advantages, not least in the psychosocial regard.

On the whole, this regulator was largely accepted. Along with other things, it had to serve the worthwhile objective of preventing a creation of a false (for example, illusionary or palliating) picture of oneself and the Other. In accordance with this ideal, the one who narrates himself, that is, his own history, commits himself to the principle of authenticity and veracity. The cultural praxis of becoming and remaining aware of one's (own) past still today follows the powerful normative commandment entrenched in psychological realism. Already Wilhelm Dilthey asserted that history told who and what a man was. Countless contemporaries and followers concurred with him on that, including current (narrative) memory psychology, which is often prone to equate a person and his/her Self or his/her identity with his/her narrated recollections (Schacter). What is generally acknowledged is at least the salience of the narratively structured recollection for the Self or the identity of a person (cf. Brockmeier and Carbaugh). This recollection is by no means only applied "rearwards." Rather, it encompasses an anticipated recollection of a future past, which is envisaged in the grammatical mode of *futurum exactum*. It operates in the mode of retention and protention. This complex cultural praxis of narrative recollection has been, and still is today, committed to the spirit of a continuous optimization of life and performance. The ever-improving knowledge of the past should throw light upon and open up the chances for future development. At the very least, it should guarantee a retrieval of lost possibilities and thus stabilize a person's action potential.

In psychiatry, psychoanalysis, and psychotherapy, the overcoming of negative, self-destructive thoughts and feelings as well as the mitigation of the distressing limitations of the potential for action—as is well known, Sigmund Freud concentrated on the abilities to work and to love—are attained through the meticulous cognitive enlightenment and emotional processing of one's own past. The famous psychoanalytical motto "remember, repeat, work through" ("*Erinnern, Wiederholen, Durcharbeiten*") has still not lost its pertinence. In depth psychology, which was initiated by Sigmund Freud (who himself developed further important considerations of Schopenhauer and Nietzsche), one engages especially in the analysis of "repressed" experiences and the unconscious motives rooted in them. Such motives originate in the past and lead their own existence, which, albeit not recognized by the actors, nevertheless conditions and often limits them. Following Freud's theoretical principle of transference (*Nachträglichkeit*), related to both memory and recollection, and his concept of psychic causality, one proceeds on the assumption that recollections have to be regarded as creative constructions. This means that, in spite of their indisputable and referential character, which also physiologically materializes in memory traces (*Erinnerungsspuren*), recollections can constantly assume new, additional, or other meanings (in the new psychosexual, social, or cognitive phases of development as well as under the impression of new experiences).

Memories change, and not least through a narrative integration in a continuously "updated" (life) story. (Personal) contents of memory are not, and cannot be, stable. They are not fixable "objects," although they have a material (physiological) basis. The contents of memory are complexes of ideas which are constructed and re-constructed in the process of recollecting, at times spontaneously and seemingly unsystematically and at other times in a deliberate and focused manner. This assumption is part of the essential inventory of narrative cognitive psychology, which regards memories—even the most personal and intimate ones—as dependent on cultural and social semantics as well as on linguistic or other symbolic repertoires and modes of expression (Brockmeier). Besides, personal memories often result from dialogues and other "co-constructions" (Pasupathi).

These ideas have long been deployed in narrative psychotherapy. Whereas psychoanalysis was initially regarded as a praxis where, in a specific social setting, a talking cure took place, at the end of which the patient was enabled to devise new stories about him- or herself and his or her life, that is, new autobiographical self stories (Schafer), the latest developments have led to broadly differentiated narrative forms of psychotherapy and therapeutic techniques (Sugiman, Gergen, Wagner, and Yamada). In spite of all the difficulties, they have in common the conviction that the therapeutically supervised *work on oneself* and the psychologically induced *constitution of the Self* often occur in the medium of a narrative. The autobiographical recollection and the conception of a new Self driven by aspirations and desires assume the form of a narrative. Those who are able to tell new, altered self stories have already developed new relationships towards themselves, others, and the world. They have begun to think of themselves in a different way, and they view and feel themselves differently. As the research and therapy of serious traumas have shown, the therapeutic effects are often due to such transformations and innovations (Crossley; see also Kansteiner and Weilnböck, this volume). The world- and self-attitude of a person is in great part narratively structured. It changes as a result of telling new self stories. The turn of attention towards these issues was not solely a contribution of good literature (and literary studies; see Neumann, this volume), but lately also of psychology and psychotherapy. These, in turn, belong to a retrospective culture which recognizes in the telling of the past and history the basis for a rational and emotionally satisfying design of the present and future (see J. Assmann, this volume).

Only few protested against the unprecedented cultural enthronement of memory and the ensuing imperative of radical, possibly gapless recollection. The objections were directed in the first place against history and historiography, namely against certain variants of an in-depth analysis of the past of a group (such as a community, an ethnie, or a nation). In his famous *On the Advantage and Disadvantage of History for Life* Nietzsche argued not so much for the usefulness as for the negative impact on life of a ("monumentalist," "antiquarian," or "critical") History. It, in his view, threatened to paralyze the will and performance of both individuals and whole peoples. Nietzsche stated that this effect was a general oppressive tendency engendered by a suicidal obsession with the past and by a certain way of dealing with past events. He turned against different variants of this "historical sense," which, in his opinion, was hostile to life, and pleaded instead for a "life-friendly" ability and will to forget. In this respect one could speak of a "culture of strengthening forgetting." This culture is strictly forward-oriented and does not place much importance on a "backward glance" in a social and temporal perspective.

Yet the voices critical of the "historical illness" as castigated by Nietzsche did not change anything for the triumphal march of the retrospective culture. The deepest conviction of the latter consisted in the idea that only a reconstruction of the past made with the help of (possibly) scientific methods was able to create an adequate picture of the present, including the vision of the Self and a personal identity, and to help in devising rational future expectations. In simple terms, someone who wants to direct a rational and realistic look forward should first take a backward glance. One who wants to present, explain, and organize what is and will be should know the past. It is all only possible, of course, within the limits set up by the human intellect. In principle, our knowledge and ability to act are limited. Still, it is true that people can emancipate themselves from a self-inflicted nonage and enhance their action potential by gaining innovative insights and working out new orientations. A rationally oriented, at least partially enlightened, and autonomous life management presupposes equal attention dedicated to the past, present, and future alike. It requires linking these analytically differential time perspectives and bringing them together in an intelligible temporal contiguity.

This holds equally true for groups of people as well as for individuals. In both cases it is necessary to decipher the "dark traces of the past" (Rüsen and Straub) in order to realistically perceive and intentionally construct the present and the future. Narrative psychology and psychotherapy both focus on individuals without limiting themselves solely to this approach. They did and still do take part in the theoretical explanation and practical application of the cultural imperative "Narrate yourself!" Accordingly, these scientific branches are subjected to the recent criticism of an indiscriminate implementation of this imperative, or at least, of the call to narrate the *complete* life of a person (Thomae). Truly remembering one's own life in its totality would mean engaging oneself in a virtually impossible enterprise. Those attempting it would have to subject themselves to a self-control and self-discipline which might overshoot the well-intentioned aim and would hardly be more than the mere promise of happiness of a "life-serving" narrative psychology.

2. Narrative Psychology and an Active, Constructive Memory

The fact that the attainments of memory are regarded as specific *active constructions* has a great deal to do with the narrative character of many recollections. An insight into the communicative or discursive character of the past as well as into its history which encompasses the present and an envisaged future is an element of a continuous and thorough representation and reflection of past events in a "memory culture." Generally, it can be said that in a retrospective culture, different modi of representing the past, present, and an expected future, which rely upon the attainments of memory and recollection, are *themselves* prominently thematized. No event, (hi)story, or time can be objectively apprehended as simple facts—*facta bruta*—and transmitted as such symbolically. Although not deliberate inventions which could be displaced into a fictional sphere, representations are viewed in this field not as natural reproductions of states or events but as results of productive epistemic actions that are both cognitively *and* emotionally, or motivationally, saturated. Such actions are performed in a symbolic medium (such as language), which inevitably gives them shape. (Basically, we are dealing here not with "media" as variable instances of *transmission*, but with *constitutive* symbolic forms without which memory and recollection would be unthinkable.) Representations are constructions, with whose help the pasts, the presents, and the envisaged futures can be *shaped*, articulated and reflected *as a story*, history, or biography. Since language (just as other symbolic media or forms) is a cultural tool, memory and recollection are also cultural phenomena.

This important recognition is a cornerstone of modern cognitive psychology and could be made thanks to Bartlett's groundbreaking research. With the help of his empirical studies, he confronted Ebbinghaus's approach, which was still dominant in the nineteenth and well into the twentieth century, with a, in many respects, superior theory (cf. Straub, "Gedächtnis"). Bartlett diverged from Ebbinghaus's endeavor to formulate a general theory of memory. Instead of searching for universal laws of an allegedly purely reproductive memory and recollection, Bartlett underscored culture's dependence on the attainments of an active, productive, or creative memory and recollection. Unlike Ebbinghaus, who carried out experiments with presumably equally neutral nonsense syllables (for example, in order to discover the laws of human ability to memorize or to forget), Bartlett, who can be deemed the first narrative and cultural psychologist, asserted in his research on memory that any recollection was basically an act of construction which would remain utterly incomprehensible without a reference to cultural praxis and the respective cognitive scripts and schemata.

People do not simply memorize objectively existing things (events, etc.), which thereafter can be neutrally perceived, captured in a universal symbolic system, and preserved in a static form. Rather, already in the act of perception and reception, they transform a given thing into a phenomenon which can be and is worth being memorized, a *meaningful* and *therefore* communicable experience. They *structure* and *organize* the material of their perception and tie it in with previous knowledge. Henceforth this remains a task of memory. This already solidly proven recognition makes the conventional idea that memory saves "what used to be," which could consequently be played back by recollection, appear simplistic and even a little naïve. It also suggests reconsidering and revising traditional theories on the "slips of memory," "distorted recollections," and the like. Memory, especially episodic or autobiographical, constantly arranges and organizes anew what we remember (in this or that situation, for this or that reason, with this or that aim, etc.). Memory is no *tabula rasa* or a blank wax tablet onto which any content may be inscribed, nor a neutral storage medium which passively records just anything and on demand reproduces it unaltered. It works and interferes with its "contents," arranging and organizing them. For this, it deploys different "schematic" possibilities, from the first operation of "conserving" to the topical re-arrangements and pragmatic-semantic re-writings. A salient feature in these operations is the narrative structuring of events.

A "scheme"—the term initially coined by Bartlett and from then on established in cognitive psychology—is an organized unit of knowledge. Stories represent such schemata (or scripts). This discovery was made by the British memory researcher as he made his test subjects read twice and later reproduce in written form quite strange stories which appeared alien to them. After reading extracts from an Indian tale, "The War of the Ghosts," the test persons recollected all the events in a form more or less familiar to them, and *not* as these were rendered in the tale. The alien was adjusted to the known, the unfamiliar was assimilated and familiarized with the help of the available schemata. *Quod erat demonstrandum*: Memory operates both actively and creatively. Recollections are meaningfully structured compositions or constructions. The one who is recollecting creates or affirms a world permeated with sense and meaning. Memory and recollection are prominently involved in people's attempts to endow their experiences with sense and meaning that conforms to socio-cultural standards (values, rules in the form of norms or conventions, habits, goals, etc.) An important part of this process consists in a narrative arrangement and integration of events into generally intelligible stories. If it is required by one's own cultural, social, and psychological "logic," one leaves out one detail or another and adds something else here or there, changing things until they assume a more or less comprehensible guise. Such "guises" circulate in the communicative praxis of a culture. They are learned, practiced, and internalized. Frequently, they take the form of ready-made stories and schematic plots (romance, comedy, tragedy, or satire are just as familiar to us as other systematizations, for example progressive or regressive plots, stories of a rise and fall, development, crisis, decline, etc.). *This* is how memory and recollection function. They depend on cultural resources, tools, and templates. In this way, they represent cultural psychic structures, processes, or functions themselves. This empirical discovery by Bartlett has attained an extreme theoretical salience, and narrative cultural psychology still adheres to it today.

Virtually all contemporary theories assume that memory does not simply preserve and retrieve on demand the "information" which once was put in and stored there. An *active* memory reconstructs the past and history from the standpoint of the present and in light of certain future expectations. Every memory-based representation employs the available cultural means of the specific present time. This present time encompasses the social situation, against the backdrop of which one speaks with others and communicates with them (be it in an oral language medium, written form, or a non-discursive, representative sign or symbolic system). A particularly important modus of this communication is storytelling. A retrospective culture can therefore be termed a *narrative culture*, even though, as pointed out by Walter Benjamin, some traditional forms and practices of storytelling as well as the social figure of the story-teller him- or herself may have become rare (cf. Echterhoff and Straub).

3. Dissociated Stories, Multiple Personalities: Cultural Schemata of a Split or a Multiple Self

Burgeoning in the latter half of the nineteenth century in Europe and North America, psychology fostered the hope that memory-based recollections and their detailed methodical analysis were not only able to deliver a more complete picture of a person's biographical past, but also could help better recognize and mold cultural, social, and psychological modi of construction, representation, and transmission of the past. In addition, modern psychology provided a scientific foundation for successfully overcoming various life problems which had emerged or become exacerbated in the process of socio-cultural life forms becoming more dynamic, individualized, and flexible. An accelerated emancipation from traditions entailed uncertainties and problems of orientation, and "individualist" psychology had to supply an institutional framework and effective means to resolve them. This branch of science soon developed considerable public power and influenced the general public consciousness. More and more often, it was recommended to those who suffered from life, and especially from the modern conditions of human existence, that they should consult scientific (or scientifically grounded) guidebooks and companions. In accordance with a systematic temporalization of the psychic sphere, scientific psychology searched for the roots of personal problems in a person's past. For this purpose, he or she had to focus on and analyze (life) stories. From the very beginning, psychology was a part of the aspiring memory sciences and has remained so up to the present day. It belonged and still belongs to the scientific sector of a retrospective, narrative culture.

Hacking elucidates this with the concept of "multiple personality," which is particularly interesting from the point of view of cultural psychology. The issue at stake is a complex and controversial clinical pattern, which emerged in the latter third of the nineteenth century. This kind of multiplicity is still usually regarded as pathological and is subsumed in the category of the dissociative personality disorders. According to the innovative view of psychiatry and psychology at that time, this historical and cultural phenomenon could only be understood through an investigation into its etiology and ontogenesis in the light of a thorough reconstruction of a person's past. This past had to be *narratively* visualized and understood in the process of a psychological analysis of the autobiographical narratives. Multiplicity as a psychological or psychopathological syndrome was assumed to be linked to an autobiographical story in the center of which stood trauma. This traumatic crisis functioned in the etiology and hermeneutics of a multiple personality as a "narrative explanans" (explanatory premise). The trauma had a decisive explanatory value. It endowed the life story with sense and meaning. The scientific explanation of multiplicity belonged to the branch of narrative cognitive psychology, in which recollections gave access to the psychic life and opened up opportunities for change.

The spectacular case of a multiple personality, which still has not lost its prominence and whose diagnostic criteria have constantly shifted and are still debatable, formidably shows how memory and recollection as well as their processing condition the psychic life of a person. Often a buried memory inaccessible to the subject preserves traumatic experiences, which make a person suffer and block his or her action potential. As assumed early on, the negative consequences of a traumatic experience are reinforced and solidified by an incapability to remember. Hence the basic therapeutic motto of "remember and talk!" It is in this very process that therapists accompany and support their clients.

Therapists always run a risk of prompting "false" memories. The "false memory syndrome" has often provided catch lines and organized public opposition to therapeutically induced exploitations of alleged traumatic experiences. Frequently, social and especially family relations have been destroyed and transformed into court cases, even though no sexual abuse had ever taken place. The False Memory Syndrome Foundation, created in 1992, provides help and support for the wrongly suspected (ostracized, convicted), although it of course does not deny sexual abuse as a distressing social fact. Narrative psychology interested in questions of cognitive psychology has to see that some purported victims of sexual abuse, often with a naïve absolving support from their therapists, constructed experiences from their early childhood which in reality had never been theirs. Without a conscious intention to lie, they appropriated an alien past. They imputed sexual abuses to their fathers (who were proved to be free of guilt) and other men, and thus presented themselves as victims who deserved attention, recognition, and reparation.

Leaving out questions of material compensation, one may see that the socio-cultural removal of taboos with regard to sexual abuse on the one hand, and public attention and compassion towards its victims on the other, tempt people to perceive and to present an alien past as their own. They simply adopt common autobiographical stories about traumatic experiences and their negative consequences, whose origins long went unrecognized. They stage a story of suffering which in no way describes their own life. The plausibility and credibility of the story result solely from its being told in a public climate of a—to some extent overdue—breaking of a taboo, and therefore mobilizes a cultural topos and a socially acknowledged plot.

Be that as it may: The work with memory is, as explicated above, the very first step on the path of psychotherapy. According to this "theory," the healing of the wounds endured and of a long-lasting injury of the Self, or at least the soothing of pain, lies in the work with memory. The mourning—Freud speaks of *Trauerarbeit*—and other psychic processes can start only after this "memory work" has been completed. Work on and with recollections takes place in a social space of narrating. It fosters new episodical and autobiographical narratives and reconfigures the old ones. It reconstructs the narrative Self. Back when the first cases of multiplicity were scientifically debated and therapeutically treated by psychiatrists and psychologists, a kind of narrative psychotherapy was already basically being practiced. It took place on the basis of an etiological-psychopathological explanation deploying an autobiographical exemplary narrative, which had to an extent already been culturally ratified towards the end of the nineteenth century.

The memories "liberated" in narrative psychotherapy (or other social contexts) are embedded into an autobiographical narrative, which follows a broadly standardized scheme. This example makes it obvious to what extent even the most intimate recollections and personal memories are constituted and encoded culturally. Without the cultural notion of a psychic trauma, multiple personalities, as known to Western psychiatry and psychology for over a century, would be utterly unthinkable. (This obviously does not address other cultural variations of "multiplicity." There are cultural ideas on the existence of multiple Selves which differ from the familiar concept of the unity of soul and body, as well as the consistency of a person and of his or her identity—however differentiated internally that may be—just as much as the form of multiple personality discussed above). Putting it in a more precise way: Not only the general concept of a trauma but also the public thematization of traumatizing sexual abuse is one of the indispensable socio-cultural preconditions for the idea of a pathological multiplication of a personality into several Selves as described above. Multiple Selves which exist, think, feel, and act completely independently from each other originate from a traumatic experience (or a series of such experiences which can lead gradually and cumulatively to their psychic consequences). Usually such an experience is sexual abuse.

Multiplicity can obviously also hinder a person from being morally and legally culpable. One can no longer apply concepts such as reliability, sanity, and criminal liability to multiple personalities. Along with unavoidable social problems, those who are affected by multiplicity are also susceptible to psychic distresses, which are basically linked to a radical loss of capabilities of orientation and performance. The apparent multiplication of possibilities which open up for the numerous Selves of a multiple personality is in reality a loss. Since the end of the nineteenth century, there has existed a narrative explanation of this loss and all the suffering which it entails. One can only say that, irrespective of its actual existence which is painfully experienced by the affected person, a "multiple personality" is principally a *discursive* and *communicational*, that is, a *narrative* phenomenon.

The narrative of the genesis of a multiple personality encompasses a "causal" explanation, which has been revised and differentiated many times by the respective sciences. This self-explanatory narrative is actually still highly disputed (Hacking) and yet as common as never before. The debates of the nineteenth century sank into oblivion to a large extent in the twentieth century and, at least publicly, were hardly present thereafter. Yet they remained important as background knowledge and offered relevant connections to later scientific research. The irritating and at the same time fascinating phenomenon of multiplicity so highly acclaimed by the "postmodern" public had an unprecedented career in the mass media. In a postmodern culture in which the "fragment" was declared by social and cultural theorists to be the key concept, a multiple personality "dissolved" into the fragmentary Selves enjoyed a favorable reception. The aforementioned narrative became from the 1970s on an increasingly successful cultural topos, first in North America and then also in some European countries. The narrative plot turned into a cultural pattern of biographical self-comprehension, which was popular in some parts of the Western world. Thus the borderline between the psychopathology of a suffering subject and the psychology of a normal postmodern person often blurs (an observation which has no relevance for this paper although this is itself a cultural phenomenon of great interest for narrative psychology).

The plot, or the narrative abbreviation, of a multiple personality belongs nowadays to a standard repertoire of narrative psychology and correlated narrative psychotherapy (cf., e.g., Crossley). Its topics are of course numerous and are by no means restricted to multiplicity alone. Autobiographical narratives frequently follow cultural patterns. This is also valid for life stories in which different kinds of traumatic experiences, life-threatening illnesses, and other decisive crises occupy the central position. Crossley demonstrates this by using numerous examples such as the typical stories of those infected with HIV/AIDS. Narrative psychology generally deals with the narrative constitution of a Self and its modification through work on memory-based narratives.

As expounded above, narrative psychology buttresses other scientific theories which in the past hundred years have been focusing on the social and cultural constitution of memory and recollections. It shows that even the presumably most intimate and personal things are constituents of social and cultural memory. What our memory absorbs and preserves are not "bare, objective facts," and memory itself is by no means a "mirror of nature." Rather, it encodes and stores things which have already been perceived and received beforehand in the light of available representational modi (terms and concepts, schemata and scripts) as well as symbolic forms. Analogously, the psychic processing and an ever-possible alteration of the memory contents resulting from recollection, that is, their decoding and rendition, are essentially a social and cultural operation. To visualize the past and history, one employs images and a language which is never completely one's own. A person recollecting past events imagines and narrates them as a member of a certain culture (for the concept of "culture," see Straub, "Kultur"). Without its symbolic forms and means one would search in vain for a specifically human memory. Without them, all those memories and narratives which help us vividly visualize and communicate the past and history of humankind, or even of one single individual, would disappear.

References

Bartlett, Frederic C. *Remembering: A Study in Experimental and Social Psychology*. Cambridge: Cambridge UP, 1932.

Brockmeier, Jens. "Introduction: Searching for Cultural Memory." *Narrative and Cultural Memory*. Spec. issue of *Culture & Psychology* 8.1 (2002): 5-14.

Brockmeier, Jens, and Donal Carbaugh, eds. *Narrative and Identity: Studies in Autobiography, Self and Culture*. Amsterdam: John Benjamins, 2001.

Bruner, Jerome. *Making Stories: Law, Literature, Life*. New York: Farrar, Straus & Giroux, 2002.

Crossley, Michele L. *Introducing Narrative Psychology: Self, Trauma and the Construction of Meaning*. Buckingham: Open UP, 2000.

Echterhoff, Gerald, and Jürgen Straub. "Narrative Psychologie: Facetten eines Forschungsprogramms. Erster Teil." *Handlung, Kultur, Interpretation: Zeitschrift für Sozial- und Kulturwissenschaften* 12.2 (2003): 317-42.

—. "Narrative Psychologie: Facetten eines Forschungsprogramms. Zweiter Teil." *Handlung, Kultur, Interpretation: Zeitschrift für Sozial- und Kulturwissenschaften* 13.1 (2004): 151-86.

Hacking, Ian. *Rewriting the Soul: Multiple Personality and the Sciences of Memory*. Princeton: Princeton UP, 1995.

Nash, Cristopher. *Narrative in Culture: The Uses of Storytelling in the Sciences, Philosophy and Literature*. London: Routledge, 1990.

Nietzsche, Friedrich Wilhelm. *Vom Nutzen und Nachtheil der Historie für das Leben*. 1874. Stuttgart: Reclam, 1970. [English: Nietzsche, Friedrich Wilhelm. *On the Advantage and Disadvantage of History for Life*. Trans. Peter Preuss. Indianapolis: Hackett, 1980.]

Pasupathi, Monisha. "The Social Construction of the Personal Past and Its Implications for Adult Development." *Psychological Bulletin* 127 (2001): 651-72.

Polkinghorne, Donald. *Narrative Knowing and the Human Sciences.* Albany: SUNY Press, 1988.

Rüsen, Jörn, and Jürgen Straub, eds. *Dark Traces of the Past: Psychoanalytic Approaches in Cultural Memory Research.* New York: Berghahn, 2008.

Sarbin, Theodore R., ed. *Narrative Psychology: The Storied Nature of Human Conduct.* New York: Praeger, 1986.

Schacter, Daniel L. *Searching for Memory: The Brain, the Mind, and the Past.* New York: Basic, 1996.

Schafer, Roy. *Retelling a Life: Narration and Dialogue in Psychoanalysis.* New York: Basic, 1992.

Spence, Donald P. *Narrative Truth and Historical Truth: Meaning and Interpretation in Psychoanalysis.* New York: Norton, 1982.

Straub, Jürgen. "Gedächtnis." *Psychologie: Eine Einführung: Grundlagen, Methoden, Perspektiven.* Eds. Jürgen Straub, Wilhelm Kempf and Hans Werbik. Munich: DTV, 1997. 249-79.

—. "Kultur." *Handbuch interkulturelle Kommunikation und Kompetenz.* Eds. Jürgen Straub, Arne Weidemann and Doris Weidemann. Stuttgart: Metzler, 2007. 7-24.

—, ed. *Narration, Identity and Historical Consciousness: The Psychological Construction of Time and History.* 1998. New York: Berghahn, 2005.

Sugiman, Toshio, Kenneth J. Gergen, Wolfgang Wagner, and Yoko Yamada, eds. *Meaning in Action: Constructions, Narratives, and Representations.* New York: Springer, 2008.

Thomae, Dieter. *Erzähle Dich selbst! Lebensgeschichte als philosophisches Problem.* Munich: Beck, 1998.

Zielke, Barbara, and Jürgen Straub. "Culture, Psychotherapy, and the Diasporic Self as Transitoric Identity." *Meaning in Action: Constructions, Narratives, and Representations.* Eds. Toshio Sugiman, Kenneth J. Gergen, Wolfgang Wagner and Yoko Yamada. New York: Springer, 2008. 49-72.

Against the Concept of Cultural Trauma

(or How I Learned to Love the Suffering of Others without the Help of Psychotherapy)

WULF KANSTEINER AND HARALD WEILNBÖCK

Handbooks celebrate the success stories of academic life. Handbook entries are supposed to be constructive and uplifting affairs which impart to future generations the academic insights of current generations, inform their readers in succinct fashion about important conceptual frameworks and methodologies, and demonstrate in what contexts and for what research agendas these intellectual tools can be applied most successfully. We will accomplish none of these objectives in the following text. Instead, we will inform you about a spectacular failure, the failure of scholars in the humanities and social sciences to develop a truly interdisciplinary trauma concept despite their many claims to the contrary. We will also present you with a culprit for this unfortunate development by blaming our colleagues for applying poststructuralist theory in rather unimaginative ways and, as a result, developing a strangely narrow and aestheticized concept of trauma.

After this announcement a short note may be in order. We hope very much that the following is not perceived as just another exercise in postmodern theory bashing. We are ourselves firmly committed to the venerable deconstructive project of questioning master narratives, exposing the ideological prejudices and blind spots of the discursive status quo, and pursuing cultural analysis in a radical self-reflexive fashion. In fact, we object to the postmodern trauma discourse, which is currently so popular in the humanities, precisely because it lacks self-reflexivity and has elevated the concept of cultural trauma into the status of a new master narrative. These negative effects are particularly pronounced in literature departments where trauma studies have contributed to the reestablishment of conventional procedures of textual exegesis as the be all and end all of the philological enterprise (Weilnböck). As a result, the very concepts that were originally developed in the context of a radical critique of traditional literary and cultural studies have been retooled and redeployed to serve these traditions. In the process, the trauma metaphor, initially adopted in a spirit of interdisciplinary collaboration, has helped reestablish literary and cultural studies as exclusive and anti-interdisciplinary academic fields.

Cathy Caruth's 1996 *Unclaimed Experience* represents the most influential, perhaps the foundational text of deconstructive trauma studies (see also Caruth, *Trauma*). All the key elements of the new trauma discourse are for the first time fully developed in this volume. Like many other scholars, Caruth defines trauma as an experience consisting of two components that the trauma victim never manages to reconcile with each other. A severe mental and maybe also physical injury which the victim seems to overcome remarkably well is followed by a belated onset of symptoms that sometimes appear to bear no causal relationship to the original injury. At first sight, Caruth thus appears to define trauma in ways that are quite compatible with psychological research on trauma and post-traumatic stress. However, unlike most of her contemporaries who study the vicissitudes of mental suffering in a clinical context, Caruth goes on to celebrate the experience and the concept of trauma as providing unprecedented insight into the human condition. Applying an interpretive strategy borrowed from Paul de Man, Caruth emphasizes that the failure of the trauma victim to come to terms with the origins and symptoms of his/her mental illness represents a rare and valuable moment of authenticity because human beings only get a chance to perceive reality directly whenever our cultural systems of signification temporarily disintegrate under their own weight. In this way, trauma is conceived as a revelation that teaches us about the limits and possibilities of human culture. Unfortunately, however, at that moment of cultural disintegration and exceptional wisdom we are unable to fully understand, let alone successfully represent our insights. Or, as Caruth states in rather apocalyptic terms, "history can be grasped only in the very inaccessibility of its occurrence" (*Unclaimed Experience* 18). For Caruth, this principal failure of representation constitutes "the truth and force of reality that trauma survivors face and quite often try to transmit to us" (*Trauma* vii).

Caruth's compact model loses a lot of its appeal if one disagrees with its de Manian premise and believes that the limits of representation can be explored and overcome in some contexts and by way of a number of different representational strategies. But even if one shares Caruth's deconstructive ethos, her model still constitutes a formidable moral conundrum that its author has neither acknowledged nor solved. From the perspective of the trauma victim whose very survival might depend on his/her ability to repair his/her trust in human systems of signification as quickly as possible, Caruth's exuberant aesthetization and valorization of trauma appears ruthless, perhaps even cynical. This problem is exacerbated by Caruth's disinterest in the therapeutic process. As other proponents of the deconstructive trauma paradigm, Caruth includes in her book extensive references to psychological studies of trauma, but this interdisciplinary gesture is immediately undermined by a very selective and often de-contextualized appropriation of the empirical literature. Caruth believes, for example, that the trauma experience will and should remain inaccessible to representation. These conclusions nicely confirm Caruth's deconstructive axioms but they are not born out in the clinical literature. Many psychologists and therapists agree that traumatic experiences may be truthfully represented in everyday narrative language, for instance as the result of successful therapy (Leys).

Intellectual suspicions about the negative, self-destructive effects of Western culture and the Enlightenment, which are reflected in Caruth's interventions, have a long and impressive tradition reaching back at least to the end of the nineteenth century. The suspicions appeared even more credible after World War II because Nazi society and its experiments in social and genetic engineering represent particularly frightful examples of human self-destruction. But the intellectual project of thinking against the grain of Western culture which still presented itself as an arduous and radically self-critical process in the writings of Adorno, Lyotard, and others has in the meantime turned into a self-important and convenient academic pursuit, especially but not exclusively in the trendy celebrations of trauma (Kansteiner). Caruth is most certainly not responsible for this development but her model has been emphatically and apodictically embraced in a wide range of academic settings, uniting poststructuralist-inclined sociologists, political scientists, educators, and many cultural and literary studies experts under the sign of trauma.

In Germany, the deconstructive trauma paradigm has a particularly enthusiastic advocate in Manfred Weinberg, a literary anthropologist at the University of Konstanz. Like Caruth, Weinberg believes that trauma is "always already inscribed in memory" and has particular epistemological value, although, again following Caruth, he quickly adds that any conscious representation of trauma remains by definition "inadequate" (205) because "trauma is the inaccessible truth of remembering" (204). Weinberg regrets that many scholars have not properly understood or fail to respect the peculiar, contradictory logic of trauma according to which truth exists but cannot and may not be spelled out. In his assessment, academic writings on philosophy and history have the purpose to "make us forget about the traumatic flipside of all memory" and in this respect differ from literary texts which are capable of exploring the interdependency between trauma and memory in more honest and productive fashion (206).

Weinberg is refreshingly honest about his disinterest, even antagonism towards psychology and psychotherapy. He does not want to improve his knowledge about the suffering and clinical treatment of trauma victims and in this way help reduce the extent of traumatic injury occurring in the world. Weinberg states explicitly that "the clinical aspect is precisely what does not interest me—or only in a marginal way—about trauma" (173). Instead, he welcomes trauma as an indispensable conceptual tool and subscribes to a poststructuralist code of ethics by promising "to do anything he can to prove trauma's incurability" and fend off any improper "abolition of trauma" (173). Weinberg's confession highlights one of the most puzzling characteristics of deconstructive trauma theory. The proponents of the deconstructive trauma paradigm draw some of their key terms and concepts from psychoanalysis and psychology but they assume a radical anti-analytical and anti-empirical posture. Caruth, Weinberg, and their many intellectual fellow travelers like to speculate in an abstract manner about the philosophical meaning of trauma and apply these concepts in their study of culture and history, but they are not interested in the empirical phenomenon of trauma and the traumatic experiences of actual people. The advocates of the concept of cultural trauma do not simply emphasize that it is extremely difficult to access and understand trauma—an assessment shared by most clinicians—; they insist categorically that for conceptual reasons trauma "must remain inaccessible to memory" and cultural representation (Weinberg 204).

Weinberg is hardly the only representative of German cultural and literary studies who embraces the deconstructive trauma concept with quasi-religious fervor. There are many other scholars in the field ready to denounce any "sacrilege" that might be committed against what they perceive as the "integrity of trauma" (Baer 27). In the face of such threats, deconstructive trauma advocates issue stern warnings about "committing a betrayal that breaches the faithfulness towards the dead" although they tend to be rather vague about the precise meaning of these terms and their criteria of judgment (Sebald 121). But let's leave the terrain of German cultural and literary studies and move to a different discipline and a different continent and see how the concept of trauma is used as a didactic tool at the University of Toronto. Roger Simon, the director of the Testimony and Historical Memory Project, has studied extensively how human rights abuses and other crises are best represented in museum exhibits. He has looked in particular at cultural memories of the Ravensbrück concentration camp, the AIDS epidemic, racially motivated lynching in the U.S., and the forced resettlement of indigenous populations in Canada. Simon seems to have approached these topics with a deep suspicion of all narrative forms of remembrance because narratives are often used to justify extreme violence, both before and after the fact. He would like to preserve the culturally disruptive effect of trauma and advocates with great pathos the creation of memorial spaces which avoid the normalizing, sedative power of narrative and call into question "the frames of certitude that ground our understandings of existence" (186). For this purpose, he reads survivor testimony looking for traces of the "absent presence" and encourages students and museum visitors to respond to representations of trauma in non-narrative formats—all the while taking considerable pride in his "risk-laden" search for new "forms of non-indifference" (187).

For somebody who is convinced about the destructive, normalizing effects of narrative the representational strategies promoted by Simon might appear very reasonable. But if one is willing to keep an open mind about narrative, as a potential tool of repression and misinformation as well as enlightenment and therapy, the didactic status quo in Toronto appears rather doctrinaire. The metaphorical fireworks of Simon's text, an excellent example of deconstructive trauma philosophy, appear to be a rather obvious attempt to advance a very specific aesthetic program by tapping into the cultural-political capital of Holocaust memory.

The disdain for narrative and the fear of attempts to sublate trauma are a stock-in-trade of deconstructive trauma studies. Caruth herself warns that any efforts to verbalize and integrate traumatic experiences will inevitably destroy the valuable precision of trauma. Even the intellectual historian Michael Roth who has shown himself to be critical of what he calls "poststructuralist trauma ontology" encourages us not to give in to "narrative lust" and, in the process, normalize and trivialize trauma (168). These statements of caution are certainly important and worth considering. Our culture produces indeed many dubious representations of trauma that might have unwelcome or even negative effects on their audiences. But the indiscriminate rejection of narrative renders the deconstructive trauma paradigm incompatible with the results of clinical research which has shown consistently that integrating traumatic experiences within narrative frameworks is an indispensable tool of psychotherapy and that narrative forms of representation help groups and collective entities to come to terms with events of violence and its mental and social consequences. In fact, anybody who encourages people to access the more troubled areas of their personal memory while at the same time preventing narrative processes from taking place potentially retraumatizes them and risks inducing a state of psychic dependency (Fischer 205).

Let's visit another outpost of trauma studies at the University of Wales at Aberystwyth where Jenny Edkins teaches in the department of international politics. Her publications on trauma and politics, especially on the legacy of 9/11, provide a great case study for the way in which deconstructive trauma advocates move quickly from an understanding of trauma as injury to specific people to the abstract, metaphorical notion of trauma as a welcome disruption of existing frameworks of social and institutional incorporation without differentiating between these two levels of analysis in any meaningful way. At the beginning of one of her texts, Edkins emphasizes appropriately that "it is people, in their physicality and their vulnerability, that [sic] experience the trauma, both bodily and psychic [sic], and it should be to them that the memories belong" (100). Edkins then embarks on an impressive theoretical excursion. First, she teaches us by ways of Lacanian psychoanalysis that all perceptions of the subject and society are social fantasies based on master signifiers which cover up the existential lack at the core of human perceptions of self and other. Then, she invokes Derrida to remind us that all truly political decisions involve a radical moment of undecidability because they require the inventions of new criteria of judgment that cannot be derived from the previous political status quo. By way of a number of additional theoretical stops, including Caruth, Agamben, and Foucault, we finally arrive at the predictable conclusion that trauma calls into question the perceptions of the world that give us a sense of security, for instance, by undermining the conventional distinctions between subject and object upon which these perceptions are based. Or, as Edkins puts it rather bluntly, events like September 11 reveal, among other things, the "indistinguishability of flesh and metal" (110).

With little deconstructive finesse, Edkins spells out the upbeat political lesson of her intervention. Since "trauma is clearly disruptive of settled stories" it threatens centralized political authority based on such stories and opens up venues for political resistance (107). Therefore, Edkins denounces president Bush's insistence on conventional narratives of heroism and sacrifice and applauds artistic attempts that undermine such narratives and insist on the interpretive void created by trauma. After all this theoretical excess and political partisanship we have conveniently lost track of the victims and their physicality and mental vulnerability. What if the survivors, to whom the memories allegedly belong, would like to embrace stories of heroism and sacrifice and renew their belief in the fictitious, yet very helpful distinction between flesh and metal? What sense does it make to advocate extending the moment of trauma simply because on an abstract metaphorical level the experience of trauma aligns very nicely with the philosophical insights of Lacan, Derrida, and others? Can we responsibly ask people after events like 9/11 to embrace their mental injury and vulnerability and question linear notions of time and temporality despite the possibility that such recommendations, if actually implemented, might constitute severe psychological risks for some individuals and collectives?

We certainly do not want to imply that Edkins intends to do harm or has actually caused harm to anybody (nor do we assume this of Caruth, Weinberg, Simon, or the other authors whose texts we refer to in this essay). We are simply puzzled that academics who display considerable interdisciplinary ambition and dexterity—after all, Lacan's and Derrida's writings are not standard components of the graduate curriculum in international relations—do not feel comfortable with or compelled to tap into the empirical literature on trauma when they study the aftermath of concrete traumatic events such as 9/11. Finally, if one is really convinced that social crises are an opportune moment to question social fictions, one might want to begin closer to home and reflect self-critically about the academic fiction of cultural trauma which poststructuralist theorists might not have invented but certainly advocate vigorously.

The last stop on our international tour brings us back to U.S. academia, the heartland of cultural trauma studies, and, more specifically, to Yale University where deconstruction has a particularly long history. But we are not visiting the French or Comparative Literature departments where de Man taught in the 1970s and 1980s, and instead look up Ron Eyerman, a sociologist who has studied the collective memory of American slavery and was part of a international group of scholars who convened at Yale in 1998/99 to study cultural trauma and collective identity (Alexander et al). Eyerman has compiled an impressive array of data about the representation of slavery in U.S. culture. But he has also committed a conceptual error that calls into question his interpretation of the data. According to Eyerman, cultural traumata—in this case the cultural trauma of slavery—are produced and reproduced through media representations which cause "a dramatic loss of identity and meaning, a tear in the social fabric of a relatively coherent group," for instance a nation or the African-American community in the U.S. (3). This definition of cultural or collective trauma reflects very nicely the common understanding of trauma as a serious form of injury but Eyerman does not present any empirical evidence for this allegedly destructive effect of films, TV shows, novels, and other cultural products which deal with the topic of slavery. Moreover, it is highly unlikely that such evidence exists. As best as we know, media texts may have a wide range of effects on their audiences but traumatic effects appear to occur extremely rarely. Finally and most important, many media representations of traumatic historical events, for instance the TV series *Roots* and *Holocaust*, have shaped group identities in ways that helped social minorities gain public recognition for past suffering. One might object to such developments for political reasons but it is misleading to describe the reconstitution of African-American and Jewish-American identity that occurred in the aftermath of these media events as cultural traumata even if the term is only applied in a metaphorical sense. Unfortunately, Eyerman's error is hardly unique; many scholars in cultural trauma studies conceptualize the relationship between trauma, media, and collective identity in similarly simplistic terms and confuse representations of violence with the presence and reproduction of trauma. The work of Eyerman and others would profit tremendously from the development of sophisticated and variegated psychological tools that could replace the blunt concept of trauma and help us design much needed empirical studies of the effects of representations of war, genocide, and violence in contemporary media societies.

At the end of our short tour we do not want to allege a global conspiracy of trauma studies but we would like to emphasize that the many parallel paths taken during the institutionalization of postmodern thought in Western academia have produced remarkably similar results in different settings. It seems to be a general characteristic of this process of institutionalization, for example, that academics over a wide range of disciplines adamantly repeat a limited set of beliefs and stop asking, let alone try to answer, the really difficult theoretical and empirical questions about the ways in which human beings individually and collectively experience trauma and respond to the traumatic experiences of others. Obviously, there are important exceptions in the field of trauma studies and in this context we would like to highlight the work of Dominick LaCapra, who has very successfully applied psychological and psychoanalytical concepts in his analyses of Holocaust memory. LaCapra has also identified one of the fundamental conceptual errors at the core of the deconstructive trauma discourse. Many advocates of the concept of cultural trauma conflate the psychological challenges that all human beings face in their everyday life, especially in the process of maturation, with the extraordinary psychological ordeal encountered, for example, by victims of extreme violence (LaCapra). As a result of this mistake, they assume that in one way or another all people partake in the experience of trauma, for instance, when they grapple with the inexpungeable relativism of all forms of human culture and communication.

Empirically speaking, however, in most societies and under most historical circumstances only a small part of the population suffers from what clinical criteria define as post-traumatic stress. Empirical studies have shown that survivors of extreme violence are particularly likely to belong to this part of the population and experience severe symptoms of mental distress. At the same time, it is also true that post-traumatic symptoms of various sorts can be caused by many different factors, including seemingly ordinary and pedestrian experiences, but that fact makes it all the more important to differentiate empirically and conceptually between different forms of violence and their social and psychological consequences.

In our assessment, the deconstructive trauma paradigm suffers from five fundamental, interrelated problems that we have tried to illustrate in this text:

- A vague, metaphorical concept of trauma, which equates the concrete suffering of victims of violence with ontological questions concerning the fundamental ambivalence of human existence and communication, obliterates the important empirical differences between the various ways that people are affected by violence, and thus constitutes a grave insult toward people who actually suffer from post-traumatic stress.
- A surprising lack of interdisciplinary curiosity; the advocates of the deconstructive trauma paradigm selectively apply psychological and psychoanalytical terminology but they do so in a curiously anti-psychological manner and almost never systematically consult recent clinical literature which reports about the theory and practice of trauma therapy and raises serious questions about the concept of cultural trauma.
- A similarly disturbing disinterest in the empirical research on media effects; advocates of the deconstructive trauma paradigm assert that cultural traumata are produced and reproduced through the media but they have not tapped into the vast scholarly literature on media effects which contradicts such simplistic assumptions.
- An almost paranoid fear of narrative based on the axiom that all narration has distorting and normalizing effects and thus destroys the fundamental pre-narrative insights revealed by trauma. This anti-narrative reflex contradicts the consensus in psychotherapy studies that narration is an indispensable tool for healing.
- A valorization and aesthetization of trauma, high art, and philosophy as sites of intangible, ethereal authenticity; this stance fosters traditional perceptions of the humanities and academia, is inherently anti-empirical, and explains the ease with which scientific resources are ignored.

In conclusion, we would like to take you on a little metaphorical excursion of our own. In our assessment, the deconstructive trauma discourse seems to be compatible with the mindset and vantage point of a certain type of bystander who was not personally involved in any event of exceptional violence yet feels compelled to contemplate the meaning of such events in abstract philosophical terms. In fact, creating distance between oneself and moments of extreme human suffering might be the whole point of the exercise because the bystander apparently wants to mentally eliminate the empirical experience of trauma by way of ontological speculation.

We think that the only plausible way to account for such intellectual ambition is to assume that the bystander is actually evading or denying some significant area of personal memory which half-consciously resonates with the historical trauma issues at hand. These mental associations, which accompany the work of the trauma theoretician, might encompass past experiences of limited mental injury or memories of committing or condoning minor violations and may appear irrelevant with hindsight. But unless the fleeting moments of violence are recognized as formative experiences, they will continue to trigger psychological defense mechanisms and curb the subject's intellectual curiosity. These speculations explain how our bystander could be troubled by an inscrutable mix of unconscious anxiety, latent guilt feelings, numbing of cognitive differentiation, and aggressive theoretical ambition. As a result, s/he begins to see theoretical trauma everywhere while refraining from talking about violence and suffering in any concrete fashion.

Obviously, the simile of the intellectual trauma theorist qua contemplative Holocaust bystander is meant as a metaphorical expression, although we consider it a more accurate and helpful metaphor than the cultural trauma metaphor itself. A lot of deconstructive trauma theory appears to represent an unsuccessful attempt to come to terms with events like the "Final Solution" and, more specifically, to work through the failure of the bystanders to prevent man-made disasters and deal with their legacies in productive ways. Our metaphor illustrates that there is no such thing as neutral by-standing—politically, personally, or scientifically—and this insight should be reflected in our scholarly work. We need to overcome the unfortunate epistemological impasse caused by contemplative trauma attachment and theoretical acting-out and develop new qualitative-empirical research tools to study the psychological effects of violence and its cultural representation with precision and theoretical dexterity.

Authors' Note

A sequel to this paper, entitled "Remembering Violence: In Favor of Qualitative Literary and Media Interaction Research," has been submitted to the open-access Internet journal *Forum Qualitative Social Research* (http://www.qualitative-research.net).

References

Alexander, Jeffrey, et al. *Cultural Trauma and Collective Identity*. Berkeley: U of California P, 2004.

Baer, Ulrich. *"Niemand zeugt für den Zeugen": Erinnerungskultur und historische Verantwortung nach der Shoah*. Frankfurt am Main: Suhrkamp, 2000.

Caruth, Cathy, ed. *Trauma: Explorations in Memory*. Baltimore: Johns Hopkins UP, 1995.

—. *Unclaimed Experience: Trauma, Narrative, and History*. Baltimore: Johns Hopkins UP, 1996.

Edkins, Jenny. "Remembering Relationality: Trauma Time and Politics." *Memory, Trauma, and World Politics: Reflections on the Relationship between Past and Present*. Ed. Duncan Bell. New York: Palgrave Macmillan, 2006. 99-115.

Eyerman, Ron. *Cultural Trauma: Slavery and the Formation of African American Identity*. New York: Cambridge UP, 2001.

Fischer, Gottfried. *"Von den Dichtern lernen . . .": Kunstpsychologie und dialektische Psychoanalyse*. Würzburg: Königshausen & Neumann, 2005.

Kansteiner, Wulf. "Genealogy of a Category Mistake: A Critical Intellectual History of the Cultural Trauma Metaphor." *Rethinking History* 8.2 (2004): 193-221.

LaCapra, Dominick. *Writing History, Writing Trauma*. Baltimore: Johns Hopkins UP, 2001.

Leys, Ruth. *Trauma: A Genealogy*. Baltimore: Johns Hopkins UP, 2000.

Roth, Michael. "Trauma, Repräsentation und historisches Bewußtsein." *Die dunkle Spur der Vergangenheit: Psychoanalytische Zugänge zum Geschichtsbewußtsein*. Eds. Jörn Rüsen and Jürgen Straub. Frankfurt am Main: Suhrkamp, 1998. 153-73.

Sebald, W. G. "Jean Améry und Primo Levi." *Über Jean Améry*. Ed. Irene Heidelberger-Leonard. Heidelberg: Winter, 1990. 115-24.

Simon, Roger. "The Pedagogical Insistence of Public Memory." *Theorizing Historical Consciousness*. Ed. Peter Seixas. Toronto: U of Toronto P, 2004. 183-201.

Weilnböck, Harald. "'Das Trauma muss dem Gedächtnis unverfügbar bleiben': Trauma-Ontologie und anderer Miss-/Brauch von Traumakonzepten in geisteswissenschaftlichen Diskursen." *Mittelweg 36* 16.2 (2007): 2-64. [English: Weilnböck, Harald. "'The Trauma Must Remain Inaccessible to Memory': Trauma Melancholia and Other (Ab-)Uses of Trauma Concepts in Literary Theory." *Mittelweg 36*. 19 March 2008. <http://www.eurozine.com/articles/2008-03-19-weilnbock-en.html>.]

Weinberg, Manfred. "Trauma—Geschichte, Gespenst, Literatur—und Gedächtnis." *Trauma: Zwischen Psychoanalyse und kulturellem Deutungsmuster*. Eds. Elizabeth Bronfen, Birgit Erdle and Sigrid Weigel. Cologne: Böhlau, 1999. 173-206.

Experience and Memory: Imaginary Futures in the Past

DAVID MIDDLETON AND STEVEN D. BROWN

1. Experience Matters

In our modern understanding of memory there is an overwhelming tension between preservation and loss. Memory itself often seems to hang by a thread, to be balanced on the cusp between recovery and dissolution. In contrast, the authors of this article address robust practices of remembering and forgetting at home and work, in public and commercial organizations, involving language and text-based communication, objects and place. Our overall aim is to provide a basis for social psychological enquiry where experience matters. We ground this discussion in classic works on memory in psychology (Frederick Bartlett), sociology (Maurice Halbwachs), and philosophy (Henri Bergson). We illustrate the significance of their ideas for our arguments with examples drawn from a range of situations where remembering and forgetting are matters of concern. We aim to move beyond experience as lived in some linear unfolding of time where memory is taken as the vehicle for linking past, present, and future. Instead, we seek to demonstrate selfhood as the shifting intersection of experiences of which our present consciousness is only the leading edge. One way to approach this is to focus on imaginary futures in the past. Experience will be demonstrated to matter not so much in terms of what happened in the past but in terms of how we build the past with the future in ways that make for the possibility of becoming different. In other words how we actualize alternative *trajectories of living.*

2. Futures in the Present and in the Past

It is easy to see how the present is dependent on the future. As Alfred North Whitehead argued in his *Adventures of Ideas*: "[C]ut away the future and the present collapses, emptied of its proper content. Immediate existence requires the insertion of the future in the crannies of the present" (223). For example, timetables, ambitions, anxieties, legal contracts are "futile gestures of consciousness" without relationships to the future. In other words, the present depends on futures.

However, can futures feature in occasions before or antecedent to them? Can the future matter in the past? We argue yes, it can in terms of imaginary futures in the past: in the ways in which we use imaginary futures. The following passage is from Primo Levi's dispassionate account of his survival in the concentration camp at Auschwitz during WW2:

> I believe it is really due to Lorenzo that I am alive today; and not so much for his material aid, as for his having constantly reminded me by his presence, by his natural and plain manner of being good, that there still existed a just world outside of our own [...] [,] something difficult to define, a remote possibility of good for which it was worth surviving. (127)

For six months, Lorenzo, an Italian civilian worker, brought bread and the remainder of his rations to Primo Levi. He gave him an old vest and wrote a postcard on Levi's behalf and brought him back a reply. As Levi puts it: "in concrete terms amounting to little" (127).

This is more than an account of survival. In tying together person and circumstance, past and present, materiality and morality, it deals with the future in an interesting way. This is not a future built out of the past. Rather it is a past built with and through the imaginary future. A future that in Alfred North Whitehead's terms is "antecedent to itself." Such accounts deal with the possibility of the things being otherwise.

3. Imaginary "Gap Filling" and Outstanding Detail

One way to think of the way in which Primo Levi deals with imaginary futures in the past is as a process of "gap filling." A camp life stripped bare of human values is rebuilt around the "outstanding" detail of Lorenzo's simple gifts and acts of altruism. Levi's post-war "effort after meaning" is imaginatively reconstructed in terms of those outstanding details. These outstanding details are enveloped in the folding together of past and present.

Frederick Bartlett discussed remembering in such terms in *Remembering: A Study in Experimental and Social Psychology*. In that classic work he argues that remembering is primarily concerned with how the past is constructed in the present to serve the needs of whatever actions we are currently engaged in. Rather than view what people remember as a window onto the content and structure of individual minds or strident attempts to retell original experience, we ought instead to be concerned with how people construct versions of the past, their position in so doing, and their use of the very notion of what it is to remember. Bartlett defines remembering as "effort after meaning," as "an imaginative reconstruction, or construction, built out of the relation of our attitude towards a whole active mass of organised past reactions or experience, and to a little outstanding detail." (213)

This approach emphasizes remembering in terms of the gap between the "mass" and the "little outstanding detail" of experience. For example, consider what is possible with the tea-soaked morsel of "petites madeleine" cake offered to Marcel Proust. It allows him to more than reclaim "lost time." He mines the potency of the past to reveal things he had not even realized he had experienced in the past. But how is such imaginative reconstruction, such gap filling accomplished? Bartlett makes clear in both *Remembering* and, later on, in *Thinking* that this reconstruction of the past is done by means of conversation. Talk is a fundamental aspect of "everyday thinking" or, as Bartlett terms it, "immediate communication thinking" (*Thinking* 164).

It might be argued that this is all well and good, but the real topic remains what people really do with their minds or really can remember, not just what they can report. However, as Edwards and Potter argue, this is an empirically difficult distinction to maintain. Descriptions of experience are endlessly variable. In addition to this, one of the main functions of such talk is to establish what it is that might have actually, possibly or definitely happened. In a sense germane to the psychology of participants, the truth of original events is the *outcome*, not the *input*, to the reasoning displayed in talk. The turn to a discursive analysis of remembering—to understand the way in which remembering is organized for and accomplished within the pragmatics of communicative action—is a legacy of Bartlett's concerns. Conversational remembering is a fundamental aspect of conduct in socially ordered settings (see, for example, Middleton and Brown; Middleton and Edwards).

4. Imaginary Gap Filling and Outstanding Detail in Communicative Action

The following example illustrates imaginative gap filling and outstanding detail in communicative action. It is taken from a reminiscence session with older people organized and recorded by Faith Gibson. Mary is talking about her experience of learning to handwrite in the early 1900s in her school.

Mary: (...) I was a bad writer ((MC laughs))

MC: well you must have got better you're very good now

Mary: no not now with my arthritis the teacher used to take me up to ((laughs)) they used to take me to the blackboard before maybe 40 of a class (.) I had to write (.) the teacher wrote on the top line you see and I was supposed to copy it as near as possible to hers until I got to be a good writer (.) and in the Irish

> School they had an enormous big certificate it had been awarded by the Vere Foster people for a team of writers from the Irish Society School (.) that was before my time (.) and the teacher took me up one day and she said to me (.) can you read that (.) and I said I can (.) and she said do you see your name there (.) and I said no I don't (.) and she said no and you never will ((other laughter)) (.) and I never did ((laughs))
>
> MC: you weren't good enough Mary
>
> Mary: no that was before my time you see but my grandfather wrote like that
>
> MC: yes
>
> Mary: he was a beautiful writer and so was my father

Mary describes how her future competency in handwriting was potentially mapped out for her at school. She was doomed to apparent failure by her teacher. Her capacity was benchmarked as different to previous generations where the craft of writing was judged differently, as evidenced in the certificate from the past in which pupils who had achieved notable levels of competency were recorded. The potency of memory is in the way she turns round on that difference in marking out her future as one that was not necessarily determined by the immediate trajectories of the teacher's judgments—"you never will." In doing this Mary builds the possibility of an alternative future back into the past where her identity as a poor hand writer is not determined. She is not to be judged in terms of what was "before my time" (MC: you weren't good enough Mary / Mary: no that was before my time). In building an imaginary future back in the past Mary accomplishes her identity as a person in the present in terms of gap filling around outstanding details of the certificate on which her name does not appear, and of the pedagogical practices of former times (i.e., the public copying of the teacher's examples). This reformulation allows for an alternative future of accountability in calling *time* into question. But what sort of time is being invoked? Is it clock time? Her life as a succession of moments?

5. Lived Time—Duration

Lives are more than the linear unfolding of a succession of moments—lives in clock time. We are compelled to live through time—a lived time or duration that is always part of something more, what Henri Bergson referred to as the "fluid continuity of the real" (*Creative Evolution*). He describes the matter out of which our worlds are formed as an "undivided flux" or a "fluid continuity of the real." Here, there is no other reality than that of a continuous, ongoing flow of change: "what is real is the continual change of form: form is only a snapshot view of transition" (302). Those forms that we perceive are akin to "snapshots" or provisional viewpoints on the "open whole" of a ceaselessly changing world. Although fundamentally we exist in a "fluid continuity of the real," we are, nevertheless, able to actively "cut out" or "isolate" discrete forms within that flux. The crucial point for Bergson is that these forms are products or outcomes relative to our particular perspectives—they are not reality itself (300-02).

Bergson argued that it is only in hesitation that we properly experience time. In other words, we experience our own durations of living. But what makes for hesitation? He argues that it is when we come against indeterminacy—"*zones of indeterminacy*" and are "made to wait." The rhythm of our particular conscious existence is interdependent with and, in some sense, built on the durations of others. To demonstrate this interdependency, we need only imagine what would happen if we were to live our own duration "at a slower rhythm." Our relationship to the world, or foothold within the real, would gradually fragment as we would experience reality directly as an "undivided flux," a constant movement of innumerable changes, with the result that we would be unable to perceive or act in an effective way (*Matter and Memory* 201-08).

Bergson's best-known example of such interdependency is discussed in *Creative Evolution*:

> If I want to mix a glass of sugar and water, I must, willy nilly, wait until the sugar melts. This little fact is big with meaning. For here the time I have to wait is not that mathematical time which would apply equally well to the entire history of the material world [...]. It coincides with my impatience, that is to say, with a certain portion of my own duration, which I cannot protract or contract as I like. It is no longer something *thought*, it is something *lived*. (9-10)

What is "big in meaning" in this example is the interdependency of our duration with that of another—in this case, the dissolving sugar. We are forced to wait for the sugar to dissolve. For the time this takes, our own duration is hooked into that of the sugar and water mix in such a way that we cannot "protract or contract it as [we] like." Bergson's point is that the growing impatience that we feel is an emerging and irreducible property of the hooking together of durations. Now, it would have been perfectly possible to have mathematically calculated in advance how long we would probably have to wait for the sugar to dissolve, but this "mathematical time" is not the time we live; our experience is not reducible to it. Indeed, what is most interesting here is the uncertainty of unfolding duration—perhaps we will become too impatient and drink the water before it is ready, perhaps we will be disturbed and the drink will be left untouched, perhaps we will realize that, after waiting, we no longer desire the sickly sweet water. For Bergson, life must be characterized by the "uncertainty" found in this small example of being made to wait: "time is this very hesitation, or it is nothing" (*Creative Evolution* 93). Properly speaking, then, our own particular duration is not really singular—it is always conjoined with others. At times, these other durations "envelop" our own, such as when we are forced to wait. Equally, our duration can envelop others.

6. Imaginary Elaboration in Hesitation at Commemorative Memorial Sites

Consider how we relate to memorial sites. Memorial sites when they "work" create hesitation out of indeterminacy. For example, the Vietnam Memorial Wall in Washington D.C. in the U.S.A. provides just such a place where imaginary elaboration is invoked in the face of zones of indeterminacy. The monument is non-figurative. On the polished black granite surface, over 58,000 names of those lost in that war are inscribed in chronological order of date of death. There are multiple zones of indeterminism. The wall is a place of "reflection"—of hesitation. We literally see ourselves reflected in and are incorporated into the wall. People are drawn into the "text" of the "wall" searching and comparing names. They leave objects of personal significance (letters, clothing, personal mementos). Objects that themselves become the source of further reflective hesitation and imaginative elaboration—"when and under what circumstances was this postcard written—was this the last message home?" Our engagement is not prescribed. It is open and the power of non-figurative monuments is that they create such zones of indeterminacy. However, the durations of living made available in hesitation are not purely subjective experience. The point is that they intersect with the durations of others and it is in that intersection that further imaginary elaboration is possible.

7. Intersecting Durations in Creating Difference

In confronting the indeterminacy of such a non-figurative memorial, where flow of experience is slowed, we are "compelled to live" (Bergson) within the duration of unfolding imaginative reconstruction. But does this make a difference? Can alternative futures be actualized out of the burden of the past in those intersecting durations where change itself is what matters in terms of the reality of experience? The final example is from Kyoko Murakami's studies of remembering and reconciliation in relation to the post-war consequences of being a prisoner of war. Murakami gathered a corpus of interviews with British Second World War veterans who were prisoners of war in the Far East. During their period of captivity, the interviewees worked to build the Thai-Burma Railway before being transferred to a copper mine in Japan. Some 50 years later, in 1992, 28 former British POWs returned to a memorial site in the vicinity of the mine. This visit was part of a whole series of events that were organized as a result of the initiative of Japanese nationals living in the U.K., veterans' associations, and people in the locality of the memorial. The aim of the visit was to promote reconciliation. The memorial site and the circumstances of its creation and maintenance became the focus of efforts in organizing the reconciliation visit for the surviving POWs to Japan.

The following is from one of the interviews with surviving veterans recorded in 1999 by Kyoko Murakami. The participants in the interview were two ex-POWs, a spouse, a Japanese contact and the interviewer—the researcher. Fred, one of the veterans, is providing an example that illustrates a change in relation to Japanese people. The account details an episode that contributed to that change. What we have is an example where durations are made to intersect. But in what ways?

F = ex-POW

M = Japanese contact

Int. = Interviewer

F: I was in Battersea Par:k some years ago (.) after the war (.) ten years after the war (.) ten years after the war (1.0) and I'm sitting out in the open air a with cup of tea at the table and two little (0.8) children running around in front of me (2.0) and I said to myself, 'oh my god > is that Japanese <' because they could be Chinese or (0.8) [Thai (.) it at [any =

Int.: [humm [humm

F: >you know what I mean < but to me they were Japanese (1.0) I thought (0.8) I didn't have to wonder very long because just behind me (there's) somebody calling out '*Oi, koi*' right? 'come here' or

Int.: humm

F: yes? I thought I know that= that means 'come here' or means 'come back' (.) I half reluctantly turned around and (at) the next table behind me was a Japanese man and woman (.) they all got up and they went down (.) stood by the lake (.) and this is the story (.) he took a picture of his wife and two children (.) she came and took a picture of him and the two children (.) and me being= I don't use the camera and all that (.) but what I would normally do in a case like that (.) and I have done it many times I would go out and say and 'Excuse me (.) do you mind if- would you like me to take a photograph of all of you?'

Int.: yes

F: I half got up and I thought 'no why should I?' and I regretted that (.) I regretted it (.) but some years later (.) when I was over at Keiko's place in Croydon (.) a Japanese man (.) lady (.) doctor?

M: Hiro?

F: and the two children they came and they stood on the stairs by Keiko's room there and I took a photograph with my camera then (.) I thought perhaps I've been redeemed at last (.) ha ha ha (.) you know that's a little thing

Int.: yes

This example occurred following a request by the researcher for the interviewees to reflect on and illustrate the consequences for them of participating in the return visit to Japan in 1992. We can see that there is a symmetry of action between the speaker's photo-taking experiences on the two different occasions—before and after the reconciliation trip. This story invokes a notion of change and presents a basis for evaluating that change. It summates the way in which the speaker, Fred, has changed due to participation in the trip. The story marks the speaker's change in attitude towards the Japanese and delineates the new perspective that Fred now possesses. This change is presented by him as a possible redemption: "I thought perhaps I've been redeemed at last," even though "you know that's a little thing." The first "story" does not stand alone. Immediately, the speaker produces the second story as a way of establishing his entitlement to being a changed person (see also Sacks). There is a sense, then, in the discursive organization of these accounts, of the ways in which local (subjective dispositions, for example) and historical issues (such as collective identities—the Japanese) are made to intersect.

What we see in this intersection is precisely the kind of "hesitation" and "elaboration" that Bergson describes. Fred is disturbed by the call "*Oi koi.*" This phrase acts as an "order word" that immediately incorporates the hearer into a recollected zone of personal relations (see Halbwachs, *On Collective Memory*; Halbwachs, *The Collective Memory*). To hear "come here" spoken in Japanese is to "feel" the visceral force of the recollection. However, in what follows next, Fred describes how he also felt compelled by the norms of politeness that correspond to the usual social relationships he inhabits. He is, in a sense, between two zones of personal relations. The tension between them is dramatized by the half getting up, that there is a hesitation, a pause. What happens in this pause? That is precisely what is at issue in the narrative. Fred is confronted with the unexpected ambiguity of seeing Japanese people play out a pleasant family scene before him. His cup of tea in Battersea Park has become something else entirely.

The hesitation on Fred's part results in precisely this experience of "waiting." For as long as Fred waits, his own duration is enveloped by that of the other—the family members who take turns to line up, smiling, in front of the camera. This juxtaposition, then, allows for an ambiguity, a possible "elaboration," as something of Fred's unfolding duration—a former POW, someone who would otherwise like to help, enjoying a cup of tea in the open air in the park—is disclosed to him. The reported event passes, Fred sits down and returns to his cup of tea.

The second event that Fred describes does not involve the same kind of interruption or pause. There is no break in the flow of activities as Fred snaps a picture of the two Japanese children on the stairs. Instead, the hesitation is between the two events as Fred subsequently contrasts the flow of the latter event with the interrupted activity of the former. In gathering up these two events together, Fred discovers a way of "slowing down" and turning around on his own duration, refusing the order that has been put on the past. This results in the imaginary elaboration or re-construction of himself as "redeemed at last." It is the juxtaposition and intersection of durations that allows for the "slowing down" and "hesitation." However, in this second example, the mediating objects are discursive—an overheard utterance, "*Oi koi*," and Fred's occasioned narrative—, which allows for the two events to be gathered up together. It is this that provides the basis for calling into question the ordering of lived experience into which Fred is subsumed and allows it to be reformulated. The utterances, no less than memorials, "contain" the difference that makes the difference.

8. Conclusions

Experience matters then not so much in terms of what happened in the past but in terms of how futures are built back into the past in ways that make for the possibility of becoming different—actualizing alternative trajectories of living. In like terms, imagination matters in terms of where the burden of the past and outstanding detail are folded together in gap-filling imaginative effort after meaning and where imaginative hesitation is a consequence of intersecting durations.

Furthermore, memory matters not as the forensic links in the continuities of persons, groups, and places, but in the ways in which we cut into the flow of experience. Remembering is therefore a discontinuous process holding back the burden of the past. In the same way, forgetting is not the frailties of memory but the return of experience to imaginative re-elaboration.

In summary, we have argued that imaginary futures in the past are a key issue in making experience matter in the study of memory as social practices of remembering and forgetting. Our aim has been to demonstrate imagination as a process of "gap filling" and "hesitating." In doing this we also discussed implications of this for time in terms of duration or the experience of lived time, of time passing. In doing this we concluded that duration is key to understanding the interactive organization of memory where overlapping durations provide the basis for imaginative hesitation. In other words, the reflexive elaboration of experience is both individually and collectively relevant.

Acknowledgements

This article is based on a plenary lecture presented at "The Colloquium on Memory and Imagination" on March 20, 2006 at the Universidade Federal de Santa Catarina, Florianopolis, Santa Caterina, Brazil. Our grateful thanks to Andréa Zanella and all those involved in organizing the conference and to Ana Smolka, Elisabeth dos Santos Braga, Luci Banks Leite, Adriana Lia Friszman de Laplane, and Marta Kohl for their constructive critical commentary and feedback.

References

Bartlett, Frederick C. *Remembering: A Study in Experimental and Social Psychology*. Cambridge: Cambridge UP, 1932.

—. *Thinking: An Experimental and Social Study*. London: Allen & Unwin, 1958.

Bergson, Henri. *Creative Evolution*. 1911. Trans. Arthur Mitchell. Mineola, NY: Dover, 1998.

—. *The Creative Mind: An Introduction to Metaphysics*. 1946. Trans. Mabelle L. Andison. New York: Citadel, 1992.

—. *Matter and Memory*. 1908. Trans. Nancy Margaret Paul and W. Scott Palmer. New York: Zone, 1991.

Edwards, Derek, and Jonathan Potter. *Discursive Psychology*. London: Sage, 1992.

Gibson, Faith. *Using Reminiscence*. London: Help the Aged, 1989.

Halbwachs, Maurice. *The Collective Memory*. 1950. Trans. Francis J. Ditter, Jr. and Vida Yazdi Ditter. New York: Harper & Row, 1980.

—. *On Collective Memory*. 1925. Ed. and trans. Lewis A. Coser. Chicago: U of Chicago P, 1992.

Levi, Primo. *If This Is a Man*. 1958. London: Penguin, 1979.

Lynch, Michael, and David Bogen. *The Spectacle of History: Speech, Text, and Memory at the Iran-Contra Hearings.* Durham: Duke UP, 1996.

Middleton, David, and Steven D. Brown. *The Social Psychology of Experience: Studies in Remembering and Forgetting.* London: Sage, 2005.

Middleton, David, and Derek Edwards. *Collective Remembering.* London: Sage, 1990.

Murakami, Kyoko. "Revisiting the Past: Social Organisation of Remembering and Reconciliation." Diss. Loughborough University, UK, 2001.

Proust, Marcel. *In Remembrance of Things Past.* 1913. Trans. C. K. Scott-Moncrieff, Terence Kilmartin and D. J. Enright. Vol. 1. Harmandsworth: Penguin, 1981.

Sacks, Harvey. "Lecture 4: Storyteller as 'Witness': Entitlement to Experience." *Lectures on Conversation.* Ed. Gail Jefferson. Vol. 2. Oxford: Blackwell, 1992. 242-48.

Whitehead, Alfred North. *Adventures of Ideas.* Harmondsworth: Penguin, 1933.

A Cognitive Taxonomy of Collective Memories

DAVID MANIER AND WILLIAM HIRST

The elasticity of the concept "collective memory" renders coherent treatment of the topic difficult. The term has been used to refer to rituals and traditions, myths, long-past historical events commemorated and memorialized in the present, and recent events remembered not just by individuals, but by mnemonic communities. How can a discussion of rituals and traditions be treated in the same way as a discussion of a community's memory of a recent event? We answer this question in part by constructing a taxonomy of collective memory, in order to appreciate better what the different uses have in common and how they differ.

As we understand it, a collective memory is not simply a memory shared across a community. It must serve a function for the community. Just as not all individual memories can properly be viewed as autobiographical memories, so also not all shared memories can be treated as collective memories. Many Americans know the approximate value of pi, but that does not make it an American collective memory. Memory for the value of pi may be relevant to the identity of members of the international community of educated men and women, and hence may be a collective memory for *this* community, but it is not pertinent to American identity and so cannot be treated as an American collective memory. Collective memories, then, are representations of the past in the minds of members of a community that contribute to the community's sense of identity. For some scholars, this representation is considered to assume a narrative form (see Brockmeier). Yet not all identity-shaping memories fit neatly into a narrative. For us, the identity of the community is constituted (in part) by community members who share not simply similar narratives, but also patterns of thought and/or lived history. Our definition of collective memory relies on group identity, not necessarily expressed in narrative form, but based on shared experience, which may or may not be explicitly articulated (see Manier).

One alternative would be to formulate a taxonomy of the memory practices used by a community, following the example of Assmann, who separated *communicative* from *cultural memory*. Communicative memories are socially mediated, based in a group, and transmitted across a community by means of everyday communication. They have a limited temporal horizon, from 80 to 100 years (four generations). On the other hand, cultural memories are maintained across generations by societal practices and initiations, such as texts, rites, monuments, commemorations, and observances, what Assmann called "figures of memory." Their temporal horizon is indefinite.

In this chapter, we want to build a taxonomy based on the work by cognitive psychologists on individual memory systems. Such a strategy might seem wrongheaded to many scholars in that it seems to conflate collective memory with individual memory. According to a common theme running through many theoretical discussions, collective memories are not mere aggregates of individual memories, and one cannot reduce principles of collective memories to principles of individual memories. Thus, Kansteiner argues that the Freudian insistence that people must "work through" their trauma in order to avoid unwanted symptoms may apply to individuals, but not nations, for "nations can repress with psychological impunity" (186). (See also Kansteiner and Weilnböck, this volume.)

However, this argument (if valid) does not imply that the principles of individual memory cannot in some ways constrain how collective memory functions. If individuals are the ones who do the actual remembering, then how a group remembers and what the group remembers will be shaped, at least in part, by the nature of individual memory. Scholars of collective memory implicitly accept this claim. They assume that collective memories are not simply faithful reproductions of the past and often base this claim on the observation that human memory (unlike computer memory) is open to distortion based on present attitude and external influence (see Bartlett). We are simply extending this line of reasoning by proposing that the distinctive structures of human individual memory may be reflected in the varieties of collective memories.

1. The Systems Approach to Subdividing Individual Memory

Psychologists have demonstrated repeatedly that human memory consists of separate but interconnected structures. Theoretically, the human memory system could be a single mechanism with the same principles governing all stages of encoding, storage, and retrieval. However, research demonstrates that multiple memory systems exist, each of which follows a distinctive set of principles. In this respect, human memory is like a computer's, which contains an array of distinct memory systems—RAM, ROM, hard drive, and so on.

Psychologists have used several conceptual frameworks to characterize the human memory system (see also Markowitsch, this volume). One scheme relies on the recollective experience accompanying a memory. In some cases, people are explicitly aware that they are remembering something, as when they claim "I remember meeting Jane last Thursday." In other instances, the past can affect the present without an accompanying recollective experience, as when people assert "I know we've met before, but I don't know where or when." The person seems familiar, but there is no conscious experience of recollecting a past event.

Using contrasts such as *recollection* versus *familiarity*, *remembering* versus *knowing*, or more commonly, *explicit* versus *implicit memory*, psychologists employ *direct* and *indirect* memory tasks as experimental probes of distinctive memory subsystems (see Schacter and Tulving). *Direct memory tasks*, used to assess *explicit* memory, involve conscious recollection. In a direct memory task known as *cued recall*, people must remember previously studied material, for example, a list of words. They may be given cues (such as that the previously studied word began with SUM___), to which they might reply with the accurate recollection SUMMIT. *Indirect memory tasks*, used to assess *implicit* memory, do not require a conscious experience of remembering. For example, in a *stem completion* task, people may be asked to complete a word stem (e.g., the letters SUM___) with the first word that comes into their minds. If participants complete the word stem with a word from the previously studied word list (SUMMIT), the list is said to have *primed* them to complete the word stem as they did. Although the two tasks are structurally similar, they differ in a critical way: Unlike cued recall, stem completion does not require having the experience of explicitly remembering that the word was on the previously studied list.

A substantial literature indicates that these two types of memory (explicit and implicit) are dissociated from each other, both at the psychological and neurological level. For instance, neurologically impaired anterograde amnesics show depressed performance in cued recall tasks, but normal levels of priming in stem completion tasks (Schacter 509). Dissociations also exist within the performance of neurologically intact individuals (Schacter 507). For example, in one study, a group of "normal" participants were asked to read a list of words and indicate for each word either (1) whether it connotes something pleasant or unpleasant (a deep orienting task), or (2) how many E's it contains (a shallow orienting task). The depth of the orienting task affected performance on a subsequent direct memory task of cued recall (with deep orienting tasks promoting better cued recall), but not on a subsequent indirect memory task (stem completion).

Brain imaging studies indicate that the explicit/implicit memory distinction has a neurological basis (Schacter and Bruckner). When participants are given a task that draws on explicit memory, greater levels of neural activation are observed in the hippocampus and related brain structures. This finding is in line with the work on amnesia, in that amnesia (which involves impairment on explicit, but not implicit, memory tasks) often arises from damage to the hippocampus. As for implicit memory tasks, the hippocampus does not play this kind of special role.

Some psychologists have based their classification framework on the content of the memory. Tulving, for instance, observed that some memories, which he called *episodic memories*, come clothed in temporal and spatial specificity and refer to personally experienced events, places, or things (see Schacter and Tulving). An example of an episodic memory would be a person's memory of eating toast for breakfast this morning. Other memories, *semantic memories*, do not possess this temporal or spatial specificity. Many people know that Napoleon was defeated at Waterloo, but they no longer remember where they learned this fact. At one time, they presumably possessed a memory of the experience of learning about this battle. Many semantic memories begin as episodic memories. But the episodic memory often fades, leaving behind only the semantic memory of what was learned.

As with the explicit-implicit memory distinction, myriad studies establish the psychological reality of the division of memory into episodic and semantic systems. Again, consider amnesic performance. Amnesics cannot remember specific events that occurred after the onset of their amnesia, but they can learn new facts. There is a striking case study of a young girl who from early infancy evidenced profound anterograde amnesia (see Vargha-Khadem et al.). Like others with this condition, she could not remember events that had just happened if asked about them only a few minutes afterwards. Yet she performed perfectly well in school, often ranking near the top of her class, so she was able to learn new facts.

Psychologists also distinguish *procedural* memories from *declarative* memories. The former refers to skills, or things that you *know how* to do (Schacter and Tulving). The latter refers to both memory for experiences and memory for facts, which are things you *know that* occurred or that constitute a fact. Thus, we can distinguish your *knowing how* to ski (a procedural memory) from your *knowing that* you frequently went skiing as a child (a declarative memory). Given the findings discussed above, it is not surprising that amnesics can acquire procedural memories at a normal rate, but have difficulty acquiring declarative memories.

Although different classification schemes have been used to arrive at each of these distinctions, the distinctions themselves have elements in common. Research with amnesics supplies an effective hook for capturing the similarities. Amnesics have difficulty with explicit, episodic, and declarative memories, but evidence normal implicit and procedural memory, and in some studies, normal semantic memory. The cluster of explicit, episodic, and declarative memory is not surprising. After all, episodic memories (which involve *knowing that* an event happened) are a subset of the class of declarative memory, and always involve an explicit recollective experience. As for the implicit, semantic, and procedural cluster, again, overlaps can easily be observed, in that procedural memories and semantic memories do not require an recollective experience of a particular event. Indeed, it may be inimical, while practicing a skill like dancing or skiing (using procedural memory), to think explicitly about the various component parts of that skill (using declarative memory).

Do these distinctions at the individual level transfer to the domain of collective memory? Are there collective analogues to the distinctions between explicit and implicit memory, episodic and semantic memory, and declarative and procedural memory? And if there are, can these subdivisions help us to understand more clearly the nature of collective memory?

2. Subdividing Collective Memory

Collective episodic memory. As with individual memory, it is possible to classify collective memories according to the recollective experiences that people have of them, as well as the spatial-temporal information they contain. Many collective memories are of events in the personal past of members of a mnemonic community. When a group of friends go to a World Cup match and see their national team play beautifully, they may form a collective memory of the game that they will share with each other for years to come. As a result, each individual memory, as well as the collective memory shared by the friends, will be clothed in a spatial-temporal context. Each friend will remember sitting in the stadium and watching the game. The memory of the experience will not only be shared, but it will also contribute to their identity as a group of friends. Of course, the nature of the remembering community may vary substantially: Fans of a sports team are one kind of community, members of a family are another, and people who lived in New York on 9/11 are a third. Moreover, one community (e.g., a set of fans) may remember the event differently from another community (e.g., fans of the opposing team). But no matter the composition of the community, shared memories of a community's experience can be constituted as a collective episodic memory.

Collective semantic memory. All the historical facts (as well as many other facts) people recite without necessarily remembering where they learned them are semantic memories, and for the most part, collective semantic memories. Some collective semantic memories are about contemporary events, places, and things. An example would be the authors' memories of the Viet Nam War. Although we were not in Viet Nam during the war, we did learn about it from the media, friends, books, teachers, and other sources while it was happening. What we learned may not properly be called episodic, since much of it lacks reference to any particular day or place in our lives, but there is a lived quality to these kinds of memories, and hence we will refer to them as *lived semantic memories.*

In contrast, many collective semantic memories refer to more distant events. The authors' memory of Washington's crossing of the Delaware is a good example of a *collective distant semantic memory* (an American collective memory). As with the Viet Nam War, we learned about Washington's military maneuver indirectly, through school, books, and an iconic painting. But unlike our lived memories about the Viet Nam War, our distant semantic memories about Washington's maneuver lack the vital impact of the former.

The impact of lived semantic memories arises, at least in part, because the remembered events have greater resonance for both individual and community. The manner in which we, as individuals, and perhaps more importantly, as members of the American community, remember the Viet Nam War instills in us a personal and communal sense of responsibility, for example, a sense of collective shame about the conduct of the war. Especially when we travel abroad, we carry this with us, the weight of our nation's bungled and sometimes disastrous foreign policies: We carry this history as an inescapable part of our collective identity as Americans.

On the other hand, distant semantic collective memories do not have this kind of effect on community members. Many Americans know about Washington's maneuver, and it could even be said that knowledge about Washington's Delaware crossing is important to the American sense of identity (see Hirsch, Kett, and Trefil). But this memory cannot be seen as involving a burden for Americans in the same way as their memories of the Viet Nam War. The memories many Americans have of the Viet Nam War carry with them a sense of responsibility towards the war refugees who fled to the U.S. and towards their descendants. But Americans do not feel any responsibility towards the descendants of America's enemies killed during the Revolutionary War, for instance, the British. Most distant collective semantic memories are just what the term suggests: Distant enough to relieve the community of the emotional burden and sense of responsibility that more recent memories may possess.

Collective Procedural or Implicit Memory. We want to contrast semantic memories (discussed above) with community traditions, practices, and rituals, which we classify as *collective procedural memories.* Although rituals serve communities in ways other than the effects they may have on memory, they no doubt can be thought of as memories, in this case of procedures rather than of facts or episodes. Some Roman Catholic parishioners may follow the procedure of the Mass without any explicit memory of what each movement symbolizes or where they learned the ritual. They *know how* to celebrate Mass, but they surely do not need to *know that* the Mass as it is celebrated today has its roots in the Council of Trent, beginning in 1545.

Rituals and traditions, or more generally, procedural memories, can serve as mnemonic tools that shape the collective identity of their practitioners, collectively reminding them of declarative memories. The celebration of Mass is intended to remind parishioners of Jesus's crucifixion. The actions entailed in a ritual or procedural memory can also create a collective feeling or attitude. The act of genuflecting creates a feeling of submission and reverence (Connerton). The movements mandated in the Mass may arise from procedural (not declarative) memories, but the result of carrying out these procedures can create the feelings that the Mass is meant to invoke.

Many people follow at least some traditions and rituals without realizing that they are learned, or even that they are rituals or traditions. They view their behavior as natural rather than as a product of experience. In such instances, one might say that the knowledge or learned procedure has become *embodied*. Embodied knowledge can exert a powerful influence on people's lives, perhaps partly because it is not explicitly recognized as something learned, but instead is taken for granted. Many elements of daily life in our own society—from the clothes we wear, to the foods we eat, to our hygienic habits, to our courtship rituals—represent this kind of embodied knowledge.

3. Summary and Conclusions

We may return now to the question with which we began this paper: How can rituals and traditions be treated in the same way as a community's memory of a recent event? Or to use the terminology developed here, how can we treat collective procedural memories and collective episodic memories as alike, that is, as like manifestations of the more general phenomenon of collective memory? The answer is as simple as the one advanced for individual memory: They are *not* the same. Although collective procedural and collective episodic memory are both examples of collective memory, they involve different types of memories, with different properties, and they should not be conflated or treated as if they were the same.

Our proposed cognitive taxonomy of collective memory sketches a way to map constraints on memory at the individual level onto constraints at the collective level. That is, we can discern distinctive principles governing collective episodic, semantic, and procedural memories by examining the principles governing their individual analogues. For example, to build on what we know about individual memory, collective episodic memories should be more susceptible to interference and more likely to be forgotten than collective semantic memories, and collective semantic memories, in turn, should be more susceptible to interference and more likely to be forgotten than procedural memories. This appears to be the case. The meaning of the Mass that parishioners learn about in catechism, that is, parishioners' collective semantic memories about the meaning of Mass, are more likely to be retained over an extended period of time than are the collective episodic memories that parishioners might form of particular Masses they have attended. Still more likely to be retained, however, are the collective procedural memories parishioners have for Mass. They may fail to remember particular Masses, or the details of the catechism, but they are likely to remember quite accurately, until they die, how to participate in the Mass. As a consequence, collective procedural memories may bear more critically on parishioners' collective identity than either their shared episodic memories or their shared knowledge of the meaning of the Mass.

We emphasize here the properties of the different types of collective memories, not the memory practices a community undertakes to utilize these memories. Memory practices can affect how well a memory is retained, but they do so within the constraints of the type of memory that is involved. Parishioners may remember the procedures of Mass in part because they practice them every week. But even in the absence of this weekly practice, the procedures will be better retained than their semantic knowledge of the catechism, or their episodic memories of particular Masses.

Such considerations can provide a more nuanced understanding of much of the current literature on different types of collective memories. Consider again Assmann's distinction between communicative and cultural memory (see also J. Assmann, this volume). Assmann claimed that communicative memories have a fixed temporal horizon of around 80 to 100 years, whereas cultural memories are more permanent. He derived this difference by considering the practices through which a memory is maintained: In the former instance through communication, in the latter instance through what he called figures of memory. But, as studies of oral tradition indicate, many communicative memories last far longer than 80 years, for example, children's counting rhymes, such as "Eenie, Meenie, Miny, Moe." On the other hand, many cultural memories (the information stored in texts or embedded in cultural artifacts), while long lasting, may not be readily accessible to a community and thus cannot legitimately be treated as part of a community's cultural memory. Assmann accepted this possibility when he discussed the two modes of cultural memory: potentiality and actuality.

We can better understand the temporal horizon of a collective memory by considering whether it is a collective episodic, semantic, or procedural memory, rather than simply whether it is a communicative or cultural memory. By definition, collective episodic memories can only last a generation. Collective semantic memories can be transmitted across generations, but are still relatively fragile. Unless they are externalized, in texts or cultural artifacts, collective semantic memories will tend to decrease from one generation to the next and may eventually be completely forgotten. However, collective procedural memory is more likely to be accessible (and available) over the long term, less likely to be distorted, and more likely to be transmitted intact from one generation to the next. Collective procedural memories (such as skills at using instruments and tools) are more likely to form the basis of a community's "actual" cultural memory than are collective semantic memories. That is, they are more likely to serve as the foundation of a community's cultural memory, and (as noted above) of the community's identity. These conclusions may not differ substantially from Assmann's, but they rest not on practices but on the characteristics of individual memory. Interestingly, when cultural memory is viewed in these terms, Nora's discussion of the replacement of memory with history can be interpreted as the replacement of (stable) collective procedural memories with (less stable) collective semantic memories.

We are not denying here the importance of considering memory practices, and their impact on the formation and maintenance of collective memories. Yet much can be gained by drawing distinctions among different types of collective memory, using a cognitive taxonomy. Such a taxonomy can further our understanding of the different types of collective memories, as well as their distinctive properties and dynamics.

Authors' Note

The order of the authors was determined by a coin toss.

References

Assmann, Jan. "Collective Memory and Cultural Identity." Trans. John Czaplicka. *New German Critique* 65 (1995): 125-33.

Bartlett, Frederick. *Remembering: A Study in Experimental and Social Psychology.* 1932. Cambridge: Cambridge UP, 1995.

Brockmeier, Jens. "Remembering and Forgetting: Narrative as Cultural Memory." *Culture and Psychology* 8 (2002): 15-43.

Connerton, Paul. *How Societies Remember.* New York: Cambridge UP, 1989.

Hirsch, E. D., Joseph F. Kett, and James Trefil. *The New Dictionary of Cultural Literacy.* 3rd ed. Boston: Houghton Mifflin, 2002.

Kansteiner, Wulf. "Finding Meaning in Memory: A Methodological Critique of Collective Memory Studies." *History and Theory* 41 (2002): 179-97.

Manier, David. "Is Memory in the Brain? Remembering as Social Behavior." *Mind, Culture, and Activity* 11.4 (2004): 251-66.

Nora, Pierre. *Realms of Memory.* New York: Columbia UP, 1996.

Schacter, Daniel L. "Implicit Memory: History and Current Status." *Journal of Experimental Psychology: Learning, Memory, and Cognition* 13 (1987): 501-18.

Schacter, Daniel L., and R. L. Bruckner. "Priming and the Brain." *Neuron* 20 (1998): 185-95.

Schacter, Daniel L., and Endel Tulving. *Memory Systems 1994.* Cambridge: MIT Press, 1994.

Vargha-Khadem, Faraneh, D. G. Gardian, K. E. Watkins, A. Connelly, W. Van Paesschen, and M. Mishkin. "Differential Effects of Early Hippocampal Pathology on Episodic and Semantic Memory." *Science* 277 (1997): 376-80.

Language and Memory: Social and Cognitive Processes

GERALD ECHTERHOFF

The possibility that the language by which one captures experience also shapes one's memory and knowledge has fascinated scholars in various disciplines, such as psychology, sociology, philosophy, linguistics, anthropology, and cultural studies. Everyday life provides us with numerous instances of how describing an experience leads to distinctive mental representations and memories concerning the experience. When the same event is verbalized or expressed differently it may also be remembered differently. For example, when a person tells a friend about a new colleague's first day at work, her verbal description of the colleague's behavior and manner as "ambitious and a bit stilted" may shape her memory representation of the colleague as well as of the events on that day (Higgins, "'Communication Game'"; Higgins, "Achieving"). Also, saying "someone stepped on my foot at the meeting yesterday" conjures up a different memory than saying "someone was aggressive to me at the meeting yesterday" (see Semin and Fiedler). In the mass media, labeling the same incident as either "an act of self-defense" or as "a reckless attack on innocent civilians" obviously evokes different representations and evaluations that may also shape how the incident is later remembered. Memories for the same historical events in nineteenth-century North America are likely (and arguably often designed) to differ depending on whether they refer to "the pioneering frontier movement" or "the expulsion and murder of the First Nations." Other examples show that when a language lacks linguistic categories to describe a stimulus, speakers of that language exhibit poorer memory for that stimulus than do speakers of a language that offers better linguistic means to capture the stimulus (see Hunt and Agnoli). (At a meta-level, of course, the following is clear: To the extent that the present article presents its information in language, without providing independent, non-verbal representations, it is essentially subject to the very biases it describes.)

Given the abundance of such examples in interpersonal communication, history, politics, and the media, one may suspect that the linguistic format can have profound effects on memory in its individual, collective, and cultural manifestations. Language, a system largely based on conventional rules, is as much a product of culture as it is a tool for people to shape culture. Thus, language effects on memory also reflect the cultural dimension of memory. This article will present theoretical approaches, key concepts, and empirical evidence bearing on these phenomena. Because the underlying perspective is that of psychological research, the article will be concerned primarily with the individual or interpersonal level rather than the macro (for example societal or cultural) level. Much of the debate will be devoted to cognitive processes which play a prominent role in language effects on memory. However, because language also serves pragmatic functions (those effects on a listener intended by a speaker) and the purpose of dialogical communication, social processes are also taken into account.

1. Foundational Issues: The Relation between Language and Memory

The concept of memory is employed to refer to a variety of processes, structures, and systems that allow events and experiences at time 1 to affect people's experiences and behaviors at time 2. A language is commonly regarded as a system of symbols that can represent people's experiences in a conventionalized and communicable format. Within the limits of certain rules (grammar), the symbols of a language can be productively combined and thus convey information that has never been conveyed before. The term language is also employed to refer to the use of such a symbol system. Many rules of natural languages can be mastered by people in an effortless fashion and at a remarkable speed.

There are at least two main ways of examining the relation between language and memory: First, one can study whether and how language shapes memory. This approach focuses on memory as the central phenomenon and how it depends on or is influenced by language and linguistic formats of representation. Second, one can also investigate how memory affects language. In this case, the focus is on language as the central phenomenon and how it depends on memory functions and processes, for instance, the ability to retrieve information about words or syntax. Drawing an analogy to experimental methodology, the first approach treats memory as the dependent variable and language as one of the potentially relevant independent variables, whereas for the second approach language is the focal dependent variable and memory one of the possible independent variables. Given the theme of this handbook, this chapter will concentrate on the first approach.

Investigations of language effects on memory are faced with the fundamental issue of the relation between the two domains. To illustrate different positions on this issue, it is helpful to refer to memory as an integral part of human cognition. The basic question is whether our cognition can at all be separated from language, that is, whether it is legitimate to treat the two as independent and separate phenomena. Without going into the details of this complex topic, suffice it to say that according to one position, language provides the essence of human thinking and memory and the mental representations entertained in our minds are inextricably linguistic. Thus, to study memory and thinking one has first and foremost to deal with language. The roots of this view can be traced back to Plato, who had Socrates declare in *Phaedo*: "I decided to take refuge in language, and study the truth of things by means of it." Along similar lines, Wittgenstein famously noted that "the limits of my language mean the limits of my world" (115). Also in the 1920s, the eminent behaviorist John Watson took the approach to an extreme by arguing that thought is merely verbal behavior that remains internal and prevocal—just below a whisper, so to speak. Since then, this position has been epitomized by the Sapir-Whorf hypothesis, named after the anthropologist Edward Sapir and his student Benjamin Lee Whorf. In its strong version, this hypothesis states that our experiences with the world are intrinsically linguistic and that cognition is inherently determined by the thinker's language (see Hunt and Agnoli).

According to a competing position, the contents and processes of the mind, including our knowledge and memory, are characteristically different and independent from the linguistic form that people use to communicate their thoughts and memories. An extreme version of this view holds that knowledge and thought transcend language. Testifying to this account, Albert Einstein, clearly a man with a highly active mind, reported that his thoughts did not come to him in words and that he tried to express them verbally only afterwards. In psychoanalysis, language has been characterized as eluding the "real," prelinguistic basis of the psyche (for example by the radical French theorist Jacques Lacan). To emphasize that the mind operates on its own terms, in a genuinely and distinctly mental mode, cognitive psychologists have postulated the existence of a universal and abstract "language of thought"—dubbed "mentalese" by the cognitive scientist Steven Pinker—that is different from natural languages and used for internal rather than external communication.

As contrary as these positions might seem, psychological research readily indicates a middle ground affording productive and sound perspectives on how language may shape memory. On the one hand, some aspects of cognition apparently can operate independently from language. For instance, pre-linguistic infants already possess higher cognitive capacities (such as causal thinking and inference), and patients with severe clinical language disorders exhibit many intact domains of cognition and memory (see Weiskrantz). Research has also indicated the important role of non-verbal modes of human cognition, such as representations based on visual, spatial, auditory, olfactory, or motor information (Rubin). It is relatively difficult to verbally describe experiences which are predominantly represented in one of these modes, such as faces, melodies, or the distinct smell of an environment. Also, researchers have identified one class of memories that typically escape verbal reports because they occur outside of people's conscious awareness. This type of memory has been dubbed non-declarative, indicating that people find it difficult or impossible to "declare" the occurrence of such memories (see Manier and Hirst, this volume). Examples include the memory for motor processes involved in riding a bicycle or priming (implicit) influences of previous exposure to stimuli.

On the other hand, language is a principal, genuinely human means of interpreting and retaining experiences. Indeed, some mental representations are impossible without language, such as the representation of one's own name. Linguistic representations are especially apt to capture experiences in abstract or higher-level formats, such as when we say that a person is "ambitious" or "aggressive," or that an incident is "an act of self-defense." It has been argued that the further mental representations are removed from low-level perceptual or motor experiences, the more important linguistic factors become (see Boroditsky). The term declarative memory is commonly used to refer to those memories that are amenable to verbalization, i.e., to memories that people can "declare." Declarative memory comprises semantic memory, memory based on acquired knowledge and concepts of the world, and episodic memory, the conscious recollection of one's previous experiences within a specifiable temporal-spatial context (see Manier and Hirst, this volume). Saying that these memories are declarative does not mean they are *only* made of words. In fact, most memory researchers would probably agree that episodic memory is to a large extent constructed on the basis of non-linguistic representations, such as visual, spatial, or auditory representations encoded at the time of the initial experience (e.g., Rubin).

One upshot of these considerations is that some cognitions and memories may indeed transcend language while not all cognition is language-based or linguistic. A picture may say more than a thousand words, yet a word may suffice to determine one of many possible interpretations of a picture. From this perspective, the debate of whether thought depends on language or vice versa is rather futile. The question of how nonlinguistic and linguistic representations interact or interfere with each other in the workings of the mind appears as psychologically more adequate and stimulating than belaboring the antagonism of extreme positions.

The role of different levels of representation will be echoed during the following presentation of different research areas on language effects on memory. For instance, one field of research, verbal overshadowing, has been concerned with how memory is affected by people's attempts to verbally describe stimuli that are predominantly processed in non-linguistic modes and thus difficult to describe (such as faces or the taste of wine). The different research fields vary in their emphasis on lexical, syntactical, or pragmatic aspects of language. Traditionally, the language-and-thought debate has focused on effects of language at the lexical level, such as whether memory for color stimuli depends on the availability (vs. lack) of certain color terms in a language. It should be noted that language can also be studied at the complex level of storytelling and narrative. Effects of narrative schemata on memory have been widely investigated (see Straub, this volume), but cannot be treated in more detail in this chapter.

Existing research has investigated differences in memory and cognition between speakers of different natural languages (between-language approach) as well as effects of different verbal expressions within the same language (within-language approach). Within-language approaches can employ experimental manipulations while between-language approaches are based on observations of existing differences. Thus, from a methodological perspective, within-language (relative to between-language) approaches provide a better basis for inferences about causal effects of language on memory (see Hardin and Banaji). Still, the often provocative claims of between-language approaches have met with no less resonance across different disciplines and areas.

2. Between-Language Approaches: Effects of General Linguistic Structures

The Sapir-Whorf hypothesis has been one of the major forces inspiring empirical research on the effects of language on thought and memory. Both Sapir and his student Whorf argued that differences in the structure of speakers' language create differences in cognition: "We see and hear and otherwise experience very largely as we do because the language habits of our community predispose certain choices of interpretation" (Sapir 69). "We dissect nature along the lines laid down by our native languages" (Whorf 213). Since the first budding of interest in the 1950s, this notion has provoked controversial debates and stimulated a substantial corpus of research, particularly on cognitive differences between speakers belonging to different language communities, such as speakers of Mandarin, English, Navajo, or Italian. Research in this field primarily addresses the extent to which the *structural* aspects of a language affect the speakers' cognition. By this view, language is predominantly treated as a tacit structure or system, much in the sense of what Chomsky called linguistic competence.

While the strong version of the Sapir-Whorf hypothesis, according to which language causally determines cognition, has long been abandoned, weaker versions, which postulate a non-deterministic relation between language and cognition, are still entertained and debated today (see Boroditsky; Kay and Regier; but see January and Kako). When researchers first started to conduct empirical studies, they considered color memory as a prototypical domain because color varies on a continuous dimension but is divided along different boundaries across languages. The Sapir-Whorf hypothesis predicts that a different linguistic division in the color space would entail differences in color cognition and memory. For instance, differences in the number of color terms offered by different languages should lead to differences in episodic memory for those colors. Between-language studies on color memory typically investigate whether speakers of languages that offer different numbers of color terms and invite different boundaries between neighboring colors exhibit different memory performance for selected color stimuli.

The initial enthusiasm for the Sapir-Whorf view in the 1950s and 1960s was considerably dampened as a result of famous studies by Eleanor Rosch Heider and others. These studies suggested that color categories in different languages are organized around universal focal colors and that these focal colors are also remembered more accurately than non-focal colors across speakers of languages with different color naming systems. However, since this serious and widely acknowledged criticism, researchers have continuously found that although color categories are subject to universal constraints, linguistic differences can entail differences in color cognition and memory. Existing evidence shows that language effects are possible even for experiences that are to a great extent universally constrained, such as color cognition, or digit span (the number of random digits people can hold in working memory), with larger digit spans in speakers of languages with shorter digit articulation (Chincotta and Underwood). Apparently, different languages can lead people to attend to different aspects of their experience so that the prelinguistic categories of their mental representation are reinforced, modulated, or even eliminated in the process of acquiring a language. A plausible notion is that the less representations are constrained by sensory (perceptual, low-level) information or human physiology, the greater is the potential influence of language (Boroditsky; Kay and Regier). Thus, between-language effects are more likely when representations are formed at an abstract, higher level or when direct sensory information is inconclusive. This is certainly the case for representations in the social, cultural, or political domain (such as when we represent or remember a person as "ambitious" or an incident as "an act of self-defense").

In an adjacent line of research, researchers have studied between-language effects on memory with bilinguals, people who have acquired two main languages for regular use in everyday life, often due to migration from one language community (country) to another. In one study, Marian and Neisser found that Russian-English bilinguals recalled more experiences from the Russian-speaking period (often from the period before their emigration to the United States) when interviewed in Russian (and vice versa when interviewed in English). Consistent with the notion of context-dependent memory, episodic memories become more accessible when the linguistic environment at retrieval matches the linguistic environment at encoding, indicating that membership in different language communities can play an important role in how we remember our personal past. Because differences in the linguistic environment are likely to entail cultural differences, a wider implication of this research is that between-language effects might also affect cultural memory.

3. Within-Language Approaches: Effects of Specific Language Use

Linguistic differences we encounter in everyday life are often due to different ways of verbalizing experiences within the same language. Several examples of such differences have been provided in the introduction of this article, such as different verbal descriptions of a person's behavior or complex incidents. A large body of research exists that has investigated the effects of such within-language differences on people's mental representations and memory. While between-language approaches draw attention to differences between general and often tacit linguistic structures or systems, within-language approaches focus on effects due to the actual and specific use of language (see Chiu, Krauss, and Lee), which is akin to what Chomsky called linguistic performance.

Among within-language approaches, researchers have predominantly investigated language effects at the level of lexical and semantic encoding or at the level of pragmatic communication. The first line of research focuses on how encoding or retrieving experiences in a verbal format affects memory and knowledge, while the second line concentrates on how interpersonal communication as a purposeful, context-dependent activity affects the communicators' memory and knowledge.

Effects at the Lexical and Semantic Level: Verbal Encoding and Retrieval. The use of words to describe or convey experiences may influence memory in different ways. First, speakers' own memory for experiences can be affected by their prior verbalization of these experiences. Such effects have been studied from different perspectives. Traditionally, memory researchers have regarded the verbal coding of input information as a means of rehearsal or additional activation. A rich body of research indeed shows that verbalization has beneficial consequences, namely the improvement and consolidation of memory for the target information. This memory advantage can be explained to some extent by the active self-generation of information (generation effect). However, studies on verbal overshadowing have shown that verbalization of experiences or stimuli that are relatively difficult to describe (such as complex visual stimuli, tastes, or music) can also have detrimental consequences on memory (Schooler, Fiore, and Brandimonte). For instance, participants who had verbally described the face of a criminal (vs. had not described the face) were subsequently less accurate at identifying the perpetrator in a photo lineup task. According to one explanation, verbally created representations of stimuli interfere with the original visual representations, rendering subsequent recognition more difficult (see Rubin). While this research revealed effects of the mere act of verbalization (relative to non-verbalization), other studies indicate that different kinds of verbalization can lead to different memories. In one study by Tversky and Marsh, memories for a story were biased in the direction of the previous retellings of that story (from either a favorable or an unfavorable perspective on a specific character in the story).

Second, the use of words may also affect the memory of recipients of a verbal message (see Hardin and Banaji). Famous experiments by Elizabeth Loftus and colleagues have shown that providing eyewitnesses of an event with different verbal information or retrieval cues about a witnessed event can bias the eyewitnesses' event memory. For instance, when eyewitnesses receive a probe containing a definite (vs. indefinite) article that falsely presupposes the presence of an object in an original event (e.g., "Did you see *the* motorcycle?" vs. "Did you see *a* motorcycle?") they are more likely to erroneously remember seeing the object during the event. Misleading details (e.g., "motorcycle helmet") that are embedded within a full-blown text or narrative can also intrude into eyewitnesses' event memory, especially when eyewitnesses do not attempt to discriminate the perceptual representations formed during the witnessed event from postevent verbal representations (Echterhoff, Hirst, and Hussy).

Various other studies have indicated that providing people with verbal labels to encode or retrieve stimuli can shape their mental representation and subsequent memory for these stimuli (see Hardin and Banaji). Verbal labels activate cognitive schemata or categories that are used to organize information in meaningful ways and subsequently guide what people remember about a target experience. Because interpersonal and social phenomena often entail representations at a relatively abstract level, human social cognition is a prototypical domain in which mental representations draw on verbal labels and categories (such as "ambitious," "introverted," "Muslim," or "Catholic"). Research drawing on the *linguistic category model* (e.g., Semin and Fiedler) has shown that even subtle linguistic differences can bias the way people recall another person's behavior. For instance, people remember and judge a target person's negative behavior more negatively when they are asked to consider it in more abstract, dispositional terms ("Person X is aggressive") versus more concrete, situational terms ("Person X shouted at Y"). To the extent that such linguistic biases or preferences both depend on and affect cultural environments, they may also be regarded as signs and carriers of cultural memory.

Effects of Pragmatic Communication: Audience Tuning and Socially Shared Reality. Language effects on memory are not confined to the lexical or semantic dimension or to the encoding and decoding of verbally represented information, but they can also be traced to the realm of pragmatic communication. From the perspective of pragmatics, language is a motivated, context-dependent means of interpersonal communication, following (explicit and implicit) rules and assumptions. Various motives of communication have been identified, such as conveying information or meaning, influencing others' behavior, maximizing beneficial social responses, accomplishing a joint task, achieving epistemic certainty, or achieving a shared understanding with others. According to common rules of the "communication game" (Higgins, "'Communication Game'"), which include Grice's maxims of conversation, communicators should convey the truth as they see it, say what is relevant, and give neither too much nor too little information, and take into account the audience's perspective, knowledge, attitudes, and preferences in their language use—a process referred to as audience tuning.

Studies employing the saying-is-believing paradigm (Echterhoff, Higgins, and Groll; Echterhoff, Higgins, Kopietz, and Groll; also see Higgins, "'Communication Game'"; Higgins, "Achieving") show that tuning to an audience's (positive or negative) attitude not only biases speakers' messages but may also affect their subsequent memory and cognitive representations of the message topic. In saying-is-believing studies, participants (assuming the communicator role) are asked to describe a target person based on a short essay that contains evaluatively ambiguous behaviors (such as a behavior that can be labeled as either "thrifty" or "stingy"). After learning that their audience either likes or dislikes the target person, participants typically perform audience tuning: They create evaluatively positive messages for an audience with a positive attitude and evaluatively negative messages for an audience with a negative attitude. The saying-is-believing effect is reflected by the finding that communicators' subsequent memory for the original target information is largely consistent with the evaluative tone of their previous message. Thus, communicators can end up believing and remembering what they said rather than what they originally learned about a target.

Importantly, audience-tuning effects on memory apparently depend to a large extent on the motives and context of interpersonal communication (Echterhoff, Higgins, and Groll; Echterhoff, Higgins, Kopietz, and Groll). Specifically, Echterhoff and colleagues have argued that such effects occur to the extent that communicators construct a socially shared reality with their audience about the topic or target (Higgins, "Achieving"). Shared reality renders previously uncertain representations of experience subjectively valid and is reflected by people's epistemic trust in the co-constructor(s). By this account, communicators reduce the uncertainty concerning the target person by taking into account the audience's attitude in producing a message about the target. Consistent with a shared-reality account, Echterhoff, Higgins, Kopietz, and Groll found that memory was biased when audience tuning was motivated by the creation of a shared reality about the target but not when it was driven by alternative, non-epistemic goals (e.g., obtaining a monetary incentive). Also, communicators tuning to an in-group audience (a fellow German), an audience they trusted as an appropriate co-constructor, incorporated the audience-tuned view into their memory, but not those who tuned their messages to an out-group audience (a Turk), an audience they did not trust sufficiently.

In these studies, the overt verbal messages and the message information available at the time of recall did *not* differ between the shared-reality conditions. What differed was the extent to which communicators felt they could trust their message as conveying a valid view about the target. Thus, differences in verbal descriptions or linguistic representations per se are not always sufficient for effects on the speakers' subsequent memory. Instead, the communicators' motives and relation to the audience are critical for the extent to which their communication shapes their mental representations of the topic.

This research also has implications for the formation of cultural knowledge. Verbal communication can disseminate knowledge, memories, and beliefs in relatively subtle ways when people actively participate as communicators, not only as passive recipients—under the proviso that they not only observe common rules (such as audience tuning) but also create and experience a shared reality with their communication partners.

Within homogeneous groups or communities, whose members regard each other as trustworthy co-constructors of reality in the face of uncertainty, such communication may affirm and even accentuate presupposed world views, including prevalent cultural stereotypes (see Lyons and Kashima), and thus fuel conflict with out-groups. Future research should seek to further integrate these cognitive, motivational, and sociocultural dimensions of how verbal communication can mold memory and knowledge.

Author's Note

I thank Gerd Bohner and Bob Krauss for providing helpful comments on drafts of this chapter.

References

Boroditsky, Lera. "Does Language Shape Thought? Mandarin and English Speakers' Conception of Time." *Cognitive Psychology* 43 (2001): 1-22.

Chincotta, Dino, and Geoffrey Underwood. "Digit Span and Articulatory Suppression: A Cross-Linguistic Comparison." *European Journal of Cognitive Psychology* 9 (1997): 89-96.

Chiu, Chi-yue, Robert M. Krauss, and Sau-lai Lee. "Communication and Social Cognition: A Post-Whorfian Approach." *Progress in Asian Social Psychology: Theoretical and Empirical Contributions.* Eds. Toshio Sugiman, Minoru Karasawa, James H. Liu and Colleen Ward. Vol. 2. Seoul: Kyoyook Kwahak Sa, 1999. 127-43.

Echterhoff, Gerald, E. Tory Higgins, and Stephan Groll. "Audience-Tuning Effects on Memory: The Role of Shared Reality." *Journal of Personality and Social Psychology* 89 (2005): 257-76.

Echterhoff, Gerald, E. Tory Higgins, René Kopietz, and Stephan Groll. "How Communication Goals Determine When Audience Tuning Biases Memory." *Journal of Experimental Psychology: General* 137.1 (2008): 3-21.

Echterhoff, Gerald, William Hirst, and Walter Hussy. "How Eyewitnesses Resist Misinformation: Social Postwarnings and the Monitoring of Memory Characteristics." *Memory & Cognition* 33 (2005): 770-82.

Hardin, Curtis D., and Mahzarin R. Banaji. "The Influence of Language on Thought." *Social Cognition* 11 (1993): 277-308.

Higgins, E. Tory. "Achieving 'Shared Reality' in the Communication Game: A Social Action That Creates Meaning." *Journal of Language and Social Psychology* 11 (1992): 107-31.

—. "The 'Communication Game': Implications for Social Cognition and Persuasion." *Social Cognition: The Ontario Symposium.* Eds. E. T. Higgins, C. P. Herman and M. P. Zanna. Vol. 1. Hillsdale, NJ: Erlbaum, 1981. 343-92.

Hunt, Earl, and Franca Agnoli. "The Whorfian Hypothesis: A Cognitive Psychology Perspective." *Psychological Review* 98 (1991): 377-89.

January, David, and Edward Kako. "Re-Evaluating Evidence for Linguistic Relativity: Reply to Boroditsky (2001)." *Cognition* 104 (2007): 417-26.

Kay, Paul, and Terry Regier. "Language, Thought and Color: Recent Developments." *Trends in Cognitive Sciences* 10 (2006): 51-54.

Lyons, Anthony, and Yoshihisa Kashima. "How are Stereotypes Maintained through Communication? The Influence of Stereotype Sharedness." *Journal of Personality and Social Psychology* 85 (2003): 989-1005.

Marian, Viorica, and Ulric Neisser. "Language-Dependent Recall of Autobiographical Memories." *Journal of Experimental Psychology: General* 129 (2000): 361-68.

Rosch Heider, Eleanor H. "Probabilities, Sampling, and Ethnographic Method: The Case of Dani Color Names." *Man* 7 (1972): 448-66.

Rubin, David C. "The Basic-Systems Model of Episodic Memory." *Perspectives on Psychological Science* 1 (2006): 277-311.

Sapir, Edward. *Culture, Language, and Personality.* 1941. Berkeley: U of California P, 1964.

Schooler, Jonathan W., Stephen M. Fiore, and Maria A. Brandimonte. "At a Loss *from* Words: Verbal Overshadowing of Perceptual Memories." *The Psychology of Learning and Motivation* 37 (1997): 291-340.

Semin, Gün R., and Klaus Fiedler. "The Inferential Properties of Interpersonal Verbs." *Language, Interaction and Social Cognition.* Eds. Gün Semin and Klaus Fiedler. Newbury Park, CA: Sage, 1992. 58-76.

Tversky, Barbara, and Elizabeth J. Marsh. "Biased Retellings of Events Yield Biased Memories." *Cognitive Psychology* 40 (2000): 1-38.

Weiskrantz, Lawrence, ed. *Thought Without Language: A Fyssen Foundation Symposium.* Oxford: Clarendon, 1988.

Whorf, Benjamin L. *Language, Thought, and Reality: Selected Writings of Benjamin Lee Whorf.* Ed. John B. Carroll. Cambridge: MIT Press, 1956.

Wittgenstein, Ludwig. *Tractatus Logico-Philosophicus.* 1922. New York: Humanities, 1961.

Cultural Memory and the Neurosciences

HANS J. MARKOWITSCH

In order to understand cultural memory it is essential first to understand memory in general. Until the 1970s scientists basically considered memory to be a unitary function which existed throughout (most of the) animal kingdom, but might vary with respect to its acquisition (learning) in gradient, capacity, differentiation, or behavioral-cognitive flexibility. Gagné saw this sequence as hierarchical, or as proceeding from simple to complex forms of learning (taxonomy of learning according to Gagné):

(1) *Signal learning or classical conditioning*
This form of learning is best known as Pavlovian conditioning. The dog who after a few pairings of a ringing bell with a piece of meat soon salivates in response to the sound alone is an example. In classical conditioning the unconditioned stimulus occurs independent of the subject's behavior.

(2) *Stimulus-response learning or instrumental conditioning*
Instrumental conditioning is dependent on the subject's behavior. The subject learns the association between a stimulus and a response.

(3) *Chaining (including verbal association)*
Chaining refers to several consecutive responses where each response determines the next. For example, only several responses which build on each other will lead to a reward.

(4) *Multiple discrimination*
Learning to differentiate between stimuli which have one or more attributes in common

(5) *Concept learning*
Learning to respond in the same way to a variety of objects or attributes of objects which have something in common

(6) *Principle learning*
Acquiring knowledge on how to master a set of problems which have common attributes

(7) *Problem solving*
Making proper use of learned principles and having insights, that is, being able to draw inferences.

Memory is, of course, by definition based on learning:

> Memory is the learning-dependent storage of ontogenetically acquired information. This information is integrated selectively and in a species-specific manner into the phylogenetic neuronal structures and can be retrieved at any given time, meaning that it can be made available for situation-appropriate behavior. Gener-

> ally formulated, memory is based on conditioned changes of the transfer properties in the neuronal "network" whereby under specific circumstances the neuromotoric signals and behavior patterns corresponding to the system modifications (engrams) can completely or partially be reproduced. (Sinz 19)

Thus, with respect to learning, "primitive" animals were seen as able to show habituation or classical conditioning ("the Pavlovian dog"). More phylogenetically advanced species could be operantly conditioned and some of the mammalian and bird species (such as dolphins, apes, and crows) were found to demonstrate imitation or insightful learning. With the appearance of Endel Tulving's book chapter on episodic and semantic memory ("Episodic and Semantic Memory"), his subsequent book on episodic memory (*Elements*), and Mishkin and Petri's chapter on memories and habits in animals, a dramatic change in viewing memory in psychology and the neurosciences occurred. This change was furthered by studying a number of amnesic patients. Warrington and Weiskrantz had observed already in 1970 that severely amnesic patients were able to correctly reidentify two-dimensional figures of objects which were presented to them as a whole initially, but only in part after a delay. Subsequently, a number of researchers detected that the memory deficits of so-called amnesic patients were not universal, but that these patients may show some limited remaining memory abilities.

From these findings and from some complementary results from experimental psychology in normal subjects, it was postulated that memory has to be divided with respect to processes and systems. Previously, scientists had only distinguished between short-term (seconds to a few minutes) and long-term memory (longer than five minutes or more than a few bits of information) (Atkinson and Shiffrin). The process division refers to implicit versus explicit memories, that is, to memories which were encoded with or without conscious reflection ("noetically" or "anoetically"). The systems approach is the most important one. It currently divides long-term memory into five basic systems. These will be explained in the following and are sketched in figure 1.

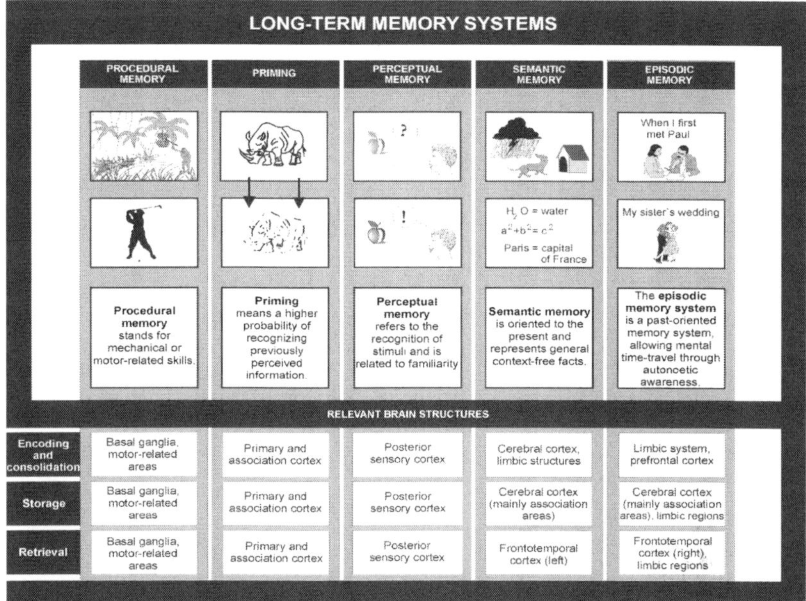

Figure 1. Sketch of the five currently accepted long-term memory systems (top) and assumed brain regions implicated in their processing (bottom). See the text for a detailed description.

Procedural memory. Psychology and the neurosciences assume that children start to memorize on the basis of motor movements: They learn that moving their hands, arms, and legs influences the environment, for example by making a mobile move. This learning is later amplified and extended to various motor-related functions, from skiing and biking to driving and playing piano or cards. All the necessary processes, retrieved during execution of such functions, proceed on an automatic, unconscious level. For instance, when asked the question of what needs to be done *first* when intending to shift gears while driving a car, many subjects will immediately respond "press the clutch," while deeper thinking may lead to the correct answer "first release the gas pedal." This example demonstrates that our procedural memory system frees us from reflecting on routine situations.

Priming. Similarly, the second memory system—priming—is a principally unconsciously acting memory system which is of help in many everyday situations. In fact, some researchers assume that we process 95% of the information we are confronted with on an unconscious level (Drachman). An example for priming: One sits in a car and listens to the radio. The played melody automatically leads to the retrieval of the melody's text. Priming is also nowadays used in radio and TV advertisements where, for example, firm A shows a spot for 20 seconds, then firms B and C each present 20-second spots, and thereafter firm A's spot is repeated, perhaps with similar but abbreviated material. The idea behind this double presentation within a short time period is that the initial (long) spot provides a prime, that is, influences the brain, but does not result in a (fully) conscious representation. Repeating the essence of the spot within a short ("contingent") time period brings the content to a conscious level and may induce purchasing of the product.

Perceptual memory. While procedural memory and priming are considered to be unconscious or anoetic memory systems, perceptual memory is regarded as a noetic system. Perceptual memory is defined as a presemantic memory system, which nevertheless allows for distinguishing or identifying an object or pattern on the basis of familiarity judgments. For example, the perceptual memory system is used to identify an apple, no matter whether it is red, yellow, or green, or half-eaten or intact, and to distinguish it from a pear or a peach.

Semantic memory. The last two long-term memory systems—semantic memory and episodic (autobiographical) memory—build on the former ones. Semantic memory refers to general facts—world knowledge, school knowledge—, facts that are present on a conscious level so that the subject can conclude "this is true" or "this is false": Oslo is the capital of Norway, but Sydney is not the capital of Australia.

Episodic-autobiographical memory. Episodic memory constitutes the highest memory system and is regarded as being autonoetic (Markowitsch, "Autonoetic Consciousness"; Tulving, "Episodic Memory and Autonoesis"). Episodic memory actually refers to mental time traveling both retrogradely (backwards) and anterogradely ("prospective memory" or "proscopia"). Autobiographical memories are usually emotional (affect-related), implying that subjects evaluate the emotional significance of the events. Therefore, autobiographical memories need a synchronization of cognitive, fact-like portions of an event and of a corresponding emotional flavoring. Furthermore, episodic memories always make reference to the self and evaluate the event with respect to the self and the social environment.

Cultural memory. After having defined these memory systems, the question arises of where cultural memory would fit into this scheme. Although one is inclined to view cultural memory as belonging to the highest of the long-term memory systems, in fact it, firstly, cannot be regarded as a unity, and, secondly, is more closely associated with the semantic and in part even with the procedural and priming memory systems. The concept of culture is based on constructs or creations which do not exist as such in nature, but are man-made. Some biologists even see culture-like features as existent in various animal species. For example, they regard the habit of washing potatoes (before eating them), which was apparently introduced to a Japanese macaque colony by an old female monkey, as such an example.

Neither such "culture-like" habits nor those of driving cars or riding bicycles would be viewed as belonging to the episodic memory system. We have, in fact, many examples of cultural memories that can be attributed to the lower memory systems—semantic, procedural, and priming. The passing down of these habits across generations, frequently accompanied by improving or refining modifications, is, however, the unique feature or attribute which distinguishes them from the genetically driven habits of lower animals, such as continuing to create "magnetic" termite hills or building complex nests. We all know that there may be many situations in which a person is unaware why he or she behaves in a given way towards other people. As an example, Elizabeth Phelps and her co-workers found that there is an unconscious racial evaluation mediated by one brain structure in particular, the amygdala. The amygdala is thought to evaluate preprocessed sensory information from all modalities (vision, audition, etc.) with respect to its biological and social significance to the individual. Damage to the amygdala as it occurs in a genetically based illness named Urbach-Wiethe disease may result in a failure to appropriately process emotional signals from the environment and consequently may lead to an impairment in interacting suitably in socio-cultural environments (Markowitsch et al., "Amygdala's Contribution"). These examples demonstrate that not only do environments shape brain processing, but that vice versa, the brain's activity (or lack of activity) influences the perception and evaluation of the environment.

Neuroscience recognizes that it needs to expand its focus from the perspective of the individual brain to that of the social world, as individuals are embedded in a social environment that shapes their brain and makes consciousness possible. In fact, as James Wertsch formulated it, it would be preferable to use the expression "collective remembering" instead of collective memory. "Remembering" indicates the process character: Old memories are recalled in the context of the present and are then re-encoded in the context and mood of the present. The state dependency of memory was already pointed out by Semon, who had a number of scientific ideas about memory encoding, representation, and recall whose value was detected and recognized only much later (cf. fig. 2).

Perception Encoding Consolidation Storage Recall/Ecphory

Figure 2. The sequence of information processing. Initially, the perceived information is encoded in the brain, then it is further fixed, embedded in and associated with already existing information (process of consolidation). That means that it is brought into synchrony with related, already stored memories. Accomplishment of final storage is assumed to occur via a neuronal network composed of components which preferentially represent facts, or emotions, or features of attentiveness and alertness. Ecphorizing the stored information is seen as being induced by external (environmental) or internal ("brain-based") cues that lead to an activation of pre-frontotemporal cortex structures which trigger or activate the neuronal networks (stored engrams) so that they come to consciousness in the context of the perceived present.

The term "ecphory" stems from Semon; Tulving (*Elements*) re-introduced and refined it much later. Semon coined this term in order to cover the process by which retrieval cues interact with stored information so that an image or a representation of the information in question appears. (Similarly, during initial encoding, all the internal and external cues, conditions, and emotional states interact with the way in which new information is perceived and processed.) The term "ecphory" is still rarely used in contemporary research (but see Calabrese et al.; Markowitsch, Thiel, Kessler, and Heiss), as many people believe in more static input-output relations. The remembering and ecphorizing of old information—including traditions and myths—is, however, always a process that depends on an interaction with the present environment and consequently—at least in many instances—with social partners and the cultural context or frame.

Seen in this way, culture and tradition form, modify, and continuously adapt both the brain's input and output. Reality may be distorted, reinvented or reconstructed. This becomes especially apparent with respect to the so-called reminiscence bump, which has frequently been described in autobiographical memory research: The majority of ecphorized memories stem from the time period beginning at about the age of 25, that is, from that epoch in life in which it is probable that (a) maturation processes are largely finished, and (b) the most significant life changes and events have already occurred. Individuals of that age gain significant knowledge about the world and of their likely status and position in their society. Matching the self with the biological and social environment results in a consolidation process which goes beyond pure memory consolidation, and instead leads to the creation of a self which is aware of his or her socio-cultural context and is able to look back into the past and forward into the future.

Thus, the prerequisites of autonoetic consciousness (Markowitsch, "Autonoetic Consciousness") are created by a concerted action of culture, communication, and brain maturation.

There are, however, two opposing tendencies: For one, the more a child is treated as an individual, the earlier it gains autonoetic awareness and self-consciousness. Children in Eastern Asia, children living in a kibbutz, and children born as the second, third, or later child all gain self-consciousness later than first-born children living in Western-style societies (cf. Harpaz-Rotem and Hirst). In Western societies, individuality—the personal style of being—is regarded as high-ranking on a scale of self-realization. On the other hand, culture in all its variants, from TV to professional activities, is much more dominant in our society than it was in former times. In consequence, our self is nowadays much more a self "in relation," or a self shaped by others, than it was in the past.

This "in relation" can be viewed from several perspectives. From sociology it is primarily regarded as related to other members of a society. It can, however, also be seen in a broader perspective. This was elucidated by Hutchins in an article entitled "How a Cockpit Remembers Its Speed." Cockpit instruments store information which can be checked by the pilot. Here, the interaction between man and machine constitutes the memory. Similarly, an individual does not have a brilliant mind—the brilliance appears only in the eyes of others when comparing intellects within their society; vice versa, it is not a society that remembers, but only the individuals within this society. Neuroscience draws similar connections, namely between a person's behavior and a person's brain. Most of the current cognitive neuroscience methodology—especially functional brain imaging—relies on this relationship, stating that the communication of nerve cells among each other in an individual brain corresponds to the behavior of the individual carrying this brain. And lastly, as mentioned above (Semon), the brain reconstructs memories, so neither individual nor collective memories correspond to the actual past; however, both kinds of memory strengthen identity. Landmarks and "timemarks" (such as ancient monuments) help in resonating communicative memories (Markowitsch, "Time"; see also Welzer, this volume). In fact, locus and time were originally regarded to be the principal constituents of episodic memories (Tulving, *Elements*); only later was a more refined definition used (see fig. 1 and Tulving, "Episodic Memory and Autonoesis").

Communicative memory also implies the existence of communicative or collective memory failure. Indeed there are examples of collective amnesia with respect to cruelties against other societies in many countries (the rape of Nanking, the massacre of Kurdish people, the Holocaust). However, there are also examples of the impact of communicative memories on an individual's brain. In 1998, Yehuda, Schmeidler, Wainberg, Binder-Brynes, and Duvdevani published a paper in which they described an increased vulnerability to posttraumatic stress disorder in adult offspring of Holocaust survivors, thereby emphasizing that communicative memories have an influence across generations and may shape the brain (as the ultimate basis of memories and traits) in a negative manner.

In conclusion, there are two complementary approaches to communicative memory. One emphasizes its existence in the outer world (monuments, language, poems, rites, cultural attainments in general), the other its existence in the individual possessors of working brains. Both approaches must work together in order to provide an understanding of the complete nature of communicative memory.

Acknowledgment

While writing this article I had a fellowship at the Hanse Institute for Advanced Study, Delmenhorst, Germany.

References

Atkinson, R. C., and R. M. Shiffrin. "Human Memory: A Proposed System and Its Control Processes." *The Psychology of Learning and Motivation: Advances in Research and Theory*. Eds. K.W. Spence and J. T. Spence. New York: Academic, 1968. 89-195.

Calabrese, P., H. J. Markowitsch, H. F. Durwen, B. Widlitzek, M. Haupts, B. Holinka, and W. Gehlen. "Right Temporofrontal Cortex as Critical Locus for the Ecphory of Old Episodic Memories." *Journal of Neurology, Neurosurgery, and Psychiatry* 61 (1996): 304-10.

Drachman, D. A. "Do We Have Brain to Spare?" *Neurology* 64 (2005): 2004-05.

Gagné, Robert M. *The Conditions of Learning*. New York: Holt, Rinehart, and Winston, 1965.

Harpaz-Rotem, Ilan, and William Hirst. "The Earliest Memories in Individuals Raised in Either Traditional and Reformed Kibbutz or Outside the Kibbutz." *Memory* 13 (2005): 51-62.

Hutchins, E. "How a Cockpit Remembers Its Speed." *Cognitive Science* 19 (1995): 265-88.

Markowitsch, Hans J. "Autonoetic Consciousness." *The Self in Neuroscience and Psychiatry*. Eds. Tilo Kircher and Anthony David. Cambridge: Cambridge UP, 2003. 180-96.

—. "Time, Memory, and Consciousness: A View from the Brain." *Endophysics, Time, Quantum, and the Subjective.* Eds. Rosolino Buccheri, Avshalom C. Elitzur and Metod Saniga. Singapore: World Scientific, 2005. 131-47.

Markowitsch, H. J., P. Calabrese, M. Würker, H. F. Durwen, J. Kessler, R. Babinsky, D. Brechtelsbauer, L. Heuser, and W. Gehlen. "The Amygdala's Contribution to Memory: A Study on Two Patients with Urbach-Wiethe Disease." *NeuroReport* 5 (1994): 1349-52.

Markowitsch, H. J., A. Thiel, J. Kessler, and W.-D. Heiss. "Ecphorizing Semi-Conscious Episodic Information via the Right Temporopolar Cortex: A PET Study." *Neurocase* 3 (1997): 445-49.

Mishkin, M., and H. L. Petri. "Memories and Habits: Some Implications for the Analysis of Learning and Retention." *Neuropsychology of Memory.* Eds. L. R. Squire and N. Butters. New York: Guilford, 1984. 287-96.

Phelps, E. A., K. J. O'Connor, W. A. Cunningham, E. S. Funayama, J. C. Gatenby, and M. R. Banji. "Performance on Indirect Measures of Race Evaluation Predicts Amygdala Activation." *Journal of Cognitive Neuroscience* 12 (2000): 729-38.

Semon, Richard. *Die Mneme als erhaltendes Prinzip im Wechsel des organischen Geschehens.* Leipzig: Engelmann, 1904.

Sinz, Rainer. *Neurobiologie und Gedächtnis.* Stuttgart: Fischer, 1979.

Tulving, Endel. *Elements of Episodic Memory.* Oxford: Clarendon, 1983.

—. "Episodic and Semantic Memory." *Organization of Memory.* Eds. E. Tulving and Wayne Donaldson. New York: Academic, 1972. 381-403.

—. "Episodic Memory and Autonoesis: Uniquely Human?" *The Missing Link in Cognition: Self-Knowing Consciousness in Man and Animals.* Eds. Herbert S. Terrace and Janet Metcalfe. New York: Oxford UP, 2005. 3-56.

Warrington, E. K., and L. Weiskrantz. "Amnesic Syndrome: Consolidation or Retrieval?" *Nature* 228 (1970): 628-30.

Wertsch, James V. "Collective Memory." *Learning and Memory: A Comprehensive Reference.* Eds. John H. Byrne and Henry Roediger. New York: Oxford UP, 2008.

Yehuda, R., J. Schmeidler, M. Wainberg, K. Binder-Brynes, and T. Duvdevani. "Vulnerability to Posttraumatic Stress Disorder in Adult Offspring of Holocaust Survivors." *American Journal of Psychiatry* 155 (1998): 1163-71.

Communicative Memory

HARALD WELZER

1. History and Development of the Concept of "Communicative Memory"

The concept of "communicative memory" arises from a differentiation of Maurice Halbwachs's concept of "collective" memory into a "cultural" and a "communicative" memory, as proposed by Aleida and Jan Assmann. "Cultural memory" is defined as a "collective concept for all knowledge that directs behavior and experience in the interactive framework of a society and one that obtains through generations in repeated societal practice and initiation" (Assmann 126).

"Communicative memory," in contrast, is an interactive practice located within the tension between individuals' and groups' recall of the past. Compared to "cultural" memory, it can be seen as the short-term memory of a society: It is bound to the existence of living bearers of memory and to the communicators of experience, and encompasses three to four generations. The temporal horizon of "communicative memory" thus shifts in relation to the given present time (Assmann 127). Contents of this memory can only be permanently fixed through "cultural formation," that is, through organized and ceremonialized communication about the past. While "communicative memory is characterized by its proximity to the everyday, cultural memory is characterized by its distance from the everyday" (Assmann 128-29). It is supported by fixed points which do not move along with the present, but are instead perceived as fateful and meaningful and are marked by texts, rites, monuments, and commemorations (Assmann 129).

"Communicative memory," on the other hand, denotes a willful agreement of the members of a group as to what they consider their own past to be, in interplay with the identity-specific grand narrative of the we-group, and what meaning they ascribe to this past. "Cultural" and "communicative memory" can only be strictly separated in a theoretical context; in the actual memory practice of individuals and social groups, their forms and methods are linked together. This also explains why the shape of "cultural memory"—at least when observed over a longer period of time—can also be seen to change: Communicative memory devalues certain aspects while placing more value on others, and also adds new elements.

This classic definition of "communicative memory" still clearly refers to the communicative practices of groups and societies, and leaves aside the question of what communicative memory is like on the level of the individual, or how the levels of mediation between the social and the autobiographical side of communicative memory can best be described. Here as well, it must be emphasized that the terminological and conceptual divisions first and foremost have an analytical function; observed empirically, the various memory forms flow into one another and form the practice of "communicative memory." This article will provide an introduction to the concepts of "social," "autobiographical," and "communicative" memory.

1.1 Social Memory

In the last two decades, the study of memory and remembering has made rapid progress overall, yet despite the extensive findings and advances in theory, there remain considerable gaps in the research on non-intentional, casual, social procedures of memory. The texture of memory seems so complex and so ephemeral that scientific instruments simply fail in attempting to determine what memory is made of and how it is created every day. At the same time, it is established knowledge that individual memory only takes on form within social and cultural frameworks, that countless aspects of the past have a direct and lasting impact on current interpretations and decisions, that there are transgenerational transmissions of experiences whose impact reaches even into the biochemistry of neuronal processes in later generations, and that non-simultaneous bonds can suddenly and unexpectedly guide action and become historically significant. The passing down of tradition, non-simultaneity, and the history of wishes and hopes form the subjective side of social memory (Fentress and Wickham; Welzer, *Das soziale Gedächtnis*). Everyday practices in dealing with those things that themselves transport history and memory—architecture, landscape, wastelands, etc.—form its objective side. "Social memory" refers to everything which transports and communicates the past and interpretations of the past in a non-intentional manner.

Four media of the social practice of forming the past can be distinguished: records, (moving) images, spaces, and direct interactions. Each refers to things which were not produced for the purpose of forming tradition, but which nonetheless transport history and shape the past in social contexts. They are described in detail below.

First, *records* which were not drawn up for the purpose of historical recall nevertheless transport subtexts of the past. This can include everything from the epigram hung in the kitchen to a sheaf of love letters in the family archives. This area of social memory encompasses all those documented expressions which historians can ennoble as sources after the fact.

Second, cultural products—plays, operas, novels, and especially *pictures and films*—have, as Gertrud Koch has said, a fundamental internal connection to the past and always also transport historical constructions or versions of the past (537). Narrative and visual media always have at least one subtext, which can suggest to the recipients a potentially completely opposite interpretation of what they have seen than the commentary with which it is shown. As such, the historical interpretation which, as an example, Leni Riefenstahl's visual imagery provided for the National Socialist system, can perhaps be relativized through an analytical commentary, but not destroyed. The same is true for historical novels or films.

But media products do not just deliver versions of the past; they also determine the perception of the present. As Goffmann pointed out, it is not merely the passing on of experience that follows such patterns and rules, but already the perception and interpretation of the event in the very moment in which it takes place. Particularly since the invention of television, soldiers have known already before their first contact with the enemy what it looks like when an enemy soldier is mortally wounded. The historian Joanna Bourke has shown how diaries, letters, and autobiographies of combatants absorb literary and filmic models into their own perception and memory (16ff.; cf. also Welzer, *Das kommunikative Gedächtnis* 185ff.).

Cultural frameworks have an effect already in the individual consciousness as a structuring matrix for the processing of information—and that means that we are faced with a circular operation when considering the phenomenon of the import of pre-formed experiences into one's own life history. For example, if, as shown in a recent study (Welzer et al.), sequences from movies prove to be adaptable to the construction of "personally experienced" war stories, then this is partly because they in turn perhaps form a sort of substrate of fragments of experiences that many former soldiers actually encountered, at least in a similar form, either completely or in part. The filmic models, after all, undoubtedly draw their narrative structure and their mise-en-scènes from narrations that precede them: the tale of the development of the simple soldier in war, the narrative structure of the adventure story, the dramaturgy of tragedy are in their turn models that are adapted by filmic media. Thus the narrative models, the experiences themselves, the reporting of experiences, and illustrations using existing visual material are all bound up in an inextricably complex relationship.

Third, *spaces* are a part of social memory. Urban planning and architecture are ensembles in which historical eras are superimposed over one another in stone, concrete, and asphalt. Of course, as not only historicism and postmodern architecture have shown, this social memory may well be a result of intentional memory politics: Architects and city planners not infrequently set out to accentuate a particular construction of a city's history, by emphasizing certain historical elements and destroying others.

For residents and passers-by, admittedly, the city presents itself as an entity that has been subject to repeated refigurations and in which layers of history paid more or less attention thus overlap. For those who live or have lived in a city, its various districts naturally also have a dimension of meaning directly related to one's life story. Interestingly, precisely that which is no longer present can have a greater effect on the memory than that which has been built over or reconstructed. Within the context of memory theory, I also find it important to point out that experiences of landscapes can be reflected in completely different ways in a person's memory, depending on his or her actual mental and physical constitution at the time. In 1917, Kurt Lewin translated his experiences as an artilleryman into a experiment of a phenomenology of the "war landscape." He argues that an observer's perception of the character of an environment depends on the military action in which the observer is involved at a particular moment. During an advance, for example, the landscape appears "directed" and its features, such as copses, hills, and houses, are defined according to their functions during combat, while the same landscape during a retreat returns to being an "undirected" peace landscape. During the advance, potential cover and emplacements are perceived, while during a retreat the hills, trenches, and fields appear in their agricultural function or simple scenic beauty (322).

Fourth and last, direct *interactions* include communicative practices which either per se concern the modes of envisioning the past or thematize the past en passant. Developmental psychology has contributed impressive explorations of the way in which an autobiographical I, which can look back onto a distinct past, can be developed in the shared practice of "memory talk" (Nelson), through increasingly discussing micro-pasts in the form of past everyday experiences. In doing so, participants "learn" that references to the past are in fact a constitutive part of shared existence, and that speaking about the past is a ubiquitous aspect of social practice. This process, the communicative actualization of experienced pasts, enjoys a lifelong continuation (Middleton and Edwards), although it should be noted that it is not actually necessary to speak explicitly about the past when the past is formed conversationally. For example, when families get together, "behind" the narrated stories, so to speak, there is also an historical associative space in which the circumstances, the zeitgeist, and the habitus of the historical actors are also communicated. Such social interaction transports history en passant, casually, and unnoticed by the speakers.

These four forms of social memory, and perhaps also social memory as a whole, can be termed an "exogrammatic memory system." It should also be noted here that human memory by no means operates solely within subjects, but also—and probably to an historically ever-increasing degree—is located outside the subjects.

Neuroscientific memory research refers to neuronal activation patterns which correspond to a mental image or a memory as "engrams." Engrams represent, one could say, the traces of all of our experiences. In contrast, "exograms" (Donald) refer to external memory content of any kind which is used to cope with current demands and to develop courses of action for the future. These can be written, oral, symbolic, representational, musical, habitual—in other words, any and every kind of content that either developed as a human device for orientation (such as language), or which can be used as such (such as using the stars for navigation). To use the language of quantum theory, such content jumps to the state of being an exogram in the moment in which it is observed and used by a subject as external memory content.

As opposed to engrams, exograms are permanent; that is, they cross the temporal and spatial borders of individual existence and the horizon of personal experience. Seen from the point of view of evolution, the deciding step in human phylogenesis was the development of symbols, because these, as Merlin Donald has shown, enrich the possibilities of human cognition by adding extremely effective memory storage. It is primarily the storage characteristics offered by engrams and exograms which must be distinguished: While engrams are "impermanent, small, hard to refine, impossible to display to awareness for any length of time, and difficult to locate and recall," exograms are "stable, permanent, virtually unlimited memory records that are infinitely reformattable" and consciously accessible (Donald 309ff.). In addition, exograms can be accessed easily and through a variety of different methods. Human consciousness thus has at its disposal two systems of representation, one internal and one external, while all other forms of life only have one internal system.

This evolutionarily decisive achievement rests on two functions of memory: first, the capability of autonoetic memory, which assumes a working memory with a certain capacity (Markowitsch and Welzer 80ff.), and second, the outsourcing of memory to other persons, institutions, or media. Memory that is autonoetic—that is, self-aware and self-reflexive—enables one to wait for better opportunities, survive problematic situations, develop more efficient solutions: In other words, it releases humans from the pressure to act immediately, and creates, in fact, precisely that space between stimulus and reaction that we call "acting."

Second, exograms allow for unique forms of representation of memory content, thus relieving humans from the pressure to act and also permitting the social transmission of memory. Humans can store and communicate information; with the invention of writing they can even pass the information on to people with whom they have no spatial or temporal connection, thereby opening up a fund of stored knowledge which radically overcomes the limitations of direct communication. This creates the possibility of the cultural transmission (Tomasello) of experiences, and that accelerates slow biological evolution through social means. Humans are able to realize their unique adaptability to changing environments because they have created a co-evolutionary environment which has emancipated them from the biological parameters of evolution. Social memory describes the exogrammatic structure of the cultural transmission process, as well as its contents.

1.2 Autobiographical Memory

Autobiographical memory is a functional system integrating the following memory systems, as postulated by the neurosciences: procedural memory, priming, perceptual memory, semantic memory, and episodic memory (see figure 1 in Markowitsch, this volume). Until recently it remained unclear as to why episodic and autobiographical memory could not be distinguished from each other on the neuronal level, even though they have decidedly different capabilities and are perceived differently on the phenomenal level. Our empirically supported suggestion would be that the autobiographical memory is to be understood as a socially constituted system which is amplified only on the content—not on the functional—level of the episodic memory. The autobiographical memory integrates the five fundamental memory systems as a functional unit and ensures that each self can be synchronized with the fluctuating groups of others.

Autobiographical memory, which more than any other determines, denotes, and guarantees our ego, develops in processes of social exchange; this applies not only to the contents, but also to the memory system, whose structure—which organizes the contents—is itself subject to social formation.

This memory, which we take to be the core of our self, exhibits many aspects which in fact were not only first formed in togetherness with others, but also only exist there. Essential aspects of our self and our decisions are bound to intuitions and associations which we do not always—

perhaps indeed only seldom—consciously control, but rather through which our actions are guided and—perhaps not so seldom—controlled. This connection between a relative individual autonomy and self-awareness on the one hand and a distinct dependence on social entities and the body on the other determine our existence, and it is the autobiographical memory that takes over the task of synthesizing this connection and creating a continuity between the two sides, one which we are not even aware of, so that we can constantly be sure of an apparently unchanging ego—across all times and all situations. This ego (and everything that we refer to as our identity, which we draw from our life history and the past of the memory community to which we belong) is in a way a self-*mis*-understanding, albeit a necessary and meaningful one. This is precisely what Hans-Georg Gadamer meant when he spoke of autobiography "reprivatizing" history (281). History does not belong to us; rather, we belong to history, as it confronts us as a totality of terms, concepts, means of orientation, and things provided by those who went before us.

The individualistic self-concept which Western societies ascribe to their members and train them in is in this view no more than a functional misunderstanding of the self. In reality, we are much more closely tied to both close and distant others than is evident in our experience of our self.

When we notice how much our self is in truth developed and lives in historical and social relation to others, it appears perhaps less independent than we would like, but nonetheless still something completely unique. And indeed, its uniqueness for each individual person of the billions in the world is composed of the conjunction of all those genetic, historical, cultural, social, and communicative conditions which, in their sum and form, only that one person alone experiences. This sequence indicates at the same time a continuum of personality development, one pole of which is fixedness and the other is variance. This continuum makes clear that the history of our communicative experiences is the element which most strongly individualizes our memory and our self. Sociality and individuality are insofar not opposites, but rather determine one another.

Ontogeny is synonymous with the ever-improving symbolic, cognitive, and temporal synchronization of the child with the other members of his or her world. The key to this synchronization, which takes place simultaneously on the levels of categorization, language, concept-building, etc., lies in the autobiographization of the memory. Only when there is a self to which experiences, observations, and thoughts can be connected can the developing person be synchronized more and more with the people in his or her environment. Individualization and socialization are thus by no means opposites, but instead concurrent. Ontogeny and sociogenesis are simply two aspects of one and the same process.

Since humans develop in a co-evolutionary environment, that which they acquire in practice consists of the newest symbolic forms: They are using the material made available by the previous generation, which they easily modify since they actively exploit their environment instead of simply adapting to it.

This provides a direct insight into the autobiographical background of a person. A co-evolutionary environment is necessarily a world of constant change; this affects human life forms in their respective historical and cultural form and thus also the ontogenetic specifications which guarantee the respective fit between those who are already there and those who come later. A species that makes use of a co-evolutionary environment needs a relay which makes its members sociable, able to connect with expanding and diversifying social groups. The autobiographical memory is just such a relay, a psycho-social entity that subjectively safeguards coherence and continuity even though the social environments and thus also the requirements demanded of the individual fluctuate. It is precisely this relay function that also explains why we can both document historically variable levels of autobiographization as well as, from an intercultural perspective, different stages of life in which ontogenetically the autobiographization, and consequently the appearance of a continuous self, begins.

Autobiographical memory allows us not only to mark memories as *our* memories; it also forms the temporal feedback matrix of our self, with which we can measure where and how we have changed and where and how we have remained the same. It also offers a matrix which allows us to coordinate the attributions, assessments, and judgments of our person that our social environment carries out almost ceaselessly.

The desire for continuity is not merely an individual wish; without the continuity of the identity of its members, a social group or society could not function, since cooperation—the central category of human existence—is only guaranteed when humans can be relied on to be the same today as they were yesterday and will still be tomorrow.

The sociologist Norbert Elias pointed out already three-quarters of a century ago that we can only sufficiently understand the psycho- and sociogenesis of humans if we grasp the underlying process as one which fundamentally and always happens within a human form that existed *before* the developing child and whose entire development after birth depends on the cultural and social behavior and methods which this form has co-evolutionarily developed. This perspective has been echoed by development psychologists as diverse as Lev Wygotsky, Daniel Stern, and Michael Tomasello, who show that humans do not "internalize" anything in their development, but rather that they, in being together with others, learn what they need in order to function in a given society and to become a full-fledged member of this specific society.

The development of memory proceeds from the social to the individual—from the infant and small child, who without an autobiographical memory exists in a universe in which things simply are as they are and does not distinguish among different sources of memories, to the preschooler, who through growing temporal differentiations gradually gains an understanding of the self in time, and finally through language and a cognitive self becomes an autobiographical I which integrates earlier and future experiences into a life story, which is simultaneously social and individual.

The regulation of the child's condition, guided by the caregiver, gradually segues into intra-personal relations: external regulations become self-regulations (Holodynski and Friedlmeier). I assume that the autobiographical memory represents the declaratively and reflexively accessible entity of self-regulation, while the other memory systems provide on a continuing basis the implicit forms of self-regulation and make them situationally accessible (Markowitsch and Welzer 80ff.).

The ontogeny of any individual child consists thus of a diachronic transformation of its situation. One transformation is historical and refers to the change in the forms of perception, communication, and upbringing (and thus also the images and ideas of what is "good for" and how one should treat a baby); the other transformation refers to the developing individual him- or herself and consists of the successive changes in his or her relationship to others and to him- or herself, or in other words, in the shift of balance between interpersonal and intrapersonal regulations.

Autobiographical memory is thus constituted far more from the "outside" than from the "inside." That it must constantly be shored up and perpetuated from outside becomes clear when, for example as a result of an injury-induced amnesia, a person can no longer synchronize his or her memories with those of others. We generally overlook this functional external side of our memory, because it does not appear to conform to our individualistic self-image. Yet also the theoretically infinite expansion of human memory space through exograms, and the meaning this has for the phylogenesis as well as the ontogeny of humans, shows that the human memory owes its full capacity not to its internal functions but rather to its external processes. Humans are thus much easier to understand when one does not consider them as individuals, but rather as interfaces in a network.

1.3 Communicative Memory

We apparently always include in our perception, interpretation, and acting many more factors than are consciously accessible to us. Against this background, an autobiography, as psychologist Mark Freeman has formulated it, is not a question of representing a life, but rather the ensemble of the manifold sources that constitute the self (40). What connects these sources is social practice, and this consists of communicative processes. A "communicative unconscious" ties these sources together and it is fundamentally predicated on more "knowledge" than is consciously available to each individual actor and also to all of them together. Essential elements of our self-esteem, our action orientations, and our memory operate on unconscious levels—not in the meaning of "repressed" or "split," but rather in the meaning of a functional unconscious which for operative reasons is located on the other side of the threshold of consciousness. The linguists George Lakoff and Mark Johnson even speak of a "cognitive unconsciousness," that is, of something which one knows and simultaneously does not know. They illustrate this using the cognitive processes which are active during every moment in which we take part in a conversation. These include (and they emphasize that these are only a small extract of the perceptions present and active during communication) being able to: identify a language from the sequence of sounds and tones and decode the grammatic structure of what is said; understand logical connections; make semantic and pragmatic sense of the entirety of spoken words and sentences; place the communication in an appropriate framework; make meaningful objections and additions; construct and test mental images of that which is being discussed; fill in gaps where something is left unsaid; anticipate the further course of the conversation; prepare the next answer; and, last but not least, draw on memories related to the topic (10ff.).

We carry out all of these cognitive processes with such flexibility and speed that they do not enter our consciousness. Only when misunderstandings arise or contradictions between the body language of our interlocutor and that which she or he is expressing verbally become apparent do we become intentionally conscious of what is guiding our behavior in the situation on the level of our communicative unconscious: a permanent, highly sensitive, and exact process of perception and interpretation which can effortlessly distinguish between the center and the periphery of the communicative situation, between its active process and its context, and among the multiple dialogues occurring simultaneously on all levels of sensory perception. If one wanted to decode all the levels of emotional and cognitive processes which go on in any given moment of any given conversation, one would soon be hopelessly lost in the thicket of simultaneity, which in itself proves that we constantly "know" more than we realize. If all of these operations were to take place under conscious control, we would be unable to act. Thus, it is high time that we ascribe to the unconscious a much more positive status than Freud and the psychoanalysts did: the unconscious is highly functional within human existence since it makes conscious acting more efficient and freer by relieving part of the load. One could in fact turn Freud's famous dictum around and say instead: "Where ego was, there shall id be," namely an unconscious that is communicatively constituted and communicatively effective in every single moment.

Conscious communicative practice is made up of each of the persons involved bringing "meaning" into the communicative situations: One deduces what the other person intends and will do even before his or her action is completed. This is evident, for example, when observing a move in a game, such as give-and-go passes in soccer, or watching a person who overhears one part of a telephone conversation and automatically tries to complete the dialogue by inferring what the person on the other end is saying. Thus, in all of our social actions and most certainly in speaking, the other is always already included.

If this communicative practice has the past and history as its object, then it is by no means merely a matter of transmitting set pieces of narrative and content that can be and are combined this way or that, but also always involves the organizational structure of these combinations, which establishes in advance in what roles which actors can appear at all, and how one should evaluate what one has experienced. Thus it is often the case that it is more the emotional dimension, the atmospheric tinge of a report that is passed on and determines the image and interpretation of the past, while the contents themselves—the circumstances of the situation, the causes, the sequences of events, etc.—can be freely altered, in a way which makes the most sense for listeners and those who retell the story. This explains why both individual life stories as well as the stories of collectives are continuously re-written in the light of new experiences and needs of the present. One could say that each present, each generation, each epoch creates for itself that past which has the highest functional value for its future orientations and options.

2. Memory as a Convergent Field: Its Problems and Surpluses

Memory and remembering as research fields are predestined for interdisciplinary approaches when one assumes that only humans can have an autobiographic memory, that this form of remembering has to be learned, and that memory has a biological basis but consists of cultural contents. We already have the first findings from interdisciplinary projects, such as one studying age-specific memory development (Markowitsch and Welzer), and more will follow. But perhaps in the medium term we are looking less at interdisciplinarity and more at the genesis of a new sub-discipline that at some point will take on the form of an elaborated "social neuroscience." Such a paradigmatic framework would be desirable, as the sophistication of the findings and theoretical approaches in the individual disciplines that address phenomena of communicative memory varies. For example, approaches in the neurosciences lack the perspective of social interaction theory and communication theory, even though on a very general level it is conceded that human brains can only be comprehended as a part of networks. Nonetheless, the neurosciences' epistemic basis is that of the individual brain. In addition, the understanding of communication in the neurosciences is based simply on the concept of information, which is inadequate in the face of the empirical reality of the communicative formation of memory content. In the humanities and social sciences, on the other hand, phenomena of memory formation are often discussed without accounting for fundamental bio-social factors. Also, in disciplines such as life-writing research or oral history, which depend on subjective evidence, it is certainly not opportune to forgo findings of neuroscientific memory research.

Current research problems include the international heterogeneity of the field. In the Anglo-American realm, the level of synthesis is for now significantly below that of the German-language discourse of memory and remembering. Seen transnationally, however, one can say that memory research in the humanities and social sciences is not seldom politically and normatively contextualized, which leads to considerable variations in national concepts and terminological frameworks. These national differences are not found in the neuroscientific research. Insofar one has to accept that from an international perspective, research into memory and remembering in the cultural fields has not reached the same level of synthesis as that in the neurosciences, which, in turn, however, does not sufficiently account for the constitutive conditions of its object of study or the implications of its own findings.

Clearly, at the end one has to see that we will never be able to sufficiently or completely comprehend through science and scholarly analysis the core of Communicative Memory, namely that core which exists in the practice of memory itself. Aesthetic approaches such as literary autobiographies (including Vladimir Nabokov's *Speak, Memory*) or movies (such as Chris Marker's *Sans Soleil*) enjoy the freedom of not having to provide proof for their reflections, and thus often come closer to the phenomenon of Communicative Memory than will ever be possible with the cumbersome tools of scientific argumentation and verification.

Translated by Sara B. Young

References

Assmann, Jan. "Collective Memory and Cultural Identity." Trans. John Czaplicka. *New German Critique* 65 (1995): 125-33. Trans. of "Kollektives Gedächtnis und kulturelle Identität." *Kultur und Gedächtnis.* Eds. Jan Assmann and Tonio Hölscher. Frankfurt am Main: Suhrkamp, 1988. 9-19.

Bourke, Joanna. *An Intimate History of Killing: Face-to-Face Killing in Twentieth Century Warfare.* London: Granta, 1999.

Donald, Merlin. *A Mind so Rare: The Evolution of Human Consciousness.* New York: Norton, 2001.

Fentress, James, and Chris Wickham. *Social Memory.* Oxford: Blackwell, 1992.

Freeman, Mark. "Tradition und Erinnerung des Selbst und der Kultur." *Das soziale Gedächtnis: Geschichte, Erinnerung, Tradierung.* Ed. Harald Welzer. Hamburg: Hamburger Edition, 2001. 25-40.

Gadamer, Hans-Georg. *Wahrheit und Methode.* By Gadamer. Vol 2. Tübingen: Mohr, 1986.

Goffmann, Erving. *Rahmenanalyse: Ein Versuch über die Organisation von Alltagserfahrungen.* Frankfurt am Main: Suhrkamp, 1979.

Holodynski, Manfred, and Wolfgang Friedlmeier. *Development of Emotions and Their Regulation.* Munich: Springer, 2005.

Koch, Gertrud. "Nachstellungen: Film und historischer Moment." *Historische Sinnbildung: Problemstellungen, Zeitkonzepte, Wahrnehmungshorizonte, Darstellungsstrategien.* Eds. Klaus E. Müller and Jörn Rüsen. Reinbek: Rowohlt, 1997. 536-51.

Lakoff, George, and Mark Johnson. *Philosophy in the Flesh: The Embodied Mind and Its Challenge to Western Thought.* New York: Basic, 1999.

Lewin, Kurt. *Werkausgabe.* Ed. Carl-Friedrich Graumann. Vol. 4. Stuttgart: Klett-Cotta, 1982.

Markowitsch, Hans-J., and Harald Welzer. *Das autobiographische Gedächtnis: Hirnorganische Grundlagen und biosoziale Entwicklung.* Stuttgart: Klett-Cotta, 2005.

Middleton, David, and Derek Edwards, eds. *Collective Remembering.* London: Sage, 1990.

Nelson, Katherine. *Language in Cognitive Development: The Emergence of the Mediated Mind.* Cambridge: Cambridge UP, 1996.

Tomasello, Michael. *The Cultural Origins of Human Cognition.* Cambridge: Harvard UP, 1999.

Trevarthen, Colwyn. "Frühe Kommunikation und autobiographisches Gedächtnis." *BIOS* 15.2 (2002): 213-40.

Welzer, Harald. *Das kommunikative Gedächtnis: Eine Theorie der Erinnerung.* Munich: Beck, 2002.

—, ed. *Das soziale Gedächtnis: Geschichte, Erinnerung, Tradierung.* Hamburg: Hamburger Edition, 2001.

Welzer, Harald, Sabine Moller, Karoline Tschuggnall, Olaf Jensen, and Torsten Koch. *"Opa war kein Nazi": Nationalsozialismus und Holocaust im Familiengedachtnis.* Frankfurt am Main: Fischer, 2002.

V. Literature and Cultural Memory

Mnemonic and Intertextual Aspects of Literature

RENATE LACHMANN

1.

When literature is considered in the light of memory, it appears as the mnemonic art par excellence. Literature is culture's memory, not as a simple recording device but as a body of commemorative actions that include the knowledge stored by a culture, and virtually all texts a culture has produced and by which a culture is constituted. Writing is both an act of memory and a new interpretation, by which every new text is etched into memory space. Involvement with the extant texts of a culture, which every new text reflects (whether as convergence or divergence, assimilation or repulsion), stands in a reciprocal relation to the conception of memory that this culture implies. The authors of texts draw on other texts, both ancient and recent, belonging to their own or another culture and refer to them in various ways. They allude to them, they quote and paraphrase them, they incorporate them. "Intertextuality" is the term conceived in literary scholarship to capture this interchange and contact, formal and semantic, between texts—literary and non-literary. Intertextuality demonstrates the process by which a culture, where "culture" is a book culture, continually rewrites and retranscribes itself, constantly redefining itself through its signs. Every concrete text, as a sketched-out memory space, connotes the macrospace of memory that either represents a culture or appears as that culture.

2.

Literature, culture's prominent (yet not only) representative of recording has affinities to other mnemonic paradigms, constitutive for a given culture. The most significant in this respect is the art of memory originating in the ancient discipline of mnemotechnics, which gave rise to a prolific tradition of representing and transmitting knowledge. Writing in its mnemonic dimension has some affinities to this art, concerning the concept of memory and the role that images play in procedures of recollection and remembering.

Mnemotechnics has a legendary source. The story of its invention by the Greek poet Simonides Melicus, passed down by Cicero and Quintilian as a prescription for acts of recollection, conceals an ancient myth narrating the development of the art of memory, at the threshold between an ancient epoch of ancestor cults and a later time when the deceased were mourned but not worshipped (Goldmann; see also Boer, this volume). The legend tells of an earthquake which caused a building in which the feasters at a banquet were seated in a certain order to collapse. It tells of the mutilation of their faces, so that it was impossible to recognize them and to remember their names. Simonides, the poet—the only one to survive the catastrophe—acts as a witness to the old, abandoned order that has been rendered unrecognizable by an epochal break. He restores this order through an "inner writing" and reading, using images that function in the same way as letters. Forgetting is the catastrophe; a given semiotic order is obliterated. It can only be restored by instituting a discipline that reestablishes semiotic "generation" and interpretation. At the beginning of memoria as art stands the effort to transform the work of mourning into a technique. The finding of images heals what has been destroyed: The art of memoria restores shape to the mutilated victims and makes them recognizable by establishing their place in life. Preserving cultural memory involves something like an apparatus for remembering by duplication, by the representation of the absent through the image (phantasma or simulacrum), by the objectification of memory (as power and ability, as a space of consciousness, or as thesaurus), and by the prevention of forgetting through the retrieval of images (the constant recuperation of lost meaning).

Several key concepts which helped to shape various styles of memoria could be seen as originating in this mythical tale: forgetting and remembering (as mechanisms that establish a culture); the storing of knowledge (as a tradition's strategy for survival); the need for cultural experience to be preserved by a bearer (of memory) as witness or as text. The myth anticipates the competition in mnemotechnics between writing and image, and the copresence of the working of memory and death.

The significance of the legend, or mythical narrative, emerges in the retellings by Cicero and Quintilian. With somewhat different accents, they both define mnemonics as imagination, as a combination of the experience of order and the invention of images. Images as representatives of things, *res*, and names, *verba*, to be remembered are registered in preordained spatial arrangements and deposited in imaginary spaces such as temples, public places, spacious rooms. When the mind traverses such depositories of mnemic images, the images are recollected, arranged in a series and then made to revert into the elements for which they substituted. The technique recommended by Cicero refers specifically to the memorization of texts.

In his interpretation of the Simonides legend, Cicero offers a new insight into the relation between image and script. He equates the fundamental factors of mnemotechnics, *locus* and *imago*, with the wax tablet, *cera*, and the letter, *littera*. These equations—wax tablet-mnemonic place, letter-image—are essential in his argument. In the second book of *De oratore* the work of memory requires the sketching of an inner image. This inner image must designate the object that is to be remembered, an object that is invisible, no longer present. The image becomes the visible sign for that object etching itself in the memory place. The images are registered in the mnemonic space—just as letters are scratched into a writing tablet.

By inserting itself into the mnemonic space between texts, a text inevitably creates a transformed mnemonic space, a textual depository whose syntax and semantics could be described in the language of the Simonidean mnemotechnics as *loci* and *imagines*. In the same way that the wax tablet is replaced by the architecture of memory, the architecture of memory is replaced by the textual space of literature. The text traverses memory spaces and settles into them. At the same time, every added text enriches the mnemonic space which new texts will traverse.

3.

The bond between mnemotechnics and literature is grounded in the double meaning of *imago* as an image of memory and as the product of imagination, the creative stimulus of literature. The image-producing activity of memory incorporates poetic imagination. The crucial problem here is to define the ways in which mnemic imagination and poetic imagination interact. They seem to mirror each other and comment upon one another. It is also plausible to assume that literary imagery necessarily appeals to mnemic imagery, that the image bank of literature is the same as the image bank of memory.

It is certainly the case that there are striking parallels between imagination (fantasy) and memory. They both represent absent objects with images. For both the image is ambiguous, both true and false. However, the alternatives may not be as clear cut; they may not radically exclude one another. In philosophical and aesthetical treatises in antiquity as well as in the works of thinkers of later periods both the parallels between fantasy and memory and their interaction in the form of a coalition between the two are pointed out. To give two instances (representing different traditions of ideas): In his essay "Pleasures of the Imagination" (1712), the English empiricist Joseph Addison defines primary pleasures as derived from sight, which he calls "the most perfect and most delightful of all our senses," and secondary pleasures as pleasures of imagination, "which flow from the ideas of visible objects, when the objects are not actually before the eye, but are called up into our memories, or formed into agreeable visions of things that are either absent or fictitious." Things absent are either due to past impressions or experiences or they are products of fantasy, fictitious. In Giambattista Vico's treatise "Szienza Nuova" (1744), a third factor enters the coalition between *phantasia* and *memoria*, namely *ingenium*. Vico defines *phantasia*, *memoria*, and *ingenium* as human capacities that are indivisible from each other. Whereas fantasy transforms what memory offers, *ingenium* is the capacity which orders and registers what has been remembered. Recollection and imagination are intertwined (Trabant).

4.

Yet there are still other parallels between the art of memory and writing as a mnemonic act when taking a closer look at intertextual procedures. When a given text enters the domain of other texts, the reference can be to entire texts, to a textual paradigm, to a genre, to certain elements of a given text, to a stylistic device, to narrative techniques, to motifs, etc. The link between the given text and the "other" text (the referent text) is the referent signal or intertext. The intertext is the very element of another text which has been incorporated, absorbed, quoted, distorted, reversed, resemanticized, etc.

The memory of the text is formed by the intertextuality of its references. Intertextuality arises in the act of writing inasmuch as each new act of writing is a traversal of the space between existing texts. The codes to which the elements intertwined in intertextual discourse belong preserve their referential character in relation to a semantic potential and to cultural experience. Cultural memory remains the source of an intertextual play that cannot be deceived; any interaction with it, including that which is skeptical about memory, becomes a product that repeatedly attests to a cultural space.

I should like to suggest three models of intertextuality, whose construction attempts to take into account the above-mentioned interrelation between mnemonics and culture: participation, troping, and transformation. In these models, writing as continuation, writing as repetition, writing as rejoinder, and rewriting are concealed.

Participation is the dialogical sharing in the texts of a culture that occurs in writing. I understand troping in the sense of Harold Bloom's concept of the trope, as a turning away from the precursor text, a tragic struggle against those other texts that necessarily write themselves into the author's own text, and an attempt to surpass, defend against, and eradicate traces of a precursor's text. In contrast, I take transformation to involve the appropriation of other texts through a process of distancing them, through a sovereign and indeed usurpatory exertion of control over them. This appropriation conceals the other texts, veils them, plays with them, renders them unrecognizable, irreverently overturns their oppositions, mixes a plethora of texts together, and demonstrates a tendency toward the esoteric and the cryptic on the one hand, and the ludic, the syncretistic, and the carnivalesque on the other.

All texts participate, repeat, and constitute acts of memory; all are products of their distancing and surpassing of precursor texts. In addition to manifest traces of other texts and obvious forms of transformation, all contain cryptic elements. All texts are stamped by the doubling of manifest and latent, whether consciously or unconsciously. All texts make use of mnemotechnic procedures, in sketching out spaces, *imagines*, and *imagines agentes*. As a collection of intertexts, the text itself is a memory place; as texture, it is memory architecture, and so forth. All texts, furthermore, are indebted to transformatory procedures that they employ either covertly or ludically and demonstratively.

In order to describe intertextual reference to elements of other texts, a metonymic type would have to be distinguished from a metaphorical one, with the help of rhetorical categories. The appropriation of texts occurs differently according to whether they are in a relation of contiguity or a relation of similarity. Here it seems evident that a tendency toward the metonymic should be ascribed to the model of participation. In quotations, anagrams, and syllepses, the borders between the previous text and the new text are shifted; the texts, in a sense, enter into one another. Metaphoric reference allows the preceding text to appear as an image within the new one; similarity evokes the original but at the same time veils and distorts it.

Troping, participation, and transformation, with their respective emphases on metonymic and metaphoric procedures, cannot be clearly distinguished with regard to the constitution of meaning in a text: They occupy a position between positive and negative semantics, between the production of semantic surplus value and semantic evacuation. Intertexts based on similarity (figures causing semantic shifts and reversals of polarity) dissolve the meaning of the text as it existed beforehand, whereas intertexts based on metonymy (participational figures) seem to preserve the pre-text. The above-mentioned models cannot be exclusively identified with metaphoric or metonymic intertextuality. One can, however, note a metonymic tendency in authors such as Pushkin, Akhmatova, and

Mandelstam, primarily in their use of anagrams, syllepses, quotations, hidden allusions, rejoinders, and repetitions, and in their surpassing of other texts as well as their attempt to identify or to merge the time of their pre-texts with the time of their own texts. In authors such as Dostoevsky, Bely, Nabokov, one also finds metonymic intertextuality; however, its repeating, preserving gesture is subverted by the syncretism of the assembled intertexts. In these authors, without a doubt, metaphoric intertextuality is more strongly developed. Semantic repolarization, achieved through the figurative or "improper" text (in the rhetorical sense of *improprie*), shifts the already present meaning of the text while simultaneously proffering another meaning. The simulacral character of metaphoric intertextuality lies in the double status of the intertextual text, being itself and another at once. Through the play of restructuring and dissimulating, it denies the presence of other texts that it nevertheless indicates at the same time. This also applies to metonymic texts, insofar as their manifest structure is subverted by a subtextual one. At the same time, the approach to another text is also a distancing of it: The other textual model—especially in Dostoevsky—is followed and simultaneously crossed out.

5.

The mnemonic capacities of literature include the representation and transmission of knowledge. Whereas the disciplines that substituted the ancient mnemotechnics tend to system formation and the creation of encyclopedic models in order to recover and accumulate knowledge (especially in the tradition initiated by Raimundus Lullus and taken up and refined by authors of the sixteenth to the eighteenth centuries), literature responds to this in a less systematic way. In quoting and discussing philosophical, aesthetic, theological, historical, and scientific knowledge, literature stores and transmits knowledge, transforming it into an element of the artistic text (exemplified by versified and prosaic texts of different periods). Literature becomes the bearer of actual and the transmitter of historical knowledge and it construes intertextual bonds between literary and non-literary texts. Furthermore, literature recovers and revives knowledge in reincorporating some of its formerly rejected unofficial or arcane traditions. The particular mode of writing which deals with such knowledge is the literature of the fantastic, especially in Romanticism. Here the fantastic operates as a mnemonic device that makes the forgotten or repressed reappear and compensates for what was lost as a result of cultural constraints. This mode of writing supported and nourished suppressed traditions of knowledge which ran as an undercurrent below the mainstream of Enlightenment. The authors of fantastic texts were fascinated by the exclusive nature of the disciplines of arcane knowledge with their doctrines and practices, the secrets of alchemy, mesmerism, the symbolic language of the kabbala as well as by their ritualistic preservation and transmission, and by the hope of regaining through them long-forgotten insights into human nature and the lost order of the world. Scientifically not fully approved techniques, such as hypnocures and hypnosis, persisted along—or "under"—the enlightened disciplines and sciences proper. A forgotten past is encountered again in fantastic literature. The recounting of that past heals an occluded memory. In this mode of writing, authors (in the "classical" fantastic and the "neo-fantastic" traditions) draw—in a most obvious manner—on other texts, recollecting stylistic strategies, plots, motifs, the personnel, the anthropological or philosophical problems the preceding texts dealt with; they transmit the structure and semantics of the genre as such (cf. the tradition including the representatives of the Gothic novel, Mary Shelley, E. T. A. Hoffmann, Nikolaj Gogol, Edgar Allan Poe, H. G. Wells, and others).

6.

Authors of literary texts like to explicate their own memory concepts. Some develop intricate "mythopoetic" theories which betray the assimilation of philosophy or literary theory. The manifests of avant-gardist movements (e.g., Italian and Russian futurism) proclaim the death of the established artistic-literary tradition in order to begin anew on its ruins. The corresponding literary theory, formulated by Russian formalism, sees literary (cultural) evolution as an alternation of systems, advocating discontinuity and disrupture as the moving force. The radical opposite to the programmatic dismissal of the past, advocated by the futurists, is to be found in the movement of the Acmeists, Anna Akhmatova and Osip Mandelstam. Instead of defending the idea of a tabula rasa, the Acmeists "yearn for the world culture" (Mandelstam) as an imperishable thesaurus, which they want to incorporate and to repeat, transforming it into a text. Their poetry is a telling example of the participation model that appears to best represent the mnemonic function of intertextuality. Participation works as revoking past texts, as sharing and repetition. Anna Akhmatova speaks of "the profound joy of recurrence." It includes a thematization of writing as a process of remembering, an equation described by Akhmatova thus: "When I write, I remember, when I remember, I write." Mandelstam in "Literary Moscow" (1922) expresses it even more pointedly: "Invention and remembering go hand in hand in poetry; to remember means the same thing as to find, and the man who remembers is the inventor. […] Poetry inhales remembering and invention with its nose and mouth." Mandelstam proposed an elaborate theory of cultural memory which owes some of its constituent ideas to Henri Bergson's notions of time, duration, evolution, and memory. The past is grasped as becoming, as deferred meaning that neither was nor is but is always being projected into the future. By treating culture as a kind of macroconsciousness, Mandelstam transposes Bergsonian concepts, which originally related to human consciousness, to the realm of culture. Retrospection is an approach to history which is carried on by writing. It is an attempt to participate in the past of a culture as a whole.

Disordered pluralism, the disengagement from divisible, measurable time, the plurivocal answer of the poetic word to the earlier times, the experience of distinct temporal strata—all these aspects of Mandelstam's conceptual imagery are echoes of Bergsonian concepts. Pure duration is heterogeneous. Remembering is not the restitution of a unified, monadic complex but the recalling of heterogeneous, interrelated strata. For Mandelstam culture is a totality that encompasses the continuous accumulation of elements, which cannot be related to one another in terms of measurable time. In order to make time into an achronic synchrony, Mandelstam extricates it from the iron rule of sequentiality. Heterogeneity is stored in the text and in memory; it is itself a phenomenon of time, just as time is a phenomenon of the heterogeneous.

In his reading of the Bergsonian concept of time as *évolution créatrice* and *durée irréversible*, Mandelstam takes into account Bergson's ideas of past, present, and future, as well as his theory of the role of memory. Bergson's notion of the accumulation of the past in the present led him to postulate a mechanism suppressing those things in memory that are unnecessary for grasping the present. Acmeist memory—deviating from Bergson at this point—is directed expressly against the forgetting of signs, against their utilitarian suppression. For them, *durée* is possible only as the storing of continually accruing layers of memory. The creative act of writing is immersed in duration. The act of writing prevents that which has been gathered in memory and in remembering from acquiring a definite identity. Mandelstam's formulaic statement in his essay "Pushkin and Skrjabin" (1919): "Memory triumphs even at the price of death! To die is to remember, to remember is to die" expresses a transindividual concept of memory. Dying as remembering means that the cultural experience stored by an individual (a writer) outlives that same person. Memory enshrined in writing is directed against the destruction of cultural experience. The locus of this transindividual, noninheritable memory is the text.

7.

In techniques such as the embedding of either other texts or foreign textual elements in the surface structure of a given text (quotations, allusions, reminiscences, and so on), or in procedures such as the mixing together and piling up of many different texts belonging to various poetic systems (cento, bricolage), or even the rewriting of, or a rejoinder to, a known text that appears in the form of a polemical response, travesty, parody, and so forth, the concern is neither with conjuring up an untouched world of literary tradition nor with demonstrating an inexhaustible erudition that is absorbed into the text as quotation. The issue concerns the semantic explosion that takes place in the collision or interfacing of texts, in the production of an aesthetic and semantic surplus. The mnemonic function of literature provokes intertextual procedures, or: the other way round, intertextuality produces and sustains literature's memory.

References

Addison, Joseph. "The Pleasures of the Imagination." *The Spectator* 411-421 (1712). Rpt. in *The Spectator*. Ed. Donald F. Bond. Vol. 3. Oxford: Clarendon, 1965. 535-82.

Akhmatova, Anna. *The Complete Poems of Anna Akhmatova.* Trans. Judith Hemschemeyer. Ed. Roberta Reeder. 2 vols. Somerville, MA: Zephyr, 1990.

Bergson, Henri. *Creative Evolution.* 1911. Trans. Arthur Mitchell. New York: Modern Library, 1944.

Bloom, Harold. *The Anxiety of Influence: A Theory of Poetry.* Oxford: Oxford UP, 1973.

Goldmann, Stefan. "'Statt Totenklage Gedächtnis': Zur Erfindung der Mnemotechnik durch Simonides von Keos." *Poetica* 21.1-2 (1989): 43-66.

Jenny, Laurent. "The Strategy of Form." *French Literary Theory Today: A Reader.* Trans. R. Carter. Ed. Tzvetan Todorov. Cambridge: Cambridge UP, 1982. 34-63.

Kristeva, Julia. "Word, Dialogue, and Novel." *Desire in Language: A Semiotic Approach to Literature and Art.* Ed. Leon S. Roudiez. Trans. Thomas Gora, Alice Jardine and Leon S. Roudiez. New York: Columbia UP, 1984. 64-91.

Lachmann, Renate. *Erzählte Phantastik: Zu Phantasiegeschichte und Semantik phantastischer Texte.* Frankfurt am Main: Suhrkamp, 2002.

—. *Gedächtnis und Literatur: Intertextualität in der russischen Moderne.* Frankfurt am Main: Suhrkamp, 1990.

—. *Memory and Literature: Intertextuality in Russian Modernism.* Trans. Roy Sellars and Anthony Wall. Minneapolis: U of Minnesota P, 1997.

Mandelstam, Osip. *The Complete Critical Prose and Letters.* Trans. Jane Gary Harris and Constance Link. Ann Arbor: Ardis, 1979.

Rossi, Paolo. *Clavis universalis: Arti della memoria e logica combinatoria da Lullo a Leibniz.* Bologna: Il Mulino, 1983.

Trabant, Jürgen. "Memoria. Fantasia. Ingegno." *Memoria: Erinnern und Vergessen.* Eds. Anselm Haverkamp and Renate Lachmann. Poetik und Hermeneutik 15. Munich: Fink, 1993. 406-24.

Yates, Frances A. *The Art of Memory.* London: Routledge, 1966.

Cultural Memory and the Literary Canon

HERBERT GRABES

Every moment while I am writing this down, a myriad of details are dropping into the past. No wonder that my memory, when attempting to store them, cannot but be highly selective. If this already pertains to personal memory, selectivity must be much increased when it comes to the storage of what is shared by a group of any size. The result of such selective processes has been called a canon (see A. Assmann, this volume).

As there are good reasons to assume that the processes of selection are generally based on evaluation, canons are objectivations of values, either individual or shared. For this reason they possess a considerable amount of prestige within the larger framework of culture. The awareness that this is so is shared keenly by the group of (mostly American) critics who, over the last few decades of the twentieth century, fiercely attacked "the canon." What these attacks show is that when collective values change, this may affect considerably the validation of canons.

We know from personal experience and from history that changes in the hierarchy of values are not uncommon, and an objective indication of such changes are the canonical shifts that can be observed over time. It is therefore not surprising that the widest field in the domain of the study of the canon has been that of the history of the concept of "canon" (cf. Gorak) and the history of such literary canons as have actually been formed (cf. Weinbrot; Kramnick; Ross; Grabes and Sichert). In view of the likelihood of change and the appearance of competing canons in one and the same culture, it seems sensible to consider them as results of evaluations shared and promoted by groups within a culture over a certain span of time.

On the other hand, canons are construed in order to last, and the history of canon formation shows that, against all odds, they quite often possess an extraordinary degree of longevity. This has to do with their central importance for the shaping and sustenance of cultural memory. In his groundbreaking 1988 essay "Kollektives Gedächtnis und kulturelle Identität" ("Collective Memory and Cultural Identity"), Jan Assmann presented a definition of cultural memory as "the characteristic store of repeatedly used texts, images and rituals in the cultivation of which each society and epoch stabilizes and imports its self-image; a collectively shared knowledge of preferably (yet not exclusively) the past, on which a group bases its awareness of unity and character" (15).

For this unifying function to come into effect, it is indispensable that a sufficient number of valuable items from the past be held in collective memory, and, alongside myths and the narratives of legendary history, canons are the most efficient means of ensuring this. The close link between canons and cultural memory has also been the reason why the embedding of canons in culture and their various cultural functions have—next to the tracing of their historical changes—found most attention in the more recent canon debate. What deserves particular mention beyond their turning the infinity of past events and achievements into a "usable past" is what, defending canons, Roger Shattuck pointed out when saying that we not only "expect to find continuity [...] in the macro realm of culture—mores, institutions, artifacts," but that "within that continuity of perception and imagination we have developed a limited number of versions of human greatness," and that "continuity and greatness are effectively conveyed and celebrated in lasting artifacts or masterworks" (90).

Howard Felperin's opinion "that the canon depends on a continuing cultural negotiation that is deeply political, a process that its successive reinscription cannot help but record" (xii) is, however, a view shared by more of those critics who participated in the canon debate. The collective canon widely determines, after all, what remains in a society's cultural memory, and this again influences the view of the present and the future. A typical example of a political approach is John Guillory's employment of Pierre Bourdieu's metaphor of "cultural capital" in dealing with *The Problem of Literary Canon Formation* (ix), and even Harold Bloom in his apocalyptic vision of the future of the "Western Canon" frankly admits that "canons always indirectly serve the social and political, and indeed the spiritual, concerns of the wealthier classes of each generation of Western society" (33). No wonder that under the aegis of the desire for an egalitarian society the vision of the dissolution of all collective canon-making has taken hold: "We all make our own canon: every teacher their own Norton [. . .]. The emergence of an infinity of canons of British literature is, perhaps, the appropriate postmodern solution (or solutions). The canon is dead: long live pick-and-mix" (Munns 26).

It is important to note that the recent canon debate has centered on the literary canon, although cultural memory comprises canons in a whole number of domains of cultural activity—for instance, in art, music, theatre, and philosophy. One reason for this can already be gathered from Jessica Munn's remark: the equation of the literary canon with the curriculum of college teaching in the U.S.A. and its heavy dependence on a few magisterial anthologies that share the market. Not that this equation was wholly beside the point: Canons can only be of some value for the functioning of cultural memory when they are handed on from generation to generation, and educational institutions are of primary importance in this process. Yet apart from the teaching canon there are many others—for instance, that of literary masterpieces on a national and international scale, a canon that is not least upheld by keeping these works in print and available in translation; there is the canon of "high" versus "popular" literature, or the broad canon of texts representing national excellence for a particular country, as is evident from many national literary histories.

At a time when both feminists and ethnic minorities were claiming a fairer share in the representation of—above all American—collective memory, the unavoidably strong selectivity of the teaching canon and the at least assumed power of the canon as "cultural capital" aroused deep feelings and much polemic in the so-called canon wars. As Robert von Hallberg put it in the introduction to his influential critical anthology, *Canons*, from 1984: "One of the issues at stake here [...] is whether canons can be adequately comprehended as the expression of the interests of one social group or class against those of another" (2). In view of the fact that one has to reckon with several "cultures of memory" existing simultaneously in one and the same society rather than with only one (and not only in a "multicultural" society), there will certainly be competition between these memorial cultures and the canons that serve as their archives. It can hardly be questioned that in the American educational system (and not only there) those "who are in positions to edit anthologies and prepare reading lists are obviously those who occupy positions of some cultural power; and their acts of evaluation—represented in what they exclude as well as what they include—constitute not merely recommendations of value but […] also determinants of value," as Barbara Herrnstein Smith remarked in her notorious anti-canonist essay "Contingencies of Value" (29). Yet this not only applies much less to the situation in Europe but also reveals a lack of distinction between the literary canon and the sacred canon of religions based on divine revelation in "holy writ." Whereas the latter can indeed serve as a scriptural paradigm of cultural power, a look at history will show that the literary canon has always been open and subject to changes brought about in complex cultural processes.

As soon as one moves away from the reductive equation of the literary canon with the teaching canon or curriculum, one becomes aware of the multitude of factors instrumental in its formation and sustenance. Later authors take up forms and themes from earlier authors, literary historians and literary critics draw attention to particular works and authors by writing about them, authors of literary histories allot much or little or no space at all to them, editors and publishers make and keep works available, and many or few people buy them and sometimes even read them, especially when urged to do so by their teachers and professors or when persuaded by friends or reviewers—or, more recently, by having seen a film version. In view of the complexity of the ensuing process, Simone Winko has suggested considering canon formation as a phenomenon of the "invisible hand," a term introduced by the economist Adam Smith in order to describe something for which it is difficult to make out its actual origin because many people have contributed to its creation, though not necessarily being aware of it. At least it can be said that canons of literature as archives of cultural memory are by no means created by critics alone—and therefore the hope of anti-canonist critics and theorists to be able to abolish them seems rather vain.

This is all the more the case since, though the literary works canons contain may be characterized by disinterestedness, the canons themselves are not. They serve societies to control what texts are kept in collective memory, are taken "seriously," and interpreted in a particular way. A perusal of almost all nineteenth-century British histories of English literature, for instance, will reveal that their hierarchical canons are meant to disseminate moral values and great pride in long-standing national excellence in order to foster national unity and identity. As for the twentieth century, Jan Gorak has shown that "canons have functioned as vehicles of national politics, as declarations of cultural independence by a critical avant-garde, as instruments to calibrate the nuances of creative excellence, and as the source of encyclopedic, mythical or historical narratives" (221). Due to their ability to negotiate between tradition and present needs by offering the literary heritage to ever new interpretation and validation, canons have proved to be so adaptable to cultural change that their survival seems guaranteed.

What is true is that the more recent focus on the negative effect of their selectivity and their "suppressive power" has overshadowed their enabling functions. One of these is the motivation and orientation the literary canon provides for authors. In Charles Altieri's words: "Canons call attention to what can be done within the literary medium. The canon is a repertory of inventions and a challenge to our capacity to further develop a genre or style [...]" (33). Furthermore, canons demarcate the field of investigation and provide qualitative guidance for literary studies. On the basis of historically contingent criteria they select what is going to count as "literature" from the thousands and thousands of extant texts, and in so doing actually create the concept of "literature." And for everyone, be it author, critic or "general reader," the canon serves the most basic and indispensable function of turning the overwhelming plenitude of what has survived into a "usable past," a corpus of texts that can be surveyed and retained in collective memory.

It is important to note that canons can serve all of these functions even when they are considered as no more than heuristic instruments. Yet because they can be given a strongly normative function in educational systems, it is understandable that they can then generate equally strong opposition. As the canons we find in literary histories are much wider than the teaching canons, and in many European countries the university curricula traditionally have not been tightly regulated, the significance of the war cry to "open up the canon" within the American canon debate can only be understood by someone who knows the extent to which the teaching of undergraduate courses is determined by the use of one of the leading anthologies that has been "introduced." What this debate has revealed is the considerable degree to which the assessment of canons depends on and is limited by personal experience and culturally determined professional practice. It is, for instance, truly amazing that, due to the fact that in American college teaching one encounters "the canon" almost exclusively in the anthologies, the canon of literary histories is hardly ever even mentioned, although it has the longest tradition of keeping texts in collective memory.

It is therefore a great improvement that the canon debate has turned more and more into a historical and systematic study of literary canons and canon formation, mostly within the broader framework of the study of cultural memory (cf. Assmann and Assmann; Gorak; Guillory; Moog-Grünewald; Kramnick; Ross; Heydebrand). What is nevertheless astonishing is the fact that the question of the extent of the canon—of how many of the texts that have come down to us from the more distant or recent past are considered worthy of being kept in cultural memory—has hardly been tackled at all, although it is of central importance for all other aspects of canonicity (cf. Grabes and Sichert). In order to get beyond making distinctions merely on the level of terminology, I would like to demonstrate which alternatives there are by taking as an example the representation of the history of writing in Britain in the national cultural memory. The most comprehensive archive would ideally comprise all Old English and medieval manuscripts and, since the introduction of printing, all published texts, and attempts to establish catalogues designed to be as complete as possible have been made at least for the early modern period with the *Short-Title Catalogues* of Pollard & Redgrave and Wing. To be as complete as possible in their documentation was already the aim of two mid-sixteenth-century antiquarians, John Leland and John Bale, who wrote the first histories of British writers and writings under the threat of a loss of the national literary tradition as a result of the dispersal and partial destruction of the holdings of the monastic libraries following the dissolution of the monasteries under Henry VIII. Leland's "Libri quatuor de viris illustribus, siue de scriptoribus Britannicis" from the earlier 1540s already offered a comparatively broad chronological canon of 674 presumed or confirmed authors of diverse kinds of writings, and the Protestant reformer John Bale was to do even much better: His *Scriptorum Illustrium maioris Brytannie, quam nunc Angliam & Scotiam uocant: Catalogus* from 1557-59 with its 1400 entries remained the most compendious work of this kind until 1748, when Bishop Thomas Tanner brought out his *Bibliotheca Britannico-Hibernica*, an epitome of a collection of writers' biographies in nine volumes that was meant to be complete up to the early seventeenth century.

In accordance with the conventions of learned works at the time, of course, early comprehensive works were written in Latin; if this precluded a wider impact, it must be said that the relatively recent *Short-Title Catalogues* have also remained sources of information merely for specialists. Yet it should also have become clear that the very broad canons of all these works are archives of cultural memory in a wider sense, because they represent the whole range of written culture, not only literary texts or, to use the older term, "poetry." As Trevor Ross has been able to show, there were, however, also various attempts to create a canon of English poetry as early as the late sixteenth and early seventeenth centuries, even if these were still rather rudimentary.

The first to publish a history of English literature with a sizeable canon covering some 150 "poets" from the twelfth to the seventeenth century was William Winstanley, with his *Lives of the Most Famous English Poets* from 1687. It is thus untrue to say that the English literary canon was first established in the eighteenth century, as is maintained by most literary historians. What is true, rather, is that Theophilus Cibber's *Lives of the Poets of Great Britain and Ireland* from 1753 with its canon of 202 chronologically arranged literary authors from Chaucer to Mary Chandler, and even Samuel Johnson's *Lives of the Most Eminent English Poets* from 1781 still follow the same structural pattern as Winstanley. Johnson's important innovation consisted in the inclusion of critical commentaries on particular works, but his canon of 54 "eminent poets" covers only the period from Shakespeare to Lyttelton.

Really innovative in a structural way was Thomas Warton's presentation of a first *grand récit* of both British cultural and literary history in his *History of English Poetry*, published between 1774 and 1781. Too ambitious with its wide-ranging excursions into cultural history, it breaks off in the earlier sixteenth century, yet with its continuous narrative it gave a new direction to the writing of literary history. Regarding the development of the canon, however, the model for almost all subsequent British literary histories of the nineteenth and earlier twentieth centuries was created by the Edinburgh historian and publisher Robert Chambers in his *History of the English Language and Literature* from 1836. Chambers's desire was to demonstrate the excellence of the "national mind" to a wider audience, and he therefore strikes a concise compromise between the qualitative and the quantitative canons, which—except for Warton's rambling narrative—had earlier been kept separate. He achieves this by giving clear priority to literary authors yet also including "Miscellaneous Writers," "Metaphysicians," "Historical, Critical and Theological Writers," "Encyclopaedias and Magazines," "Biographers," "Travellers," "Political Economists," "Popular Publications," and even "Writers of Science." This combination of a qualitative canon of "literature" in a narrower sense with a broader canon representing national written culture in its various discourses was to become the dominant tradition of British writing of national literary history, finding its epitome in the fifteen volumes of the *Cambridge History of English Literature* from the early twentieth century (1907-16). It should be added that this tradition is still very much alive, as is shown not only by the already published volumes of the spacious *New Cambridge History of English Literature* and new *Oxford English Literary History*, but also by such one-volume works as the *Short Oxford History of English Literature* by Andrew Sanders.

Typical of this tradition is a rather stable "core canon" made up of Chaucer, Spenser, Shakespeare, Milton, Dryden, Pope, Dr Johnson, Wordsworth, Dickens and Tennyson, with Jane Austen, George Eliot, T. S. Eliot, Joyce, and Beckett being added in the course of the twentieth century. The surrounding canon of authors considered still eminent tends to be much broader and reacts much more to changing trends in literary criticism. Even more changes occur on a still lower hierarchical level of authors who receive at least some kind of commentary; at the lowest level of attention, there may be little more than a cursory presentation of names and titles—a level that quite obviously has the sole function of reminding us that there is still so much more of note in written culture.

Regarding the demand to "open up the canon" it can thus be said that the canon of traditional British literary histories in this respect has always been wide open. What cannot be warded off, however, is the reproach that it has been "a vehicle for national, racial and gender superiority" (Gorak 235), especially in the nineteenth and earlier twentieth centuries. But it can be said that the canons of more recent British literary histories, beginning with the *Sphere History of Literature in the English Language* (1970), the *Macmillan History of English Literature* (1982), and the *Longman Literature in English Series* (1985-) do pay cognizance to the existence of postcolonial literatures, some to a significant degree, and—mainly due to the sterling work done by feminist historians and critics, and to the pressure exerted by them—also include many more women authors.

It may be true that literary historians tend to be rather fond of tradition, hence slower in their responses to cultural change than theoretically minded critics who always want to be on the "cutting edge." That this need not be so, however, is shown by the fact that in recent years, with Michael Alexander's *History of English Literature* (2000) and the *Brief History of English Literature* (2002) by John Peck and Martin Coyle, some new literary histories have appeared in Britain that present a canon devoted almost exclusively to "literature" in a narrower sense. At a time when the upcoming culturalism seems to threaten the privileged position of imaginative writing in cultural memory, it is these literary historians who are bucking the trend. This goes to show that in a dynamic culture which is constantly changing, the contest over which of the cultural achievements of the more distant or more recent past will be able to secure a position in cultural memory finds its most prominent expression in the competing canons that serve as its archives. To abandon the canon would mean to jettison cultural memory. And even critics seem to become aware of this again. In 2004 there even appeared a work with the title *Pleasure and Change: The Aesthetics of Canon*, something that would have been practically unthinkable ten years earlier, and it presents the more recent views of Frank Kermode on the canon. So despite all temporarily quite fierce anti-canonist arguments, the canon will not die. Too strong is the desire to be canonized, too useful the canonizing for cultural memory, and too welcome the need to constantly rewrite it for literary and cultural historians.

References

Altieri, Charles. *Canons and Consequences: Reflections on the Ethical Force of Imaginative Ideals.* Evanston: Northwestern UP, 1990.

Assmann, Aleida, and Jan Assmann, eds. *Kanon und Zensur.* Munich: Fink, 1987.

Assmann, Jan. "Kollektives Gedächtnis und kulturelle Identität." *Kultur und Gedächtnis.* Eds. Jan Assmann and Tonio Hölscher. Frankfurt am Main: Fischer, 1988. 9-19. [English: Assmann, Jan. "Collective Memory and Cultural Identity." Trans. John Czaplicka. *New German Critique* 65 (1995): 125-33.]

Bloom, Harold. *The Western Canon: The Books and School of the Ages.* New York: Harcourt Brace, 1994.

Felperin, Howard. *The Uses of the Canon: Elizabethan Literature and Contemporary Theory.* Oxford: Clarendon, 1990.

Gorak, Jan. *The Making of the Modern Canon: Genesis and Crisis of a Literary Idea.* London: Athlone, 1991.

Grabes, Herbert, and Margit Sichert. "Literaturgeschichte, Kanon und nationale Identität." *Gedächtniskonzepte der Literaturwissenschaft: Theoretische Grundlegung und Anwendungsperspektiven.* Eds. Astrid Erll and Ansgar Nünning. Berlin: de Gruyter, 2005. 297-314.

Guillory, John. *Cultural Capital: The Problem of Literary Canon Formation.* Chicago: U of Chicago P, 1993.

Hallberg, Robert von, ed. *Canons.* Chicago: U of Chicago P, 1984.

Herrnstein Smith, Barbara. "Contingencies of Value." *Canons.* Ed. Robert von Hallberg. Chicago: U of Chicago P, 1984. 5-40.

Heydebrand, Renate von, ed. *Kanon—Macht—Kultur: Theoretische, historische und soziale Aspekte ästhetischer Kanonbildungen.* Stuttgart: Metzler, 1998.

Kermode, Frank. *Pleasure and Change: The Aesthetics of Canon.* Ed. Robert Alter. Oxford: Oxford UP, 2004.

Kramnick, Jonathan Brody. *Making the English Canon: Print-Capitalism and the Cultural Past, 1700-1770.* Cambridge: Cambridge UP, 1998.

Moog-Grünewald, Maria, ed. *Kanon und Theorie.* Heidelberg: Winter, 1997.

Munns, Jessica. "Cannon Fodder: Women's Studies and the (British) Literary Canon." *Canon vs. Culture: Reflections on the Current Debate.* Ed. Jan Gorak. New York: Garland, 2001. 17-27.

Ross, Trevor. *The English Literary Canon: From the Middle Ages to the Late Eighteenth Century.* Montreal: McGill-Queen's UP, 1998.

Shattuck, Roger. "Perplexing Lessons: Is There a Core Tradition in the Humanities?" *The Hospitable Canon.* Eds. Virgil Nemoianu and Robert Royal. Philadelphia: John Benjamins, 1991. 85-96.

Weinbrot, Howard. *Britannia's Issue: The Rise of British Literature from Dryden to Ossian.* Cambridge: Cambridge UP, 1993.

Winko, Simone. "Literatur-Kanon als *invisible hand*-Phänomen." *Literarische Kanonbildung.* Ed. Heinz Ludwig Arnold. Munich: Edition Text + Kritik, 2002. 9-24.

Life-Writing, Cultural Memory, and Literary Studies

MAX SAUNDERS

"Life-writing" is a contentious term. It covers a wide range of texts and forms. Indeed, its contentiousness arises at least partly because it seems, to some, to cover too many. As one leading British biographer, Hermione Lee, writes, it is sometimes used "when different ways of telling a life-story—memoir, autobiography, biography, diary, letters, autobiographical fiction—are being discussed together" (100). This is the main sense in which I shall be using it. Though, as Lee notes, another main usage is "when the distinction between biography and autobiography is being deliberately blurred" (100). Critics sometimes use the term "auto/biography" to indicate this generic fusion (or, again, as a shorthand for talking of the genres autobiography and biography together). The term "autobiography" was coined as Romanticism took shape towards the end of the eighteenth century. Paradoxically, this is also the period in which the view began to emerge that all writing had an autobiographical dimension. According to this view, which became increasingly consolidated through the nineteenth century, and which is even shared by Postmodernism, the distinction between autobiography and other forms such as biography or fiction is thus always already blurred. The two senses distinguished by Lee are then not as distinct as they might have seemed. A memoir of someone else, by virtue of the fact that you are writing about them because they were important in your life, will be part of your autobiography. That scholars are prepared to spend years of their lives immersing themselves in the biographies of others tells you something about their biographies. To some extent they are writing displaced autobiographies; and that vector of displacement is what lends even the most scrupulously factual biography its admixture of fictionality.

In his seminal essay "Autobiography as De-Facement," Paul de Man theorized this question of autobiographical readings by arguing that autobiography is not a genre at all, but precisely a mode of reading. A sentence in a biography may purport to refer to its subject—Dr. Johnson, say—but we are at liberty to read it as autobiographical: as telling us instead about Boswell. Such generic blurring is characteristic in another way, though. Life-writing is fundamentally inter-textual (see Lachmann, this volume). Biographies will quote freely from their subjects' letters or diaries or speeches where available. Memoirists will quote conversation they claim to remember verbatim. One might think autobiography would provide the greatest generic purity, relying only on acts of memory for its sources. Yet autobiographers too will quote documents, others' biographies, their own journals or novels. Though of course, by the same principle of generic fusion, such sources will themselves be already fused. Siegfried Sassoon's *Memoirs of an Infantry Officer* (1930), say, which offers a fictionalized account of Sassoon's life as "George Sherston" (who shares Sassoon's war experiences, but not his poetic vocation), quotes from his diaries written in the trenches. The effect is to ground the narrative in immediate testimony. Yet Sassoon's own diaries, which have since been published, reveal something arresting. He often describes himself in the third person, as if he needed to view himself as a character in a novel, in order to write about his experiences. The diary is thus already fictionalized. The diary extracts in the *Memoirs* have then been re-written—re-fictionalized—in order to make them sound more autobiographical. Not all life-writing plays such complex games with intertextuality and inter-generity, but most examples do something of the sort.

Such generic problems posed by life-writing have important theoretical ramifications, especially for the study of cultural memory. Much recent theory of autobiography in particular, pioneered by Philippe Lejeune, has focused on the notion of a "contract" between author and reader, guaranteeing that the person named on the title page is actually the subject of the book as well as the corresponding real person. But such an argument only serves to raise the question of the legitimacy of a literary contract, as well as that of what to do about cases which do not fit the contractual model—what one might call non-contractual autobiography, as found in third-person autobiography (such as *The Education of Henry Adams*, 1918), pseudonymous publication (such as *The Autobiography of Mark Rutherford*, by William Hale White, 1881), and the vast genre of the autobiographical novel.

This destabilizing of genres frustrates attempts to see life-writing as possessing a direct connection with subjective experience and individual memory. Yet from another point of view, such problematization presents an opportunity. If other genres or sub-genres or forms can be read as life-writing—such as novels, poems, short stories, travel writings, topographical books, historiography—they can all be used as routes into cultural memory. But of course if we are to use such literary texts as evidence for cultural memory studies, clearly we cannot use them naively, as historical "documents" or "sources" of first-hand testimony. Indeed, we must approach them as literary critics, aware that what we are dealing with are, precisely, texts. That is, rather than studying memory-texts for historical fact, in the way nineteenth-century historians sought to establish "wie es eigentlich gewesen," our object of study is, instead, modes of writing. Rather than giving us direct access to unmediated memory, what such texts reveal is, instead, memory cultures. When we study life-writing as a source for cultural memory, that is, our conclusions will also be literary-critical ones: interpretations of the ways in which memory was produced, constructed, written, and circulated.

This may appear a trivializing limitation, one which frustrates the historian's desire to know the past, substituting instead discussions of how the past was mediated. Yet once again an apparent limitation can also be seen as an advantage, since one thing life-writing shows is that while we may think of memory as somehow prior to auto/biography, or literature, or any form of textuality, our memories are always already textualized. They are by definition "after the event," but also, as representations or mediations or narrativizations of the event, they have always begun to turn the event into something else (see Straub, this volume). Even journals (those less artful than Sassoon's, anyway) which seem immediate, are mediated by short-term memory. Clinical talk of "false memory syndrome" has the unfortunate side-effect of implying that memory ought to deliver truth. Of course the truth of narrated memories can be argued over, and some will be found more consonant with other forms of evidence, and some less so. But from one point of view all memory partakes of falsification, to the extent that it is necessarily a transformation of the remembered event or experience. Thus studying literary life-writing texts as sources for cultural memory can make us more sophisticated cultural historians, and more sophisticated students of memory.

It can also make us more sophisticated literary critics, since to read biography or autobiography in terms of cultural memory is to some extent to read them against the grain. Both forms define their scope in terms of the individual life, and claim to offer unparalleled access to the mind and experience and memories of their subjects. That is precisely their lure for historians and cultural mnemologists. One of the most haunting passages of William Wordsworth's *The Prelude* describes how, as a young boy, he found a small boat one evening, and surreptitiously rowed it out into the lake (1805 text, bk. 1, lines 372-427). As he does so, he is facing the shore, and notices that a cliff, set back from the shore so he had not seen it earlier, appears to rise up into view as he keeps rowing. He becomes terrified, imagining the cliff as rearing up to pursue him, and he hurries back to the shore, not only feeling contrite, but coming to feel that the episode is an example of the way his moral sense has been developed not by people, or religious teaching, but by nature herself. It is a crucial episode, and offers insight into a formative memory; one which has retained its power over the adult poet, and which stands as a landmark in his biographical development. Modern autobiography is centrally concerned with such attempts to write the self, to represent subjectivity, interiority, personal memory.

However, read from the point of view of cultural memory, even if *The Prelude* gives us the record of an unusually free and unstructured individual childhood, it gives us an unparalleled account of how it was possible to *be* as a child in the late eighteenth century, and of how childhood was being reconfigured as something to be remembered in particular ways through the nineteenth century. To read *The Prelude* thus is to treat it (naively, as suggested above) as any other historical document; as written testimony to individual memory, which can be tessellated with other individual memories to build up a pattern of memories across a whole culture: in short, to read autobiography as a component of a culture's memory; as its reflection. But a literary work like *The Prelude* has a different status from the kind of unpublished sources beloved by historians, such as diaries or letters. As it passed into public consciousness, it also contributed to the *production* of cultural memory.

It is such works of autobiography which have tended to attract the most theoretical attention; not autobiographies of the obscure, so much as texts by already canonical figures. The high poststructuralist theory of critics like de Man tends to focus on Romanticism: Its foundational texts of modern life-writing are *The Prelude* or Rousseau's *Confessions* (1781-88); works in which the subject's uniqueness is axiomatic, and in which the emphasis on self-expression is the primary impulse. However, an exclusive focus on such texts can occlude the ways in which other life-writing practices have historically also had a strong cultural function. Recently letters, diaries, and travel narratives, all of which are heavily invested in the production and representing of sociability, have begun to receive more theoretical attention. Biography in particular has been a central form of cultural memory production. This is in part anthropological. Biography has been regarded as a form of ancestor worship, and certainly the early examples of lives of rulers such as Plutarch's *Lives* are animated by veneration. They also have the function of defining and celebrating the values of their society—a society which they tend to show in the process of formation. They also have a marked moral function, something which is seen more clearly in hagiography, in which it is the religious life that is celebrated, in order to furnish moral examples.

As Western societies became increasingly secularized from the Enlightenment, the cultural function of biography developed in antithetical ways. One strand, which essentially modernizes the ancient veneration function, is represented by Thomas Carlyle's famous dictum of 1840 that "[t]he history of the world is but the Biography of great men" (29). Such great men are accorded honor for the way the force of their personalities changed the course of history. Besides the elision of even the possibility of the great woman, there are three aspects of this relevant to our discussion.

First, the greatness of the great man is a mark of his singularity; his individuality. To this extent, Carlyle's is a Romantic notion of individual "genius"; one who merely works out his energies in the sphere of history rather than art. Second, and following from this, though such lives are "exemplary," what they are examples of is the apogee of human achievement, and thus by definition of achievement which cannot be matched by the ungreat. Indeed, Carlyle's strategy can be seen as a characteristic Victorian intellectual response to industrialization and democratization as forces which are felt as leveling humanity downwards. Third, though the lives told are individual, they contribute to the collective "history." Here the statement is a paradox: it fragments "history" into individual biography; but it simultaneously appears to value great lives for their contribution to the collective human story. In a sense such paradoxes can be seen to anticipate the emergence of impersonal, materialist history, associated (ironically) with the person of Marx, later in the nineteenth century. According to Marxist dialectical materialism, individual lives are the result of economically determined historical processes, not the cause of history; and the idea that great men shape history is an ideological mystification.

The other strand of secularized life-writing, instead of celebrating the exceptional man, celebrates representative man or woman. If this is less apparent in biography—books on the unknown would be harder to sell—it is more so in autobiography. Writers such as John Stuart Mill or H. G. Wells, while telling their stories of intellectual achievements extraordinary by any standard, nonetheless insist that there was little exceptional about their intelligence; it was merely their training or circumstances which gave them an advantage. Such strategies are at least in part designed to save autobiography from its nemesis, egotism. But they perhaps also evince an anxiety that the increasingly psychological turn of the humanities and human sciences through the nineteenth century was tending to represent self-hood as increasingly private and solipsistic. When Emerson wrote that "[a]ll history becomes subjective; in other words, there is properly no history, only biography" (15), he meant that it was only in the individual mind that the universal had its existence, because the individual partook of the universal mind. But to our post-modern therapeutic culture that has lost confidence in totalizing grand narratives, only the private and confessional are thought meaningful. The very notion of "cultural memory," paradoxical though it is, might be thought of as trying to preserve this Emersonian idealist notion of universalized individualism.

The subsequent fate of life-writing is probably best understood in terms of a series of theoretical challenges, especially from Psychoanalysis, Marxism, Feminism, (Post) Structuralism, and Postcolonialism, each of which has produced new turns in the biography of auto/biography. And it is with a sketch of these challenges that this essay will conclude.

The challenge of psychoanalysis is not that it disputed the value of interpreting the individual life, but that it entirely transformed the nature of such interpretation. First, because it offers a radically fragmented picture of the self; and because one of the components, the unconscious, cannot be represented directly. Autobiographers no longer have access to their full subjectivity; biographers have a new reason to mistrust their subjects, who not only do not know the full stories of themselves, but may produce unconscious distortions in recounting what they do know, or think they know. Thus the psychoanalytically minded biographer, or even autobiographer, assumes the role of analyst, listening to their subject for signs of repression, displacement, or slippage, while also (if they are scrupulous) recognizing that life-writing can never be the same as a formal psychoanalytic interaction. It was pioneering, psychoanalytically inflected work like Lytton Strachey's that Virginia Woolf had in mind when she announced "The New Biography" in 1927. Strachey‘s landmark volume *Eminent Victorians* (1918) anatomizes four establishment icons—Cardinal Manning, Florence Nightingale, the educationalist Dr. Arnold, and General Gordon—in slyly subversive, ironic sketches. However, it was not until the 1970s that it became possible to discuss sexuality explicitly in auto/biographies as opposed to case histories.

The "New Biography" produced a new enthusiasm for the form. As Laura Marcus argues: "The rise in popularity of biographies was linked to the perception that biography had been reinvented for the twentieth century, requiring a new level of critical self-awareness" ("The Newness" 193-94). But the New Biography's celebration of "personality" and "character," however newly presented, coincides with Modernism's doctrine of *im*personality, and its fragmentation of character into a montage of voices. As the New Biography responded to such Modernist experiments, the Modernists were reacting against biography in turn; and not just its Victorian forms, but the New Biography too. It may have been precisely the sense of a renaissance of the literature of personality that led Eliot to write (in the year following *Eminent Victorians*): "Poetry is […] not the expression of personality, but an escape from personality" (21).

The formalism of Eliot's "impersonal theory" represented another challenge to the authority of life-writing. If, as Eliot argued, "the more perfect the artist, the more completely separate in him will be the man who suffers and the mind which creates," the biography of artists who matter can tell us nothing about their creative minds or the art they create (18). Eliot's ideas were taken up into the American "New Criticism" of critics like W. K. Wimsatt, who, with Monroe C. Beardsley, denounced what they labeled "the Intentional Fallacy": the attempt to move from a work of art to a putative biographical intention behind it. This doctrine, together with the Cambridge "Practical Criticism" of I. A. Richards, William Empson, and F. R. Leavis, sought to focus attention on "the words on the page" rather than on the personality of their author. The criticism and theory of life-writing diminished in the mid-twentieth century, largely due to the prestige of such strictures.

Marxism (which, though it predates these positions, became most influential in literary and cultural studies in the 1960s and 1970s) voices two related objections in particular. First, that the *form* of auto/biography is essentially conservative: an expression of liberal individualism and bourgeois ideology. Second, that its *function* is to preserve a false consciousness: that its presentation of a totalized, coherent, and significant individual life is an illusion in a world of alienated capitalism. Yet life-writings have provided invaluable data for social historians of actual social experience of class struggle.

Feminism too turned to life-writings to redress a kind of cultural amnesia—to write the cultural memory of the women whose contribution to history had been all but obliterated. Also, as Carolyn Heilbrun argues, the development of feminism has meant that it is only in the twentieth century that women have been able to approach full "truth-telling" in their life-writing, and address what the Victorians passed over: female desire, independence, power, anger, bodies. Three main strategies of feminist life-writings are discernible. First, to write auto/biographies of women. Second, to produce reference works such as the *Feminist Companion to Literature in English* (1990). Third, to contribute such material to reference works: both established, such as the *Dictionary of National Biography* or the *Oxford Companion to English Literature* (edited by Margaret Drabble since 1985); or to new projects such as *Edwardian Fiction: An Oxford Companion*, edited by Sandra Kemp, Charlotte Mitchell and David Trotter (1997).

Just as feminism has rehabilitated life-writing, so other forms of identity politics have found it essential to their causes. The histories of sexual, racial, and class identities have all been enriched by the recovery of letters, diaries, and memoirs, as well as by the establishing of biographical counter-cultures. Such work is often avowedly inspirational in its aim, offering a sense of historical solidarity for oppressed minorities, and seeking to record counter-cultural memories that official cultures tend to repress or try to forget.

Fiction often performs this ideological rescue-work too of course. But the historical traumas of the twentieth century have seemed to exact from their survivors the giving of testimony, bearing witness. If Adorno's assertion that "writing poetry after Auschwitz is barbaric" seems too categorical, the attempts to fictionalize events which cultural memory has tended to sacralize have proved controversial. In the literary reports upon the First World War or the Holocaust, it is autobiographical writings which have often become the canonical texts, such as the memoirs of Robert Graves, Vera Brittain, Primo Levi, or Elie Wiesel. Yet the most iconic of Holocaust texts is one written by a victim who did not survive, and which ends before its author was arrested and deported to the death camp. Anne Frank's diary bears witness to a life of persecution and terror. But the pathos of her story comes from her portrayal of an intensely felt individual life, all the more pathetic for the promise of her extraordinary precocity which she is doomed not to be able to fulfill. We read it knowing that the death she fears as an ever-present possibility is her fate. But this individual fate has also become, in cultural memory, a synecdoche for the collective victims of the Holocaust.

The testimonial paradigm for life-writing—what one might call the death-witnessing of the author—is diametrically opposed to the major (post)structuralist challenges to literary biography, first crystallized in Roland Barthes's famous essay "The Death of the Author" (1967). Barthes opposed the biographical tradition on the grounds that it had a reactionary influence upon interpretation. The New Critics thought biography a distraction from a text's meaning, but they still thought meaning was determinate. For Barthes, what is wrong with the biographical is precisely that it tried to fix meaning, by joining it to the author. Instead he celebrates a textual pleasure liberated from authorial control; a rush of plurality. Authors have an authority function, analogous to other patriarchs such as God, prophets, or kings. Barthes's proclamation of the death of the author is the textual equivalent of Nietzsche's enunciation of the death of God. His essay still precipitates nervous assertions that reports of authors' deaths have been exaggerated. But that is to miss Barthes's point, which was to sketch a utopian revolution of reading. Michel Foucault's essay "What Is an Author?" (1969) approaches the issue from another perspective. Where Barthes's author is a tyrant of meaning, Foucault is, as always, concerned with discourse: the discourse of authorship; "the author" as a means of organizing knowledge; making the system of writing intelligible according to a specific categorization.

One response to such poststructuralist challenges is for auto/biography to become postmodern; more conscious of its own narrativity, fictionality, impossibility (as in Barthes's own thematically organized *Roland Barthes par Roland Barthes*). This turn, coinciding with the increasingly auto/biographic turn in twentieth-century fiction, has produced writing which nomadically crosses the borders between biography and fiction. "Faction" or non-fiction novels—like Truman Capote's *In Cold*

Blood (1966) or Norman Mailer's *The Executioner's Song* (1979)—narrate real-life content in novelistic forms and styles. Edmund White's term "autofiction" similarly claims a different mode of generic fusion, in which rather than saying a novel is based on autobiographical fact, it is intimated that selfhood is itself already fictionalized. Postmodern biographies too have used the apparently historical form to contain fictionalized material. Peter Ackroyd's *Dickens* (1990) includes fantasy inter-chapters in which Dickens has conversations with his own characters or with Oscar Wilde and T. S. Eliot. Edmund Morris's *Dutch: A Memoir of Ronald Reagan* (1999) was even more controversial. Despite his status as Reagan's "official biographer," Morris includes several invented characters, including a fictionalized version of himself describing events at which he was not actually present. Arguably in both cases the blurring of fact and fiction reflects the fictionalizing powers of their subjects.

Given the force of these challenges, it is not surprising that life-writing was late in receiving the attention of literary theorists. But, paradoxically, at this point of maximum skepticism about the ability of texts to represent selves, a renaissance was discernible in the study of life-writings. This has in part come about as writing biography became increasingly accepted once more within the academy, and as its practitioners have written critically and theoretically about the form. Key examples include Holmes, Batchelor, Gould and Staley, and Lee.

Works of this kind are mostly accounts of a craft rather than elaborations of literary theory. But critics have, over the last three decades, begun to appreciate the theoretical interest of life-writing in its various forms. Though it took half a century after the modernist explorations of writers like Woolf, the "New Biography" eventually gave rise to what we might call the "New Biotheory," exemplified by the following studies: Backscheider, Barthes, Heilbrun, France and St. Clair, and Jolly.

Of course, for the reasons given at the start of this essay, "biotheory" is necessarily also "auto/biotheory." The best recent life-writing theory has tended to be focused on autobiography, or on the relations between autobiography and adjacent modes such as biography or fiction. Selected examples here include de Man, Anderson, Lejeune, Marcus, Olney, Stanley, and Swindells.

To conclude: After its nineteenth-century heyday, life-writing tended to be treated with condescension through much of the twentieth century, as a form of belles-lettres irrelevant to the study of either literature or society. Formalist critics saw it as ephemeral bric-a-brac which needed to be cleared away to allow access to the primary creative works of poems, novels or plays; political critics saw it as an anachronistic ideological falsification. In the late twentieth century, two opposing theoretical developments have accorded it a new relevance. For New Historicists, such contextual material has come to seem an inextricable part of a text's production and reception, and thus part of its interpretation. By contrast, the poststructuralist argument that there is nothing outside textuality implied that life-writings appear not so much as contexts but as other texts, material susceptible of the same kind of analysis as the primary texts. There was always a tendency to consider some life-writing in this way. Works like Keats's magnificent letters, say, were effectively treated as creative works in their own right; as essentially poetic works that just happened to be written in letter form. While New Historicism has a strong strain of foundationalism in it, poststructuralism is anti-foundational, relentlessly skeptical about the possibility of grounding specific meanings and facts. One advantage of the concept of cultural memory is its ability to hedge its bets on this contest, since it is concerned not with actual events but their cultural repercussions; not with actual memories but with memories as representations, and with representations of memories. As a result of these critical developments, the hierarchy of texts has been questioned. Life-writing texts take their places as other texts, just as valid or authoritative as anything else. Indeed, they are often the texts that question generic boundaries with the greatest force.

References

Anderson, Linda. *Autobiography*. London: Routledge, 2001.

Backscheider, Paula R. *Reflections on Biography*. Oxford: Oxford UP, 1999.

Barthes, Roland. "The Death of the Author." Trans. Richard Howard. *Aspen Magazine* 5-6 (1967): n. pag.

Batchelor, John, ed. *The Art of Literary Biography*. New York: Oxford UP, 1995.

Carlyle, Thomas. "Lecture on the Hero as Divinity." *Heroes, Hero-Worship and the Heroic in History*. 1841. London: Chapman and Hall, 1904. 1-41.

de Man, Paul. "Autobiography as De-Facement." *The Rhetoric of Romanticism*. New York: Columbia UP, 1984.

Eliot, T. S. "Tradition and the Individual Talent." 1919. *Selected Essays*. 3rd, enl. ed. London: Faber and Faber, 1951. 13-22.

Emerson, Ralph Waldo. "History." *Essays*. Cambridge, MA: Riverside, 1865. 7-44.

France, Peter, and William St. Clair, eds. *Mapping Lives: The Uses of Biography*. Oxford: Oxford UP, 2002.

Gould, Warwick, and Thomas F. Staley, eds. *Writing the Lives of Writers*. London: Macmillan; New York: St. Martin's, 1998.

Heilbrun, Carolyn. *Writing a Woman's Life*. New York: Norton, 1988.
Holmes, Richard. *Footsteps: Adventures of a Romantic Biographer*. London: Hodder and Stoughton, 1985.
Jolly, Margaretta, ed. *Encyclopedia of Life Writing: Autobiographical and Biographical Forms*. 2 vols. London: Fitzroy Dearborn, 2002.
Lee, Hermione. *Body Parts*. London: Chatto and Windus, 2005.
Lejeune, Philippe. *Le pacte autobiographique*. Paris: Éditions du Seuil, 1975.
Marcus, Laura. *Auto/Biographical Discourses*. Manchester: Manchester UP, 1994.
—. "The Newness of the 'New Biography': Biographical Theory and Practice in the Early Twentieth Century." *Mapping Lives: The Uses of Biography*. Eds. Peter France and William St. Clair. Oxford: Oxford UP, 2002. 193-218.
Olney, James. *Metaphors of Self: The Meaning of Autobiography*. Princeton: Princeton UP, 1972.
Stanley, Liz. *The Autobiographical I*. Manchester: Manchester UP, 1995.
Swindells, Julia, ed. *The Uses of Autobiography*. London: Taylor and Francis, 1995.

The Literary Representation of Memory

BIRGIT NEUMANN

Memory and processes of remembering have always been an important, indeed a dominant, topic in literature. Numerous texts portray how individuals and groups remember their past and how they construct identities on the basis of the recollected memories. They are concerned with the mnemonic presence of the past in the present, they re-examine the relationship between the past and the present, and they illuminate the manifold functions that memories fulfill for the constitution of identity. Such texts highlight that our memories are highly selective, and that the rendering of memories potentially tells us more about the rememberer's present, his or her desire and denial, than about the actual past events. This is particularly true for cultural memories because they involve intentional fashioning to a greater extent than do individual memories. Hence, literary fictions disseminate influential models of both individual and cultural memories as well as of the nature and functions of memory.

The study of literary representations of individual processes of memory has always been one of the central epistemological interests in literary studies. Numerous studies of various epochs and authors have shown that literature, both thematically and formally, is closely interwoven with the thematic complex of memory and identity. While the study of representations of individual memory has long been an established approach, only recently have scholars begun investigating literary representations of collective memory (cf. Erll). Narratology, which has been extensively involved in the discussion of forms of literary memory (cf. Löschnigg; Henke; Erll and Nünning; Basseler and Birke), has proven to be of great value in the exploration of the representation of memory. Narratological approaches draw attention to formal-aesthetic characteristics of literature and thereby bring into view the fictional possibilities for world- or memory-creation. Such approaches are based on the assumption that works of fiction have specific, genuinely literary techniques at hand to plumb the connection between memory and identity. Not only can literature make the nexus of memory and identity the object of explicit reflections, but it can also represent this nexus implicitly—that is, through a variety of semanticized forms. As the concept of the "semanticization of literary forms" makes clear, narrative techniques of representation function as independent carriers of meaning (cf. Nünning, "Semantisierung"), which make a central, semantically multi-dimensional contribution to the constitution of meaning and thereby provide productive interpretative possibilities. True, literature draws upon the extra-textual reality. However, as a depragmaticized medium, it represents a constructive way to encounter the world, and creates its own memory worlds with specifically literary techniques.

For a long time, no genre designation existed for texts which represent processes of remembering. However, recently critics proposed the term "fictions of memory" (Nünning, *Fictions*; Neumann) to designate such works. The term "fictions of memory" deliberately alludes to the double meaning of fiction. First, the phrase refers to literary, non-referential narratives that depict the workings of memory. Second, in a broader sense, the term "fictions of memory" refers to the stories that individuals or cultures tell about their past to answer the question "who am I?", or, collectively, "who are we?" These stories can also be called "fictions of memory" because, more often than not, they turn out to be an imaginative (re)construction of the past in response to current needs. Such conceptual and ideological fictions of memory consist of predispositions, biases, and values, which provide agreed-upon codes for understanding the past and present and which find their most succinct expression in literary plot-lines and myths (cf. Nünning, "Editorial" 5).

1. The Mimesis of Memory

In fictions of memory, the process of remembering is evoked by what literary critics have called "mimesis of memory" (Neumann): This term refers to the ensemble of narrative forms and aesthetic techniques through which literary texts stage and reflect the workings of memory. Rather than indicating a mimetic quality of literature, the term points to its productive quality: Novels do not imitate existing versions of memory, but produce, in the act of discourse, that very past which they purport to describe. Genette points out that "no narrative can show or imitate the story it tells. [...] Language signifies without imitating" (164). All it can do, therefore, is tell a story in a manner which is detailed, precise, and alive, and in that way create the "illusion of mimesis." True, as suggested by Ricœur's concept of a three-level mimesis, literary representations of memory are always prefigured by culture-specific configurations of memory and current discourses about the operation of memory. However, on the textual level, novels create new models of memory. They configure memory representations because they select and edit elements of culturally given discourse: They combine the real and the imaginary, the remembered and the forgotten, and, by means of narrative devices, imaginatively explore the workings of memory, thus offering new perspectives on the past. Such imaginative explorations can influence readers' understanding of the past and thus refigure culturally prevailing versions of memory. Literature is therefore never a simple reflection of pre-existing cultural discourses; rather, it proactively contributes to the negotiation of cultural memory.

If one starts from the premise that literature is not a closed system, but a part of the principal meaning-making processes of a culture, interacting with other symbol systems, then an analysis of literary stagings of memory can provide information about a culture's predominant memorial concepts. Literature represents a "reintegrative interdiscourse" (Jürgen Link) which is interwoven with other systems such as psychology, historiography, law or religion, and which draws on contents and concepts of memory that already circulate in a culture. In their world-creation, literary works resort to culturally predominant ideas of memory, and, through their literary techniques, represent these ideas in an aesthetically condensed form. This cultural preformation of literature also implies that narrative techniques are not transhistorical constants, but rather historically variable strategies which offer interpretive patterns specific to particular epochs. Literature represents a form of expression of the cultural appropriation of reality which has at its disposal specific means of exploration that are marked as fictional. In light of this specific referentiality of literary works—that is, cultural preformation on the one hand and possibilities of imaginative formation on the other hand—a study of fictional representations of memory yields insight into culturally prevalent concepts of memory, into stereotypical ideas of self and other, and into both sanctioned and unsanctioned memories.

In this staging of individual and cultural memory, narrative texts can fall back on a broad spectrum of aesthetic techniques, ranging from characteristic features of narrative mediation, to the representation of the inner world, time and space, to intertextuality or the design of plot patterns. These narrative devices are semanticized to the extent that they implicitly convey culture-specific notions of the workings of individual and collective memory. What follows is a discussion of some of the most prominent techniques that can be employed by narratives to stage the processes of remembering. Furthermore, it will be shown that such techniques, for instance the representation of time and narrative mediation, allow specific conclusions concerning culturally prevailing notions of memory.

Characteristically, fictions of memory are presented by a reminiscing narrator or figure who looks back on his or her past, trying to impose meaning on the surfacing memories from a present point of view. Thus, the typical pattern for the literary representation of memories is retrospection or analepsis (Genette 40). Events that took place in the past are recollected only later, i.e., in the present, and are represented as the memories experienced by a narrator or a figure. The constitutive characteristic of all fictions of memory is therefore their operating with co-present time perspectives: The multi-temporal levels of the past and the present intermingle in manifold and complex ways. This kind of organisation does not merely establish a consecutive order, not merely a chain of elements along the arrow of time, but a reference frame in which each event is related to others in both a forward and backward direction: Each event is both marked by all preceding events and evokes expectations about events to come.

Fictions of memory vary greatly with regard to the ordering of the analepses. Typically, the analepses are ordered chronologically, thus successively bridging the gap between a specific past event, the figure's own memory-created starting point, and a moment in the present at which the process of remembering is initiated. Such a completing analepsis (Genette 51) is particularly conducive to portraying the psychological development of a fictional character, whose memories seem to fall into place within a meaningful life-narrative. It is found most often in classical fictional autobiographies, which seem to presuppose the possibility of a coherent construction of the past (cf. Basseler and Birke). Yet, especially in contemporary fictions of memory, this chronological order is dissolved at the expense of the subjective experience of time. In such instances the strict sequence of events is undercut by the constant oscillation between different time levels. Deviations in sequential ordering (anachronies) are often semanticized because they illustrate the haphazard workings of memory and thus contribute substantially to highlighting the memory-like quality of narratives.

With conspicuous frequency, the interplay between individual memory and identity is staged through the tension—constitutive for homodiegetic narration—between the experiencing or remembered and narrating or remembering I. This construction also implies a considerable temporal tension. The central challenge that the retrospective I faces is the meaning-creating reconciliation of the temporal and cognitive-emotional discrepancy—that is, the meaningful connection of this past to the current situation in which the memory is retrieved. In terms of the close interrelationship between memory and identity, the retrospective narration corresponds to the process of constructing a diachronic and narrative identity on the basis of one's episodic, i.e., autobiographical memories. The remembering I constitutes his or her own identity in the dialog with his or her past self, a process within which the differential aspects of identity are, ideally, integrated into a temporal continuum in the narrative modus, and are displayed as a relative unity. To the extent that the narrative is successful at establishing a significant relationship between past experiences and the present, the continuity-creating potential of memory narrations, in the sense of a meaningful synthesis of heterogeneous elements, is revealed. If, on the other hand, the remembering I is not able to adjust his memories to his current needs in a meaning-creating manner, then the stability of his identity is often called into question. The missing connection to the past indicates cognitive and emotional ambiguities and thereby tends to be a narrative formation which points to a biographical break. The failure to join together temporally differential dimensions goes along with a dissolution into disparate fragments of memory which indicate the instability of the meaning-making process.

Broadly speaking, the tension between the narrating I and the experiencing I can be designed in two basic ways that can be located on a continuum: At one end of the scale, the present context of remembering is scarcely fleshed out and the temporal interval between the remembering and remembered I is primarily indicated by the use of past tense. To the extent that the concurrent situation of recollection is pushed into the background by the representation of the past, the reconstructive character of meaning-making, including its dependency on co-present conditions, is dissimulated. At the other end of the scale, the context and motivation underlying the present act of autobiographical retelling are highly salient and distinct. In these instances of homodiegetic narration, the focus is shifted from the diegetic to the extradiegetic level of the retelling. Accordingly, the narrative focus often alternates between the simple chronological succession of the frame narrative and the multi-temporal levels of the embedded memory streams, thus self-reflexively depicting memories as intertwined with the contexts in which they are recalled. Generally, a self-reflexive disclosure of the meaning-making process highlights memories' connection to the present, thus laying bare a specific process of narrative mediation.

If one takes a look at contemporary literature, one sees a clear increase in the number of such self-reflexive novels, which is evidence of a growing consciousness of the fundamental problems and the limits of the identity-creating appropriation of the past. Many contemporary novels problematize the processes of remembering on a meta-level and foreground the ways in which memories are constructed. Such fictions of meta-memory, as one could aptly call them, combine personally engaged memories with critically reflective perspectives on the functioning of memory, thus rendering the question of how we remember the central content of remembering. The story and discourse continually transact with and against each other, continually produce, enlarge and question each other's meaning through their very antagonism. Due to this paradoxical structure, they confront closure with its inherent contradictions, and engage the reader in an ongoing dialogue with different avenues to interpreting the literary past. In accordance with recent approaches to memory, such novels intimate that meaningful memories do not exist prior to the process of remembering and narrating the past, but that they are constituted by the active creation of self-narrations. The revelation of the constructed nature of memory does not offer evidence of the past's insignificance; however, it makes memory subject to debate.

This difficulty in appropriating the past is also often accentuated by use of techniques of unreliable narration as well as through the dissolution of the unique plot into possible worlds. The concept of unreliable narration is based on the reader's recognition of textual or normative inconsistency. Particularly in contemporary fictions of memory, narrative instances often actively interpret, re-interpret, and continually re-create the individual past and the identity built on this past in the act of narration. Textual incongruities, ambiguities, (self-) contradictions or the representation of deviant norms are most likely to be attributed to the narrator's unreliability. Reinterpretations of the past and the related pluralization of the remembered world make clear the polyvalence, indeed the elusiveness, of past experiences and underscore that acts of memory offer every bit as much an insight into the factual conditions of the past as into current schemes of interpretation. It shows that any autobiographical narrative is bound to be fictionalized through processes of selection, appropriation, and evaluation, thus accentuating that remembering primarily means the identity-creating constructions of a "usable past."

In novels in which the appropriation not of the individual but rather the collective past is represented, a fundamental device that allows for the negotiation of collective memories, identities, and value hierarchies is perspective structure. Figures and anthropomorphized narrative instances are generally endowed with a particular perspective, which offers insight into their level of information and psychological dispositions as well as the norms which govern their actions. Texts with a multi-perspectival narration or focalization provide insight into the memories of several narrative instances or figures and in this way they can reveal the functioning and problems of collective memory-creation. An analysis of the perspective structure provides information about the social structure of the fictional world and about the importance or value of specific versions of the past: Which versions of memory are articulated, which remain underrepresented? Who or what is remembered by whom? Are there convergences between the individual memory perspectives or are they incompatible opposites in the battle for interpretative sovereignty?

A fundamental privilege of fictional texts is to integrate culturally separated memory versions by means of mutual perspectivization, bringing together things remembered and things tabooed and testing the memory-cultural relevance of commonly marginalized versions of memory. By giving voice to those previously silenced fictions of memory, they constitute an imaginative counter-memory, thereby challenging the hegemonic memory culture and questioning the socially established boundary between remembering and forgetting (cf. Singh, Sherrett, and Hogan). Through a multi-perspectival expansion of the remembered world, fictions of memory can design a panorama of co-existing collective memories: Shared interpretations of the past, but also incompatible memories of the shared collective past, become visible. In this process, the degree of convergence of the individual perspectives generally correlates with the stability of the shared creation of meaning. The gradual, intersubjective validation of the individual perspectives offers an integrative image of the collective past and underscores the commonality of experience in terms of a collective identity. In contrast, divergent, perspectively refracted memories mark the undeniable plurality of memory creation and the characteristic stratification of memory cultures. Where the common past dissolves into a multitude of heterogeneous memory versions, the rifts and competitions within the fictional memory world are revealed, and characteristic features of today's memory cultures become observable. Contradictory, mutually relativizing perspectives face each other in an antagonistic relationship in the struggle for memorial sovereignty, and challenge the idea that there is a prevailing, unifying, and binding memory.

The social pluralization of competing versions of the past can be further augmented through forms of structural multi-perspectivity, that is, through intertextual and intermedial references to the material dimension of memory culture. Intermedial references can illustrate the synchronous plurality of culturally circulating media of memory and versions of the past. They evoke traces of the past and turn the text into an "echochamber" (Barthes 78) of the past, in which the complex cultural heritage continues to resonate up to the present. Allusions to legends, fairy tales, myths, and other stories of dubious historical authenticity suggest that fact and fiction intermingle in cultural memory and that these fictions should thus be treated as cultural documents in their own right as they shed light on what is actually remembered as a culture's past. Furthermore, techniques of intermedialization reveal the reality-constituting character of media and show that for the individual only those memories are possible for which the culture provides external supports. Thus it becomes apparent that the appropriation of the past is also limited by conditions of medial dissemination and that the question as to whose memory versions will prevail in the fight for historical definitional power depends on the memory-cultural effectiveness of the specific medium of memory (see Rigney, this volume). A pluralization of the perspectives by means of intertextual and intermedial references thus points to both the social dimension of memory and also the functioning of the material dimension, and accentuates the importance of media for collective memory-creation.

The time structure, the narrative mediation, and the perspective structure of narrative texts are the central literary forms which permit the staging and reflection of memory-creation. The privileges of novels within the memory culture include experimentation with new concepts of memory, giving voice to hitherto marginalized memories and ultimately making visible the processes of individual and collective memory-creation. Clearly, this overview of the narrative techniques that are relevant to the staging of memory is not exhaustive. Semanticization of space or the use of metaphors of memory are, for instance, two further constituents of the mimesis of memory which are exploited by many novels to represent processes of remembering. Fictions of memory may exploit the representation of space as a symbolic manifestation of individual or collective memories. Space may not only provide a cue triggering individual, often repressed, past experiences; it may also conjure up innumerable echoes and undertones of a community's past. Hence, space serves to symbolically mediate past events, underlining the constant, physical presence of the multilayered cultural past, which is even inscribed in the landscape and in the architecture. The affinity between space and memory is also reflected in the important role of spatial metaphors in the rhetoric of remembering (cf. Assmann 158-65). Buildings or parts of buildings, such as the attic, often visually represent memories, thus echoing the close connection between space and memory that goes back to antiquity. Whereas spatial order often indicates the easy accessibility of the past, spatial disorder suggests that the access to the past is difficult, intricate or even impossible.

Moreover, a more extensive discussion should also take into account that processes of remembering are not only represented in novels, but also in numerous dramas (so called memory-plays) as well as in poetry (cf. Gymnich). Dramas may resort to dialogues in order to portray specific versions of the past or re-enact past events through the use of flashbacks (which are typically highlighted by theatrical effects such as the fading out of the stage lights). The action of the past can be understood as a sequence of episodic memories and thus as a dramatic analogue to the narrative representation of consciousness. Finally, in poems, speakers may figure as representatives of a particular memory culture and articulate both individual and collective memories. Memory poetry is characterized by a pronounced heteroreferentiality and thus spurs a fictitious collective audience to recall fateful events of the shared past. Due to their specific metrics and often rhymes, poems are particularly apt to affect and shape cultural memory. Given these differences between novel, drama, and poetry, future investigations in this domain should take into account the genre-specific mimesis of memory, i.e., the genre-specific devices that are employed in literary texts to represent memories.

2. The Functions of Literature in the Formation of Memory

Because literature is interwoven with other systems of memory culture, it not only draws on pre-existing discourse systems but is also in a position to productively influence these systems. The approaches of *Funktionsgeschichte* (the history of the changing functions of fiction) (cf. Fluck) emphasize that literature, as a part of the prevailing processes of creating memory, is endowed with a (memory-)cultural effectiveness and can contribute to a new perspectivization of extra-textual orders of knowledge and hierarchies of values. The concepts of memory staged within the medium of fiction may influence the extra-literary memory culture—given that they are also actualized by the recipients. Thus, these concepts can influence the creation and reflection of individual as well as collective images of the past. As a medium of cultural self-reflection, literature—through its aesthetic structure—paves the way for cultural change.

Narrative psychologists have pointed out that novels, with their conventionalized plot-lines and highly suggestive myths, provide powerful, often normative models for our own self-narration and interpretation of the past (see Straub, this volume). Apparently, when interpreting our own experience, we constantly, and often unconsciously, draw on pre-existing narrative patterns as supplied by literature. Thus, by disseminating new interpretations of the past and new models of identity, fictions of memory may also influence how we, as readers, narrate our pasts and ourselves into existence. Fictions of memory may symbolically empower the culturally marginalized or forgotten and thus figure as an imaginative counter-discourse. By bringing together multiple, even incompatible versions of the past, they can keep alive conflict about what exactly the collective past stands for and how it should be remembered. Moreover, to the extent that many fictions of memory link the hegemonic discourse to the unrealized and inexpressible possibilities of the past, they can become a force of continual innovation and cultural self-renewal. Thus, far from merely perpetuating culturally pre-existing memories, fictions of memory have a considerable share in reinforcing new concepts of memory. Literature becomes a formative medium within the memory culture which, on the basis of symbol-specific characteristics, can fulfill particular functions, functions which cannot be served by other symbol systems. Viewed in this way, we may conclude that the study of fictional narratives is not only wedded to particular lifeworlds, but turns into a laboratory in which we can experiment with the possibilities for culturally admissible constructions of the past.

References

Assmann, Aleida. *Erinnerungsräume: Formen und Wandlungen des kulturellen Gedächtnisses*. Munich: Beck, 1999.

Barthes, Roland. *Roland Barthes par Roland Barthes*. Paris: Seuil, 1975.

Basseler, Michael, and Dorothee Birke. "Mimesis des Erinnerns." *Gedächtniskonzepte der Literaturwissenschaft: Theoretische Grundlegung und Anwendungsperspektiven*. Eds. Astrid Erll and Ansgar Nünning. Berlin: de Gruyter, 2005. 123-48.

Erll, Astrid. *Gedächtnisromane: Literatur über den Ersten Weltkrieg als Medium englischer und deutscher Erinnerungskulturen in den 1920er Jahren*. Trier: WVT, 2003.

Erll, Astrid, and Ansgar Nünning, eds. *Gedächtniskonzepte der Literaturwissenschaft: Theoretische Grundlegung und Anwendungsperspektiven*. Berlin: de Gruyter, 2005.

Fluck, Winfried. *Das kulturelle Imaginäre: Eine Funktionsgeschichte des amerikanischen Romans 1790-1900*. Frankfurt am Main: Suhrkamp, 1997.

Genette, Gérard. *Narrative Discourse*. 1972. Oxford: Basil Backwell, 1980.

Gymnich, Marion. "Individuelle Identität und Erinnerung aus Sicht von Identitätstheorie und Gedächtnisforschung sowie als Gegenstand literarischer Inszenierung." *Literatur, Erinnerung und Identität: Theoriekonzeptionen und Fallstudien*. Eds. Astrid Erll, Marion Gymnich and Ansgar Nünning. Trier: WVT, 2003. 29-48.

Henke, Christoph. "Remembering Selves, Constructing Selves: Memory and Identity in Contemporary British Fiction." *Fictions of Memory*. Ed. Ansgar Nünning. Spec. issue of *Journal for the Study of British Cultures* 10.1 (2003): 77-100.

Löschnigg, Martin. "'The Prismatic Hues of Memory': Autobiographische Modellierung und die Rhetorik der Erinnerung in Dickens' *David Copperfield*." *Poetica* 31 (1999): 175-200.

Neumann, Birgit. *Erinnerung—Identität—Narration: Gattungstypologie und Funktionen kanadischer Fictions of Memory*. Berlin: de Gruyter. 2005.

Nünning, Ansgar. "Editorial: New Directions in the Study of Individual and Cultural Memory and Memorial Cultures." *Fictions of Memory*. Ed. Ansgar Nünning. Spec. issue of *Journal for the Study of British Cultures* 10.1 (2003): 3-9.

—, ed. *Fictions of Memory*. Spec. issue of *Journal for the Study of British Cultures* 10.1 (2003).

—. "Semantisierung literarischer Formen." *Metzler Lexikon Literatur- und Kulturtheorie: Ansätze—Personen—Grundbegriffe.* 1998. Ed. Ansgar Nünning. Stuttgart: Metzler, 2001. 579-80.

Ricœur, Paul. *Time and Narrative.* 3 vols. Chicago: U of Chicago P, 1984-88.

Singh, Amritjit, Joseph Skerrett, and Robert Hogan, eds. *Memory, Narrative, and Identity: New Essays in Ethnic American Literatures.* Boston: Northeastern UP, 1994.

The Dynamics of Remembrance: Texts Between Monumentality and Morphing

ANN RIGNEY

1. Memory Studies: From "Sites" to "Dynamics"

When collective memory first rose to prominence on the academic agenda in the late 1980s, the emphasis was on the "sites" which act as common points of reference within memory communities. Such "sites" (as discussed in earlier sections of this collection) do not always take the form of actual locations, but they have in common the fact that, by encapsulating multifarious experience in a limited repertoire of figures, they provide a placeholder for the exchange and transfer of memories among contemporaries and across generations.

As we know from recent work, memory sites neither come "naturally" into being nor all at once. Instead, they are the product of a selection process that has privileged some "figures of memory" above others (J. Assmann) and, linked to this, of multiple acts of remembrance in a variety of genres and media. For it is only through the mediation of cultural practices that figures of memory can acquire shape, meaning, and a high public profile within particular communities. The repertoire of such cultural practices changes over time together with technological and aesthetic innovations: The historical novel was at the forefront of new mnemonic practices in the first decades of the nineteenth century, for example, but this role is arguably now being played by graphic novels like Art Spiegelman's *Maus* (1973, 1986) or Joe Sacco's *Safe Area Goražde* (2000) and by virtual memorials using the new digital media.

Although it has proven useful as a conceptual tool, the metaphor of "memory site" can become misleading if it is interpreted to mean that collective remembrance becomes permanently tied down to particular figures, icons, or monuments. As the performative aspect of the term "remembrance" suggests, collective memory is constantly "in the works" and, like a swimmer, has to keep moving even just to stay afloat. To bring remembrance to a conclusion is de facto already to forget. While putting down a monument may seem like a way of ensuring long-term memory, it may in fact turn out to mark the beginning of amnesia unless the monument in question is continuously invested with new meaning (Koselleck).

In light of these considerations, it seems inevitable that attention should have turned in recent years from memory sites as such to the cultural dynamics in which they function (Olick and Robbins 122-30; Rigney,

"Plenitude"). The distinction made by Jan Assmann between "communicative" and "cultural" memory already indicated that cultural remembrance is subject to a certain internal dynamic or lifespan: It evolves from the relatively unorganized exchange of stories among contemporaries and eyewitnesses to the increasingly selective focus on "canonical" sites which work as points of reference across generations. Other scholars have considered how the development of cultural remembrance is affected by the changing social frameworks that influence what is considered relevant enough to remember at any given time (Irwin-Zarecka). Research has shown that the canon of memory sites with which a community identifies is regularly subject to revision by groups who seek to replace, supplement, or revise dominant representations of the past as a way of asserting their own identity (Olick and Robbins 122-28).

In this ongoing process, existing memory sites become invested with new meanings and gain a new lease of life. But they may also be upstaged by alternative sites and become effectively obsolete or inert. Indeed, the "dynamic" perspective on cultural remembrance suggests that "memory sites," while they come into being as points where many acts of remembrance converge, only stay alive as long as people consider it worthwhile to argue about their meaning. One of the paradoxes of collective remembrance may be that consensus ("we all recollect the same way") is ultimately the road to amnesia and that that it is ironically a lack of unanimity that keeps some memory sites alive.

The current interest in the dynamics of cultural remembrance provides a new perspective on the role of art, including literature, in the formation of collective memory. Moreover, as we shall see, this shift from "sites" to "dynamics" within memory studies runs parallel to a larger shift of attention within cultural studies from products to processes, from a focus on cultural artifacts to an interest in the way those artifacts circulate and influence their environment.

2. Literary Studies: From "Products" to "Processes"

Given the historical importance of writing as a medium of cultural memory, it is not surprising that there should be widespread interest in cultural memory studies among literary scholars (for a summary, see Erll). The focus has mainly been on individual texts, and the ways in which the textual medium is used to shape remembrance by paying attention to certain things rather than others, to structure information in certain ways, and to encourage readers to reflect on their own position in relation to the events presented.

One especially fruitful line of inquiry has picked up on earlier discussions within the philosophy of history and addressed the role played by narrative structures in the recollection of real events. As Hayden White had shown from the 1970s on, events do not "naturally" take the form of a story, meaning that whoever narrates events is in fact involved in actively shaping experience into an intelligible pattern with a beginning, middle, and end, and with an economy of antipathy and sympathy centered on particular human figures. These insights into the "value of narrativity in the representation of reality" (White) have led to an interesting body of research into the use of narration as an interpretative tool that is wielded both by historians and those working in other fields of remembrance. Within more recent discussions, moreover, narrativization has emerged, not just as an interpretative tool, but also as a specifically *mnemonic* one. Stories "stick." They help make particular events *memorable* by figuring the past in a structured way that engages the sympathies of the reader or viewer (Rigney, "Portable"). Arguably, all other forms of remembrance (monuments, commemorations, museums) derive their meaning from some narrativizing act of remembrance in which individual figures struggle, succumb, or survive.

One of the issues that inevitably crops up in discussions of the role of narrative in cultural memory is the relation between historiography and fiction. While the difference between factual accounts and, say, novels has come to seem less absolute than it once seemed (since even factual accounts are based on a narrative structuring of information), the freedom to invent information, and not merely structure it, nevertheless gives to fiction a flexibility which is absent in other forms of remembrance. Studies have shown that fiction (as in the historical novel) is a great help when it comes to narrativizing events since narrators who are free to design their own stories can more easily evoke vivid characters and give closure to events (Rigney, *Imperfect Histories* 13-58). Those who "stick to the facts" may paradoxically end up with a more historical and authentic story, but also a less memorable one, than the producers of fiction. The latter not only enjoy poetic license when narrativizing their materials, but also often have creative, specifically literary skills that help give an added aesthetic value to their work. This aesthetic dimension means that they can attract and hold the attention of groups without a prior interest in the topic, but with a readiness to enjoy a good story and suspend their disbelief (Landsberg 25-48).

More research needs to be done on the relation between memorability, aesthetic power, and cultural longevity. But there is already evidence to show that "inauthentic" versions of the past may end up with more cultural staying power than the work of less skilled narrators or of more disciplined ones who stay faithful to what their personal memories or the archive allow them to say. Whatever their shortcomings as history, fictional works like Tolstoy's *War and Peace* (1865-69) or Spielberg's *Schindler's List* (1993) have enjoyed a high public profile and undeniably provided cultural frames for collective recollections of the Napoleonic era and World War Two respectively. To the extent that they are fictions, the status of such narratives is chronically ambivalent, meaning that they are continuously open to challenge by non-fictional recollections of the past. In practice, however, fictions often prove difficult to displace because it is not easy to come up with a non-fictionalized account that has the same narrativizing and aesthetic power (Rigney, *Imperfect Histories*). In the case of traumatic events, moreover, the freedoms offered by fictional genres and literary modes of expression may simply provide the *only* forum available for recalling certain experiences that are difficult to bring into the realm of public remembrance or that are simply too difficult to articulate in any other way (see Kansteiner and Weilnböck, this volume). Indeed, what may distinguish literary narratives from fictional narratives as such is their expressiveness: their power to say and evoke more because of the writer's imagination and unique mastery of the medium.

The idea that literature, along with the other arts, has a privileged role to play in giving voice to what has been overlooked in other forms of remembrance is a recurring theme (see Rigney, "Portable"). Indeed, literature and the other arts often appear specifically as a privileged medium of *oppositional* memory, as a "counter-memorial" and critical force that undermines hegemonic views of the past (Hartman). This line of reasoning, reflecting the moral authority of writers even at the present day, is deeply rooted in the dominant tradition of twentieth-century criticism in which artistic value is correlated with the defamiliarization of received ideas and in which the close reading of individual, highly-regarded texts is pitched towards showing how they subvert dominant views and envision alternatives (e.g., Bal and Crewe).

As indicated above, however, the "dynamic" turn in memory studies is itself part of a larger shift within culture studies away from such a focus on individual products to a focus on the processes in which those products are caught up and in which they play a role. Behind this shift in emphasis within literary studies lies among other things the idea, associated with New Historicism, that individual products are part of the social circulation of meanings and the idea, associated generally with post-structuralism, that meaning as such is never fixed once and for all, but is something that *happens* in the way events, texts, and other cultural products are appropriated (over and over again, always with a difference). This dynamic turn has led recently to an increase of interest in the way texts give rise to commentaries, counter-narratives, translations into other languages, adaptations to other media, adaptations to other discursive genres, and even to particular actions on the part of individuals and groups. Adaptation, translation, reception, appropriation have thus become key words, with the cultural power of an artistic work being located in the cultural activities it gives rise to, rather than in what it is in itself. The *Mona Lisa*, for example, is culturally significant, not "in itself," but as a result of its reception, including all the appreciative commentaries, parodies, imitations, and so on that it has spawned. Artistic works are not just artifacts, but also agents (Gell).

When the various approaches to literary works (as product, as agent) are taken together, then a double picture emerges of their role in cultural remembrance. Firstly, literary works resemble monuments in that they provide fixed points of reference. They are "textual monuments" which can be reprinted time and again in new editions even as the environment around them changes (Rigney, "Portable"). And interestingly, monumentality in this sense applies not just to those works that are themselves acts of recollection (like *War and Peace*), but also to all other works that have gained a monumental status as part of the literary canon (see Grabes, this volume). At the same time as they may enjoy this monumentality, however, literary works continuously morph into the many other cultural products that recall, adapt, and revise them in both overt and indirect ways.

This combination of monumentality and morphing, of persistence and malleability, can be illustrated by the case of Walter Scott's *Ivanhoe* (1819). This novel has been reprinted countless times and thus exists as a "textual monument" to which we can refer (even here it proves useful as a common point of reference). At the same time, the original narrative has been re-written and reshaped in various other media (theater, comic books, film, digital games, re-enactments) and by many other writers, including both historians inspired by Scott's example and those intent on replacing his account of the Middle Ages by a more accurate one. Thus the medievalist Jacques Le Goff recently claimed in an interview in *Lire.fr* (May 2005) that his whole oeuvre as a historian "began" with his reading of Scott's novel: "c'est à partir de là que tout a commence."

The line from *Ivanhoe* (1819) to Le Goff's *Héros et merveilles au Moyen Âge* (2005) is long and winding, but its existence bears witness both to the persistence and the mutability of stories.

3. Texts: Both "Monuments" and "Agents"

It is clear from the above that the role of literary works in cultural remembrance is a complex one. To understand it fully one needs to go beyond the analysis of individual works to the study of their reception and their interactions with other acts of remembrance in a variety of media and genres. When literature is located within this broader dynamics, traditional themes can be revisited in the light of the various roles played by literary works in the performance of cultural memory. As least five interrelated roles can be discerned, some of which apply to all fictional narratives, irrespective of medium, while others are more specifically linked to literary works with recognized cultural value:

1. *Relay stations*: Fictional narratives often build on or recycle earlier forms of remembrance (Rigney, "Plenitude") and, in this sense, they can be described as relay stations in the circulation of memories. It is because figures are relayed across media (image, texts), across discursive genres (literary, historiographical, judicial) and across practices (commemorations, judicial procedures, private reading) that they can end up becoming collective points of reference for individuals inhabiting different locations. Thus Victor Hugo's vivid evocation of the cathedral in *Notre-Dame de Paris* (1831) not only "reiterates" in textual form the actual Gothic building, but also picks up on contemporary discussions regarding its preservation (Friedrich). In this way, fictional narratives can be seen as one of the many channels through which figures of memory are circulated and given a high profile. Indeed, they are arguably the most important of relay stations given their wide circulation and their broad appeal.
2. *Stabilizers*: Fictional narratives, as was mentioned earlier, can succeed in figuring particular periods in a memorable way and so provide a cultural frame for later recollections. Their sticking power as narratives and as aesthetic artifacts thus works as a stabilizing factor (A. Assmann) in cultural remembrance. Thus Walter Scott's novel *Old Mortality* (1816) became a privileged point of reference, if only as a punch bag, in discussions of the seventeenth-century Scottish civil war (Rigney, *Imperfect Histories* 13-58); Erich Maria Remarque's *Im Westen nichts Neues* (1929) has played a comparable role with respect to the First World War. Illustrating the fact that the memory *of* culture represents a specific field within collective remembrance (alongside events like war) the literary canon itself has also traditionally functioned as a stabilizer of remembrance: The celebration of literary "monuments" from the past (whether or not these themselves have a mnemonic dimension) helps reinforce communality in the present.

3. *Catalysts*: Thanks to the imaginative powers of their creators, fictions seem to have a particular role to play in drawing attention to "new" topics or ones hitherto neglected in cultural remembrance. In such cases, they are not merely relay stations, but may be actually instrumental in establishing a topic *as* a socially relevant topic and in setting off multiple acts of recollection relating to it. Thus the publication of Louis de Bernière's *Captain Corelli's Mandolin* (1994) provided an occasion for commemorating the Italian experience in Greece during World War Two, while Günter Grass's novel *Im Krebsgang* (2002) contributed to the intensification of discussions on the plight of German refugees at the end of World War Two.
4. *Objects of recollection*: Literary texts do not just work as media of remembrance, but themselves become objects of recollection in other media and forms of expression (Erll 159). The basic point is illustrated by the extensive celebrations that took place in Dublin in 2004 to commemorate the centenary of the (fictional) story set in 1904 that James Joyce narrated in *Ulysses* (1922). But literature is not only an object of recollection in this formalized way. "Remakes" of earlier texts, revisions of earlier texts, and the remediation of early texts in new media also represent important means of keeping earlier narratives "up to date," that is, memorable according to the norms of the new group. Research into the way in which stories are morphed in new media and appropriated in new contexts is still at an early stage (Sanders), but has already opened new perspectives for cultural memory studies. It gives us insight into the cultural life of stories and the way in which the latter may mutate into something new or become eroded by "over-exposure." While recursivity ensures that certain stories become known, it also means that they can end up exhausted from having been repeated in increasingly reduced form, from theater and film to souvenirs and other tie-ins. By the time Walter Scott's *Waverley* (1814) is only known as the name of a cinema in Manhattan, for example, we are no longer dealing with a story that is still actively shaping the course of collective remembrance.
5. *Calibrators*: Canonical literary "monuments" also have a specific role to play as a benchmark for reflecting critically on dominant memorial practices. Indeed, *revisioning* canonical texts (as distinct from merely remediating them; see 4) represents an important memorial practice, especially within the framework of a postmodern literary culture where originality is sought in the re-writing of earlier texts rather than in novelty as such (see Lachmann, this volume). Familiar figures from earlier texts function as coat stands on which to hang new, often radically opposing versions of the past or as a wedge to break open up a

hitherto neglected theme. Thus J. M. Coetzee re-wrote Defoe's *Robinson Crusoe* (1719-20) in his novel *Foe* (1986), which is a post-colonial palimpsest of the earlier story; while Chinua Achebe's *Things Fall Apart* (1958) and V. S. Naipaul's *A Bend in the River* (1979) can both be seen as critical rewritings of Conrad's *Heart of Darkness* (1899) (see Plate for many other examples). The result is a critical form of cultural remembrance that is arguably distinct to artistic practices whereby writers exploit the monumentality and malleability of earlier works in order to reflect critically on those earlier accounts and the memory they have shaped.

4. In Conclusion

Locating literary practice within the larger framework of cultural memory studies has shown up some of the complex processes involved in the circulation of stories and the evolution of collective remembrance: both the convergence of remembrance on particular sites and the gradual erosion of those sites. In many respects, literary texts and other works of art can be considered as simply one form of remembrance alongside others. At the same time, however, they are capable of exercising a particular aesthetic and narrative "staying power" that ensures that they are not always simply superseded by later acts of remembrance. Whether as objects to be remembered or as stories to be revised, literary texts exemplify the fact that memorial dynamics do not just work in a linear or accumulative way. Instead, they progress through all sorts of loopings back to cultural products that are not simply media of memory (relay stations and catalysts) but also objects of recall and revision.

References

Assmann, Aleida. *Erinnerungsräume: Formen und Wandlungen des kulturellen Gedächtnisses.* Munich: Beck, 1999.

Assmann, Jan. *Das kulturelle Gedächtnis: Schrift, Erinnerung und politische Identität in frühen Hochkulturen.* 1992. Munich: Beck, 1997.

Bal, Mieke, and Jonathan Crewe, eds. *Acts of Memory: Cultural Recall in the Present.* Hanover, NH: UP of New England, 1999.

Erll, Astrid. *Kollektives Gedächtnis und Erinnerungskulturen.* Stuttgart: Metzler, 2005.

Friedrich, Sabine. "Erinnerung als Auslöschung: Zum Verhältnis zwischen kulturellen Gedächtnisräumen und ihrer medialen Vermittlung in

Victor Hugos *Notre-Dame de Paris* und *Les Misérables*." *Arcadia: Zeitschrift für vergleichende Literaturwissenschaft* 40.1 (2005): 61-78.

Gell, Alfred. *Art and Agency: An Anthropological Theory*. Oxford: Oxford UP, 1998.

Hartman, Geoffrey H. "Public Memory and Its Discontents." *The Uses of Literary History*. Ed. Marshall Brown. Durham: Duke UP, 1995. 73-91.

Irwin-Zarecka, Iwona. *Frames of Remembrance: The Dynamics of Collective Memory*. New Brunswick, NJ: Transaction, 1994.

Koselleck, Reinhart. "Kriegerdenkmale als Identitätsstiftungen der Überlebenden." *Identität*. Eds. Odo Marquard and Karlheinz Stierle. Poetik und Hermeneutik 8. Munich: Fink, 1979. 255-76.

Landsberg, Alison. *Prosthetic Memory: The Transformation of American Remembrance in the Age of Mass Culture*. New York: Columbia UP, 2004.

Olick, Jeffrey K., and Joyce Robbins. "Social Memory Studies: From 'Collective Memory' to the Historical Sociology of Mnemonic Practices." *Annual Review of Sociology* 24 (1998): 105-40.

Plate, Liedeke. "Women Readers Write Back: Rewriting and/as Reception." *SPIEL* 19.1 (2000): 155-67.

Rigney, Ann. *Imperfect Histories: The Elusive Past and the Legacy of Romantic Historicism*. Ithaca: Cornell UP, 2001.

—. "Plenitude, Scarcity and the Circulation of Cultural Memory." *Journal of European Studies* 35.1 (2005): 209-26.

—. "Portable Monuments: Literature, Cultural Memory, and the Case of Jeanie Deans." *Poetics Today* 25.2 (2004): 361-96.

Sanders, Julie. *Adaptation and Appropriation*. London: Routledge, 2006.

White, Hayden. *The Content of the Form: Narrative Discourse and Historical Representation*. 1981. Baltimore: Johns Hopkins UP, 1987.

VI. Media and Cultural Memory

The Texture of Memory: Holocaust Memorials in History

JAMES E. YOUNG

As the events of the Holocaust have been chronicled and shaped in the survivors' diaries and memoirs, in their children's films, novels, and artworks, public memory of this time is being molded in a proliferating number of memorial images and spaces. Depending on where these memorials are constructed and by whom, these sites remember the past according to a variety of national myths, ideals, and political needs. Some recall war dead, others resistance, and still others mass murder. All reflect both the past experiences and current lives of their communities, as well as the State's memory of itself. At a more specific level, these memorials also reflect the temper of the memory-artists' time, their place in aesthetic discourse, their media and materials.

Memory of the Holocaust is never shaped in a vacuum, and the motives for such memory are never pure. Both the reasons given for Holocaust memorials and museums and the kinds of memory they generate are as various as the sites themselves. Some are built in response to traditional Jewish injunctions to remember, others according to a government's need to explain a nation's past to itself. Where the aim of some memorials is to educate the next generation and to inculcate in it a sense of shared experience and destiny, other memorials are conceived as expiations of guilt or as self-aggrandizement. Still others are intended to attract tourists. In addition to traditional Jewish memorial iconography, every state has its own institutional forms of remembrance. As a result, Holocaust memorials inevitably mix national and Jewish figures, political and religious imagery.

The relationship between a state and its Holocaust memorials is not one-sided, however. On the one hand, official agencies are in a position to shape memory explicitly as they see fit, memory that best serves a national interest. On the other hand, once created, memorials take on lives of their own, often stubbornly resistant to the state's original intentions. In some cases, memorials created in the image of a state's ideals actually turn around to recast these ideals in the memorial's own image. New generations visit memorials under new circumstances and invest them with new meanings. The result is an evolution in these memorials' significance, generated in the new times and company in which they find themselves.

In Poland, for example, countless memorials in former death camps at Auschwitz, Majdanek, Belzec, and Treblinka (among others), and across the countryside commemorate the whole of Polish destruction through the figure of its murdered Jewish part. The mass murder of Jews in Poland is recalled as an intrinsic part of Poland's own national landscape of martyrdom, often through images of irreparable breaches and shattered vessels. In Israel, where half the state's population on its founding in 1948 were survivors of the Holocaust, martyrs and heroes are remembered side by side. The national Holocaust remembrance day in Israel—Yom Hasho'ah Vehagvurah—thus commemorates both the mass murder of Europe's Jews and the heroism of ghetto fighters—all seemingly redeemed by the birth of the State. With the ingathering of hundreds of thousands of new immigrants from the former Soviet Union, Israel's memory of the Holocaust has also grown more plural and inclusive, as reflected in the new and magnificent redesign of Yad Vashem, Israel's national Holocaust memorial museum.

As the shape Holocaust memory takes in Europe and Israel is determined by political, aesthetic and religious coordinates, that in America is guided no less by distinctly American ideals and experiences—such as liberty, pluralism, and immigration. Whether found on Boston's Freedom Trail, or at Liberty State Park in New Jersey, or just off the National Mall in Washington, D.C., or nestled in Miami's community of Latin American immigrants, American Holocaust memorials enshrine not just the history of the Holocaust but also American democratic and egalitarian ideals as they counterpoint the Holocaust. In such memorials, American memory itself is enlarged to include the histories of its immigrants, the memory of events on distant shores that drove these immigrants to America in the first place.

It is in Germany, however, where the issues surrounding Holocaust memorialization come into the sharpest, most painful relief. In the land of what Saul Friedlander has called "redemptory anti-Semitism" (3), the possibility that art might redeem mass murder with beauty (or with ugliness), or that memorials might somehow redeem this past with the instrumentalization of its memory, continues to haunt a post-war generation of memory-artists. Moreover, these artists in Germany are both plagued and inspired by a series of impossible memorial questions: How does a state incorporate shame into its national memorial landscape? How does a state recite, much less commemorate, the litany of its misdeeds, making them part of its reason for being? Under what memorial aegis, whose rules, does a nation remember its own barbarity (see Langenohl; Meyer; both this volume)? Where is the tradition for memorial mea culpa? Where are the national memorials to the genocide of Native Americans, to the millions of Africans enslaved and murdered in the Americas? Unlike state-sponsored memorials built by victimized nations and peoples to themselves in Poland, Holland, or Israel, those in Germany are necessarily those of the persecutor remembering its victims. In the face of this necessary breach in the conventional "memorial code," it is little wonder that German national memory of the Holocaust remains so torn and convoluted. Germany's "Jewish question" is now a two-pronged memorial question: How does a nation mourn the victims of a mass murder perpetrated in its name? How does a nation re-unite itself on the bedrock memory of its horrendous crimes? These questions constitute the conflicted heart of Germany's struggle with its national memory of the Holocaust.

One of the most compelling results of Germany's memorial conundrum has been the advent of its "counter-monuments": brazen, painfully self-conscious memorial spaces conceived to challenge the very premises of their being. Contemporary German memory-artists are heirs to a double-edged postwar legacy: a deep distrust of monumental forms in light of their systematic exploitation by the Nazis and a profound desire to distinguish their generation from that of the killers through memory (see Reulecke, this volume). In their eyes, the didactic logic of monuments—their demagogical rigidity and certainty of history—continues to recall too closely traits associated with fascism itself. A monument against fascism, therefore, would have to be a monument against itself: against the traditionally didactic function of monuments, against their tendency to displace the past they would have us contemplate—and finally, against the authoritarian propensity in monumental spaces that reduces viewers to passive spectators.

Rather than attempting to resolve such memorial questions in their designs, contemporary artists and architects—such as Jochen Gerz and Esther Shalev, Horst Hoheisel and Hans Haacke, Renata Stih and Frieder Schnock, Sol LeWitt and Richard Serra, Daniel Libeskind, and Peter Eisenman—have striven for formal articulation of the questions themselves. For example, in Jochen Gerz and Esther Shalev's 1986 "Monument against Fascism" in Harburg-Hamburg, a 12-meter-high, lead-covered column was sunk into the ground as people inscribed their names (and much else) onto its surface; on its complete disappearance in 1994, the artists hoped that it would return the burden of memory to those who came looking for it. With audacious simplicity, their "counter-monument" thus flouted a number of memorial conventions: Its aim was not to console but to provoke; not to remain fixed but to change; not to be everlasting but to disappear; not to be ignored by its passersby but to demand interaction; not to remain pristine but to invite its own violation; not to accept graciously the burden of memory but to throw it back at the town's feet. How better to remember a now-absent people than by a vanishing monument?

In a similar vein, Horst Hoheisel has commemorated the void left behind by Europe's missing Jews in his "negative-form memorial" (Aschrott-Brunnen, 1986) in Kassel, as well in his proposal to blow up the Brandenburger Tor for the 1995 competition for Germany's national Memorial for Europe's Murdered Jews. Here, Hoheisel would mark one destruction with another. In other installations by Micha Ullman and Rachel Whiteread, the artists have also turned to both bookish themes and negative spaces in order to represent the void left behind by the "people of the book." Still other artists in Germany have attempted to re-animate otherwise amnesiac sites with the dark light of their pasts, reminding us that the history of such sites also includes their own forgetfulness, their own lapses of memory. Berlin artists Renata Stih and Frieder Schnock thus mounted 80 signposts on the corners, streets and sidewalks near Berlin's *Bayerische Platz*. Each includes a simple image of an everyday object on one side and a short text on the other, excerpted from Germany's anti-Jewish laws of the 1930s and 1940s. Where past citizens once navigated their lives according to these laws, present citizens would now navigate their lives according to the memory of such laws.

For these and other artists and architects, the possibility that memory of events so grave might be reduced to exhibitions of public craftsmanship or cheap pathos remains intolerable. They contemptuously reject the traditional forms and reasons for public memorial art, those spaces that either console viewers or redeem such tragic events, or indulge in a facile kind of *Wiedergutmachung* or purport to mend the memory of a murdered people. Instead of searing memory into public consciousness, they fear, conventional memorials seal memory off from awareness altogether; instead of embodying memory, they find that memorials may only displace memory. These artists fear rightly that to the extent that we encourage monuments to do our memory-work for us, we become that much more forgetful. They believe, in effect, that the initial impulse to memorialize events like the Holocaust may actually spring from an opposite and equal desire to forget them.

Indeed, in the eyes of many contemporary artists and critics, the traditional monument's essential stiffness and grandiose pretensions to permanence thus doom it to an archaic, premodern status. Even worse, by insisting that its meaning is as fixed as its place in the landscape, the monument seems oblivious to the essential mutability in all cultural artifacts, the ways the significance in all art evolves over time. In this way, monuments have long sought to provide a naturalizing locus for memory, in which a state's triumphs and martyrs, its ideals and founding myths are cast as naturally true as the landscape in which they stand. These are the monument's sustaining illusions, the principles of its seeming longevity and power. But in fact, as several generations of artists—modern and post-modern alike—have made scathingly clear, neither the monument nor its meaning is really everlasting. Both a monument and its significance are constructed in particular times and places, contingent on the political, historical, and aesthetic realities of the moment.

In fact, as many contemporary artists have long recognized, the process of the memorial competition itself is often at least as rewarding as the final result. For Holocaust memory is always "contested" as long as more than one group or individual remembers. Not only does an open memorial competition make such competing memories palpable, but it also throws into relief the complex, nearly impossible questions facing every artist or architect attempting to conceive of such a monument. Among the dilemmas for contemporary Holocaust memorial designers are: How to remember horribly real events in the abstract gestures of geometric forms? How to create a focal point for remembrance among ruins without desecrating the space itself? How to embody remembrance without seeming to displace it?

These questions and others arose with the very first open competition for a memorial at Auschwitz-Birkenau in 1957. "The choice of a monument to commemorate Auschwitz has not been an easy task," the sculptor Henry Moore wrote as head of the internationally acclaimed design jury assembled for the Auschwitz competition. "Essentially, what has been attempted here has been the creation [...] of a monument to crime and ugliness, to murder and to horror. The crime was of such stupendous proportions that any work of art must be on an appropriate scale. But apart from this, is it in fact possible to create a work of art that can express the emotions engendered by Auschwitz?" (Moore).

As was clear to Moore in 1957 and to many critics and artists since then, public art in general, and Holocaust memorials in particular, tend to beg traditional art historical inquiry. Most discussions of Holocaust memorial spaces ignore the essentially public dimension of their performance, remaining either formally aestheticist or almost piously historical. So while it is true that a sculptor like Nathan Rapoport (designer of the Warsaw Ghetto Memorial) will never be regarded by art historians as highly as his contemporaries, Jacques Lipshitz and Henry Moore, neither can his work be dismissed solely on the basis of its popular appeal. Unabashedly figurative, heroic, and referential, his work seems to be doomed critically by precisely those qualities—public accessibility and historical referentiality—that make it monumental. But in fact, it may be just this public appeal that finally constitutes the monument's aesthetic performance—and that leads such memorials to demand public and historical disclosure, even as they condemn themselves to critical obscurity. Instead of stopping at formal questions, or at issues of historical referentiality, we must go on to ask how memorial representations of history may finally weave themselves into the course of ongoing events.

While questions of high and low art continue to inform the discussion surrounding Holocaust monuments, they no longer dictate their critical discussion. Instead, we might keep in mind the reductive—occasionally vulgar—excesses in popular memorial representations, even as we qualify our definitions of kitsch and challenge its usefulness as a critical category for the discussion of public monuments. Rather than patronizing mass tastes, we recognize the sheer weight of public taste and that certain conventional forms in avowedly public art may eventually have consequences for public memory—whether or not we think they should. This is to acknowledge the unfashionable, often archaic aspects of so many Holocaust memorials, even as we look beyond them. It is also to recognize that public art like this demands additional critical criteria if the lives and meanings of such works are to be sustained—and not oppressed—by art historical discourse.

For there is a difference between avowedly public art—exemplified in public monuments like these—and art produced almost exclusively for the art world, its critics, other artists, and galleries, which has yet to be properly recognized. People do not come to Holocaust memorials because they are new, cutting edge, or fashionable; as the critics are quick to note, most of these memorials are none of these. Where contemporary art is produced as self- or medium-reflexive, public Holocaust monuments are produced specifically to be historically referential, to lead viewers beyond themselves to an understanding or evocation of events. As *public* monuments, these memorials generally avoid referring hermetically to the processes that brought them into being. Where contemporary art invites viewers and critics to contemplate its own materiality, or its relationship to other works before and after itself, the aim of memorials is not to remark their own presence so much as past events *because* they are no longer present. In this sense, Holocaust memorials would point immediately beyond themselves.

In their fusion of public art and popular culture, historical memory and political consequences, therefore, Holocaust memorials demand an alternative critique that goes beyond questions of high and low art, tastefulness and vulgarity. Rather than merely identifying the movements and forms out on which public memory is borne, or asking whether or not these monuments reflect past history accurately or fashionably, we turn to the many ways this art suggests itself as a basis for political and social action. That is, we might ask here not only how the monument-maker's era and training shaped memory at the time, and how the monument would reflect past history, but most important, what role it now plays in current history.

We might now concern ourselves less with whether this is good or bad art, and more with what the consequences of public memorial art are for the people. This is to propose that like any public art space, Holocaust memorials are neither benign nor irrelevant, but suggest themselves as the basis for political and communal action. The aim here will be to explore not just the relations between people and their monuments but the consequences of these relations in historical time. Whereas some art historians have traditionally dismissed such approaches to art as anthropological, social, or psychological, others have opened their inquiry to include larger issues of the sociology of art: Public memorials in this case are exemplary of an art work's social life, its life in society's mind. The question becomes not just: How are people moved by these memorials? But also: To what end have they been moved, to what historical conclusions, to what understanding and actions in their own lives? This is to suggest that we cannot separate the monument from its public life, that the social function of such art *is* its aesthetic performance (see Rigney, this volume).

Often it seems as if a monument's life in the communal mind is as hard and polished as its exterior form, its significance as fixed as its place in the landscape. But precisely because monuments seem to remember everything but their own past, their own creation, the critic's aim might now be to reinvest the monument with memory of its own coming into being. By returning to the memorial some memory of its own genesis, we remind ourselves of the memorial's essential fragility, its dependence on others for its life, that it was made by human hands in human times and places, that it is no more a natural piece of the landscape than we are. For unlike words on a page, always gesturing at something beyond the ink and paper giving them form, memorial icons seem to embody ideas, inviting viewers to mistake material presence and weight for immutable permanence. Such a critique might thus save our *icons* of remembrance from hardening into *idols* of remembrance.

For too often, a community's monuments assume the polished, finished veneer of a death mask, unreflective of current memory, unresponsive to contemporary issues. Instead of enshrining an already enshrined memory, such an approach might provide a uniquely instructive glimpse of the monument's inner life—the tempestuous social, political and aesthetic forces—normally hidden by a monument's taciturn exterior. By drawing back into view the memorial-making process, we invigorate the very idea of the monument, thereby reminding all such cultural artifacts of their coming into being.

To this end, we might enlarge the life and texture of Holocaust memorials to include: the times and places in which they were conceived; their literal construction amid historical and political realities; their finished forms in public spaces; their places in the constellation of national memory; and their ever-evolving lives in the minds of their communities and of the Jewish people over time; even their eventual destruction. With these dimensions in mind, we look not only at the ways individual monuments create and reinforce particular memory of the Holocaust period, but also at the ways events re-enter political life shaped by monuments.

On a more general level, we might ask of all memorials what meanings are generated when the temporal realm is converted to material form, when time collapses into space, a trope by which it is then measured and grasped. How do memorials emplot time and memory? How do they impose borders on time, a facade on memory? What is the relationship of time to place, place to memory, memory to time? Finally, two fundamentally inter-related questions: How does a particular place shape our memory of a particular time? And how does this memory of a past time shape our understanding of the present moment?

In such questions, we also recognize the integral part visitors play in the memorial text: How and what we remember in the company of a monument depends very much on who we are, why we care to remember, and how we see. All of which is to suggest the fundamentally interactive, dialogical quality of Holocaust memorials. For public memory and its meanings depend not just on the forms and figures in these memorials, but on the viewers' responses to them. Through this attention to the activity of memorialization, we might also remind ourselves that public memory is constructed, that understanding of events depends on memory's construction, and that there are worldly consequences in the kinds of historical understanding generated by monuments. In this light, we find that the performance of Holocaust memorials depends not on some measured distance between history and its monumental representations, but in the conflation of private and public memory, in the memorial activity by which minds reflecting on the past inevitably precipitate in the present historical moment.

Taken together, these stages comprise a genuine activity of memory, by which artifacts of ages past are invigorated by the present moment, even as they condition our understanding of the world around us. Instead of allowing the past to rigidify in its monumental forms, we would vivify memory through the memory-work itself—whereby events, their recollection, and the role monuments play in our lives remain animate, never completed. It is not enough to ask whether or not our memorials remember the Holocaust, or even how they remember it. We should also ask to what ends we have remembered. That is, how do we respond to the current moment in light of our remembered past? This is to recognize that the shape of memory cannot be divorced from the actions taken in its behalf, and that memory without consequences contains the seeds of its own destruction.

References

Foundation of the Memorial to the Murdered Jews of Europe. *Materials on the Memorial to the Murdered Jews of Europe.* Berlin: Nicolai, 2005.

Frahm, Klaus. *Denkmal für die ermordeten Juden Europas/Memorial to the Murdered Jews of Europe.* Berlin: Nicolai, 2005.

Friedlander, Saul. *Nazi Germany and the Jews, Volume I: The Years of Persecution, 1933-1939.* New York: Harper Collins, 1997.

Hoheisel, Horst, and Andreas Knitz. *Zermahlene Geschichte: Kunst als Umweg.* Weimar: Schriften des Thüringischen Hauptstaatsarchivs, 1999.

Huyssen, Andreas. *Twilight Memories: Marking Time in a Culture of Amnesia.* New York: Routledge, 1995.

Jeisman, Michael, ed. *Mahnmal Mitte: Eine Kontroverse.* Cologne: Dumont, 1999.

Konneke, Achim, ed. *Das Harburger Mahnmal gegen Faschismus/The Harburg Monument against Fascism.* Hamburg: Hatje, 1994.

Linenthal, Edward T. *Preserving Memory: The Struggle to Create America's Holocaust Museum.* New York: Viking, 1995.

Moore, Henry. *The Auschwitz Competition.* Auschwitz: State Museum of Auschwitz, 1964. N. pag.

Rieth, Adolph. *Monuments to the Victims of Tyranny.* New York: Praeger, 1969.

Winzen, Matthias. "The Need for Public Representation and the Burden of the German Past." *Art Journal* 48 (1989): 309-14.

Young, James E., ed. *The Art of Memory: Holocaust Memorials in History.* Munich: Prestel, 1994.

—. *At Memory's Edge: After-Images of the Holocaust in Contemporary Art and Architecture.* New Haven: Yale UP, 2000.

—. "Memory and Counter-Memory: Towards a Social Aesthetic of Holocaust Memorials." *After Auschwitz: Responses to the Holocaust in Contemporary Art.* Ed. Monica Bohm-Duchen. London: Lund Humphries, 1995. 78-102.

—. *The Texture of Memory: Holocaust Memorials and Meaning.* New Haven: Yale UP, 1993.

The Photograph as Externalization and Trace

JENS RUCHATZ

If memory is intrinsically social, as Maurice Halbwachs has pointed out, then the formation of any memory does rely fundamentally on means of exchanging and sharing knowledge (cf. Assmann, *Erinnerungsräume* 132). It cannot do without symbols that represent or embody knowledge of the past and are capable of circulating in a social group. In other words, the extension and complexity of collective memory is to a large extent dependent on the available media. This contribution will take the case of photography to show how memory and media interact.

1. Externalization

There seem to be two fundamentally opposed ways of relating media and memory: *externalization* and *trace*. Whereas the concept of externalization foregrounds the instrumental and social character of media, the conception as trace stresses the autonomy of media technology. *Externalization* is the established and, one could say, literal notion of media as memory: Accordingly texts or forms in one medium (or a medium as a whole) are related to human memory either as a way of storing its contents or as analogous in structure. Other scholars have suggested similar terms, such as "exteriorization" (Leroi-Gourhan 257) or "excarnation" (Assmann, "Exkarnation"), to discuss the merit of certain technologies to store information outside the human body that otherwise would have to be preserved neutrally or—more probably—forgotten. In their function of enhancing memory's capacity, technologies of externalization follow and supplement the internal techniques of mnemonics.

The affinity of memory and media has become manifest in a plenitude of metaphors which construe media as memory or vice versa. Regarding photography one cannot but quote the famous description of the daguerreotype, photography on a "silver-plated sheet of copper," as "the mirror with a memory" (Holmes 54), which was coined in 1859. In *Civilization and its Discontents* Sigmund Freud (38) conceives technology in general as a cultural program that is aimed at generating "prostheses" in order to compensate for the deficiencies of human organs. From this perspective the camera and the gramophone come to be improved "materializations" of the human capacity to remember, both capturing fleeting sensations (for more such metaphors cf. Stiegler, *Bilder* 102-05). To the same extent that storage media have been compared or even equated with the functions of memory, the human capacity to remember has been understood through the metaphors that new media technologies offered. The Dutch historian of psychology Douwe Draaisma has shown how strongly the unavoidably metaphorical conceptions of human memory relied on the evolution of media technology: After the invention of photography, human memory "became a photographic plate, prepared for the recording and reproduction of visual experience" (120). Likewise, the expression "photographic memory" testifies to the urge to use media as cognitive models to understand the operations of memory.

In addition to media and "natural" memory regularly being used to shed light on each other, the assumed affinity of media and memory also informs anthropology and cultural history. The French anthropologist André Leroi-Gourhan, to give but one example (for more cf. Ruchatz, "Externalisierungen"), has shown the cultural evolution of mankind to be founded—substantially, even if not exclusively—on a history of media which permitted the formation of a "social memory." Whereas animals could not transcend instinctive behavior, man could liberate himself from the biological memory of the species and externalize his "action programs" in the form of symbolic representations that render possible a comparison of different options for acting: Anthropological evolution is hence bound to the means that expand the amount of knowledge that can be simultaneously made available (Leroi-Gourhan 219-35). The transition from exclusively oral to literal cultures marks the beginning of the "exteriorization" of knowledge. Writing easily exceeds the limits of the brain as it allows for a preservation of experience and knowledge in a material form of virtually boundless capacity. All in all Leroi-Gourhan distinguishes five periods in the history of collective memory: "that of oral transmission, that of written transmission using tables or an index, that of simple index cards, that of mechanography [i.e., largely punch cards], and that of electronic serial transmission [i.e., modern computers]" (258). Human evolution is in this respect founded on a rapidly growing body of knowledge that soon requires innovative ways of ordering (libraries' "index cards"), finally leading to the "machine brain" of the computer that, according to Leroi-Gourhan, threatens to challenge the human monopoly on thinking.

The capacity of media to support or even smoothly replace the work of "natural" memory has frequently been called into question. In a famous critique Plato (274e-276d) opined that while writing could figure as an individual aide-memoire for a speaker, it could not aspire to act as communicative memory in itself (see J. Assmann, this volume). Paradoxically, the very same qualities that render technological storage a valuable supplement to "natural" memory also distinguish it from the latter. Writing, on the one hand, stores information that can be read in contexts locally and temporally apart from its origin, thus inevitably changing the meaning, as Plato complained. On the other hand, every bit of information that is encoded in written form remains stable and—at least materially—forever unaltered, whereas in human memory old and new "input" coexist and interact, forming a dynamic, ever-changing context. It is obvious, however, that, if media kept information exactly like the human brain, there would be no point in using them. These objections, which distance the mind from its externalizations, are reflected more openly in the view of media as trace.

2. Trace

If one takes into account that photography itself has been conceived as memory, it becomes even less comprehensible that it has only rarely figured in media histories of memory. Neither Leroi-Gourhan nor Assmann and Assmann pay tribute to photography's significance. The periodization is usually confined to orality, writing, and print, concluding with the digital age. The media of analogous recording—most prominently photography, phonography, and film—are situated at the margins if included at all. This omission can be readily explained by the insight that photography is considered so radical an externalization that it stretches the concept beyond its limits. One could argue that not just the retention of knowledge, but also perception had been externalized, thus eluding human intervention in the whole process.

French film critic André Bazin attributed to pictures the task of "mummification," that is, the function of symbolically saving humans from death by immortalizing their appearance. Photographic media could lay claim to an increased power in recalling the past because the automatic formation of the picture omitted interpretation and therefore emancipated memory from subjectivity. According to Bazin "all the arts are based on the presence of man, only photography derives an advantage from his absence" (13). Likewise, Siegfried Kracauer has elaborated the difference between human memory and photographic records:

> Photography grasps what is given as a spatial (or temporal) continuum, memory images retain what is given only insofar as it has significance. Since what is significant is not reducible to either merely spatial or merely temporal terms, memory images are at odds with photographic representation. (50-51)

Manual modes of representation—writing, drawing, or painting—may increase a society's or individual's "storage" capacity, thus minimizing the need to single out what is worth keeping, but photographic exposure bypasses human intervention on all levels. This blindness to selectivity is the quality that the expression "photographic memory" means: a memory that does not filter according to relevance and retains even the apparently insignificant.

In this respect, the photograph refers to the past not as externalization but as a trace (Ruchatz, "Fotografische" 89-92). Making sense of a photograph as a trace means to take it as evidence of what is shown on it and to reconstruct the situation of its origin. When a photograph refers to the past not as its representation but as its product, it functions more as a reminder that triggers or guides remembering than as a memory in itself. Because traces are taken to be generated unintentionally they are regarded as particularly authentic and trustworthy testimonies of the past. This stance has, however, to be qualified: As soon as a trace is identified as such, it is removed from the sphere of the authentic and displaced to culture. Traces are not defined as carriers of meaning from the start (as are convention-based sign systems like speech), but it nonetheless takes cultural knowledge to mark objects (for example, fingerprints) as meaningful traces. And even more: Although the production of traces is presumed to be devoid of cultural encoding, their "reading" is, as the word itself betrays, paradoxically an act of "decoding." Even if the knowledge consulted to "read" traces is rarely ever properly conventionalized, the singular event that led to the formation of a particular trace can only be reconstructed by resorting to a more general knowledge, for example by reducing the singularity to typical and decodable traits. A trace remains "authentic" only as long as it has not been read.

With regard to photography's relation to memory the concept of the trace proves fruitful, as it points to photography's specific temporality. Different from iterable conventional signs, a photograph refers to a particular and singular moment in time that is inevitably past when the finished print is looked at. Photography is as profoundly marked by this fugaciousness as it brings it to view. What is certified to have been present, but is no more, can be looked at as if it still was. According to Roland Barthes, photography brings about an "anthropological revolution in man's history" because it gives not so much an impression of the presence of a thing but "an awareness of its having-been-there" ("Rhetoric" 44). This intricate mingling of past and present, presence and absence, distinguishes photography not only from manual ways of representation but also from the moving image of film, which, as Barthes contends, gives an impression of presence. Accordingly the photographic trace may be the only representation of an event that incorporates its absence. It is of course necessary to clarify that, if any photograph *can* be viewed as a relic of the past, this mode of use does not prevail in all contexts: Photos in family albums are more likely to be seen this way than photographic illustrations in field guides or cookbooks, which are not meant to be viewed as singular traces of something particular, but as exemplary depictions that show a specimen representative of a class of things.

Neither photography as a medium nor a single photograph can be tied down exclusively—or even ontologically—to one exclusive mode of signification. It goes without saying that every photo is not just automatically produced, but also subject to a number of significant decisions: The choice of the object, its framing and the moment of exposure, the use of a certain lens and a particular photographic material all shape how the picture will look in the end. The same holds true for the actions following the exposure, in particular the production of the prints. But all these voluntary acts only surround the moment of exposure when light forms the image on the film and the photographer cannot intervene (Dubois 47). Consequently any photographic picture consists to different ratios of a mixture of selection and accident, of significant and insignificant elements. Photography produces an exceptional class of traces, insofar as they are regularly and intentionally produced as well as conventionally recognized as significant and signifying: Photographs show—but do not explain—what has caused them.

To clarify how photography acts as a sign it is helpful to take recourse to Charles Sanders Peirce's triadic distinction of signs (cf. Dubois 17-53): In this terminology photographic traces function as *index*—a sign that signifies by its relation to its origin—and the externalized and encoded messages as *symbol*—a sign that signifies by virtue of conventions. Somehow sandwiched between these opposites figures the most prominent quality of photography: As *icons* photos signify by similarity. The light that is reflected onto the light-sensitive emulsion delineates the objects in front of the lens in such a manner that no code is required to recognize them. More often than not two or more of these modes of signification combine when photographs are looked at: Before photographs can take on a symbolic meaning, for example, the objects in them have to be recognized by way of their iconicity.

Likewise, trace and externalization do not necessarily exclude each other, stressing either the cultural or the technological aspect of a photograph. The concepts rather help to distinguish two modes of photographic signification that can be found even in the same picture. The difference between externalization and trace distinguishes two functions of medial artifacts that pertain not only to photography, but can—to a greater or lesser extent—be observed wherever media are used for retaining the past. In the following I want to take a look at the functions photographs perform in processes of individual and collective remembering. It will be observed that private photographs tend to be used as traces, that is, read indexically, whereas collective memory favors photographs that support a symbolical reading and thus can be appropriated as externalization.

3. Private Photography

Private photographs are expressly taken for the single purpose to serve as future aide-memoires (Starl 23). They address either the photographing individual him- or herself or the family he or she belongs to. This fact poses serious problems for the uninvolved observer. If private photographs, on the one hand, do not look personal or individual, but rather "interchangeable" (Hirsch, *Familial Gaze* xiii), the stereotypical mise-en-scène and choice of subjects do not exhaust their meaning. They rather serve as anchors (Barthes, "Rhetoric" 39-41) and starting points for remembering what is actually not visible in the pictures. By applying the distinction of *users* and *readers* to private photography, Patricia Holland (107) has elaborated this observation. Users, the proper addressees of any given set of private photos, know the context of what is visible on a photo either from personal experience or from conversations with relatives or friends. By contrast, readers cannot penetrate the surface of the photographic image, because they have no access to this private knowledge, and therefore try to make sense of it by identifying the social codes that are present. The pictures then lose their specific meaning in favor of more general insights into social and cultural conventions.

In his famous empirical study undertaken in the 1960s, Pierre Bourdieu showed to what extent the practice of private photography is social. What are worthy occasions for photography (rites of passage like baptism or marriage, holidays, etc.) and how to frame, place, and pose a subject can be considered collectively pre-structured choices. "Thus when we photograph ourselves in a familial setting, we do not do so in a vacuum; we respond to dominant mythologies of family life, to conceptions we have inherited, to images we see on television, in advertising, in film" (Hirsch, *Familial Gaze* xvi). Private photography is obviously interspersed with and structured by social presettings. Photography-based private memory thus offers a perfect example for Halbwachs's point that individual memory is social as it does rely on collective framings.

When readers look at private photographs they generally take them as externalizations that betray the implicit ideologies and codings of collective memory. Users tend to see their own private photographs as traces that offer a material starting point for recalling what happened at the time of exposure. For them the ideological side of their own practice will remain more or less obscure. Whereas readers will tend to break up a photograph into different layers of signification (framing, posing, etc.), users will more probably regard the photograph in its entirety as a trace of a past event. In the user's eyes the main purpose of the photographs is to provide a kind of visual evidence that prompts and anchors acts of remembering. If photography's iconic abilities may be supportive, in the end they are of only secondary importance. Even blurry, under-exposed or in other ways failed photographs can do service insofar as they are tied physically to the event that produced them (Starl 23).

In order to establish a link to the past, photographs need not be accepted as externalizations of personal impressions. Private photographs may be experienced as such when they seem to agree with somebody's very own impressions or perceptions—in short: when the likeness is considered striking. Photography's ability to record events in bypassing subjectivity has, however, raised suspicion that it might not recall but rather replace lived experience. Barthes has pointed out that the photograph was "never, in essence, a memory," but rather blocked remembrance and easily turned into a "counter-memory" (Barthes, *Camera* 91). By repeatedly using photographs to trigger memories, what is remembered mentally could converge with what is retained pictorially—if photographs are regarded as externalizations they would have to be internalized first. Photographic pictures have the power not just to prompt but also to redirect and change memories according to what is iconically perceived and indexically authenticated.

In the private context photographs are used to intentionally retrieve memories. In the stabilized sequence of an album the pictures can form a kind of pictorial autobiography that its owners employ to ascertain their identity, the photographic narrative serving as material proof (see Straub, this volume). The knowledge brought to bear on private photographs may stem from one's own experiences, but can also extend to the communicative memory of a family when it concerns familial events that happened before one's birth: This second form of photographically founded recollection, which is neither autobiographical memory nor impersonal history, has been termed "postmemory" (Hirsch, *Family Frames* 22).

4. Public Photographs as Icons

In contrast to private photography, publicly distributed photographs are usually produced for instant consumption. Only a very small fraction of the photographs published every year survive the time of their publication and enter collective memory—and they do so not due to the photographer's intention, but by accident. Photographs that are collectively revered and memorized are usually called "icons"—icons, however, not in the Peircean sense, for photographic icons are characterized precisely by their bias towards the realm of the symbolic.

Up to now the term "photographic icon" just designates pictures that attract strong collective attention and emotional reaction. It has yet to be developed into a clear-cut concept (Brink 232-38). Unanimity exists, however, that iconic photographs foreground symbolic values. If in principle photographs can claim "instant convertibility into a symbol" (Goldberg 135; also cf. Brink 15), the question still remains why some pictures do transform more easily into a symbol than others. There are at least three factors that support this conversion of a trace that refers to a singular event (confirming that it has happened) into a carrier of a cultural meaning:

1. It helps if the composition of a photograph corresponds with pictorial and rhetorical traditions, that is, when it can subconsciously be identified as an externalization of established modes of organizing collective knowledge (Edwards and Winkler 290-91; Bertelsen 85-89). Symbolization can, however, be taken too far. Roland Barthes ("Shock") has argued that so-called shock photos fail to impress, because the photographer has too obviously taken the place of the recipients and inscribed his moral judgment into the pictures. Photography's troubling ambiguities, due to the lack of a semiotic code in the trace, got buried under a superficial, speechlike message that could only be affirmed by the viewers. A successful photographic icon balances trace and presumed externalizations, so that the symbolic dimension appears to belong to reality itself: It shows that "life can surpass art" (Bertelsen 83). How important assumptions like these are is evident in the never-ending discussions of whether Robert Capa's *Death of a Spanish Loyalist* or Joe Rosenthal's photo of the flag-raising on Iwo Jima were staged or not (Griffin 137-40, 143f.; Goldberg 144).
2. The presentation of photographs can downplay their reference to the particular events of which they are a trace. In a magazine or a newspaper, photographs can be accompanied either by a straightforward *caption*, stressing the indexical quality by detailing place and date of the exposure, or by a *title* that encourages an interpretation of a more general kind, which surpasses the concrete event presented in the photograph (Scott 46-74). The adoption of a press photo into collective memory very often goes together with the renunciation of exact captions (Wiedenmann 323-27; Zelizer 102-11).

3. Repeated publication automatically loosens the tie of a photograph to a specific point in historic time (Griffin 140). If it is continuously republished a picture is gradually depleted of its indexical reference to the particular event of its origin. It becomes instead linked more and more to its prior uses, turning into a sign that signifies by social convention. This process of abstraction and the canonization go hand in hand and mutually reinforce each other, because the more the unambiguous, symbolical meaning of a photo is consolidated, the more likely it is to be republished. In the end, a photo can turn into a visual token, a mnemonic, that stands for an event as a whole, a series of events or even a historical epoch, like Rosenthal's photo of Iwo Jima for World War II in the Pacific (see also Erll, this volume). To what extent this picture has become conventional is demonstrated by its permanent appropriations in a range of visual media. Starting in 1945 the picture was published on postage stamps and posters; it was taken as model for the U. S. Marine Corps Memorial in Arlington in 1954, which pop artist Edward Kienholz complemented by a critical replica; it became the focus of the novel *Flags of Our Fathers* and Clint Eastwood's film of the same title (Dülffer). It even cut the links to WW II and became a "visual ideograph" that could be adapted freely to other historical contexts, be it in editorial cartoons (Edwards and Winkler) or in a photograph of the New York firemen on 9/11.

Photographs can become canonized as veritable *lieux de mémoire* that enter cultural memory, and end up in history textbooks (see also Hebel, this volume). Photo historian Vicki Goldberg has argued that photographic images increasingly function as summaries of complex historical phenomena, "partially displacing the public monument" (135). The prevalence of moving images has even strengthened photography's importance, because the still image then renders the easily graspable version, as it condenses a course of events into one single moment (Goldberg 218-19, 226).

Whether and how the advent and success of digital photography will affect the connection of photography and memory remains a crucial, but to this day open, question. It is often argued that when the light-sensitive chemistry of traditional photography is replaced by digitized bits that can easily be manipulated one by one, photographs will no longer be regarded as traces, since their authenticity is fundamentally called into question. In the future it might happen that the iconic look of photographic pictures will be no longer be bound to either indexical authenticity nor an origin in a definite past, but to a temporally indifferent externalization (Stiegler, "Digitale"). Without the fundamental aspect of the trace that secured the temporal specificity of the photographic image, the salient position of photography in visual memory would be seriously endangered.

References

Assmann, Aleida. *Erinnerungsräume: Formen und Wandlungen des kulturellen Gedächtnisses.* Munich: Beck, 1999.

—. "Exkarnation: Gedanken zur Grenze zwischen Körper und Schrift." *Raum und Verfahren: Interventionen 2.* Eds. Jörg Huber and Alois Martin Müller. Basel: Stroemfeld/Roter Stern, 1993. 133-57.

Assmann, Aleida, and Jan Assmann. "Das Gestern im Heute: Medien und soziales Gedächtnis." *Die Wirklichkeit der Medien: Eine Einführung in die Kommunikationswissenschaft.* Eds. Klaus Merten, Siegfried J. Schmidt and Siegfried Weischenberg. Opladen: Westdeutscher Verlag, 1994. 114-40.

Barthes, Roland. *Camera Lucida.* London: Fontana, 1984.

—. "The Rhetoric of the Image." *Image, Music, Text.* Trans. Stephen Heath. London: Fontana, 1977. 32-51.

—. "Shock Photos." *The Eiffel Tower and Other Mythologies.* New York: Hall and Wang, 1979. 71-74.

Bazin, André. "The Ontology of the Photographic Image." *What is Cinema?* Trans. Hugh Gray. Vol. 1. Berkeley: U of California P, 1967. 9-16.

Bertelsen, Lance. "Icons on Iwo." *Journal of Popular Culture* 22.2 (1989): 79-95.

Bourdieu, Pierre. *Photography: A Middle-Brow Art.* Trans. Shaun Whiteside. Stanford: Stanford UP, 1990. Trans. of *Un art moyen: Essai sur les usages sociaux de la photographie.* Paris: Les Éditions de Minuit, 1965.

Brink, Cornelia. *Ikonen der Vernichtung: Öffentlicher Gebrauch von Fotografien aus nationalsozialistischen Konzentrationslagern nach 1945.* Berlin: Akademie, 1997.

Draaisma, Douwe. *Metaphors of Memory: A History of Ideas about the Mind.* Cambridge: Cambridge UP, 2000.

Dubois, Philippe. *L'Acte photographique et autres essais.* Paris: Nathan, 1990.

Dülffer, Jost. "Über-Helden—Das Bild von Iwo Jima in der Repräsentation des Sieges: Eine Studie zur US-amerikanischen Erinnerungskultur seit 1945." *Zeithistorische Forschungen/Studies in Contemporary History* 3.2 (2006). 7 Nov. 2007 <http://www.zeithistorische-forschungen.de/16126041-Duelffer-2-2006>.

Edwards, Janis, and Carol K. Winkler. "Representative Form and Visual Ideograph: The Iwo Jima Image in Editorial Cartoons." *The Quarterly Journal of Speech* 83 (1997): 289-310.

Freud, Sigmund. *Civilization and Its Discontents.* New York: Norton, 1962.

Goldberg, Vicki. *The Power of Photography: How Photographs Changed Our Lives.* New York: Abbeville, 1991.

Griffin, Michael. "The Great War Photographs: Constructing Myths of History and Photojournalism." *Picturing the Past: Media, History and Photography.* Eds. Bonnie Brennen and Hanno Hardt. Urbana: U of Illinois P, 1999. 122-57.

Hirsch, Marianne, ed. *The Familial Gaze.* Hanover, NH: UP of New England, 1999.

—. *Family Frames: Photography, Narrative, and Postmemory.* Cambridge: Harvard UP, 1997.

Holland, Patricia. "'Sweet it is to scan ...': Personal Photographs and Popular Photography." *Photography: A Critical Introduction.* Ed. Liz Wells. London: Routledge, 1997. 103-50.

Holmes, Oliver Wendell. "The Stereoscope and the Stereograph." 1859. *Photography: Essays and Images.* Ed. Beaumont Newhall. London: Secker & Warburg, 1980. 53-62.

Kracauer, Siegfried. "Photography." 1927. *The Mass Ornament: Weimar Essays.* Ed. Thomas Y. Levin. Cambridge: Harvard UP, 1995. 47-63.

Leroi-Gourhan, André. *Gesture and Speech.* Cambridge: MIT Press, 1993.

Plato. "Phaedrus." Trans. R. Hackforth. *The Collected Dialogues of Plato Including the Letters.* 1961. Eds. Edith Hamilton and Huntington Cairns. Princeton: Princeton UP, 1989. 475-525.

Ruchatz, Jens. "Externalisierungen: Gedächtnisforschung als mediale Anthropologie." *Handlung Kultur Interpretation* 12.1 (2003): 94-118.

—. "Fotografische Gedächtnisse: Ein Panorama medienwissenschaftlicher Fragestellungen." *Medien des kollektiven Gedächtnisses: Konstruktivität—Historizität—Kulturspezifität.* Eds. Astrid Erll and Ansgar Nünning. Berlin: de Gruyter, 2004. 83-105.

Scott, Clive. *The Spoken Image: Photography and Language.* London: Reaktion, 1999.

Starl, Timm. *Knipser: Die Bildgeschichte der privaten Fotografie in Deutschland und Österreich von 1880 bis 1980.* Berlin: Koehler & Amelang, 1995.

Stiegler, Bernd. *Bilder der Photographie: Ein Album photographischer Metaphern.* Frankfurt am Main: Suhrkamp, 2006.

—. "Digitale Photographie als epistemologischer Bruch und historische Wende." *Das Gesicht der Welt: Medien in der digitalen Kultur.* Munich: Fink, 2004. 105-25.

Wiedenmann, Nicole. "'So ist das, was das Bild dokumentiert, das Gegenteil dessen, was es symbolisiert': Holocaustfotografien im Spannungsfeld zwischen Geschichtswissenschaft und Kulturellem Gedächtnis." *Die Medien der Geschichte: Historizität und Medialität in interdisziplinärer Perspektive.* Eds. Fabio Crivellari, Kay Kirchmann, Marcus Sandl and Rudolf Schlögl. Konstanz: UVK, 2004. 317-49.

Zelizer, Barbie. "From the Image of Record to the Image of Memory: Holocaust Photography, Then and Now." *Picturing the Past: Media, History and Photography.* Eds. Bonnie Brennen and Hanno Hardt. Urbana: U of Illinois P, 1999. 98-121.

Journalism's Memory Work

BARBIE ZELIZER

Of the numerous social and cultural settings involved in the establishment and maintenance of collective memory, the environment associated with journalism is perhaps among the least obvious vehicles of memory. And yet journalists play a systematic and ongoing role in shaping the ways in which we think about the past. This chapter considers the scholarship tracking the relationship between journalism and memory, and in doing so it addresses how that relationship both strengthens and weakens each of its constituent parts.

1. Why the Journalism-Memory Link is Problematic—and Inevitable

When seen from the perspective of what journalists themselves deem important about their work, journalism appears to be an ill-suited setting to offer an independent tracking of the past. For as long as journalism has been around, the popular assumption has been that it provides a first, rather than final, draft of history, leaving to the historians the final processing of journalism's raw events. Against such a division of labor, journalism has come to be seen as a setting driven more by its emphasis on the here-and-now than on the there-and-then, restricted by temporal limitations associated with rapidly overturning deadlines. Journalism distinguishes itself from history by aspiring to a sense of newsworthiness that is derived from proximity, topicality, and novelty, and it is motivated by an ongoing need to fill a depleting news-hole despite high stakes, a frantic pace, and uncertain resources. In this regard, the past seems somewhat beyond the boundaries of what journalists can and ought to do in accomplishing their work goals.

The degree to which the present drives journalism seems to position journalism's alignment with memory—and indeed, with all things associated with the past—at odds with its own sense of self. As Edy succinctly states:

> [T]he fact that news media make use of historical events at all is somewhat counterintuitive. Journalists have traditionally placed a high value on being the first to publicize new information. Extra editions, news flashes, and program interruptions for important new information all testify to a desire to present the

> latest information to audiences. Many stories go out of date and cannot be used if there is not space in the news product for them on the day that they occur. (74)

Not surprisingly, then, memory is seen as outside the parameters of journalists' attention.

But does journalism really leave the past to others? The burgeoning of the literature on collective memory during the mid-1980s helped promote a turn in scholarly recognition of journalism's involvement with the past, for as work by Maurice Halbwachs, Jacques le Goff, Pierre Nora and others was translated and widely disseminated, there grew a recognition that journalism's alignment with the past reflected a slightly more complicated relationship than that suggested by traditional notions of history. Scholars began to pay attention to the fact that collective recollections and reconstructions of the past were set in place by agents with their own agendas to promote and—particularly among sociologists like Schwartz, Schudson ("Dynamics of Distortion"), and Wagner-Pacifici—that memories existed on the level of groups. This made memory work a fruitful way to think about journalists' involvement in the past, and scholars began to address journalism's persistent, though unstated, predilection for times earlier than the unfolding of contemporary events. As Lang and Lang argued, memory work drew from "a stock of images of the past that, insofar as they continue to be mediated, [...] lose little of their importance with the passage of time" (138). They suggested that in journalism

> even cursory perusal reveals many references to events no longer new and hence not news in the journalistic sense. This past and future together frame the reporting of current events. Just what part of the past and what kind of future are brought into play depends on what editors and journalists believe legitimately belongs within the public domain, on journalistic conventions, and of course on personal ideologies. (126)

Understanding journalism as one kind of memory work offered scholars broadened ways of explaining journalism. References to the past came to be seen as helping journalists regularly make sense of the present. In Lang and Lang's view, such references came to fill many functions for journalists trying to make sense of rapidly evolving events. They helped journalists build connections, suggest inferences, create story pegs, act as yardsticks for gauging an event's magnitude and impact, offer analogies, and provide short-hand explanations. The past came to be seen as so central to journalism that it emerged as an unspoken backdrop against which the contemporary record-keeping of the news could take place.

All of this is a roundabout way of stating that a close attendance to how journalism works reveals that journalists rarely concede the past to others. Although much has been made of journalists' so-called reliance on the commandment questions of news—the who, what, where, when, and how of journalism, with not enough emphasis on the "why" (Carey)—a necessary attachment to the explanatory paradigms underlying current events is always there for the taking in journalism. The past remains one of the richest repositories available to journalists for explaining current events, and scholars have begun to track the variant ways in which the past helps journalists interpret the present.

A recognition of journalists' work as engaged with memory thereby proceeds by definition against journalists' own rhetoric of what they claim to do. And yet, journalists' role in making and keeping memory alive ranks uppermost in the list of those institutional actors and settings critical to its establishment (Zelizer, "News"; Zelizer, "Reading the Past"). Equally relevant, how the past sneaks into journalism plays to the recognition of collective memory more actively than an embrace of traditional notions of history. Journalists provide a particularly useful example of how memory work takes shape among those who produce recollections of the past, in that when journalists are involved in record-keeping about the past, they reflect larger impulses that complicate its ownership. Acting on what Warren Susman long ago observed—that "history [...] is not something to be left to historians" (5)—the ascendance of the past in journalism enhances the possibility for journalists to act as amateur historians and sleuths of the past—in events as wide-ranging as the Kennedy assassination (Zelizer, *"Covering the Body"*), Watergate (Schudson, *Watergate*), and recollections of Richard Nixon (Johnson)—in a way that accommodates the ever-changing nature of the past and its variations across the technologies of modern media. This means that collective memory, rather than history, is a useful frame through which to consider journalism.

2. Characteristics of the Journalism-Memory Link

The specific relationship that draws journalism and memory into close quarters has numerous characteristics that derive from the fundamental fact that much of journalism is crafted beyond the reach and scrutiny of others. This means that when journalists resist conceding their grip on public events, there is little to offset their efforts. Practices like rewrites, revisits to old events, commemorative or anniversary journalism, and even investigations of seemingly "historical" events and happenings are regular occurrences in the daily register of newsmaking (Zelizer, "News"; Edy).

One of the first scholarly endeavors to look at memory and the news was Lang and Lang's 1989 consideration of how the public opinion process is shaped by past events, and it was indicative of a key entry point for thinking about journalism and memory—through the audience and journalism's impact on the public's perception of the past (e.g., Volkmer). As memory continued to draw attention as a prism through which to consider journalism, however, more scholars began to approach journalistic work itself as a topic relevant to memory alongside its role in audience perception and response.

This has not always been a visible characteristic of work on journalism and memory. For instance, many scholars have tended to address the link between them by eclipsing the journalistic project within broader discussions of media, at times providing wide-ranging considerations of a past covered by journalism as one of numerous memory agents. Edgerton and Rollins discussed the various treatments of the past provided by television in general, while Doherty tracked the role of visuals in shaping the Army-McCarthy Hearings of the 1950s. While a substantial body of literature has emerged, then, not all of it has been identifiable for its consideration of the linkage between journalism and memory. This has in effect understated the particular role that journalism plays in helping us track the past.

What does journalism bring to an understanding of memory work that differs from that of other memory agents? Much existing literature has followed two intertwined strands—thinking about the form and content of memory—in conjunction with journalism.

3. Invoking Memory Through Form and Content

The particular rules and conventions of remembrance that characterize journalism make it well-suited to invoking memory in certain ways but limited in others. Many scholars have focused on journalistic work as a kind of recounting that strategically weaves past and present by upholding journalism's reverence for truth and reality (Schudson, *Watergate*; Zelizer, *"Covering the Body"*; Huxford), all the while drawing on the singular characteristics of memory work—its processual nature, unpredictability, partiality, usability, simultaneous particularity and universality, and materiality (Zelizer, "Reading the Past"). This twinning is seen as producing a tension in the kind of memory work journalism can produce, which has not always been the most effective tool for reconsidering the past. A gravitation toward simplistic narratives, recounting without context, and a minimization of nuance and the grey areas of a phenomenon all make journalistic accounting a somewhat restricted approach to the past. Against this tension, journalists' mnemonic work tends to be driven through variations on the relationship between journalism's content and its form, which forces different kinds of engagement with the past. As Wagner-Pacifici notes, "there is no natural dialogue between content and form. Everything waits to be decided" (302). How decisions take shape depend on a wide array of factors that are central to newsmaking.

4. When Memory Draws From Content

In that journalism's charter is to explain events in the public sphere, drawing from memory and the past offers an obvious source through which to understand topical events. Meyers, for instance, showed how the news treatments of Israel's national celebrations were shaped by references to earlier celebrations. Kitch (*Pages from the Past*) tracked how U.S. magazines recycled celebrity stories and stories of a certain kind of nation-state as the predictable repository of content across time. Wardle considered stories of child murder against the historical contingencies that forced a similar story into differential shapes across time periods.

News topics often are given a look backward simply because attending to the topic forces an engagement with the past. Obituaries, for instance, are modes of engaging with the past as a way of coming to grips with its finality. Events involving death often themselves make good news stories, and journalists often look to memory when the public needs help in recovering from the trauma surrounding death. The U.S. response to September 11, for instance, was crafted in conjunction with the news media's capacity to move the story of grief toward one of recovery (Kitch, "Mourning in America").

Journalism's institutional memory is nurtured by the tensions surrounding the critical incidents of the public sphere, and so the presence of contestation and debate is often a reliable predictor that memory work will at some point begin. This suggests that when the event itself is contested, as is often the case with the news of war, crime, terror, and natural disaster, journalists look to the stories of memory as a way to guide its retelling.

5. When Memory Draws From Form

At times it is the available form of memory rather than the news story that makes engagement with the past attractive. Certain forms of journalism's look to the past suggest some attendance to memory though they do not insist on its presence. This includes forms that use the past as a way to understand journalism's topicality. Using history or events of the past as a way to understand the present is basic to the scholarly projects associated with collective memory, but it is built in pragmatic ways into journalism as well. The past offers a point of comparison, an opportunity for analogy, an invitation to nostalgia, a redress to earlier events.

Most often, engagement with the past takes the shape of historical analogies, as in *Time*'s labeling of its coverage of the Iraq War as "Gulf War II" (Zelizer, "When War") or in discussions of the Columbia Shuttle disaster as a repeat of the Challenger explosion (Edy and Daradanova). Predictably, the past is at times remembered erroneously. One discussion of the U.S. coverage of the Vietnam and first Gulf Wars showed how the news media labeled war protestors as "anti-troop" not during the Vietnam War but during the first Gulf War, as a way of strategically misremembering war dissidence so as to better fit journalistic discussions of the later conflict (Beamish, Molotch and Flacks).

Scholars have invested efforts in tracking the coverage of particular news events and the historical analogies from which they draw. Zelizer discussed how historical references were used by journalists to recount the present-past relationship in visual terms, showing how atrocities in Bosnia and Rwanda (1998) and the war in Iraq (2004) were illustrated through images of earlier events.

6. When Form Necessitates Memory

At times, journalism is driven by those journalistic forms which exist by virtue of the ease with which they can produce memories. Themselves dependent on periodic reinstatement (Schwartz), these include various kinds of commemorative discourse, retrospective issues, and other modes of anniversary journalism. Edy, for instance, suggested that journalists connect with the past in three main ways—commemoration, historical analogies, and historical contexts. In each case, the argument can be made that the journalistic project would not exist were it not for some kind of a priori engagement with the past.

Journalism tends to produce mnemonic work through those news organizations with the most extensive archives, and in this regard certain kinds of news institutions, organizations, and individuals are better attuned than others to be producing memory work. For instance, Kitch ("'Useful Memory'") showed how Time Inc. became a predictable repository for crafting memories of the past by virtue of its extensive and accessible data retrieval system. Even individual journalists who tend to address the past are those who were themselves involved in the past being addressed: Dan Rather has been at the helm of mnemonic addresses to the Kennedy assassination, which he covered as a cub reporter (Zelizer, *"Covering the Body"*); the story of Watergate has been recounted over the years through the celebrated persona of Woodward and Bernstein (Schudson, *Watergate*).

This work can be grouped by two categories. On the one hand are the special projects produced by news organizations that strategically address the past and are produced for that aim. They include both the publication and broadcast of retrospective issues, programs, special broadcasts, books, and volumes that track a general past—as in the state of a particular news organization, particular news medium or journalism writ broadly over time—and those that follow a specific past, as in the coverage of a particular news event or social issue over time. On the other hand, journalists make extensive effort to track the past by explicitly and strategically following journalism's own earlier projects. Grainge offered a thoughtful analysis of *Time*'s various attempts to track the hundred most influential people of the twentieth century. He found, not surprisingly, that the 100 list read as a "particular kind of memory text, a figuration of collective cultural inheritance" which *Time* sought to promulgate as a "memory of democratic and capitalistic achievement" (204). Zelizer ("Journalists") found that journalists do a kind of "double-time" on the events that they report, allowing them to correct in later coverage what they missed earlier: Thus, they adapted earlier reportage of both McCarthyism and Watergate into stories that better fit their evolving understandings of the events.

The scholarship that attends to these explicit forms of mnemonic engagement suggests that attending to the past is an integral part of journalism. In essence, it provides a "time-out" in the flow of news (Zelizer, "Collective Memory"), by which both journalists and the organizations that employ them are able to predict and control the erratic quality of news flow. In this regard, they echo the more general role of collective memory in lending coherence, however temporary, to ever-present contestations over the past.

7. On Journalism and Memory

By drawing from content, drawing from form, and accommodating forms that necessitate an address to the past, journalism's memory work is both widespread and multi-faceted. Recounting the present is laced with an intricate repertoire of practices that involve an often obscured engagement with the past. This renders journalism a key agent of memory work, even if journalists themselves are adverse to admitting it as part of what they do.

What all of this suggests is that we are far from knowing what journalism can tell us more broadly about how memory takes shape. As journalism continues to function as one of contemporary society's main institutions of recording and remembering, we need to invest more efforts in understanding how it remembers and why it remembers in the ways that it does.

Acknowledgement

Thanks to Dan Berger for assistance with this manuscript. An earlier version of this manuscript appeared in Vita Fortunati and Elena Agazzi, eds., *Ricordare: Percorsi transdisciplinari attraverso la memoria*. Rome: Meltemi, 2006.

References

Beamish, Thomas D., Harvey Molotch, and Richard Flacks. "Who Supports the Troops? Vietnam, the Gulf War, and the Making of Collective Memory." *Social Problems* 42.3 (1995): 344-60.

Carey, James. "The Dark Continent of American Journalism." *Reading the News*. Eds. Robert Manoff and Michael Schudson. New York: Pantheon, 1986. 146-96.

Doherty, Thomas. *Cold War, Cool Medium: Television, McCarthyism and American Culture*. New York: Columbia UP, 2003.

Edgerton, Gary R., and Peter C. Rollins. *Television Histories: Shaping Collective Memory in the Media Age*. Lexington: UP of Kentucky, 2001.

Edy, Jill A. "Journalistic Uses of Collective Memory." *Journal of Communication* 49.2 (1999): 71-85.

Edy, Jill A., and Miglena Daradanova. "Reporting the Present Through the Lens of the Past: From Challenger to Columbia." *Journalism: Theory, Practice and Criticism* 7.2 (2006): 131-51.

Grainge, Paul. "Remembering the 'American Century': Media Memory and the *Time* 100 List." *International Journal of Cultural Studies* 5.2 (2002): 201-19.

Huxford, John. "Beyond the Referential: Uses of Visual Symbolism in the Press." *Journalism: Theory, Practice and Criticism* 2.1 (2001): 45-72.

Johnson, Thomas J. *The Rehabilitation of Richard Nixon: The Media's Effect on Collective Memory*. New York: Garland, 1995.

Kitch, Carolyn. "Mourning in America: Ritual, Redemption, and Recovery in News Narrative after September 11." *Journalism Studies* 4.2 (2003): 213-24.

—. *Pages From the Past: History and Memory in American Magazines*. Chapel Hill: U of North Carolina P, 2005.

—. "'Useful Memory' in Time Inc Magazines." *Journalism Studies* 7.1 (2006): 94-110.

Lang, Kurt, and Gladys Engel Lang. "Collective Memory and the News." *Communication* 11 (1989): 123-39.

Meyers, Oren. "Still Photographs, Dynamic Memories: An Analysis of the Visual Presentation of Israel's History in Commemorative Newspaper Supplements." *Communication Review* 5.3 (2002): 179-205.

Schudson, Michael. "Dynamics of Distortion in Collective Memory." *Memory Distortion: How Minds, Brains and Societies Reconstruct the Past.* Ed. Daniel Schacter. Cambridge: Harvard UP, 1995. 346-64.

—. *Watergate in American Memory: How We Remember, Forget and Reconstruct the Past.* New York: Basic, 1992.

Schwartz, Barry. "The Social Context of Commemoration: A Study in Collective Memory." *Social Forces* 61.2 (1982): 374-402.

Susman, Warren. *Culture as History.* New York: Pantheon, 1984.

Volkmer, Ingrid, ed. *News in Public Memory.* New York: Lang, 2006.

Wagner-Pacifici, Robin. "Memories in the Making: The Shape of Things That Went." *Qualitative Sociology* 19.3 (1996): 301-20.

Wardle, Claire. "Monsters and Angels: Visual Press Coverage of Child Murders in the US and UK, 1930-1990." *Journalism: Theory, Practice and Criticism* 8.3 (2007): 263-84.

Zelizer, Barbie. "Collective Memory as 'Time-Out': Repairing the Time-Community Link." *Communication and Community.* Eds. Gregory J. Shepherd and Eric W. Rothenbuhler. Mahwah, NJ: Erlbaum, 2001. 181-89.

—. *"Covering the Body": The Kennedy Assassination, the Media and the Shaping of Collective Memory.* Chicago: U of Chicago P, 1992.

—. "Journalists as Interpretive Communities." *Critical Studies in Mass Communication* 10 (1993): 219-37.

—. "News: First or Final Draft of History?" *Mosaic* 2 (1993): 2-3.

—. "Reading the Past Against the Grain: The Shape of Memory Studies." *Critical Studies in Mass Communication* 12.2 (1995): 215-39.

—. *Remembering To Forget: Holocaust Memory Through the Camera's Eye.* Chicago: U of Chicago P, 1998.

—. "When War is Reduced to a Photograph." *Reporting War: Journalism in Wartime.* Eds. Stuart Allan and Barbie Zelizer. London: Routledge, 2004. 115-35.

Literature, Film, and the Mediality of Cultural Memory

ASTRID ERLL

1. The Power of Fiction: Novels and Films as Media of Cultural Memory

Cultural memory is based on communication through media. Shared versions of the past are invariably generated by means of "medial externalization" (see A. Assmann, this volume), the most basic form of which is oral speech, and the most common setting arguably that of grandparents telling children about the "old days." More sophisticated media technologies, such as writing, film, and the Internet, broaden the temporal and spatial range of remembrance. Cultural memory is constituted by a host of different media, operating within various symbolic systems: religious texts, historical painting, historiography, TV documentaries, monuments, and commemorative rituals, for example. Each of these media has its specific way of remembering and will leave its trace on the memory it creates. What kinds of cultural memory, then, are produced by literature and film?

Fictional media, such as novels and feature films, are characterized by their power to shape the collective imagination of the past in a way that is truly fascinating for the literary scholar (and somewhat alarming for the historian). Two of the best-known examples are Erich Maria Remarque's *Im Westen nichts Neues* (1929; *All Quiet on the Western Front*) and Margaret Mitchell's *Gone with the Wind* (1936). Both were initially tremendously popular novels, with astronomic circulation figures, and both were turned into even more successful movies. The First World War and the American South—for many people even today these are "All Quiet on the Western Front" and "Gone with the Wind." Fictions, both novelistic and filmic, possess the potential to generate and mold images of the past which will be retained by whole generations. Historical accuracy is not one of the concerns of such "memory-making" novels and movies; instead, they cater to the public with what is variously termed "authenticity" or "truthfulness." They create images of the past which resonate with cultural memory. Usually, such fictions can neither be called "valuable literature," nor do they enter the canon of artistic masterpieces (see A. Assmann; Grabes; both this volume). And often, too, they will disappear as quickly as they appeared on the scene.

With a view to cultural memory studies, these observations call for two methodological moves or shifts in attention: firstly, from high culture to popular culture; and secondly, from the time-bound media of storage, which allow cultural memories to travel across centuries and even become themselves objects of remembrance (Shakespeare's historical plays would be an example), to the space-bound media of circulation, which can reach large audiences almost simultaneously, make cultural memories today and are forgotten tomorrow (cf. Innis).

The key question I am asking here is: What is it that turns *some* media (and not *others*) into powerful "media of cultural memory," meaning media which create and mold collective images of the past? Using examples mainly from war literature and war cinema, this article will provide three answers in three steps: I will look firstly at their *intra*-medial "rhetoric of collective memory"; secondly at their *inter*-medial dynamics, that is, the interplay with earlier and later representations; and thirdly at the *pluri*-medial contexts in which memory-making novels and films appear and exert their influence. In short, I am concerned here with phenomena *within*, *between*, and *around* those media which have the power to produce and shape cultural memory.

2. The Rhetoric of Collective Memory: How War Novels Create Modes of Remembering

Whenever the past is represented, the choice of media and forms has an effect on the kind of memory that is created: For example, a war which is orally represented, in an anecdote told by an old neighbor, seems to become part of lived, contemporary history; but as an object of a Wagnerian opera, the same war can be transformed into an apparently timeless, mythical event. In literature as in film, there are different modes of representation which may elicit different modes of cultural remembering in the audience.

With regard to novels of the First World War, I have distinguished four modes of a "rhetoric of collective memory": the experiential, the mythical, the antagonistic, and the reflexive mode (*Gedächtnisromane*). Experiential modes are constituted by literary forms which represent the past as a recent, lived-through experience. They are closely connected to what is called "communicative memory" (see J. Assmann, this volume). The specific qualities of communicative memory are often staged in literary texts by first-person narrative, thus indicating "life writing" (see Saunders, this volume). Siegfried Sassoon's and Robert Graves's fictions of the Great War make use of this strategy. Another typical form to represent war, used especially by modernist writers (such as Ford Madox Ford and Virginia Woolf), are stream-of-consciousness techniques, which convey the specific inner experientiality of the trenches, combat, and trauma. And finally, a very detailed depiction of everyday life in the war and the representation of oral speech—especially sociolect, such as soldiers' slang—may serve to create what may be termed (with a nod to Roland Barthes) authenticating *effets de mémoire.* This strategy can be studied in Frederic Manning's war novel *The Middle Parts of Fortune* (1929).

Mythicizing modes are constituted by literary forms that resemble representations of the past within the framework of Jan Assmann's "cultural memory," that is, the remembrance of foundational events which are situated in a faraway, mythical past. Typical of this tendency is Ernst Jünger's novel *In Stahlgewittern* (1920; *The Storm of Steel*), in which German soldiers are transformed into figures of Germanic mythology. But also Francis Ford Coppola's highly acclaimed Vietnam War movie *Apocalypse Now* (1979) mythicizes the historical events by means of intertextual references and the creation of a primordial atmosphere, using an array of visual and sound effects.

Literary forms that help to maintain one version of the past and reject another constitute an antagonistic mode. Negative stereotyping (such as calling the Germans "the Hun" or "beasts" in early English poetry of the Great War) is the most obvious technique of establishing an antagonistic mode. More elaborate is the resort to biased perspective structures: Only the memories of a certain group are presented as true, while the versions articulated by members of conflicting memory cultures are deconstructed as false. Authors of the "lost generation," Ernest Hemingway and Richard Aldington for example, make ample use of these strategies. Resorting to we-narration may underscore the antagonistic potential of a novel. This is actually one of the most striking narrative features in Remarque's requiem on the lost generation, *All Quiet on the Western Front.* Here, we-narration creates a collective identity for a generation of young front-line soldiers, who are set apart from the old, war-mongering generation at home.

Literature usually allows its readers both a first- and a second-order observation: It gives us the illusion of glimpsing the past (in an experiential, mythical, or antagonistic way) and is—often at the same time—a major medium of critical reflection upon these very processes of representation. Literature is a medium that simultaneously builds and observes memory. Prominent reflexive modes are constituted by forms which draw attention to processes and problems of remembering. One of these forms is the explicit narratorial comment on the workings of memory, found, for example, in Marcel Proust's famous novel of memory, *A la recherche du temps perdu* (1913-27). Other strategies include the montage of different versions of the past, which can be studied in Edlef Koeppen's *Heeresbericht* (1930), the best German novel to have come out of the First World War.

Even more experimental forms appear in the literature of the Second World War, such as Kurt Vonnegut's inversion of chronology in *Slaughterhouse-Five* (1969) as a way to represent the bombardment of Dresden.

These different modes of representing the past—here zooming in to everyday experience, there zooming out to timeless myth; here taking part in contestation, there staying aloof and adopting a reflexive stance—are not restricted to war novels, or even to historical fiction. A rhetoric of collective memory can be found in all literary genres which represent the past, from romance to gothic novels and to crime thrillers, and of course also in other media such as feature films. Conversely, modes of remembering need not necessarily be established by verbal, literary, and narrative forms. Non-fictional media such as historiography and journalism (see Zelizer, this volume) and visual media such as painting and photography (see Ruchatz, this volume) have developed their own "rhetorics of collective memory."

3. Premediation and Remediation: The Inter-Medial Dynamics of Memory

Not only *intra*-medial strategies, such as the rhetoric of collective memory, but also *inter*-medial relations are involved in the process that turns fictions into media of cultural memory. The inter-medial dynamics of cultural memory is usually characterized by a double movement, by the interaction of what can be called "premediation" and "remediation" (cf. Bolter and Grusin; Hoskins; Erll, *Prämediation*; Rigney, this volume). With the term "remediation" I refer to the fact that memorable events are usually represented again and again, over decades and centuries, in different media: in newspaper articles, photography, diaries, historiography, novels, films, etc. What is known about a war, a revolution, or any other event which has been turned into a site of memory, therefore, seems to refer not so much to what one might cautiously call the "actual events," but instead to a canon of existent medial constructions, to the narratives and images circulating in a media culture. Remembered events are transmedial phenomena, that is, their representation is not tied to one specific medium. Therefore, they can be represented across the spectrum of available media. And this is precisely what creates a powerful site of memory (cf. Rigney).

The term "premediation" draws attention to the fact that existent media which circulate in a given society provide schemata for future experience and its representation. In this way, the representations of colonial wars premediated the First World War, and the First World War, in turn, was used as a model for the Second World War. But not only depictions of earlier, yet somehow comparable events shape our understanding of later events. Media which belong to even more remote cultural spheres, such as art, mythology, religion, or law, can exert great power as premediators, too. John Bunyan's *The Pilgrim's Progress* (1678), with its "Valley of the Shadow and Death" episode, premediated many journals and letters written during the First World War, as Paul Fussell has shown. (At the same time it was itself a remediation of Biblical accounts.) The American understanding and representation of 9/11 was clearly premediated by disaster movies, the crusader narrative, and Biblical stories. Premediation therefore refers to cultural practices of looking, naming, and narrating. It is the effect of *and* the starting point for mediatized memories.

With regard to the "Indian Mutiny" of 1857 (an uprising in colonial India against British rule) I have shown how witnesses' letters, newspaper articles, and drawings made on the spot were remediated in historiography, novels, and painting, thus endowing these later media with the atmosphere of experientiality and authenticity usually associated with contemporary media. At the same time, these representations were heavily premediated by earlier colonial accounts of violent encounters with rebellious subjects, by pictorial conventions derived from Renaissance painting, and by a long tradition of religious and literary writing (Erll, *Prämediation*).

Paradoxically, even despite antagonistic and reflexive forms of representation, remediation tends to solidify cultural memory, creating and stabilizing certain narratives and icons of the past. Such stabilizing effects of remediation can be observed in the emergence of "9/11" as an American, and indeed transnational, *lieu de mémoire* (see Hebel, this volume). The burning twin towers quickly crystallized into the one iconic image of the event, and this icon has been remediated ever since: in television news, photography, movies, comic strips, etc. But such iconization is not restricted to visual media. Another example connected with 9/11 is the icon of the "falling man," which remembers those people who were trapped by the fire on the upper floors of the World Trade Center and decided to jump rather than die in the flames. The "falling man" was first represented by a photograph taken by Richard Drew. In September 2003, this photograph was remediated in a story written by Tom Junod and published in *Esquire* magazine. In March 2006, Henry Singer and Richard Numeroff turned the "falling man" into a documentary (*9/11: The Falling Man*). And in 2007, Don DeLillo's novel *Falling Man* appeared on the literary market. These are only a few examples of its remediation, which feature text and image as well as very different stories and meanings, but at the same time all contribute to the stabilization of the "falling man" as an icon of "9/11."

Remediation is not restricted to icons and narratives, but can even choose actual media products and media technologies as its objects. It is especially in the cinema of cultural memory that we find such manifest forms of remediation. Actual, historical documentary material is incorporated in new movies, and this integration of photographic and filmic media serves to create an *effet de réel*: The fictional story seems indexically linked to the historical events it depicts (see also Ruchatz, this volume). However, the boundaries between documentary material and fictional reenactment (cf. Sturken) are often blurred in the course of remediation. One example is the famous Iwo Jima photograph, which was taken by Joe Rosenthal on February 23, 1945. It shows a group of U.S. marines raising the American flag on a Japanese island south of Tokyo. When it appeared in the *New York Times* shortly thereafter, it brought hope to the war-tired Americans. Still today, this photograph stands in U.S. memory for American heroism and the victory that is about to be won. Since its publication, the press photograph has been remediated countless times: by a memorial, several statues, books, songs, rituals, postal stamps, and other photographs. And it has been integrated (sometimes by filming the photograph itself, sometimes by reenactment) into a great number of popular war movies, among them *Sands of Iwo Jima* (1949, with John Wayne). The most recent variation of its cinematic remediation is Clint Eastwood's movie *Flags of Our Fathers* (2006), in which Hollywood movie stars reenact the raising of the flag. A film still of this reenactment which resembles precisely the original photograph (except that it is in color) appears as the cinema poster. It is probably only a question of time until the still of Eastwood's reenactment will appear somewhere as authentic "source material" and be itself remediated, in order to make another representation appear authentic.

Flags of Our Fathers is also an example of how specific media technologies can be remediated: The intentionally bleached-out colors remind the audience of the monochrome news coverage during the Second World War and of course also of Rosenthal's original black-and-white photograph. What is often integrated via remediation into film versions of the past is therefore not merely actual documentary material, but also its specific "look" (which usually derives from the media technology of the time, but also from historical aesthetics). Parts of the Vietnam War movie *Platoon* (1986), for example, imitate the shaky camera movement characteristic of war journalism at the front and thus the look of news coverage in the 1960s and 1970s. Another example is *Saving Private Ryan* (1998), a movie about the Second World War, for which key episodes were shot in the grainy style of 16mm color film, thus emulating the cinematography of 1940s documentaries (cf. Westwell 78, 92).

It is the double dynamics of the premediation of remediation, of the medial preformation and re-shaping of events, which links each representation of the past with the history of media memories. First and foremost, these processes make the past intelligible; at the same time, they endow medial representations with the aura of authenticity; and, finally, they play a decisive role in stabilizing the memory of historical events into *lieux de mémoire*.

4. Film and Cultural Memory: Pluri-Medial Networks

Asking once again what it is that turns some novels and movies into powerful memory-making fictions, a preliminary answer can now be given: Certain intra- and inter-medial strategies (as considered in sections 2 and 3 of this article) are responsible for marking them out as media of cultural memory. However, such strategies endow fictions only with a *potential* for memory-making. This potential has to be *realized* in the process of reception: Novels and movies must be read and viewed by a community *as* media of cultural memory. Films that are not watched or books that are not read may provide the most intriguing images of the past, yet they will not have any effect in memory cultures. The specific form of reception which turns fictions into memory-making fictions is not an individual, but a collective phenomenon. What is needed is a certain kind of *context*, in which novels and films are prepared and received as memory-shaping media.

Taking as an example contemporary filmmaking, such contexts have been reconstructed in detail by an interdisciplinary group of researchers at the University of Giessen (cf. Erll and Wodianka). We took a close look at some popular German history movies, such as *Der Untergang* (2004, *The Downfall*), a film about the last days of Adolf Hitler, and *Das Leben der Anderen* (2006, *The Lives of Others*), a film about life in the German Democratic Republic. There is actually a current boom of history films, a filmic memory conjuncture, which can be observed especially in—but is certainly not restricted to—Germany. Movies, TV serials, fictional, documentary, and semi-documentary formats have, in the course of the past fifteen years, virtually become obsessed with the representation of contemporary history: Films about the "Third Reich," the Holocaust, the Second World War and its aftermath abound. Judging from its prevalence and impact, "film" seems to have become the leading medium of popular cultural memory.

Scrutinizing the cultural practices surrounding history movies we determined that it is not in the first place the medial and inter-medial strategies that turn a "film about history" into a "memory-making film," but instead what has been established around them: A tight network of other medial representations (and medially represented actions) prepare the ground for the movies, lead reception along certain paths, open up and channel public discussion, and thus endow films with their memorial meaning. With regard to the two examples mentioned above, we followed reviews in national and international newspapers and movie magazines, special features on TV, carefully targeted marketing strategies, merchandise, the DVD versions (including the "making of" segments, interviews with producers and actors, historical background information, etc.), awards (*The Lives of Others* received an Academy Award in 2007), political speeches, academic controversies (especially among historians with regard to *The Downfall*, on the question of the ethics of representing Hitler as a movie protagonist and thus humanizing him), the publication of a book about or a book based on the film (and its censorship, as in the case of *The Lives of Others*), and finally all those didactic formats which have turned both movies into teaching units in German classrooms.

All those advertisements, comments, discussions, and controversies constitute the collective contexts which channel a movie's reception and potentially turn it into a medium of cultural memory. Moreover, all these expressions are circulated by means of media. Therefore we call these contexts "*pluri*-medial networks." To sum up: While the potential of fictions to be turned into media of cultural memory is developed by certain strategies on intra-medial and inter-medial levels, those potentialities can only be turned into actualities within pluri-medial contexts. The "memory-making film" as well as the "memory-making novel" are made *in* and *by* the media networks surrounding them.

5. Conclusion

Literature and film can have effects on both levels of cultural memory: the individual *and* the collective (see for this distinction the introduction of this volume). On a collective level, fictional texts and movies can become powerful media, whose versions of the past circulate in large parts of society, and even internationally. These media of cultural memory, however, are rarely uncontroversial. Their memory-making effect lies not in the unity, coherence, and ideological unambiguousness of the images they convey, but instead in the fact that they serve as cues for the discussion of those images, thus centering a memory culture on certain medial representations and sets of questions connected with them. With a view to these complex collective processes an intensified dialogue between representatives from literary and media studies and historians and sociologists promises to provide further insights into how the circulation of media, their reception, critical discussion, institutionalization, and canonization works.

On an individual level, media representations provide those schemata and scripts which allow us to create in our minds certain images of the past and which may even shape our own experience and autobiographical memories (see the articles by Markowitsch and Welzer, this volume). The "cultural mind" is in many ways a "medial mind": It is the patterns derived from the media cultures we live in, especially (albeit often unintentionally) from fictions, that shape our idea of reality and our memories. This insight calls for interdisciplinary collaboration between what may seem to be disciplines situated farthest apart on the spectrum of memory studies: literary and media studies on the one hand and psychology and the neurosciences on the other.

References

Assmann, Aleida. *Erinnerungsräume: Formen und Wandlungen des kulturellen Gedächtnisses.* Munich: Beck, 1999.

Assmann, Jan. *Das kulturelle Gedächtnis: Schrift, Erinnerung und politische Identität in frühen Hochkulturen.* Munich: Beck, 1992.

Bolter, Jay David, and Richard Grusin, eds. *Remediation: Understanding New Media.* Cambridge: MIT Press, 1999.

Cook, Pam. *Screening the Past: Memory and Nostalgia in Cinema.* London: Routledge, 2005.

Erll, Astrid. *Gedächtnisromane: Literatur über den Ersten Weltkrieg als Medium englischer und deutscher Erinnerungskulturen in den 1920er Jahren.* Trier: WVT, 2003.

—. *Prämediation—Remediation: Repräsentationen des indischen Aufstands in imperialen und post-kolonialen Medienkulturen (von 1857 bis zur Gegenwart).* Trier: WVT, 2007.

Erll, Astrid, and Ann Rigney, eds. *Mediation, Remediation, and the Dynamics of Cultural Memory.* Berlin: de Gruyter, 2008 (in press).

Erll, Astrid, and Stephanie Wodianka, eds. *Plurimediale Konstellationen: Film und kulturelle Erinnerung.* Berlin: de Gruyter, 2008 (in press).

Fussell, Paul. *The Great War and Modern Memory.* Oxford: Oxford UP, 1975.

Hoskins, Andrew. *Televising War: From Vietnam to Iraq.* London: Continuum, 2004.

Innis, Harold A. *The Bias of Communication.* Toronto: U of Toronto P, 1951.

Rigney, Ann. "Plenitude, Scarcity and the Circulation of Cultural Memory." *Journal of European Studies* 35.1-2 (2005): 209-26.

Sturken, Marita. *Tangled Memories: The Vietnam War, the AIDS Epidemic, and the Politics of Remembering.* Berkeley: U of California P, 1997.

Westwell, Guy. *War Cinema: Hollywood on the Front Line.* London: Wallflower, 2006.

Memory and Media Cultures

MARTIN ZIEROLD

The relevance of the media for individual and social forms of memory is widely acknowledged by representatives of memory studies. A relatively recent perspective, which analyzes the connection between memory and current media cultures, is based on this close relationship between the media and processes of remembrance, but it emphasizes topics that have been largely neglected thus far in the discourse. The starting point is a specific interest in the theoretical and empirical description and analysis of social memory under the conditions of *present-day* media cultures.

This perspective is a relatively young and rather amorphous field of research, which at present can neither be described by an established label nor is it based on a homogenous canon of basic texts, concepts, or models. Nevertheless, there is a growing tendency in the field of cultural memory studies to attempt to find new ways of integrating the analysis of *contemporary* media developments into the study of social memory.

Previous analyses of the connection between media and social memory often focused on media history rather than on media theory or contemporary developments. For example, a number of comprehensive and detailed analyses dealt with the different forms of social memory in oral and early written cultures. The current media-cultural conditions concerning social memory, however, have been examined only briefly, fragmentarily, and often with a very pessimistic view: Some scholars fear that modern societies could even become oblivious to the presuppositions of their present and forget their past. The latest developments of the media, such as the boom of electronic media or digitalization, are often blamed for this alleged disappearance of memory.

More recent attempts to analyze current media systems and their influences on social memory are dissatisfied with such generalizations, which do not do justice to the complex and often paradoxical development of present-day media systems. Consequently, international scholars are trying to develop an advanced interdisciplinary theory and empiricism that can be counted as part of a media-cultural studies approach to memory studies. Among them are Astrid Erll, who has contributed a refined model of media for cultural memory studies (*Kollektives Gedächtnis* 130ff.), and Franziska Sick, who calls for a precise study of the systemic connection between media technologies and their application (44ff). The early criticism of memory studies by historians such as Kerwin Lee Klein (127ff.) and Alon Confino (1386ff.; see also his article in this volume) are important starting points for new approaches, as is empirical research on memory in journalism by scholars such as Michael Schudson and Barbie Zelizer (see her article in this volume). I have recently tried to contribute a first draft of an integrative theoretical concept from a media-cultural studies perspective, which combines theories from cultural studies and the social sciences. Obviously, a first step towards establishing a new perspective is a critical evaluation of previous research and a systematic analysis regarding its suitability for the description of current developments.

1. A Critical Review of Research So Far

The crisis of memory diagnosed by representatives of memory studies obviously depends on the posited concept of memory and its criteria. However, the sheer number of television documentaries about history, for example, could also lead to the opposite conclusion that memory in today's societies is booming. One of the main reasons for this paradox seems to be the lack of explicit terminology and the vagueness of the criteria as to what can be considered to be functional social memory and what is thought to be an alarming development. In the international, Anglo-American-dominated discourse, some aspects of memory studies have been radically criticized. The most important aspect so far is still the question whether memory studies' theories are adequately explicit. To sum up the criticism, very often the usage of the terms "memory" or "remembrance" under discussion seem to be vague or even arbitrary. Some memory studies scholars emphasize that they intentionally do not aim at the elaboration of a *theory* of cultural memory (cf., e.g., Assmann 16). The avoidance of an explicit theory seems to be a flexible and open attitude and has been productive to a certain extent, but with the increasing establishment of this field of research it has become highly problematic.

The American historian Kerwin Lee Klein was among the first to lament the indistinct, arbitrary usage of the word "memory" which finally renders the word inexplicable (129). The American historian Alon Confino fundamentally criticizes the debate even as he admits that memory studies has led to numerous seminal results. But he concludes that the usage of the term "memory" is inflationary and lacks a clear focus and a critical reflection of methods and theories (1387).

This basic criticism of the American discourse also applies to European research, although in comparison the terminology used by scholars such as Aleida and Jan Assmann seems to be relatively precise and elaborate (see their articles in this volume). Nevertheless, it is problematic that their distinction between different systems of memory such as "cultural memory" and "communicative memory" is described in detail, whereas basic terms such as "culture" or even "memory" and "remembrance" are simply taken for granted.

This lack of explicitness in previous models is especially evident where the question of the "location" of collective memory is concerned. Confino doubts the value of the use of the term "memory" in social contexts if employed independently of individual actors (1387). As long as it is not evident how the respective authors model "collective memory," there is a risk of interpreting it as an ontological entity instead of an academic construction. The Israeli historians Noa Gedi and Yigal Elam, for example, accuse Pierre Nora of representing just such an idea (34). Klein also points out how problematic it can be to almost mystically transfer individual psychological phenomena onto imaginary collectives (135).

But this criticism of memory studies' concepts is not only based on the common lack of explicitness but can also refer to the genesis of the theories and concepts. Here, the terminology of Aleida and Jan Assmann is a good example of a concept that has been developed mainly by studying pre-modern societies. However, it seems to be taken for granted that it is equally suitable for the comprehensive explanation of present societies. But if Jan Assmann's definition of "cultural memory" is taken seriously, recent memory processes in fact cannot be discussed as part of "cultural memory," as this is defined as referring to founding myths of an absolute past. The last 80 to 100 years and with them nearly all occasions of memory transmitted by electronic media cannot be analyzed with the terminology of cultural memory. But that does not necessarily mean an end of remembrance as such. Considering the acceleration processes of modern media, it merely becomes obvious that the coordinates of time for social processes of memory have shifted.

Thus, despite all its merits, it can be doubted if the Assmanns' model, with its specific genesis, is suitable for modern forms of society. This also applies to the increasing expansion of terminology which can be observed at present. An increasing tendency to introduce further terms into the discourse can be registered, terms which are rooted in but in some way expand on the first definition of communicative and cultural memory by Aleida and Jan Assmann. This expansion is oriented towards concepts from neurobiological and psychological memory research, but often lacks an adequate reflection of their implications. Where neuroscience can always claim that the location of memory is the brain (see Markowitsch, this volume), even in the most recent concepts memory studies often fails to explain its model for the location of memory in societies.

With the introduction of a further concept, that of the media, which, like the terms collective, cultural, and social memory, tends to be used vaguely and indistinctly, the problems become even more evident. The development of media history illustrates how the evolution of media revolutionizes a concept of memory which might have been plausible for oral communities. In early oral societies, the memory of individuals corresponds to a great extent with an abstract common memory, which is established and stabilized by mutual experiences and special celebrations and rites and is almost entirely known to every single member. Even in more advanced oral societies the socially relevant memory can also be considered to be attached to specialized professionals and their memory. However, with the development of writing the problem of the location of an alleged common memory becomes paramount, and the further differentiation of society and of the media at hand render any terminology obsolete that does not adequately explain and reflect its terms, which have been metaphorically transferred from psychology. Furthermore, Erll points out that in memory studies the term "the media" is often used arbitrarily, referring to very different levels—as instruments of communication but also as different genres—and that the functions attributed to them vary considerably ("Medium" 6ff.).

Finally, generalizations that claim that *one* media technology is responsible for the end of all memory are highly problematic: The demise of print does not mean the end of books and even less the end of writing or reading. An adequate analysis of the relationship between the media of a society and the conditions of social forms of memory can neither be achieved by generalizations nor by a minute analysis of individual media offers (*Medienangebote*), that is, the actual media products, such as a book, a film, or a newspaper article, which, according to Siegfried J. Schmidt, are an offer to communicate and provide media users with different opportunities for various levels of engagement. A more promising field of research would be an analysis of the connection between the media and memory in the context of a complex media system that includes writing and print, but also radio, television, and the Internet, and which is open to contrary and even paradoxical developments. I believe that the occasionally almost apocalyptical scenarios of the end of all remembrance in view of modern media technologies are to a high degree due to a normative and static concept of cultural memory. With a definitive notion of what social memory should be, one cannot explain why in modern societies remembrance may be improbable, but still occurs massively. Such concepts can only state a crisis where changes ought to be depicted. A more abstract, non-normative concept of memory which accepts that the forms of social memory change together with the development of the media broadens the horizons and brings into focus just those kinds of contrary and paradoxical developments we experience today.

2. An Alternative Perspective for Cultural Memory Studies

A more abstract understanding of social memory could be an alternative to some of the previous, rather problematic static models. Recently, I have tried to develop a concept based partly on work by Astrid Erll and Siegfried J. Schmidt (see their articles in this volume). It is the intention of this integrative perspective, which combines social sciences, media studies, and models from cultural studies, to be compatible with interdisciplinary research. It does not claim to offer a more "correct" concept than other models, but merely an alternative with a specific focus. The terminology developed in this concept is designed to offer a potential for analyzing modern societies without replacing other approaches. Basic thoughts of this alternative perspective are presented by Siegfried J. Schmidt's essay in this handbook (see also Schmidt, *Kalte Faszination*; Schmidt, *Geschichten & Diskurse*; Zierold 106ff.).

Here, I want to focus on the integrative concept of media as one basis for a new perspective that replaces isolated analyses with a survey of the comprehensive interdependence of the media systems of a society. Erll's suggestion of a new model of media for memory studies, which is based on Schmidt's theory, is an important foundation of such a systemic analysis.

Erll distinguishes between the material and social dimensions of media. By material dimensions she means semiotic instruments of communication (such as language, images, or sounds), media technologies (such as print, radio, television, or the World Wide Web), and finally media offers for remembrance (including specific newspaper articles, TV shows, and Internet sites). In the social dimension, at least two contexts have to be regarded separately: the production and distribution of a media offer and the reception and use of the media offer, which often takes place much later and under totally different historical conditions. Contrary to the systemic homogenous production and distribution, the reception and use of media offers cannot be understood as socially homogenous. Which offers are used for individually relevant processes of remembrance is decided within the differentiated social systems of society. The same media offer can be employed completely differently in divergent systemic contexts. It is important when regarding social contexts, however, to keep in mind that reception and use are always shaped by the specific options that the instruments of communication and media technologies open up or inhibit.

Such an integrative but also explicitly differentiated concept of "the media" seems to be especially appropriate for a discussion of the connection between the media and social forms of memory because it enables a complex analysis. With this concept, scholars can explicitly state which specific aspect of the relation of the media and memory they want to focus upon, and they are also forced to clarify which aspects are left out.

If this concept is taken seriously, a fragmentary analysis of a single aspect of the media is insufficient; instead, the relationships among various phenomena have to be observed and described. Consequently, the analysis of a certain media offer has to be considered against the background of the conditions of its production and distribution, and it has to be taken into account that various manners of reception and use in different social systems can follow. The instruments of communication and media technologies used for the production of media offers are decisive factors on every level. There is an ambivalent relationship between media technologies and their users in the production and in the reception/use of media offers, too: On the one hand, it makes no sense to conceive of media without users, but on the other hand, the complex connections between the different aspects of media show that the possible uses of media are not completely unlimited. In relation to processes of remembrance, the influences of media have to be regarded in a multi-faceted way. An investigation of the effects of media in the interplay of all available media technologies is also indispensable and especially relevant to an analysis of social forms of memory. Regarding media and remembrance it is interesting to consider which media from the wide spectrum of available technologies are used for socially relevant occasions for remembrance, which forms of elaborations of remembrance they allow, which are realized, how they are received and used, etc.

This differentiation of the concept of media shows that no single aspect of the integrative connection of a complex concept of media can be regarded independently of the others. The effects of technologies always depend on the specific applications in the production and use of media offers, which are always contingent and culturally variable. Regardless of the starting point of an analysis, with a differentiated concept of media the interdependence of the different dimensions must always be kept in mind, and even if a total analysis is not possible, it has to include as many relations as possible and should explicitly mark which questions are left unanswered.

These basic reflections also suggest that it is highly probable that new media technologies, which have been examined only rather negligently and indistinctly in the past, are likely to cause quite contrary developments. They allow new forms of processes of remembrance for the individual and an easy availability of media offers on the Internet. Still, the concern about the long-term availability of digital information is legitimate. It has to be considered, however, that this question largely depends on the use of technology and its further development. It is not only a matter of technology, but also of the cultural uses a society makes of its media systems. In the near future it will be decided whether commercial aspects of the use of media will have priority over cultural interests. Digital technologies enable an extensive distribution of media offers, but they also make possible a restrictive regulation of their use that was previously unknown. Today open source projects and Creative Commons licenses on the one hand and restrictive new copyright and digital rights management on the other hand leave all options open. It will depend on social decisions concerning these matters how in ten, twenty, or even a hundred years we will be able to use these currently new technologies for processes of remembrance. These developments are not pre-determined, which emphasizes the importance of a long-term social politics of remembrance that is not simply pessimistic, but acts on the basis of a differentiated analysis.

Issues concerning the policy of remembrance exist on all levels. Referring to technology it has to be decided how the regular transfer of information into new file formats and systems of storage can be guaranteed, and if the commercialization of the rights of computer languages, file standards, and of single bits of information or even of whole archives will be limited. On the level of production it is also important not to lament the end of all memory, but to analyze who is in a position to influence the politics of memory, that is, who selects historic subjects to be represented in the media and which strategies of staging these stories are used. The representation of the past in the media is an important factor that determines whose special occasions for remembrance and elaborations will be considered to be relevant and which (media) offers of remembrance have a chance to be socially accepted.

The users can only use those occasions of remembrance which are available in the media. In the course of the differentiation of occasions of remembrance inconsistent uses are to be expected. Social processes of remembrance are closely connected with the identity of social groups, which has to be regenerated and negotiated all the time, and therefore they can be interpreted as political instruments of power.

3. Future Topics for Research

The first thoughts depicted so far are simply a starting point for research concerning the connection between modern media and memory. It is crucial that the theoretical discussion be intensified in the future and that existing models be improved and further suggestions made. Considering the various contrary tendencies and the trend towards a pluralization of processes of remembrances in society, the connection between the media and memory cannot be described only in a theoretical manner but must also be observed in detail empirically. There is a demand for studies which substantiate the initial theoretical concepts empirically, which examine processes of remembrance under the conditions of modern media systems.

The renunciation of normative judgments in favor of a detailed non-normative and dynamic description of the changes of social processes of memory is only a first necessary step. However, such an observation, which is free of any value judgment, need not be the last. The present criticism concerning the current development of processes of remembrance may be too general, yet it is not totally unfounded. The increasing commercialization, for example, can indeed cause severe restrictions on our handling of the past and our politics of identity. Research should not refrain from criticism altogether. It is an important task for the future to develop a position which allows us to describe society in a critical yet sufficiently complex and differentiated way. The question of how societies deal with their past in the media system of the present will be an important aspect for the development of a reflected critical theory of media cultures.

References

Assmann, Aleida. *Erinnerungsräume: Formen und Wandlungen des kulturellen Gedächtnisses.* Munich: Beck, 1996.

Confino, Alon. "Collective Memory and Cultural History: Problems of Method." *The American Historical Review* 102.5 (1997): 1386-403.

Erll, Astrid. *Kollektives Gedächtnis und Erinnerungskulturen: Eine Einführung.* Stuttgart: Metzler, 2005.

—. "Medium des kollektiven Gedächtnisses—ein (erinnerungs-) kulturwissenschaftlicher Kompaktbegriff." *Medien des kollektiven Gedächtnisses: Konstruktivität—Historizität—Kulturspezifität.* Eds. Astrid Erll and Ansgar Nünning. Berlin: de Gruyter, 2004. 3-22.

Gedi, Noa, and Yigal Elam. "Collective Memory—What Is It?" *History & Memory* 8.1 (1996): 30-50.

Hejl, Peter M. "Wie Gesellschaften Erfahrungen machen oder: Was Gesellschaftstheorie zum Verständnis des Gedächtnisproblems beitragen kann." *Gedächtnis: Probleme und Perspektiven der interdisziplinären Gedächtnisforschung.* Ed. Siegfried J. Schmidt. Frankfurt am Main: Suhrkamp, 1991. 293-336.

Klein, Kerwin Lee. "On the Emergence of Memory in Historical Discourse." *Representations* 69 (2000): 127-50.

Reinhardt, Jan D., and Michael Jäckel. "Massenmedien als Gedächtnis- und Erinnerungs'generatoren'—Mythos und Realität einer 'Mediengesellschaft'." *Mythen der Mediengesellschaft/The Media Society and its Myths.* Eds. Patrick Rössler and Friedrich Krotz. Konstanz: UVK, 2005. 93-112.

Schmidt, Siegfried J. *Geschichten & Diskurse: Abschied vom Konstruktivismus.* Reinbek: Rowohlt, 2003.

—. *Kalte Faszination: Medien, Kultur, Wissenschaft in der Mediengesellschaft.* Weilerswist: Velbrück Wissenschaft, 2000.

Schudson, Michael. *Watergate in American Memory: How We Remember, Forget, and Reconstruct the Past.* New York: Basic, 1992.

Sick, Franziska. "Digitales Recht und digitales Gedächtnis." *Medium und Gedächtnis: Von der Überbietung der Grenzen.* Eds. Franziska Sick and Beate Ochsner. Frankfurt am Main: Lang, 2004. 43-69.

Thompson, John B. *The Media and Modernity: A Social Theory of the Media.* Cambridge: Polity, 2003.

Zelizer, Barbie. "Reading the Past Against the Grain: The Shape of Memory Studies." *Critical Studies in Mass Communication* 12 (1995): 214-39.

Zierold, Martin. *Gesellschaftliche Erinnerung: Eine medienkulturwissenschaftliche Perspektive.* Berlin: de Gruyter, 2006.

Index of Names

Index of Terms

Notes on Contributors

ALEIDA ASSMANN studied English literature and Egyptology at the universities of Heidelberg und Tübingen. Since 1993 she has been Professor of English Literature and Literary Theory at the University of Konstanz. Her research interests are the history of writing and reading, the media of cultural memory, and the development of collective memory in post-war Germany. Her publications include: *Zeit und Tradition* (1999); *Erinnerungsräume: Formen und Wandlungen des kulturellen Gedächtnisses* (3rd edition 2006); *Geschichtsvergessenenheit/Geschichtsversessenheit: Über den Umgang mit deutschen Vergangenheiten seit 1945* (with Ute Frevert, 1999); *Einführung in die Kulturwissenschaft: Grundbegriffe, Themen, Fragestellungen* (2006); *Der lange Schatten der Vergangenheit: Erinnerungskultur und Geschichtspolitik* (2006); *Geschichte im Gedächtnis: Von der individuellen Erfahrung zur öffentlichen Inszenierung* (2007).

JAN ASSMANN was Professor of Egyptology at the University of Heidelberg from 1976 to 2003 and is now Honorary Professor of Cultural and Religious Studies at the University of Konstanz. He has published on ancient Egyptian religion, literature, and history, but also in the areas of cultural theory (cultural memory), history of religion (monotheism and cosmotheism), literary theory, and historical anthropology. His books include: *Das kulturelle Gedächtnis: Schrift, Erinnerung und politische Identität in frühen Hochkulturen* (Beck, 1992); *Moses the Egyptian* (Harvard, 1997); *Ägypten: Eine Sinngeschichte* (Beck, 1996), translated as *The Mind of Egypt: History and Meaning in the Time of the Pharaohs* (Harvard, 2003); *The Search for God in Ancient Egypt* (Cornell, 2002); *Death and Salvation in Ancient Egypt* (Cornell, 2006); and *Of God and Gods: Egypt, Israel, and the Rise of Monotheism* (University of Wisconsin Press 2008, in press).

PIM DEN BOER is Professor of European Cultural History at the University of Amsterdam. He studied history at the University of Leiden and at the École des Hautes Études en Sciences Sociales in Paris. He has been a fellow at the Netherlands Institute for Advanced Study at Wassenaar (1994-1995) and a visiting fellow at the Remarque Institute for European History, New York University (2006). Among his publications are: *History as a Profession: The Study of History in France 1818-1914* (Princeton University Press, 1998); *Lieux de mémoire et identités nationales* (Amsterdam University Press, 1993); *Beschaving: Studies over de begrippen hoofsheid, heusheid, beschaving en cultuur* (Amsterdam University Press, 2001); *Simon Stevin: Het burgherlick leven; Vita Politica (1590)* (Bijleveld, 2001; French translation 2005; English translation in preparation); *Europa: De geschiedenis van een idee* (Prometheus, 5th revised edition 2007).

STEVEN D. BROWN is Professor of Organizational and Social Psychology at the University of Leicester, UK and Visiting Professor at the Universiteit voor Humanistiek, Netherlands. His research develops a social and critical psychological approach to collective remembering across a variety of empirical settings. He is co-author, with David Middleton, of *The Social Psychology of Experience: Studies in Remembering and Forgetting* (Sage, 2005) and, with Paul Stenner, of *Psychology without Foundations: Constructionism, Mediation and Critical Psychology* (Sage, 2008). Current projects include a study of memorial practices around the 2005 London Bombings and studies of memory, mediation, and identity in social networking technologies. He is currently an associate editor of the *British Journal of Social Psychology*.

ALON CONFINO is Professor of Modern German and European History and the Director of the Jewish Studies Program at the University of Virginia, USA. He has written extensively on memory, nationhood, and historical method. He is the author of *The Nation As a Local Metaphor: Württemberg, Imperial Germany, and National Memory, 1871-1918* (University of North Carolina Press, 1997), *Germany as a Culture of Remembrance: Promises and Limits of Writing History* (University of North Carolina Press, 2006), and the forthcoming *Foundational Pasts: An Essay on the Holocaust and Historical Understanding*. His essay "History and Memory" in *The Oxford History of Historical Writing* and co-edited book *Between Mass Death and Individual Loss: The Place of the Dead in Twentieth-Century Germany* are to appear soon.

GERALD ECHTERHOFF, Dr. habil., received his Ph.D. from the New School for Social Research, New York in 2000 and was a postdoctoral fellow at Columbia University in 2001. He was Assistant Professor in the Department of Psychology at the University of Bielefeld, Germany until 2008, and is currently Visiting Professor at the University of Cologne. His research interests include social influence on memory, social cognition, interpersonal communication, shared reality, language and thought, and the cultural and political contexts of remembering. He has authored articles in international high-impact journals such as *Journal of Experimental Psychology: General*, *Journal of Personality and Social Psychology*, *Memory & Cognition*, and *Social Cognition*, and is the editor of several volumes, including *Kontexte und Kulturen des Erinnerns* (with Martin Saar, 2002).

ASTRID ERLL is Professor of English Literature and Culture at the University of Wuppertal, Germany. Her main fields of interest are British literary and cultural history, cultural memory studies, postcolonial studies, media theory, and narratology. Her publications include: *Gedächtnisromane* (WVT, 2003); *Kollektives Gedächtnis und Erinnerungskulturen* (Metzler, 2005); and *Prämediation—Remediation*, a book on the medial representations of the "Indian Mutiny" (WVT, 2007). Together with Ansgar Nünning she is general editor of the series *Media and Cultural Memory/Medien und kulturelle Erinnerung* (MCM, de Gruyter, since 2004) and co-editor of *Medien des kollektiven Gedächtnisses* (MCM 1, 2004) and *Gedächtniskonzepte der Literaturwissenschaft* (MCM 2, 2005). Together with Ann Rigney she edited *Literature and the Production of Cultural Memory* (*European Journal of English Studies* 10.1 (2005)) and *Mediation, Remediation and the Dynamics of Cultural Memory* (MCM 10, 2008, in press).

ELENA ESPOSITO is Professor of Sociology at the University of Modena-Reggio Emilia, Italy. She has published several works on the theory of social systems, media theory, and sociology of memory, among them: *Soziales Vergessen: Formen und Medien des Gedächtnisses der Gesellschaft* (Suhrkamp, 2002); *Die Verbindlichkeit des Vorübergehenden: Paradoxien der Mode* (Suhrkamp, 2004); and *Die Fiktion der wahrscheinlichen Realität* (Suhrkamp, 2007).

VITA FORTUNATI is Professor of English Literature at the University of Bologna, Italy. Her main areas of research are modernism, utopian literature, women's studies, and cultural memory. Since 2006 she has been the coordinator of *ACUME 2: A European Thematic Network on Interfacing Sciences, Literature and Humanities*. She has published on verbal and visual representations of the body (*The Controversial Women's Body: Images and Representations in Literature and Art*, with Annamaria Lamarra and Eleonora Federici, Bologna University Press, 2003); female aging between culture and medicine; memory from a female perspective (*Studi di genere e memoria culturale/Women and Cultural Memory*, edited with Gilberta Golinelli and Rita Monticelli, Clueb, 2004); memory and trauma ("The Impact of the First World War on Private Lives: A Comparison of European and American Writers: Ford, Hemingway, and Remarque," in *History and Representation in Ford Madox Ford's Writings*, ed. Joseph Wiesenfarth, Rodopi, 2004); the notion of critical nostalgia ("Memory, Desire and Utopia: a New Perspective on the Notion of Critical Utopia," in *Time Refigured: Myths, Foundation Texts and Imagined Communities*, eds. Martin Procházka and Ondřej Pilný, Litteraria Pragensia, 2005). With Elena Agazzi, she has recently edited *Memoria e Saperi: Percorsi transdisciplinari*, Meltemi, 2007.

HERBERT GRABES is Professor of English at the University of Giessen, Germany. He has published widely on English and American literature and literary theory, including monographs on the history of the mirror metaphor, Nabokov's novels, theoretical conceptions of literature, the history of early English pamphleteering, and the history of American drama. He is co-editor of the yearbook *REAL* and currently working on the history of histories of English literature. The most recent of the many books he has edited are *Writing the Early Modern English Nation* (2001); *Innovation and Continuity in English Studies: A Critical Jubilee* (2001); *Literary History/Cultural History: Force-Fields and Tensions* (2001); *Literature, Literary History, and Cultural Memory* (2005); and *The Wider Scope of English* (with Wolfgang Viereck, 2006).

DIETRICH HARTH studied German literature, classics and sociology at the universities of Frankfurt am Main and Tübingen. After his *Habilitation* at the University of Erlangen he was appointed Professor of Modern German and Comparative Literature at the University of Heidelberg. He has also been invited to lecture on literary theory and history of ideas by various university departments in Italy, France, Spain, China, and England. His main research topics include the theory of literature, ritual studies, cultural anthropology, memory studies, and the history of European historiography. He is one of the founders of the publishing house Synchron Publishers Heidelberg (www.synchron-publishers.com) and of the Collaborative Research Center "Dynamics of Ritual" (www.ritualdynamik.uni-hd.de). Selected publications include: *Kultur und Konflikt* (co-editor, 1990); *Mnemosyne. Formen und Funktionen der kulturellen Erinnerung* (co-editor, 1991); *Kultur als Lebenswelt und Monument* (co-editor, 1991); *Die Erfindung des Gedächtnisses* (1991); *Revolution und Mythos* (co-editor, 1992); *Das Gedächtnis der Kulturwissenschaften* (1998); "Are Cultures Readable?" (2004); *Ritualdynamik: Kulturübergreifende Studien zur Theorie und Geschichte rituellen Handelns* (co-editor, 2004); "Rituale, Texte, Diskurse: Eine formtheoretische Betrachtung" (2005); "Ritual and Other Forms of Social Action" (2006); "'Alle Kultur nach Auschwitz ist Müll': Zerrformen des kulturellen Gedächtnisses" (2006); and *Ritual und Gedächtnis* (forthcoming).

UDO J. HEBEL is Professor and Chair of American Studies at the University of Regensburg, Germany. He taught at the universities of Mainz, Potsdam, and Freiburg, and was Distinguished Max Kade Visiting Professor at Colorado College, Colorado Springs, USA. He was a Visiting Scholar at the University of Michigan and Harvard University. He published *Romaninterpretation als Textarchäologie* (1989), *Intertextuality, Allusion, Quotation* (1989), *Transatlantic Encounters* (co-editor, 1995), *"Those Images of Jealuosie": Identitäten und Alteritäten im puritanischen Neuengland* (1997), *The Construction and Contestation of American Cultures and Identities in the Early Na-*

tional Period (editor, 1999), *Sites of Memory in American Literatures and Cultures* (editor, 2003), *Visual Culture in the American Studies Classroom* (co-editor, 2005), *Twentieth-Century American One-Act Plays* (2006). His articles focus on U.S.-American cultures of memory, colonial New England, twentieth-century American fiction and drama, African American drama and theater, German-American images, visual cultures, American suburbia, and theories of American Studies. He served as Vice President of the German Association for American Studies and as Deputy Director of the Bavarian American Academy; he currently is a member of the boards of both organizations. He is general editor of *Amerikastudien/American Studies* and an elected member of the American Antiquarian Society.

WILLIAM HIRST is Professor of Psychology at the New School for Social Research, USA. His graduate training was at Cornell University. He taught at Rockefeller University, Princeton University, and Cornell University before coming to the New School. He has edited three volumes and published numerous articles, in topics as wide ranging as attention, amnesia, and social aspects of memory, including recent papers on collective memory in *Memory* (co-authored with David Manier) and *Social Research* (co-authored with Gerald Echterhoff).

MARIO ISNENGHI has taught at the universities of Padua and Turin, Italy, and is currently Professsor of Contemporary History at the University of Venedig Ca' Foscari. He is a specialist in the history of the First World War and author of *Il mito della grande Guerra* (Bari, 1970; currently in the seventh edition). There have also been multiple editions of his works *Le guerre degli Italiani: Parole immagini ricordi 1848-1945* (Mondadori, 1989) and *L'Italia in piazza: I luoghi della vita pubblica dal 1848 ai giorni nostri* (Mondadori, 1994). He edited the three-volume work on Italian sites of memory, *I luoghi della memoria* (Laterza, 1996-97); a French translation was published in 2006. His most recent publication is *Garibaldi fu ferito: Storia e mito di un rivoluzionario disciplinato* (Donzelli, 2007). He is also one of the general editors of the journal *Belfagor*, founded in 2008.

MAUREEN JUNKER-KENNY studied at the University of Tübingen, received her doctorate in theology from the University of Münster, and her *Habilitation* from the University of Tübingen. She is a Fellow of Trinity College Dublin and Associate Professor of Theology in the School of Religions and Theology, Trinity College Dublin. Her main research interests are conditions of theology in modernity, foundations of ethics, moral and religious identity, and biomedical ethics. She is co-editor of the *International Journal of Practical Theology*, of *Ethics and Education*, and of the series

Practical Theology in the Discourse of the Humanities (de Gruyter). Her publications include: *Creating Identity: Biographical, Moral, Religious* (edited with Hermann Häring and Dietmar Mieth, SCM Press, 2000) and *Memory, Narrativity, Self, and the Challenge to Think God: The Reception within Theology of the Recent Work of Paul Ricoeur* (contributor and edited with Peter Kenny, LIT-Verlag, 2004). Two book projects she is currently working on are *Religion and Public Reason* (de Gruyter) and *Habermas for Theologians* (Continuum/ T & T Clark).

ELENA LAMBERTI is Professore a contratto for Anglo-American Literatures at the University of Bologna. In 2000, she received the Annual Book Award from the Italian Association for Canadian Studies ("Young Scholars" category) for *Marshall McLuhan: Tra arte letteratura e media* (Mondadori, 2000). She edited *Interpreting/Translating Modernism: A Comparative Perspective* (Compositori Grafiche, 2001), and is the author of *Ford Madox Ford and The Republic of Letters* (with Vita Fortunati, Clueb, 2002). Elena Lamberti was responsible for the design and development of ACUME: Cultural Memory in European Countries: An Interdisciplinary Approach (three-year European Thematic Network, 2002-05) as assistant to the General Coordinator. Her areas of research include English literature (twentieth-century fiction, modernism, postmodernism); Canadian literature (twentieth century); twentieth-century criticism; comparative literature; and interdisciplinary studies: literature, media, and technology (information technologies).

WULF KANSTEINER is Associate Professor of History and Judaic Studies at Binghamton University (SUNY), USA, where he teaches contemporary European history, media history, and historical theory. He studied at UCLA and the University of Bochum, Germany. He is the author of *In Pursuit of German Memory: History, Television, and Politics after Auschwitz* (Ohio University Press, 2006), co-editor (with Ned Lebow and Claudio Fogu) of *The Politics of Memory in Postwar Europe* (Duke University Press, 2006), and has published essays on historiography, trauma theory, and the representation of history in film and television. He is also co-editor of the Sage journal *Memory Studies*. He is currently working on a collection of essays on the limits of Holocaust culture.

RENATE LACHMANN is Professor emerita of Slavic Literatures and Comparative Literature at the University of Konstanz, Germany and a member of the Heidelberg Academy of Science and Humanities. Her main fields of interest are the history and theory of rhetoric, mnemonic concepts, semiotic of culture, literature of the fantastic, and the representation of knowledge. Since 1990, she has published: *Gedächtnis und Literatur: Intertextualität in der russischen Moderne* (Suhrkamp, 1990), translated as *Memory and Literature* (translators Roy Sellars and Anthony Wall, University of Minnesota Press, 1997); *Die Zerstörung der schönen Rede: Rhetorische Tradition und Konzepte des Poetischen* (Fink, 1994); *Erzählte Phantastik: Zu Phantasiegeschichte und Semantik phantastischer Texte* (Suhrkamp, 2002); *Memoria: Vergessen und Erinnern* (edited with Anselm Haverkamp, Fink, 1993); *Gedächtniskunst: Raum-Bild-Schrift: Studien zur Mnemotechnik* (Suhrkamp, 1991); and *Rhetorik als kulturelle Praxis* (edited with Riccardo Nicolosi and Susanne Strätling, Fink, 2008).

ANDREAS LANGENOHL studied sociology and Slavic linguistics. He received his doctorate and *Habilitation* in sociology from the University of Giessen, Germany. His work covers modernization theory; practices of collective memory, especially in Russia; processes of cultural transnationalization; and the sociology of finance. Since 2003 he has been directing the research project "The Market Time of Globalization," part of the Collaborative Research Center "Memory Cultures" at the University of Giessen. Since 2007 he has directed the research group "Idioms of Social Analysis" in the Center of Excellence "Cultural Foundations of Integration" at the University of Konstanz. Recent publications include: "How to Change Other People's Institutions: Discursive Entrepreneurship and the Boundary Object of Competition/Competitiveness in the German Banking Sector," *Economy and Society* 37 (2008) 1; "A Critique of Organizational Capitalism: The Enabling Fiction of Market Efficiency in Financial Professionals' Narratives" (in *Économistes et anthropologistes à face de la mondialisation*, vol. 2: *La mondialisation au risque des travailleurs*, eds. Laurent Bazin, et al., L'Harmattan, 2008); "Technology and (Post-)Sociality in the Financial Market: A Re-Evaluation" (with Kerstin Schmidt-Beck, in *Science, Technology and Innovation Studies* 3.1 (2007)).

JACQUES LE RIDER is Professor (Directeur d'études) of German Cultural History at the École pratique des Hautes Études (Sorbonne, Paris). In the field of cultural memory studies, he has published *Transnationale Gedächtnisorte in Zentraleuropa* (edited with Moritz Csáky and Monika Sommer, Studien Verlag, 2002). His book *Modernité viennoise et crises de l'identité* (Paris, 1990) was translated by Rosemary Morris as *Modernity and Crises of Identity: Culture and Society in Fin-de-siècle Vienna* (Polity Press/Continuum, 1993). Recent publications include: *Nietzsche en France, de la fin du XIXe siècle au temps présent* (Presses Universitaires de France, 1999); *Journaux intimes viennois* (Presses Universitaires de France, 2000); *Freud, de l'Acropole au Sinaï* (Presses Universitaires de France, 2002); *Arthur Schnitzler ou La Belle Époque viennoise* (Belin, 2003); *Malwida von Meysenbug: Une Européenne du XIXe siècle*

(Bartillat, 2005); *L'Allemagne au temps du réalisme (1848-1890)* (Albin Michel, 2008).

DAVID MANIER is Associate Professor of Psychology at Lehman College, City University of New York. A clinical psychologist by training, he completed his doctorate at the New School for Social Research, USA, and his postdoctoral training at the National Center for PTSD (U.S. Department of Veterans Affairs) in Honolulu. He has published widely in the fields of collective memory, stress, and trauma, including a recent paper in *Memory* (co-authored with William Hirst).

JEAN-CHRISTOPHE MARCEL is Maître de conférences of Sociology at the University of Paris-Sorbonne, France. His main fields of interest are the history of French and American sociology, the sociology of the Durkheimian school and especially Halbwachs's work, sociology of knowledge, and methods of inquiry. His publications include: "Les derniers soubresauts du rationalisme durkheimien: Une théorie de 'l'instinct social de survie' chez Maurice Halbwachs" (in *Maurice Halbwachs: Espaces, mémoires et psychologie collective*, eds. Yves Déloye and Claudine Haroche, Publications de la Sorbonne, 2004); "Le déploiement de la recherche au Centre d'Études Sociologiques (1945-1960)" (in *La Revue pour l'histoire du CNRS* 13 (2005)); "Gurvitch et la reconstruction de la sociologie française" (in *Anamnèse* 1 (2005)); "André Davidovitch (1912-1986) et le deuxième âge de la sociologie durkheimienne" (with Laurent Mucchielli, in *L'Année Sociologique* 57.1 (2006)); "Mémoire, espace et connaissance chez Maurice Halbwachs" (in *Maurice Halbwachs, sociologue retrouvé*, eds. Marie Jaisson and Christian Baudelot, Presses de l'ENS, 2007); and "Le temps des groupes sociaux: Gurvitch critique d'Halbwachs" (in press).

HANS J. MARKOWITSCH is Professor of Physiological Psychology at the University of Bielefeld, Germany. He studied psychology and biology at the University of Konstanz, had professorships for biopsychology and physiological psychology at the universities of Konstanz, Bochum, and Bielefeld, and was offered chairs of psychology and neuroscience at universities in Australia and Canada. He co-operates with scientists from universities and Max Planck institutes in Germany and North America. His research centers on the neural and psychic bases of memory disorders and consciousness. He is author, co-author, or editor of more than twenty books and has written about 500 scientific articles and book chapters. Book publications include: *Intellectual Functions and the Brain* (Hogrefe & Huber, 1992); *Neuropsychologie des Gedächtnisses* (Hogrefe, 1992); *Gedächtnisstörungen* (Kohlhammer, 1999); *Gehirn und Verhalten* (with Monika Pritzel and Matthias Brand, Spektrum, 2003); *Dem Gedächtnis auf der Spur: Vom Erinnern und Vergessen* (Wissenschaftliche Buchgesellschaft/PRIMUS Verlag, 2002/05); *Gedächtnisstörungen nach Hirnschäden* (Hogrefe, 2004); *Das autobiographische Gedächtnis* (with Harald Welzer, 2005); *Tatort Gehirn: Auf der Suche nach dem Ursprung des Verbrechens* (Campus, 2007); *Falsche Erinnerungen* (with Sina Kühnel, Spektrum, 2008); and *Gedächtnis* (Beck, 2009, forthcoming).

ERIK MEYER is a research associate at the Collaborative Research Center "Memory Cultures" at the University of Giessen, Germany. His main fields of interest are the politics of memory, memory and digital media, and political communication and popular culture. Publications include a book with Claus Leggewie on the Holocaust-Memorial in Berlin (*"Ein Ort, an den man gerne geht": Das Holocaust-Mahnmal und die deutsche Geschichtspolitik nach 1989*, Hanser, 2005) and several articles on commemoration, recently "Ort und Bild als Medien historischen Lernens" (in *Soldaten und andere Opfer?*, ed. Ellen Ueberschär, Evangelische Akademie Loccum, 2007).

DAVID MIDDLETON is a research consultant and Honorary Reader in Psychology at Loughborough University, UK, where he taught discursive and socio-cultural psychology (1976-2003). He has research affiliations with the Loughborough Discourse and Rhetoric Group (DARG provides a forum for research and discussion in discursive psychology); as a Research Fellow on the UK Economic and Social Research Council's Teaching Learning Research Programme project "Learning in and for Interagency Learning" (2004-2008); as an affiliate member of the Centre for Sociocultural and Activity Theory Research (CSAT) at the University of Bath, UK; and as a Guest Professor at the University of Oslo at the interdisciplinary research center investigating design, communication, and learning in digital environments (InterMedia). His research focuses on the social use of remembering and forgetting in vernacular and institutional settings. His published work includes *The Social Psychology of Experience: Studies in Remembering and Forgetting* (with Steven D. Brown, Sage, 2005); "Cognition and Communication at Work" (with Yrjo Engeström, Cambridge University Press, 1996); and *Collective Remembering* (with Derek Edwards, Sage, 1990).

LAURENT MUCCHIELLI is Senior Research Fellow at the Centre National de la Recherche Scientifique and Associate Professor at the University of Versailles Saint-Quentin, France. He is the founder and an associate editor of the *Revue d'Histoire des Sciences Humaines*. His two fields of interest are the history of social sciences and the sociology of crime and penal institutions.

In the first field, he has edited *Histoire de la criminologie française* (L'Harmattan, 1994); *La sociologie et sa method: Les Règles de Durkheim un siècle après* (L'Harmattan, 1995); *La Découverte du Social: Naissance de la Sociologie en France* (La Découverte, 1998); *Le cas Spencer: Religion, science et politique* (Presses Universitaires de France, 1998); and *Mythes et histoire des sciences humaines* (La Découverte, 2004). He now works mainly in the second field.

BIRGIT NEUMANN teaches English Literature and Culture at the University of Giessen, Germany. Since 2006 she has been Principal Investigator at the International Graduate Center for the Study of Culture (GCSC) in Giessen. From 2005 to 2007 she was Associate Director of the Collaborative Research Center "Memory Cultures" at the University of Giessen. She has published on memory, cultural knowledge, and identity and alterity, including book-length studies on fictions of memory (*Erinnerung—Identität—Narration: Gattungstypologie und Funktionen kanadischer Fictions of Memory*, de Gruyter, 2005), on the rhetoric of the nation in eighteenth-century literature (*Nationale Fremd- und Selbstbilder in britischen Medien des 18. Jahrhunderts: Die Rhetorik der Nation*, WVT, 2008, in press), and on the study of narrative fiction (with Ansgar Nünning, Klett, 2008, in press).

ANSGAR NÜNNING has been Professor of English and American Literature and Cultural Studies at the University of Giessen, Germany since 1996. He is the founding director of the Giessen Graduate School for the Humanities and of the International Graduate Center for the Study of Culture (GCSC) as well as the academic director of the International Ph.D. Program (IPP) "Literary and Cultural Studies" and a member of the Collaborative Research Center "Memory Cultures." He has published widely on English and American literature, cultures of memory, narratology, and literary and cultural theory. His most recent book publications include: *Metzler Lexikon Literatur- und Kulturtheorie* (4th edition 2008); *Introduction to the Study of Narrative Fiction* (with Birgit Neumann, 2008); *Einführung in die Kulturwissenschaften* (edited with Vera Nünning, 2003); *Medienereignisse der Moderne* (edited with Friedrich Lenger, 2008); *Metzler Handbuch Promotion: Forschung—Förderung—Finanzierung* (edited with Roy Sommer, 2007); *Englische Literatur unterrichten: Grundlagen und Methoden* (with Carola Surkamp, 2006); *An Introduction to the Study of English and American Literature* (with Vera Nünning, 2004, 4th edition 2007); *Kulturwissenschaftliche Literaturwissenschaft* (edited with Roy Sommer, 2004); *Erzähltextanalyse und Gender Studies* (edited with Vera Nünning, 2004). He is editor of the series *Uni Wissen Anglistik/Amerikanistik*, *Uni Wissen Kernkompetenzen*; *WVT-Handbücher zum literaturwissenschaftlichen Studium* and *ELCH: English Literary and Cultural History* (both with Vera Nünning); *MCM: Media and Cultural Me-*

mory/Medien und kulturelle Erinnerung (with Astrid Erll); and *WVT-Handbücher zur Literatur- und Kulturdidaktik* (with Wolfgang Hallet).

JEFFREY OLICK is Professor of Sociology and History at the University of Virginia, USA. His books include: *States of Memory: Continuities, Conflicts and Transformations in National Retrospection* (Duke University Press, 2003); *In the House of the Hangman: The Agonies of German Defeat, 1943-1949* (University of Chicago Press, 2005); and *The Politics of Regret: On Collective Memory and Historical Responsibility* (Routledge, 2007). Together with Daniel Levy and Vered Vinitzky-Seroussi, he is editing *The Collective Memory Reader* (Oxford, forthcoming).

JÜRGEN REULECKE was Professor of Modern and Contemporary History at the University of Siegen, Germany from 1984 to 2003, and since 2003 has been Professor of Contemporary History at the University of Giessen as well as Director of the Collaborative Research Center "Memory Cultures." His areas of research are in particular the history of social policy and social movements and urbanization since the end of the eighteenth century, as well as contemporary cultural history, focusing especially on youth and generational history in the twentieth century. Recent publications include: *Generationaliät und Lebensgeschichte im 20. Jahrhundert* (editor, 2003); *Söhne ohne Väter: Erfahrungen der Kriegsgeneration* (co-editor, 2004); *Das Konstrukt "Bevölkerung" vor, im und nach dem Dritten Reich* (co-editor, 2005), *Erinnerungen an Kriegskindheiten* (co-editor, 2006), *Good-bye memories? Lieder im Generationengedächtnis des 20. Jahrhunderts* (co-editor, 2007), *Weimars transatlantischer Mäzen: Die Lincoln-Stiftung 1927 bis 1934* (co-editor, 2008).

ANN RIGNEY, Professor of Comparative Literature at Utrecht University, Netherlands, has published widely in the fields of historical and narrative theory, nineteenth-century historiography, and cultural memory studies. She is author of *The Rhetoric of Historical Representation: Three Narrative Histories of the French Revolution* (Cambridge University Press, 1990) and *Imperfect Histories: The Elusive Past and the Legacy of Romantic Historicism* (Cornell University Press, 2001). She is co-editor (with Astrid Erll) of *Mediation, Remediation, and the Dynamics of Cultural Memory* (de Gruyter, 2008, in press) and is currently working on a study of the afterlife of Walter Scott as a case study in cultural remembrance and obsolescence in the age of mass media.

JENS RUCHATZ is Assistant Professor of Theater and Media Studies at the University of Erlangen, Germany. His main interests are the theory and history of the media in general, in particular the history and theory of photography, the history of telecommunication, media and individualization, uses of the interview, and the theory of exemplarity. His publications include *Licht und Wahrheit: Eine Mediumgeschichte der fotografischen Projektion* (Fink, 2003). Together with Nicolas Pethes he edited *Gedächtnis und Erinnerung: Ein interdisziplinäres Lexikon* (Rowohlt, 2001) and a special issue of the journal *Handlung, Kultur, Interpretation. Zeitschrift für Sozial- und Kulturwissenschaften* entitled *Gedächtnis disziplinär* (12.1 (2003)).

MAX SAUNDERS is Professor of English at King's College London, where he teaches modern English, European, and American literature, and is Director of the Centre for Life-Writing Research. He studied at Cambridge University and Harvard, and was a Research Fellow and then College Lecturer at Selwyn College, Cambridge. He is the author of the biography *Ford Madox Ford: A Dual Life*, 2 vols. (Oxford University Press, 1996), the editor of Ford's *Selected Poems* (Carcanet, 1997); *War Prose* (Carcanet, 1999); and *Critical Essays* (with Richard Stang, Carcanet, 2002), and has published essays on life-writing, on impressionism, and on Ford, Conrad, James, Forster, Eliot, Joyce, Rosamond Lehmann, Richard Aldington, May Sinclair, Lawrence, Freud, Pound, Ruskin, Anthony Burgess, and others. He is also general editor of *International Ford Madox Ford Studies.* He is currently completing a study of the relations between modern literature and life-writing.

SIEGFRIED J. SCHMIDT is Professor emeritus at the University of Münster, Germany. His main fields of interest are constructivism, communication theory, and media culture. Recent publications include: *Kommunikationswissenschaft: Systematik und Ziele* (with Guido Zurstiege, 2007); *Histories & Discourses: Rewriting Constructivism* (2007); *Beobachtungsmanagement: Über die Endgültigkeit der Vorläufigkeit* (Audio-CD, 2007); *Kulturschutt: Über das Recycling von Theorien und Kulturen* (edited with Christoph Jacke and Eva Kimminich, 2006); *Zwiespältige Begierden: Aspekte der Medienkultur* (2004); *Unternehmenskultur: Die Grundlage für den wirtschaftlichen Erfolg von Unternehmen* (2004); *Erfahrungen: Österreichische Texte beobachtend* (2002).

JÜRGEN STRAUB has been Professor of Social Theory and Social Psychology at the University of Bochum, Germany since 2008. He held a professorship at the University of Erlangen-Nuremberg and at the University of Witten-Herdecke until 2002, and was Chair of Intercultural Communication in the School of Humanities and Social Sciences at the Chemnitz University of Technology from 2002 to 2008. He was also a fellow at the Center for Interdisciplinary Research at the University of Bielefeld (1994-1995) and a fellow at the Institute for Advanced Study in the Humanities (KWI) in Essen. Together with Jörn Rüsen (former president of the

KWI), he has since 2004 been Director of the Graduate School for Intercultural Communication and Intercultural Competence, housed at the KWI. Since 2004 he has also served as Executive Director of the Stiftung für Kulturwissenschaften (Foundation for the Humanities) in Essen and on the Academic Advisory Board of the Sigmund Freud Institute in Frankfurt am Main. He has published extensively in his fields of research: cultural and cross-cultural psychology, intercultural communication and competence, violence in modern societies, action theory, identity, (personal and collective) memory, historical consciousness, narrative psychology, long-term psychosocial and cultural effects of the Shoah, migration research, theory, methodology, and methods of qualitative social research.

HARALD WEILNBÖCK received his Ph.D. in German Studies and training as a research psychoanalyst at the University of California Los Angeles, after which he joined the UCLA Critical Theory Program in Paris. In his dissertation, he applied concepts from recent clinical psychology and psychoanalysis to texts from Hölderlin and Heidegger. He worked in a German Research Foundation project on reading and media biography. His *Habilitation* is from the University of Leipzig, Germany. In an upcoming book he investigates narrative patterns of "borderline literary interaction" in Ernst Jünger. Drawing from further psychotherapy training he developed a novel approach to the teaching of culture, the Group-Analytic Reading Seminar. He is currently conducting a European Union research project, "Reading and Media Interaction as Trauma Therapy," in the Department of Clinical Psychology at the University of Zurich, employing methods of biography studies and qualitative psychology. He works in counseling and team supervision. He has written on issues of media research, literary theory, psychological readings of film and literature, interdisciplinary narratology, and psychotherapy research.

HARALD WELZER is Director of the Center for Interdisciplinary Memory Research at the Institute for Advanced Study in the Humanities (KWI) in Essen, Germany and Research Professor of Social Psychology at the University of Witten/Herdecke. His most important publications in recent years include: *"Opa war kein Nazi!": Nationalsozialismus und Holocaust im Familiengedächtnis* (with Karoline Tschuggnall und Sabine Moller, Fischer, 2002); *Das kommunikative Gedächtnis: Eine Theorie der Erinnerung* (Beck, 2005); *Täter: Wie aus ganz normalen Menschen Massenmörder werden* (Fischer, 2005); and *Klimakriege: Wofür im 21. Jahrhundert getötet wird* (Fischer, 2008).

JAY WINTER, Charles J. Stille Professor of History, joined the Yale faculty in 2001. From 1979 to 2001, he was Reader in Modern History and Fellow of Pembroke College, Cambridge. He holds Ph.D. and DLitt degrees from Cambridge. He is an historian of the First World War, and is the author of *Sites of Memory, Sites of Mourning: The Great War in European Cultural History* (Cambridge University Press, 1995). He was co-producer and won an Emmy for the 1996 BBC/PBS television series "The Great War and the Shaping of the Twentieth Century." In 2006 Yale University Press published two of his books: *Remembering War: The Great War between Memory and History in the Twentieth Century* and *Dreams of Peace and Freedom: Utopian Movements in the Twentieth Century.*

JAMES E. YOUNG is Professor of English and Judaic Studies at the University of Massachusetts, Amherst, where he has taught since 1988, and currently Chair of the Department of Judaic and Near Eastern Studies. He is the author of *Writing and Rewriting the Holocaust* (Indiana University Press, 1988); *The Texture of Memory* (Yale University Press, 1993), which won the National Jewish Book Award in 1994; and *At Memory's Edge: After-Images of the Holocaust in Contemporary Art and Architecture* (Yale University Press, 2000). He was also the Guest Curator of an exhibition at the Jewish Museum in New York City, entitled "The Art of Memory: Holocaust Memorials in History" (March-August 1994, with venues in Berlin and Munich, September 1994-June 1995) and was the editor of *The Art of Memory* (Prestel, 1994), the exhibition catalogue for this show. In 1997, Professor Young was appointed by the Berlin Senate to the five-member *Findungskommission* for Germany's national "Memorial to Europe's Murdered Jews," which selected Peter Eisenman's design, finished and dedicated in May 2005. Most recently, he was appointed by the Lower Manhattan Development Corporation to the jury for the World Trade Center Site Memorial competition, won by Michael Arad and Peter Walker, and now under construction.

SARA B. YOUNG is a translator and doctoral candidate in the Department of German at the University of Wisconsin-Madison, USA, writing her dissertation on memory and the representation of the built environment in East German novels. She has taught courses in the Department of English at the University of Giessen, Germany, and in the Departments of German at Giessen and Wisconsin. Her fields of interest are German literature of the twentieth and twenty-first centuries, particularly of the GDR; the representation of space; and literary representations of cultural memory.

BARBIE ZELIZER is the Raymond Williams Professor of Communication and Director of the Scholars Program in Culture and Communication at the University of Pennsylvania's Annenberg School for Communication. A former journalist, Zelizer is known for her work in the area of journalism, culture, memory, and images, particularly in times of crisis. She has authored or edited seven books, including the award-winning *Remembering to Forget: Holocaust Memory Through the Camera's Eye* (University of Chicago Press, 1998); *Covering the Body: The Kennedy Assassination, the Media, and the Shaping of Collective Memory* (University of Chicago Press, 1992); and *Journalism After September 11* (with Stuart Allan, Routledge, 2002). In 2004, she published *Taking Journalism Seriously: News and the Academy* (Sage) and *Reporting War: Journalism in Wartime* (with Stuart Allan, Routledge). A recipient of a Guggenheim Fellowship, a Freedom Forum Center Research Fellowship, and a Fellowship from Harvard University's Joan Shorenstein Center on the Press, Politics, and Public Policy, Zelizer is also a media critic, whose work has appeared in The Nation, the Jim Lehrer News Hour, Newsday, and Radio National of Australia. Coeditor of *Journalism: Theory, Practice and Criticism* and currently President-Elect/Select of the International Communication Association, she is presently working on a book on about-to-die photographs and journalism.

MARTIN ZIEROLD is Associate Director of the International Graduate Center for the Study of Culture (GCSC) at the University of Giessen, Germany. Among his fields of interest are cultural memory studies, media and communication theory, cultural theory, and arts management. He has published the monograph *Gesellschaftliche Erinnerung* (2006) and a number of articles on modern media and memory. He is co-editor of a special issue of the magazine *SPIEL* on *Memory and Popular Culture* (2008), and together with the other members of GCSC's Executive Board will be general editor of the new series *Giessen Contributions to the Study of Culture* (WVT, from 2008).